# Malevolent Legalities

# The Fairleigh Dickinson University Press
## Series in Law, Culture, and the Humanities

Series Editor: Caroline Joan "Kay" S. Picart, M.Phil. (Cantab), Ph.D., J.D., Esquire Attorney at Law; Adjunct Professor, FAMU College of Law; former English & HUM professor, FSU

The Fairleigh Dickinson University Press Series in Law, Culture, and the Humanities publishes scholarly works in which the field of Law intersects with, among others, Film, Criminology, Sociology, Communication, Critical/Cultural Studies, Literature, History, Philosophy, and the Humanities.

*On the Web at* http://www.fdu.edu/fdupress

### Publications

Kevin S. Jobe, *Malevolent Legalities: Discriminatology and the Specters of Scalia* (2024)

Linda Myrsiades, *From Treason to Runaway Slaves: Legal Culture in New Republic Trials, 1783–1808* (2023)

Eamon P.H. Keane and Peter Robson, *The Ian Willock Collection on Law and Justice in the Twenty-First Century* (2023)

Peter Robson and Ferdinando Spina, *Vigilante Justice in Society and Popular Culture: A Global Perspective* (2022)

Joel Silverman, *The Legal Exhibitionist: Morris Ernst, Jewish Identity, and the Modern Celebrity Lawyer* (2022)

Matthew Sorrento and David Ryan, *David Fincher's* Zodiac: *Cinema of Investigation and (Mis)Interpretation* (2021)

T. Patrick Hill, *No Place for Ethics: Judicial Review, Legal Positivism, and the Supreme Court of the United States* (2021)

Caroline Joan "Kay" S. Picart, *Monsters, Law, Crime: Explorations in Gothic Criminology* (2020)

Elaine Wood, *Gender Justice and the Law: Theoretical Practices of Intersectional Identity* (2020)

Orit Kamir, *Betraying Dignity: The Toxic Seduction of Social Media, Shaming, and Radicalization* (2019)

Marouf A. Hasian, Jr., *Lawfare and the Ovaherero and Nama Pursuit of Restorative Justice, 1918–2018* (2019)

George Pate, *Enter the Undead Author: Intellectual Property, the Ideology of Authorship, and Performance Practices since the 1960s* (2019)

# Malevolent Legalities

## Discriminatology and the Specters of Scalia

Kevin S. Jobe

FAIRLEIGH DICKINSON UNIVERSITY PRESS
*Vancouver • Madison • Teaneck • Wroxton*

Published by Fairleigh Dickinson University Press
Copublished by The Rowman & Littlefield Publishing Group, Inc.
4501 Forbes Boulevard, Suite 200, Lanham, Maryland 20706
www.rowman.com

86-90 Paul Street, London EC2A 4NE

Copyright © 2025 by The Rowman & Littlefield Publishing Group, Inc.

*All rights reserved.* No part of this book may be reproduced in any form or by any electronic or mechanical means, including information storage and retrieval systems, without written permission from the publisher, except by a reviewer who may quote passages in a review.

*Fairleigh Dickinson University Press gratefully acknowledges the support received for scholarly publishing from the Friends of FDU Press.*

British Library Cataloguing in Publication Information Available

**Library of Congress Cataloging-in-Publication Data**

Names: Jobe, Kevin S., 1984- author.
Title: Malevolent legalities : discriminatology and the specters of Scalia / Kevin S. Jobe.
Description: Lexington : Fairleigh Dickinson University Press, 2024. | Series: The fairleigh dickinson university press series in law, culture, and the humanities | Includes bibliographical references and index.
Identifiers: LCCN 2024032688 (print) | LCCN 2024032689 (ebook) | ISBN 9781683934028 (cloth) | ISBN 9781683934035 (epub)
Subjects: LCSH: Discrimination in justice administration--United States. | Scalia, Antonin, 1936-2016--Political and social views.
Classification: LCC KF8700 .J625 2024 (print) | LCC KF8700 (ebook) | DDC 342.7308/7--dc23/eng/20240716
LC record available at https://lccn.loc.gov/2024032688
LC ebook record available at https://lccn.loc.gov/2024032689

∞™ The paper used in this publication meets the minimum requirements of American National Standard for Information Sciences—Permanence of Paper for Printed Library Materials, ANSI/NISO Z39.48-1992.

# Contents

Acknowledgments — vii

Preface — ix

Introduction — 1

## PART 1: "PRUDENT EVIL" — 75

**1** *Edwards v. Aguillard* (1987): Humpty Dumpty Had a Fall — 79

**2** *St. Mary's Honor Ctr. v. Hicks* (1993): "Injustice is the Game" — 105

**3** *Romer v. Evans* (1996): "The Written Law Killeth, but the Spirit Giveth Life" — 135

## PART II: "A REGIME OF STATIC LAW" — 153

**4** *Reno v. Bossier Parish* (2000): "Preventing Progress" — 157

**5** *Abbott v. Perez* (2018): Severing the Memory of Discrimination — 177

**6** *Students for Fair Admission v. Harvard* (2023): Colorblindness by Legal Fiat — 207

Conclusion: *303 Creative LLC v. Elenis* (2023): The Specters of Scalia — 233

Bibliography — 245

Index — 253

About the Author — 257

# Acknowledgments

I wish to thank Edwin Moloy, Sarah Wharton, and the helpful and knowledgeable team of archivists at the Harvard Law School Historical and Special Collections for hosting my research visit to the Scalia Papers in November 2023. Sarah and the team guided and facilitated all the steps of the archive process, from online database requests and retrieval of materials to the organization and supervision of the access to materials in the Harvard Law Reading Room. The archival research conducted for this book was made possible through funding from the College of Liberal Arts at the University of Texas-Rio Grande Valley. Therefore, I wish to extend my thanks to Dean Walter Diaz, Russel Skowronek, and Monica Denny for facilitating and encouraging this research with support from the College of Liberal Arts. I also thank my faculty mentor Cory Wimberly, professor of philosophy at the University of Texas-Rio Grande Valley, for planting the idea that archival research *is* philosophical research.

I also want to thank the many scholars who have provided feedback and commentary on the text, including Eduardo Mendieta, Naomi Zack, Erin Kelley, Wendy Salkin, Nathifa Green, and the internal reviewers and editors at Fairleigh Dickinson University Press. This book would not have been possible without the editor of the *Law, Culture and Humanities* Series at FDU Press, Caroline "Kay" Picart. At every stage of the process, Caroline has guided and encouraged the book's trajectory, completion, and success. I would also like to thank my editor at Rowman & Littlefield, Zachary Nycum, for working so diligently together with FDU Press in bringing this book to completion.

# Preface

**W**hat is a preface to a text? What function does it serve, and why is it deemed necessary? Why not simply proceed directly to the text? One answer suggested by the thrust of this book is that the preface is a sort of "prelude," a performative inauguration or announcement of the author's work or "act" being performed. The preface therefore links the *act* (the work itself) to its *performance* in a particular space, time, historical context, and/or to a certain purpose and the author's intent. This performative reading of preface as prelude has been described by performance theorists as "setting the stage" of a performance, at once a form of theatre (performance) and a type of speech-act (performativity).[1] Moreover, if Plato's Athenian in *The Laws* is correct, then "All speeches, and whatever things involve the voice, are preceded by preludes, which are . . . a sort of warm-up, and which provide a sort-of craft-like preparation, within the province of the relevant craft, that is useful for the coming performance."[2]

This suggested link between law and music, in fact, serves as the basis for Plato's construction of the laws of the city of Magnesia, where Plato equates laws of the city with temporal modes or "measures" (*nomoi*). As the Athenian tells us in *The Laws*,

> I think, in fact, that of the songs sung to the lyre, the so-called *nomoi*, indeed all music, are preceded by preludes that are composed with amazing seriousness. But in the case of what are really and truly *nomoi*, the laws that we say are political, no one has either given voice to a prelude, or composed one and published it, as if it were natural for there not to be one. It seems to me, though . . . that it *is* natural; and the laws stated in double fashion seemed to me just now not to be double in a somehow simple way, but rather to be two things: a law and a prelude to the law.[3]

As the Athenian observes, lawmakers do not normally give preludes in addition to the text of the laws they make. The surprisingly contemporary implication of Plato's observation is therefore the following: all written laws established by lawmakers have an implicit prelude, or *pre-text*, as part of their "double" character: laws (*nomoi*) simultaneously enact a written speech as text (*logon*) while also setting into motion a path (*prooimia*) that the speech announces and encourages the citizen-audience to follow. By distinguishing between the *text* of the law and its *prelude*, Plato underscores the performative character of law that cannot be separated from written legal texts.

Plato's distinction in *The Laws* between text and prelude draws our attention to the fact that a prelude is a sort of hidden mode of speech act that signals a message *prior to* the written text of the law—text that often conceals or fails to reveal the ultimate purposes, intentions, rationales, or goals of law and policy. In legal terms, then, a prelude can be described as a kind of *pre-text*: the hidden speech that precedes or is concealed by the *face* of the text of the law. In the fields of pragmatics and legal interpretation, we distinguish between communicative meaning that is made explicit on the face of the text and meaning that is *implicit* or unstated on the face of the text. In this way, a pre-face is simply a pre-text: that which goes before or is concealed by the face of the text. Plato's crucial insight in *The Laws*—that law has a "double" meaning as both text and pretext—serves as this book's motivating theoretical insight for understanding discriminatory speech. Indeed, the central problem I analyze in the book is the problem of what I call *performative discrimination*, understood as modes of discrimination in which the text itself facilitates (i) the masking or concealment of discriminatory speech and (ii) the resignification of discriminatory speech as "neutral" action performed in "good faith." Without attending to the *performativity* and *performances* of law (its pretexts and preludes), we miss the ways that the text performs that which is left *unsaid*. If the text of law always implies, as Plato suggests, a performance of that which is left unsaid, then any theory of legal interpretation that relies exclusively on the "plain" or "ordinary" meaning of the text while rejecting "extratextual," pretextual, or contextual sources of meaning will fail to capture the true meaning of any text.

As for Plato's "preludes" (*prooimion*), philologists have argued that *prooimion* in fact constitute an entire speech genre in ancient Greek culture and language that indicates an "opening whose execution determines the success of the following speech or undertaking."[4] Boris Maslov argues that *prooimion* derive their meaning from the root οἶμος, meaning "path" or "way." As Maslov concludes, "The proper meaning of the compound *pro-oimion* would be 'what one says before setting out on one's way,' with the extended meaning 'proper speech act preceding an undertaking.'"[5] This eminently performative understanding of preludes as preparatory speech-acts inaugurating an epic or song or journey illuminates the extremely rich domain served by a prelude. As a theatrical device, a prelude "sets the stage" for the performance ahead; as a type of speech-act, a prelude announces and inaugurates the beginning of a path through which an author wishes to take the reader. As part of a musical mode or measure [*nomoi*], a prelude "sets the tone" by setting into motion (*anakinesis*) a temporal mode of organization through which the performance will unfold.

In *The Rhetoric*, Aristotle observes that the preludes (*prooimia*) of flute-playing that Plato uses in *The Laws* to speak of legal "pretexts" are structurally equivalent to the *exordium*, or introduction of a speech. For Aristotle, all these forms of speech share a common structural feature. He writes, "The exordium [*proomion*] is the beginning of a speech [*arkhē logou*], as the prologue in poetry and the prelude in flute-playing; for all these are beginnings [*arkhai*], and as it were a paving the way for what follows."[6] For Aristotle, *arkhai* refer to the *beginnings* or *origins* of a thing, the first principles that explain the genesis of something's coming-to-be. Thus, we come full circle—by pursuing the theme of pretext, we discover that pretext is a sort of prelude, which in turn is a beginning or original explanatory principle for the *coming-to-be* of a text. To give a sufficient explanation for the meaning of a text, therefore, we must pay attention to the *origin* (*arkhe*), the original explanatory principle for understanding how a text comes-to-be.

Ironically, we have arrived at a familiar thesis in statutory interpretation—namely, the notion that to fully understand a congressional statute, we must consult the original meaning or original intent of the statute. This is the theory of constitutional interpretation known as "originalism." It seems, then, that by pursuing a skeptical inquiry into what lurks behind every text in its pretext, we have simply arrived back where we started: the modern view that when interpreting legal texts, we should consult the original meaning. But are these two theses truly identical? Is consulting the original meaning of a text the same inquiry as pursuing an inquiry into its pretextual *arkhai*, the origins or beginnings of a text's *coming-to-be?*

The central methodological argument of this book is that they are *not*, in fact, the same. On the contrary, as Preus's Greek historical lexicon reminds us, the meaning of *arche* in ancient Greek may refer to "Origin, beginning, source, rule."[7] Alex McAuley's historical study of the term *arche* in ancient Greek politics reveals that "The Greek vocabulary of office-holding is derived from the verb *archein*, generally translated as 'to rule, govern, or command.'"[8] In Hannah Arendt's famous formulation, *arkhai* refers to both a *beginning* and a form of *rule* proper to the political domain of action.[9] Therefore, *arkhai* is at once an epistemological principle for understanding the original "source" of the genesis or *coming-to-be* of something as well as a *political* concept referring to the *archon*, the "rulers" or "governors" of ancient Greek city-states who ruled over the various spheres of political life.

Since every pretext can be understood as both *origin* and *rule* (*arkhe*) of the coming-to-be of a text, we can also say that every text presupposes an inquiry into not only the pretextual origin of a text but also the pretextual *rule* of the text. In this way, following Plato, we can say that every text implies a pretext, and that a pretext should be understood as both an origin and rule that precedes, hides behind, or is concealed by the text of the law.

The conclusion that we may draw, therefore, is that, with Plato, every legal text implies a prior rule (*arkhe*) that helps explain its coming-to-be. A proper understanding of any legal text must necessarily involve an inquiry not only into the original meaning or intent of the text (one thesis of "textualist-originalism") but also into the *pretextual rule* that has *already been decided* or made by a political authority prior to *and hidden by* the enactment of the text. The pretextual rule hidden by the text, therefore, explains the genesis or coming-to-be of the text itself. This thesis stands in direct opposition to the judicial philosophy of textualist-originalism, which states that the understanding of legal texts is *not* a political or legislative activity since the judicial role is simply to interpret the words of the text, instructed by the original meaning of the words at the time of enactment (originalism). Instead, our pursuit of the theme of pretext suggests that the "origins" of any legal texts must be explained in terms of the application of rules made by a sovereign *prior* to the text, that is, rules involving political decisions *that are performed through the text*—precisely the thesis that the judicial philosophy of textualism denies. To study the "origin" (*arkhe*) of a text is to study the pretext of the sovereign.

The judicial philosophy of textualism that is the object of critique in this book can be contrasted with a judicial philosophy of *textual skepticism*, which recognizes, as with Plato's Athenian, that texts always imply a pretext: that which is left *unsaid* or *unstated* on the face of the text itself. The legal ontology of textualism, which denies the existence of discriminatory purpose, is contrasted with the methodological insights in this book, namely that discrimination (1) is performed through the law, (2) persists through time, and (3) is a product of strategic manipulation of legal speech. Discrimination, in a real sense, takes on a legal life of its own.

The battle over competing judicial philosophies (i.e., "originalism" versus "purposivism") has largely defined the major controversies on the U. S. Supreme Court since Ronald Reagan's nomination of Justice Antonin Scalia in 1986. Most recently, these judicial philosophies clashed in the Supreme Court's announcement of the success of its "colorblind" jurisprudence in *Students for Fair Admission v. Harvard* (2023). Here, the court split over the fundamental question of whether the Fourteenth Amendment's Equal Protection Clause should be understood "purposively" through its legislative history as a *remedial purpose* for addressing the temporal persistence of racial discrimination, or whether the clause should be read "textually" as a "race-neutral" rule prohibiting whatsoever any government classification using race. As the majority argued, the text of the clause does not include textual reference to race, and therefore equal protection merely means that the government must be "color-blind" with respect to racial preferences. In contrast, the dissent argued that the Fourteenth Amendment's *purpose* has always been remedial, aimed at the persistence of racial discrimination that unlawfully subordinates others on the basis of race. The battle over the colorblind Constitution, as I show, is largely an extension of the debate over text versus pretext: whether antidiscrimination laws should be read as *texts* prescribing abstract rules against racial classification, or whether antidiscrimination laws should be read as a *prelude* containing historical memory, legislative purposes, social directives, and political promises that we in the present bear responsibility for inheriting, executing, and carrying forward. Therefore, the debate between text and pretext is also a debate over the *temporal* function of law and legal reality. Is the law simply a set of texts whose explicit words prescribe abstract rules, regardless of their historical purpose or meaning? Or is the law first and foremost an historical, cultural artifact that can be understood only through its preludes, its historical movements, motivations, and purposes that bind us together as political subjects?

As a prelude to the "path" that unfolds in these pages, I hope the reader will appreciate the pretextual foray into the rich domain of preludes outlined in this prefatory performance. In what follows, I trust the reader will come to see, as the Athenian wrote in *The Laws*, that every speech (including this one) implies a prelude.

## NOTES

1. Magela Cáffaro Geraldo, "The preface as stage: the theatrical trope and the performance of authorial identities in the nineteenth century," *Ilha Do Desterro: A Journal of English Language, Literatures in English and Cultural Studies* 70, no. 1 (2017): 265–74.
2. Plato, *The Laws*, trans. C. D. C. Reeve (Indianapolis, IN: Cambridge, 2022), 722d2, 131.
3. Plato, *The Laws*, 722d5.
4. Boris Maslov, "The Real Life of the Genre of *Prooimion*," *Classical Philology* 107, no. 3 (2012): 196.
5. Maslov, "The Real Life of the Genre of *Prooimion*," 202.
6. Aristotle, *Art of Rhetoric*, trans. J. H. Freese, Loeb Classical Library 193 (Cambridge: Harvard University Press, 1926), 427.

7. Anthony Preus, *Historical Dictionary of Ancient Greek Philosophy* (New York: Rowman & Littlefield, 2015), 59.

8. Alex McAuley, "Officials and Office-Holding," in *A Companion to Ancient Greek Government*, ed. Hans Beck (Oxford: Wiley-Blackwell, 2013), 179.

9. Hannah Arendt, *The Promise of Politics* (New York: Schocken Books, 2005), 45–46.

# Introduction

## Malevolent Legalities

Beginning in 2021, the radical conservative think-tank Claremont Institute published a series of "originalist" hit-pieces or salvos calling for a Christian Nationalist "counter-revolution" dismantling America's "anti-discrimination regime" and "Overturning the existing post-American order."[1] Targeting the "the false and pernicious" value of *diversity*, the authors call for the "purge" of antidiscrimination laws by reestablishing the "ancient principles" of the American founding, concluding that, "until America is refounded either on the woke gods or the God of Abraham, Isaac, and Jacob—regime-level battles will keep occurring—and with increasing intensity."[2] According to the Claremont Institute, a Christian Nationalist dismantling of antidiscrimination laws would result in a "truly colorblind Constitution." Fortunately for the institute, the US Supreme Court in June 2023 had just validated the Claremont Institute's vision in its overturning of affirmative action based on "an originalist defense of the colorblind Constitution."[3] According to the majority of the court, the Fourteenth Amendment is a completely "race-neutral" text, and the Constitution's "original founding" demands colorblind laws.

The question this book aims to address is how did we arrive at this point? How has the judicial philosophy of "originalism" or "textualism" been weaponized against antidiscrimination law—indeed as a weapon of discrimination *itself*? In the Supreme Court's decision in *Shelby County v. Holder* (2013) invalidating Section 5 of the Voting Rights Act, Justice Ginsburg likened post–civil rights era discrimination to "battling the Hydra. Whenever one form of voting discrimination was identified and prohibited, others sprang up in its place."[4] Justice Ginsburg was referring to the mythical nine-headed serpent Hydra from Greek mythology, depicted on the cover of this book, that regenerated two new heads in place of each one that Heracles lopped off with his sword. Ginsburg had identified what I refer to as *performative discrimination*—the uncanny ability of legal actors to utilize the law to regenerate or reanimate discrimination in novel forms of legal reality. To investigate and dissect the Hydra of discrimination, one must turn a critical eye to the field of legal interpretation. I therefore draw on archival and legal research in conducting a study of the intellectual influence of Justice Antonin Scalia (1936–2016) in constructing the legal ontology of textualism that has dramatically shaped the interpretation and practice of antidiscrimination law and is now arguably the dominant method of legal interpretation on the US Supreme Court. By examining the philosophical foundations and performative procedures of textualism, the book explores the ways in which the "specters" of Justice Scalia's textualism continue to transform the way we think about discrimination and our collective relationship to law, time, and constitutional memory.

The main argument of the book, grounded in archival and legal materials, is that "textualist-originalism" (a) makes it lawful for discrimination to be performed through the text, and (b) explicitly seeks to prevent progress in antidiscrimination law by enacting a regime of "static law." My overall argument is advanced in two parts, each containing an analysis of three US Supreme Court cases. Each of the six cases examined in the book represents its own line of cases directly traceable to Scalia's textualist philosophy. Part 1 explores the philosophical basis of Scalia's textualism in providing the groundwork for the performative practices of *malevolent legality*. Chapter 1 examines Scalia's rejection of the Supreme Court's "purpose" doctrine in *Edwards* (1987) and its undermining of the court's "discriminatory purpose" doctrine. Chapter 2 examines Scalia's majority opinion in *St. Mary's Honor Ctr v. Hicks* (1993) announcing the court's "pretext plus" doctrine and its sanctioning of performative lying by "bad faith" actors in employment discrimination. Chapter 3 examines Scalia's dissenting opinion in *Romer v. Evans* (1996) in light of the direct influence of Frederick Charles von Savigny's notion of the *volkgeist* on Scalia's use of the "traditions of the people" as an "unwritten constitution," Overall, part 1 of the book argues that since textualism rejects judicial scrutiny into "extratextual" purposes not made textually explicit, and because injustice is performed by discrimination not made textually explicit, it follows that textualism results in injustice ("Scalia's Argument for Textualist Injustice").

Part 2 of the book explores the *temporal* character of Scalia's textualist-originalism and its continuing influence on the post-Scalia Supreme Court. Chapter 4 examines Scalia's majority opinion in *Reno v. Bossier Parish School Board* (2000) and argues that Scalia's textualist opposition to the "progressive" congressional purpose of the Voting Rights Act was an extension of Scalia's activist judicial philosophy that aimed to "prevent progress" by enacting a regime of static law. Chapters 5 and 6 examine two post-Scalia

Supreme Court decisions. Chapter 5 examines how Scalia's attack on the purpose of the Voting Rights Act and his court's invalidation of Section 5 provided precedent for the court's conclusion in *Abbott v. Perez* (2018) that the history of discrimination is irrelevant for interpreting the "good faith" presumption of the Texas legislature. Finally, chapter 6 examines the court's "colorblind" decision in *Students for Fair Admission v. Harvard* (2023) invalidating affirmative action through a "race-neutral" textualist reading of the Fourteenth Amendment. In part 2, then, I argue that the self-described goal of Scalia's activist judicial philosophy of originalism is to prevent progress by enacting a regime of static law ("Scalia's Argument for Preventing Progress").

Methodologically, the book develops a unique framework for studying how discrimination: (1) is *performed* through the law, (2) persists through *time*, and (3) is a product of strategic *manipulation* of legal speech. The methodology developed for the book's analysis is called *discriminatology*, understood as the theoretical study of the temporality, performativity, and pragmatics of discrimination. When applied to the judicial philosophy of textualist-originalism, this methodology illuminates the ways in which textualist-originalism has dramatically shaped antidiscrimination doctrine and jurisprudence by advancing an activist judicial philosophy that allows discrimination to be performed through the text and seeks to prevent progress by enacting a regime of static law.

My main argument both converges with and departs from the insights of Critical Legal Studies (CLS). First, it converges with the CLS thesis that in many cases judicial decisions are more akin to "ideological choice" than to determinate outcomes applying legal rules and materials. In *A Critique of Adjudication*, Duncan Kennedy made the argument that "some part of judicial law making in adjudication is best described as ideological choice carried on in a discourse with a strong convention denying choice, and carried on by actors many of whom are in bad faith."[5] However, while Kennedy's claim is a broad generalization covering the entire field of adjudication including "conservative" and "liberal" jurisprudence (i.e., "originalism" and "purposivism"), the argument and focus of this book is more modest. In particular, the book takes as its primary focus the specific brand of interpretation developed by what Justice Scalia he called textualist-originalism.[6] Furthermore, the conclusion the book reaches about Scalia's jurisprudence—namely that textualist-originalism is grounded in the performance of a sovereign exceptionalism of legal meaning—is a far more modest and narrower claim about a particular form of legal interpretation. In contrast, Kennedy's overall contention regarding adjudication is a broad generalization not merely about legal interpretation but about the nature of *legal rules themselves*. Kennedy writes, "the system of legal rules contains gaps, conflicts, and ambiguities that get resolved by judges pursuing conscious, half-conscious, or unconscious ideological projects."[7] Here, the book parts ways with the CLS generalization about the inevitable indeterminacy of legal rules themselves. Rather, careful research into debates over legal meaning reveals that the indeterminacy of legal rules is *not* an inevitable feature of the law itself. What the archival and legal research conducted for this book suggests is that legal rules are *manipulated* by more or less performative theories of *interpretation*. The more performative the theory of interpretation (i.e., "textualist-originalism"), the more likely that legal rules will appear to contain "gaps, conflicts, and ambiguities that get resolved by judges pursuing conscious, half-conscious, or unconscious ideological projects."[8] It is here that Scalia's use of "original public meaning" and rejection of legislative purpose takes on central importance. If the meaning of a legal text can be severed from its congressional record and historical policy context and instead be selected from Webster's dictionary, a Dr. Seuss rhyme, or the "traditions of the people," then it follows that *any* legal text—no matter how clear—can be manipulated in bad faith to advance any number of ideological and/or discriminatory projects. But if the meaning of a law must always be informed by the concrete, social policy purpose it was designed by Congress to solve (for example), then there will at least be a set of agreed-upon legislative materials that may be consulted that will not simply be left up to individual judges to include or exclude by his or her sovereign whim. This demonstrates that the so-called indeterminacy of legal rules highly depends on the particular theory of interpretation with which one approaches the law in the first place.

Finally, given that textualism has arguably become the main prism through which lawyers, judges, and law students are trained to approach the so-called "science" of reading case law, it is incumbent to scrutinize how textualism has transformed how we think about the law. Indeed, as Professor William Baude declared in the 2023 Scalia Lecture at Harvard Law School, "One could say that textualism has won, and we have Justice Scalia to thank for it."[9] Thus, if the game of legal interpretation is over and the battle is won, we must ask: what has been the collateral damage to our understanding of law? If textualism has won, what has been lost?

## "NOT THE COURT"

In October of 2023, Justice Amy Coney Barrett, who replaced Ruth Bader Ginsburg on the court with her nomination by President Trump in 2020, delivered the annual Stein Lecture at the University of Minnesota. As Justice

Barrett began the lecture, student protestors interrupted the lecture hall, chanting *"Not the court. Not the state. People must decide their fate."*[10] The moderator immediately displayed on a screen the text of Minnesota statutes prohibiting trespass and interfering with public property, indicating that the protestors were subject to arrest by university police. The protestors vacated the lecture hall, and the Stein lecture continued, where Barrett spoke about her long-time clerkship for Justice Scalia and the judicial philosophy of textualism she shared with Scalia. For the self-proclaimed textualist Barrett, the incident and the students' slogan, *"Not the Court,"* pointed to what seemed like a stark contradiction. Justice Barrett, in her speech accepting President Trump's nomination in 2020, had clarified the origins of her textualist judicial philosophy, which claims to set aside any political questions of policymaking:

> I clerked for Justice Scalia more than 20 years ago, but the lessons I learned still resonate. His judicial philosophy is mine, too. A judge must apply the law as written. Judges are not policymakers, and they must be resolute in setting aside any policy views they might hold.[11]

On the textualist view, the only authoritative source for interpreting the meaning of a text is *the text itself*—all "extratextual" sources are prohibited, most of all the personal policy preference of the judge. As Scalia and Garner write in their widely cited 2012 treatise on statutory interpretation, *Reading Law*, textualism "reject[s] judicial speculation about both the drafters' extratextually derived purposes and the desirability of the fair reading's anticipated consequences."[12] Weighing policy consequences is the job of the legislature, not the courts. Laws mean what they *say*, and *not* what they do *not* say, regardless of the intended purpose of the legislature. This was the clear message of a principled textualist judge.

However, the October 2022 term was marked by turmoil and controversy. First, in June 2022, Barrett had joined a 6–3 textualist majority opinion of Alito, Thomas, Gorsuch, Kavanaugh, and Roberts, arguing that the right to abortion "is not a fundamental constitutional right because such a right has no basis in the Constitution's text."[13] In the same term, the court held in *303 Creative LLC v. Elenis* (2023) that a business's discriminatory refusal of service to same-sex couples qualified as "protected" speech under the First Amendment. In June 2023, Barrett again joined a 6–3 textualist majority who argued that affirmative action is unconstitutional because, according to the majority, the Fourteenth Amendment contains "no textual reference to race"[14] and therefore is "a wholly race-neutral text."[15] One month later, in July 2023, the Associated Press obtained thousands of documents revealing that "justices spanning the court's ideological divide have lent the prestige of their positions to partisan activity, headlining speaking events with prominent politicians, or advanced their own personal interests."[16] These revelations led to the creation of the first-ever "Code of Conduct" for the Supreme Court, announced in November 2023. For textualists who claimed to strictly adhere to the separation of powers doctrine in leaving the court *out* of the legislative business of "policymaking," the contradiction appeared stark. While textualists have always claimed they are merely interpreting the written words of the Constitution's text, public perception indicated a belief that the court was going well beyond the text: *Not the court. Not the state. People must decide their fate.*

This public perception that the majority was enforcing its own policy views upon the nation could also be seen in the divisions of the court itself. In a scathing dissent in the court's invalidation of affirmative action, Justice Ketanji Brown Jackson argued that the court's textualist "race-neutral" reading of the Fourteenth Amendment had enforced a legally mandated ignorance of race and therefore completely detached itself from American history. Jackson concluded of the majority, "With let-them-eat-cake obliviousness, today, the majority pulls the ripcord and announces "colorblindness for all" by legal fiat."[17] Justice Sotomayor penned a separate dissent attacking the majority's "perverse, ahistorical, and counterproductive outcome."[18] Jackson noted the court's temporal desire to "turn back time," observing, "Turning back the clock . . . the Court indulges those who either do not know our Nation's history or long to repeat it. Simply put, the race-blind admissions stance the Court mandates from this day forward is unmoored from critical real-life circumstances."[19] This controversial ruling invalidating affirmative action was therefore a bookend on a highly "political" and arguably policy-oriented 2022/2023 term for the court—precisely the kind of policy questions that textualist judges *claimed* must be "set aside." As Judge Barrett has said, "Judges are not policymakers." But could one seriously argue that the judges in these cases were not making (or remaking) policy?

Attempts to explain the apparent contradiction between what textualists claim and the court's policy outcomes often trace the problem to President Ronald Reagan's nomination of conservative justices (most notably Rehnquist and Scalia), who were allegedly tasked with a mission to roll back the socially liberal policy created in the wake of the Warren Court of the 1950s and 1960s. According to this narrative, Justice Scalia (for example) should be seen as a "counterrevolutionary" reacting against the cultural values of the previous era of 1960s social movements.[20] Under this view, Scalia and the conservative justices nominated in the wake of the Reagan era were simply pursuing a roll-back of gay rights, sex discrimination, affirmative action, and other socially liberal policies under the cover of "sticking to the text." Bruce Allen Murphy argues in *Scalia: A Court of One* that after Justice Bork's failed confirmation in 1986, Scalia

> began the process of politicizing the Court and launching the partisan warfare among the justices . . . Scalia now saw his mission as leading the war to change the Supreme Court from the liberal activism of the Warren Court of the 1960s and waffling moderate conservatism of the Burger Court in the 1970s and 1980s to the dedicated, unwavering conservative-oriented search for the original meaning of the Constitution after 1986. He just needed to persuade people in speeches and writings off the Court that textualism and originalism were the proper ways to decide cases.[21]

Therefore, according to a political "liberal versus conservative" policy narrative, Reagan's nominations to the court were simply covert conservatives "legislating" from the bench to roll back decades of liberal social policy.

However, this "liberal versus conservative" social policy narrative runs up against several problems. One objection to such a narrative is that Justices Anthony Kennedy and Sandra Day O'Connor, also nominated as Scalia was by Ronald Reagan, were essential in advancing the protection of LGBTQ rights.[22] Kennedy penned the majority opinion in *Lawrence v. Texas* (2003) invalidating state laws criminalizing same-sex sexual intimacy. In that ruling, President Reagan's nominations split the decision exactly 2-2: Kennedy and O'Connor joined the majority protecting same-sex rights, while Scalia and Rehnquist joined the dissent. Scalia not only disagreed with Kennedy's majority opinion but disagreed vehemently. Justice Scalia's dissent (correctly) predicted that the court's reasoning would lead to the legalization of same-sex marriage, which later came to fruition in *Obergefell v. Hodges* (2015), a decision in which (again) Kennedy joined the "liberal" majority in protecting the rights of same-sex couples.

Furthermore, the court's "textualist" methods have produced results exactly contrary to conservative social policy outcomes. In the court's opinion in *Bostock v. Clayton County* (2020), President Donald Trump's 2017 nominee and avowed textualist Neil Gorsuch shocked many by penning a majority opinion which argued that "Title VII's plain text" of the Civil Rights Act prohibiting employment discrimination on the basis of sex also applies to homosexual and transgender individuals.[23] To the surprise of many conservatives, Gorsuch forcefully presented a tour-de-force "textualist" argument in favor of protecting the rights of homosexual and transgender individuals against employment discrimination. Writing the 6–3 majority opinion, Gorsuch not only cited Justice Scalia's major treatise on textualist legal interpretation[24] but also declared, in the spirit of Scalia himself, "Only the written word is the law, and all persons are entitled to its benefit."[25] Justice Gorsuch's textualist opinion thus drew on a tradition of conservative justices who have been essential in protecting the federal constitutional rights of same-sex and transgender individuals.

The most significant problem with the narrative that textualists are simply covert social conservatives, however, is the fact that the specific methods of textualism and originalism have become incorporated as a norm for "liberal" justices as well.[26] Textualism has been used by liberal-leaning judges to argue for the disqualification of Donald Trump from the 2024 presidential election. Textualism has become a central feature of Justice Sotomayor's reasoning, justifying her opinions "based on the plain text of the statute,"[27] often clarifying her own approach by writing that "statutory interpretation 'begins with the text.'"[28] Justice Kagan, who famously declared in 2015 that "we're all textualists now,"[29] is often quoted by all members of the court, including liberal justices, with her remark, "Statutory interpretation, as we always say, begins with the text."[30] Liberal constitutional lawyers and scholars have argued that originalism even *requires* the possibility of progressive judicial thought. Thus, while textualist methods have led more conservative justices such as Kennedy, O'Connor, and Gorsuch to support constitutional rights for LGBTQ individuals, textualism has also provided a framework for the reasoning of "liberal" justices Kagan, Sotomayor, and has led some to argue that such methods *require* progressive outcomes within the canon of judicial thought. For many of these reasons, it has been observed that, as of the October 2023 term, textualism is the Supreme Court's dominant interpretive theory.[31]

While textualist-originalist methods of interpretation have become the norm in judicial interpretation across the political spectrum, I will argue that one reason for its success is that textualism is a *performative* theory of the text that allows any interpreter to disguise the arbitrary sovereign exclusion of legal meaning in the "neutrality" of the text. While textualist-originalism claims its methods are a neutral and objective interpretation of "the text," in fact, the method allows for the application of a *pretextual* rule hidden by the text itself. It is this feature of textualism I refer to as *sovereign exceptionalism*. While Scalia's textualism has been criticized for not being applied consistently or being utilized "opportunistically" to achieve conservative policy preferences, many analyses still implicitly accept the idea that a "pure" textualist method exists in theory that can supply neutral criteria for adjudicating legal disputes and thus maintain a "science of statutory construction." In contrast, the methodology I advance questions the fundamental notion that a "scientific" neutral method of interpretation exists in the first place. As a host of legal scholars, historians, and biographers of Scalia have argued, textualism is in fact a normative, rhetorical method with a distinct "malleability" or "flexibility" that allows judges to achieve results they prefer through a "opportunistic" and "selective" interpretive procedure. What is less understood or studied, however, is *how* the specific procedures of textualism facilitate the performativity required for the malleability and flexibility that textualism affords the interpreter.

The performative flexibility of textualism is what allows textualist judges to contradict one another, even on the same legal issue or case. In early 2024, textualism's contradictory methods were illustrated in real time in the wake of the US Supreme Court's ruling on the disqualification of Donald Trump from running in the 2024 presidential election.[32] The central legal issue in the runup to the election was the text of Section Three of the Fourteenth Amendment that prohibits running for office any representative who has engaged in insurrection or rebellion against the Constitution.[33] Due to Trump's involvement with the January 6 insurrection at the US Capitol, numerous states have attempted to remove Trump from the ballot. In response, these actions have been challenged by Trump's legal team. In its findings of fact, the district court had determined that Trump engaged in insurrection on January 6, 2023. However, Democratic-appointed Judge Sarah B. Wallace concluded that the text of Section Three of the Fourteenth Amendment did *not* apply to the office of the president and therefore could not be used to disqualify former President Trump. However, as the court noted, Section Three does *not* explicitly mention federal offices such as the president but rather refers to state representatives and state electors. Therefore, according to the District Court, the text of the Constitution allows a former president who engaged in insurrection to run again for president. However, in its appellate ruling disqualifying Trump from the Colorado ballot, the Supreme Court of Colorado cited the "plain language" and "ordinary meaning" of the word "office," concluding that the office of president clearly falls within the ordinary meaning of the text.[34] Therefore, the court ruled, the text *does* disqualify Trump from running. This ruling was taken up on *certiori* by the US Supreme Court which decided in favor of former President Trump in March of 2024.[35]

What is striking about these two contradictory conclusions—that Section Three does and does not disqualify Trump—is that each is grounded in textualist legal interpretation. Because the president is not explicitly mentioned in the text, the district court concludes Trump is not excluded from running. And because the ordinary meaning of the text includes the president, the Colorado Supreme Court concludes that Trump is excluded from running. In fact, both methods of interpretation are part of the textualist toolbox: the Constitution must be interpreted to mean what it says and *not* what it does not say, and the text should be interpreted in its "ordinary meaning" at its time of enactment. But how could opposite conclusions be reached by textualist methods?

In fact, such contradictory outcomes are built into textualism according to its most ardent and influential architect, the late Justice Antonin Scalia. In his treatise on *Reading Law*, Scalia explained:

> Imagine a Supreme Court comprising Justice Scalia and eight near clones. That Court would find lots of cases to be hard; this book shows the sorts of interpretive issues that might cause the Justice Scalia of 2011 to disagree with the Justice Scalia of 2012. It would grant review of those hard cases and decide many of them five to four.[36]

For Scalia, the "reason why textualists are bound to disagree among themselves is built into the rule that meaning depends on the enacted text rather than what the text's authors meant, intended, planned or expected the text to accomplish."[37] For Scalia, textualism rejects the hermeneutic scrutiny into the motives, intentions, or purposes of law that are not made explicit on the face of the text itself. Scalia outlines in a speech on "Realism and the Religion Clauses" "the four supporting pillars of constitutional construction":

> (1) Text. The Constitution says what it says, and does not say what it does not say. (2) Original Meaning. Text is to be given the same meaning, and the same application to facts, that it had when it was adopted-not some new meaning or application favored by later times. (3) Tradition. Where the original meaning or application of the text cannot be determined, it should be interpreted and applied as it is reflected in the traditional practices of the people. (4) Immutability. We have an enduring Constitution, not a living one. If social conditions require that its dispositions be changed, there is an amendment process prescribed for that purpose.[38]

Scalia's judicial philosophy of what he called textualist-originalism therefore centered the written text itself as the sole, singular authority for interpreting the meaning of a constitutional text. However, for Scalia, the meaning of "the text" could also be interpreted using time-specific dictionary definitions of the words of the text itself and/or the *unwritten* "traditional practices of the people" at the time of a law's enactment. For this reason, the textualist must dive down into the hermeneutic depths of "the interpretive community alive at the time of the text's adoption."[39] This meant that for Scalia, sometimes a textualist judge must look to the "unwritten" original meaning. Indeed, the "original meaning" of a text may be embodied in the unwritten "traditions of the people," a notion influenced by von Savigny's notion of the "spirit of the people," or *volkgeist* (as discussed in chapter 3). Within these hermeneutic depths, a textualist of 2011 may disagree with the textualist of 2012, just as textualist judges conclude that Section Three of the Fourteenth Amendment may disqualify and not disqualify Trump from running for president.

Therefore, the text may mean one thing for textualist A, and another thing for textualist B. Scalia disagrees with Scalia.

In this way, I examine the specific kinds of performative practices that continue to make textualism so successful and ubiquitous throughout the legal community and which has established itself as the dominant method of interpretation on the Supreme Court. I argue that textualism is grounded in a certain *performance* of the text that hides the application of pretextual rules, and it is precisely through its *performativity* that judicial decisions may then be presented with "neutrality" and objectivity. The performative procedures of textualism outlined in the book therefore facilitate what I refer to as *malevolent legality*. In order to demonstrate how textualism is grounded in the application of pretextual rules, let us examine the case of Dino.

## THE CASE OF DINO

Dino Villareal was born a biological female named Diana but was raised as and identified as a male for all his adult life. In 1994, Dino moved in with his romantic partner, Sandra Sandoval. In 2002, Sandoval adopted two babies from a couple whose parental rights had been terminated. Dino and Sandoval lived together and shared "actual care, control, and possession" of the children from 1994 until their separation in January 2011. Therefore, because Dino had actual care, control, and possession of the children for at least six months, Dino had standing under the Texas Family Code during that period to apply for parentage but never applied. After their separation, Dino filed a petition to adjudicate his parentage in 2013 after Sandoval prohibited any contact between Dino and the children. In 2013, a court denied Dino's petition for standing. However, in 2014, Dino obtained a legal Order Granting Change of Identity,

> which acknowledged his name change from Diana to Dino, and included the following finding: "3. Petitioner's sex is male." Following the trial court's findings, the order concluded, "IT IS ORDERED that Petitioner's identity is changed from female to male."[40] With this order granting Dino the status of being legally "male," Dino then filed a second petition to adjudicate his parentage under Texas Family Code 160 which allows standing for "a man whose paternity of the child is to be adjudicated."[41]

Therefore, with the court order granting Dino's legal status as "male," Dino argued

> that because the Order Granting Change of Identity, signed on January 3, 2014, was in place prior to his filing the second suit to adjudicate parentage, he now

has standing to maintain suit. Dino contends that his Order Granting Change of Identity is legally sufficient to confer statutory standing to adjudicate his legal paternity to Sandoval's adopted children under subsection 160.602(a)(3).[42]

However, the court denied Dino's second petition, rejecting the argument that he had standing despite his legal status of "male" being granted prior to the filing of the second petition. In its reasoning, the court relied on the fact that the legislature does not define the word "male." As a result, the court proceeded to engage in a textualist interpretation of "ordinary meaning" in which it defines "male" in exclusively biological terms. As the court reasoned,

> The Texas Family Code defines "man" as "a male individual of any age.". . . The Texas Family Code does not, however, define the term "male." "When the legislature fails to define a word or term, we will apply its ordinary meaning." *Id.* In this court's March 11, 2015 opinion, we cited Webster's Dictionary which defines "male" as "an individual that produces small usually motile gametes . . . which fertilize the eggs of a female." *Id.* That definition has not changed and is controlling in this mandamus. Therefore, regardless of his possession of a court order changing his identity, Villarreal still does not meet the statutory definition of "man" under the Texas Family Code.[43]

In a concurring opinion, Judge Patricia Alvarez—a liberal, Democratic member of the court—supported the court's conclusion with a textualist justification while acknowledging that the result was "sad," "heart-wrenching," and "incredibly unfair." As Judge Alvarez wrote,

> Although I agree that the Texas Family Code's definition of man results in an incredibly unfair situation for Villarreal, this court is bound by the language of the statute and not by what we think is fair. . . . Although Villarreal's inability to legally establish standing to assert his parental rights over these children is heart-wrenching and sad, an appellate court is bound by the law and not emotions.[44]

The court thus explains its conclusion as the natural and inevitable result of simply "applying the statute" and the "ordinary meaning" of the word "male."

However, in Dino's first petition, the same Court cited not one *but two* diverging definitions of the word male. Immediately after citing the biological, Webster's Dictionary definition ("male = gamete producing"), the court observed that "Black's Law Dictionary defines male as "of the masculine sex." BLACK'S LAW DICTIONARY 862 (5th ed.) (1979)."[45] However, in Dino's second petition, this far more inclusive dictionary definition is not even mentioned, and only the narrow, biological Webster's definition is cited. Instead of giving explanation of why the Webster's biological definition is better or has more fidelity to the legislature's intention or purpose than the Black's definition, the court simply declares, "That definition has not changed and is controlling in this mandamus." No mention or justification is given as to why the more inclusive Black's definition is excluded.

As the dissent in the case pointed out, nothing forced the court to define "male" according to the Webster's Dictionary definition. In fact, nothing in the Texas Family Code compels a court to read the statute in a narrow, technical sense such that "male" is defined by "gametes which fertilize eggs." Even though the court cited two different dictionary definitions of "male," one narrow and exclusive and one broader and inclusive, the court selected the one definition (without explanation) that excluded the petitioner's standing and then concluded that the court is merely following the "ordinary" language of the statute. Therefore, the "heart-wrenching" and "incredibly unfair" outcome was *not* the result of the court sticking to the "clear language" or "ordinary meaning" of the words—rather, the court selected *precisely* the meaning of the statute that excluded the plaintiff's right to standing. Notice that the court equates the neutrality and objectivity of "the law" with its *own* selective, unjustified definition of "male" (Webster's), which enables it to claim that it is simply applying law rather than (for example) engaging in unwarranted discrimination on the basis of sex and/or gender. Only *after* excluding the dictionary definition it disfavors ("male = masculine sex") and presenting the one it favors (without justification) does the court then conclude that its reasoning is simply giving effect to the "ordinary meaning" of the word, concluding that it is "bound by the law and not emotions." Rather than simply acknowledging that "male" means "male" in Texas family law, the court twists itself into knots to conclude, "even if considered a man from birth for legal purposes, Dino's status as a man is not sufficient to confer statutory standing as, "a man whose paternity of the child is to be adjudicated."[46] That is, even though Dino is a man, and has legal status as a man, *he is not a man*. X does *not* equal X.

This case is intended to show *not* that textualism inherently has a conservative or liberal bias but rather the contrary: textualism necessarily allows the interpreter, indeed any interpreter, to apply a *pretextual* rule of exclusion prior to the application of "the law" itself—a pretextual rule that is concealed under the cover of an "objective" application of the "plain language" of the text. Even though the court order granted Dino legal status as "male," the court said he does not qualify as a "male" according to the statute. But if a court grants an individual's change of legal identity to a "male," how can they *not* be considered a "male," legally speaking? As the dissent points out, the most likely explanation is that *transgender* individuals are excluded from the definition. Thus, the *pretextual* legal rule seems to be: "male = male, except for trans individuals." Thus, even when trans individuals have been *legally ordered* "male," a textualist reserves for himself the power not to go beyond the text but rather *before* the text (*pretext*), introducing textual exceptions and discriminations where there were none. Indeed, if a "male" by statute counts as a "male" by court order, then it is obvious that Dino has a right of standing by the "ordinary language" of the statute. According to a textualist, however, a "male" by court order does *not* mean a "male" by statute. For a textualist, "male" fails to mean "male" in *this* case because textualism allows the application of a *pretextual rule* excluding any definitions it disfavors under the guise of objective, neutral methods. If a textualist judge dislikes the fact that certain individuals might be legally included in the definition of "male," a textualist may simply apply a pretextual rule that *excises* or *defines out* of textual existence that which he wants to exclude. The result of this *sovereign excision* is "the text," presented as an objective rendering according to the sovereign decision of the textualist judge.

## TEXTUALISM AS SOVEREIGN EXCEPTIONALISM

In this respect, Dino's case exemplifies a kind of sovereign exceptionalism that forms the basis of the judicial method of textualism. As I use the term, sovereign exceptionalism in judicial interpretation refers to the unilateral selection of a single, determinate legal meaning by making arbitrary sovereign exceptions to a specific universe of legal meaning. As I argue below, sovereign exceptionalism is *required* in making textualist determinations regarding the meaning of any legal text. In this way, I argue that textualism is a *performative* theory of the text that requires the inclusion/exclusion of social meaning through sovereign exception.

In *The History of Sexuality*, Michel Foucault traced the origins of sovereign power to the Roman *pater familias*, grounded in the legal right to decide whether the subjects of the household may live or die. Through the Middle Ages up to its modern form in the absolute sovereignty of the king or monarch, Foucault argued, the art of government was still modeled on the family, with the "sovereign" conceived as the *pater familias*.[47] In the feudal state, sovereign power referred to "essentially a right of seizure: of things, time, bodies, and ultimately life itself; it culminated in the privilege to seize hold of life in order to suppress it."[48] For Foucault, the modern juridical system of law functions on the basis of sovereign power because "Law cannot help but be armed, and its arm, *par excellence,* is death; to those who transgress it, it replies, at least as a last resort, with that absolute menace. The law always refers to the sword."[49] However, with the emergence of what Foucault had called "bio-politics" and the economic problem of population in the eighteenth century,[50] sovereign power underwent a "juridical regression" as the absolute power of the king's sword was increasingly displaced by "tactics of government" regulating the market, the economy, sexuality, health, reproduction, epidemics, and public health.[51] Thus for Foucault, whereas sovereign power achieved obedience simply by imposing the law upon its subjects by the sword, the governmental state of the eighteenth century pursues the ends of administering the population by "employing tactics rather than laws".[52] In Foucault's estimation, however, the emergence of "government" in no way reduced the role of sovereign power. In fact, for Foucault, the question of how sovereign power exerts itself in this new governmental state is made even more urgent, because the proliferation of the "tactics of government" poses the question of "what juridical form, what institutional form, and what legal basis could be given to the sovereignty typical of the state."[53] As a result, Foucault makes clear that, "sovereignty is absolutely not eliminated by the emergence of a new art of government that has crossed the threshold of political science. The problem of sovereignty is not eliminated; on the contrary, it is made more acute than ever."[54]

In *Precarious Life,* Judith Butler takes up the urgent question of sovereign power in the wake of the post-9/11 authorization of the Patriot Act.[55] For Butler, the legal authorization of indefinite detention in Guantanamo Bay should be understood as a legal suspension of the law, and therefore as an exercise of what Giorgio Agamben has described as a sovereign "state of exception." In *State of Exception,* Agamben defined the domain of the *state of exception* as a "consistent set of legal phenomena" developed by nation-states since World World I, which consist in the suspension of the legal order.[56] Drawing upon Carl Schmitt's formulation, Agamben takes up an analysis of the sovereign as "he who decides on the exception."[57] As Schmitt had argued in *Political Theology,* the mark of sovereign power is the characteristic of being both inside and outside the legal order. Schmitt writes, "Although he stands outside the normally valid legal system, he nevertheless belongs to it, for it is he who must decide whether the constitution needs to be suspended in its entirety."[58] For Agamben, one of the essential features of the state of exception is the collapse of the distinction between legislative, executive, and judicial functions of power such that the sovereign exception is determined by the sovereign decision itself.[59] Therefore, Agamben describes the sovereign state of exception as an *inclusive exclusion* whereby sovereign authority in the modern state excludes that which is determined to be an exception to the legal order. As Agamben had argued, the sovereign state of exception has become a normalized, common technique of government, whereby the very exercise of government entails the sovereign decision to decide on the *exception* to the legal order. Indeed, for Schmitt, the exception referred to "a general concept in the theory of the state, and not merely to a construct applied to any emergency decree or state of siege."[60] For Agamben, the normalization of the state of exception reached its peak in the camps of Nazi-occupied during World War II and can be illustrated in the normalization of the figures of the undocumented (*sans-papiers*), detainees in Guantanamo Bay, and (we might add) homeless populations, and migrant caravans crossing the US-Mexico border, among many other "surplus" populations deemed to be "exceptional."

In a chapter of *Indefinite Detention*, Butler examines contemporary "tactics of government" as a manifestation of sovereign power in the contemporary state. Remarking on Agamben's thesis that the state of exception has become a normalized technique of government, Butler writes that the example of Guantanamo Bay illustrates that "Not only is law treated as a tactic, but it is also suspended in order to heighten the discretionary power of those who are asked to rely on their own judgment to decide fundamental matters of justice, life and death."[61] Responding to Foucault's question about how sovereign power manifests itself in our contemporary governmental state, Butler writes that the various states of exception we are seeing today point to "a broader phenomenon, namely, that sovereignty is reintroduced in the very acts by which state suspends law, or contorts law to its own uses. In this way, the state extends its own domain, its own necessity, and the means by which its self-justification occurs."[62] According to Butler, sovereign power is exercised in our contemporary governmental state by the *self-conferral* of power exercised by "rogue" representatives of sovereignty distributed throughout a web of governmental decision-makers. Within this web of decision-makers, Butler writes,

> sovereignty is exercised in the act of suspension, but also in the self-allocation of legal prerogative; governmentality denotes an operation of administration power that is extra-legal, even as it can and does return to law as a field of tactical operations . . . the state is not subject to the rule of law, but law can be suspended or deployed tactically and partially to suit the requirements of a state that seeks more and more to allocate sovereign power to its executive and administrative powers.[63]

Therefore, for Butler, the answer to Foucault's question about how sovereign power is exercised within the web of "tactics" deployed by government is the following:

> Petty sovereigns abound, reigning in the midst of bureaucratic army institutions mobilized by aims and tactics of power they do not inaugurate or fully control. And yet such figures are delegated with the power to render unilateral decision,

accountable to no law and without any legitimate authority. The resurrected sovereignty is thus not the sovereignty of unified power under the conditions of legitimacy, the form of power that guarantees the representative status of political institutions. It is, rather, a lawless and prerogatory power, a 'rogue' power *par excellence*.[64]

In other words, for Butler, the contemporary governmental state exercises sovereign power by delegating sovereign authority to make unilateral decisions to a network of "petty sovereigns" whose function is the self-allocation and justification of the legitimacy and authority of the state. In this way, for Butler, sovereign power in the governmental state relies upon the "tactics of government" in justifying its own authority through practices of unilateral and arbitrary self-conferral.

Justice Scalia himself was keenly aware of the undemocratic, arbitrary nature of "sovereign" power wielded by judges. In his 2012 treatise *Reading Law*, Justice Scalia remarked on the undemocratic nature of unelected judges deciding fundamental issues of justice for the entire nation. Scalia writes, "Only in the theater of the absurd does an aristocratic, life-tenured, unelected council of elders set aside laws enacted by the people's chosen representatives on the ground that the people do not want those laws."[65] Again, commenting on the undemocratic nature of judges deciding on what the "spirit" of the law means, Scalia writes elsewhere that, "It is simply not compatible with democratic theory that laws mean whatever they ought to mean, and that unelected judges decide what that is."[66] Here, Scalia was criticizing his rival interpretive theories (namely purposivism and consequentialism) for holding undemocratic views of an "activist" judiciary. For Scalia, if judges are not constrained by the text itself, then judges will be able to create any number of "purposes" or "policy consequences" to justify their own reading of the text that might be contrary to the wishes of "the people." Therefore, the criticism goes, the broad discretion allowed by other interpretive theories is undemocratic, since such discretion allows judges the sovereign power to unilaterally decide the outcome using "extratextual" sources not authorized by the people such as personal interest or policy preference. In contrast, Scalia argued, textualism is the most democratic theory of interpretation since textualist judges are always constrained by the written text enacted by the people. Whereas "purposivists" are not constrained by the text and can manipulate the outcome according to "extralegal" considerations, Scalia claimed, textualism simply gives effect to the written text and therefore constrains the judge from relying on extralegal considerations.

However, what Scalia had failed to fully appreciate is that his *own* method of textualism was even more susceptible to precisely the same criticism of "judicial discretion." In their 2012 treatise, *Reading Law*, Scalia and Garner had articulated 57 statutory canons of construction that are described as "principles of expression that are as universal as principles of logic."[67] For Scalia, a textualist utilizes these canons of construction to interpret the meaning that is intelligently expressed in the law. However, as early as January 1987, Scalia had openly acknowledged that all judicial canons of construction could be "manipulated" just as easily as the purposivist's use of legislative history and historical record. Criticizing judges' reliance on legislative purpose or history, Scalia writes, "So you can manipulate legislative history as well as you can manipulate the canons of construction."[68] Therefore, Scalia himself even recognized that the same "absurd" level of undemocratic judicial "discretion" he saw in purposivism could just as easily be achieved by utilizing the very canons of construction Scalia presented as "universal" principles of textualist interpretation.

Even in the wake of the publication of Scalia and Garner's treatise, there were clear signs that Scalia's specific brand of "textualist-originalist interpretation"[69] was being used by judges of many different political stripes as a kind of sovereign exceptionalism in making unilateral, discretionary determinations on the social meaning of "the text." The arbitrary nature of textualism's sovereign exceptionalism was illustrated in *Yates v. United States* (2015), where the Supreme Court faced the question of whether a fish qualified as a "tangible object" for purposes of federal criminal law. Writing for the majority, Justice Ginsburg explained that the purpose of the criminal law in question was to preserve information rather than prevent destruction of all physical objects in the universe, and that the meaning of words "does not turn solely on dictionary definitions of its component words."[70] However, the liberal justice Elena Kagan joined Justices Scalia and Thomas in arguing that, on the contrary, the dictionary definition leads to the conclusion that a "fish" was in fact a tangible object. Writing for the dissent, Justice Kagan explained the textualist view that a fish qualified as a "tangible object." Citing none other than Scalia and Garner's *Reading Law*,[71] Kagan argued that statutory construction begins with the "ordinary meaning" of the text. Kagan then writes, "A fish is, of course, a discrete thing that possesses physical form. See generally Dr. Seuss, One Fish Two Fish Red Fish Blue Fish (1960). So the ordinary meaning of the term "tangible object" in §1519, as no one here disputes, covers fish (including too-small red grouper)."[72]

Kagan's reasoning regarding the "ordinary meaning" of the word *fish* is fascinating because it reveals the vast field of meanings available to the textualist searching for ordinary meaning. When giving justification for the ordinary meaning of a legal term in a federal criminal statute, Kagan cites for authority none other than Dr. Seuss, and one is struck by the arbitrariness of the source Kagan cites—why should the legal meaning of a federal criminal statute depend upon a Dr. Seuss rhyme? For a textualist, such sources supposedly indicate the public meaning of the term at the time of enactment and thus provide evidence for the ordinary meaning. But the sheer arbitrariness of Kagan's citation of Dr. Seuss (why not Shel Silverstein, Beverly Cleary, or Judy Blume) demonstrates the degree of sovereign exceptionalism *required* in making textualist determinations regarding ordinary meaning. Why should Dr. Seuss be presented in support of one's preferred definition of *fish* but Shel Silverstein's allegorical poem about fish should be excluded? One could argue that in Shel Silverstein's poem "Fish?"[73] a fish is a *metaphor* for human behavior and therefore a fish does *not* clearly and unambiguously qualify as a tangible object. In this way, Kagan's citation of Dr. Seuss and exclusion of other readings and sources begins to appear as completely arbitrary, revealing the fact that the textualist's selection of "ordinary" meaning is drawn from a vast field of possible public meanings that can be selected according to one's preferred, preselected definition. Alternatively, a textualist may draw open this vast field of "public" meanings precisely to exclude any textual definitions one disfavors. In this way, Scalia's specific brand of "textualist-originalist interpretation"[74] not only allows but *requires* a kind of sovereign exceptionalism in making unilateral, discretionary determinations on the social meaning of any text. Given the vast array of potential meanings of the term "ordinary meaning," a textualist *must* become a sovereign exceptionalist, making the final, arbitrary determinations on what to exclude based simply on his or her preferred definition of what should be the ordinary meaning of the text for *all* legal subjects.

Because the textualist toolbox of "ordinary meaning" opens a vast field of competing social meanings (dictionary definitions, public meanings, "traditional practices," Dr. Seuss rhymes, etc.), and because "the text" is presented as natural and objective, it follows that the selection of any specific definition to serve as the "ordinary meaning" will always disguise a certain degree of arbitrariness in what meanings are included or excluded by the sovereign judicial selection of meaning. Just as in *Yates* (2015), Kagan excludes any disfavored textual definitions by the citation of Dr. Seuss, the court in Dino's case excludes the definition that would have given Dino standing by citing Webster's definition as simply "the ordinary meaning." In this way, textualism requires the application of a *pretextual rule of exception* that is hidden by the sovereign determination of ordinary meaning of the text. For Scalia, the ordinary meaning of a text may refer to (a) the written text itself, (b) a dictionary definition of one's selection, or (c) the unwritten "traditional practices" of the people, such that any selection of a definition or a tradition then becomes an "inclusive exclusion" of any disfavored definitions. In Scalia's words, the resultant ordinary meaning becomes "the only objective standard of interpretation even competing for acceptance."[75]

Schmitt's description of the sovereign exception provides insight into the judicial logic of textualism. In Dino's case, the sovereign inclusive exclusion of Dino's legal standing as a "male" (even though he had legal standing as male) was achieved by the textualist use of a *pretextual* rule—namely the rule that "male = male, *except* for trans individuals." Even while Dino had been *legally ordered* male, the textualist reserves the power to introduce a textual discrimination *before* the text (pretext). Only by this exclusion of trans individuals can the court conclude that Dino (male) is *not* a male in Texas family law. But how can a male in Texas family law fail to mean a male in Texas family law? In *Political Theology*, Schmitt gives us an answer:

> All law is "situational law." The sovereign produces and guarantees the situation in its totality. He has the monopoly over this last decision. Therein resides the essence of the state's sovereignty, which must be juristically defined correctly, not as the monopoly to coerce or to rule but as the monopoly to decide. The exception reveals most clearly the essence of the state's authority. The decision parts here from the legal norm, and (to formulate it paradoxically) authority proves that to produce law it need not be based on law.[76]

In this passage, Schmitt argues that the foundation of sovereignty in the modern state lies *not* in legal norms such as rule of law or equality under law but rather in the unilateral decision itself. For Schmitt, the essence of sovereignty resides not in the predictability or transparency of legal norms and rules but in the sovereign decision determining what constitutes threats to the public order. As a result, it is not a problem for Schmitt if the word male fails to mean male in Texas family law. If a textualist judge determines that trans individuals should not count as male, then the textualist judge may exercise a sovereign decision to exclude these individuals. If trans individuals are excluded from the law, that is simply because sovereignty for a textualist resides not in legal norms like equality under law but in the textualist judge's sovereign power to decide on the exception.

In this way, a pretextual rule of exception is hidden by the "objective standard" of the court's "ordinary meaning." Only by applying a pretextual rule of exception that excludes the definition that includes the plaintiff may the court then conclude that it is simply applying the ordinary meaning of the word male. Indeed, the "natural meaning" or "plain meaning" of the text is always the result of a certain kind of sovereign textualism that reserves for itself the power to exclude any textual definitions it disfavors merely by judicial fiat. In this respect, *all* social meanings for a textualist become possible objects for sovereign exception. Textualist meaning determination is therefore a kind of "black box": it is impossible to identify a textualist's reasons or "inputs" for arriving at the legal outcomes or "outputs" of textualist decisions.

The argument that textualism requires a kind of sovereign exceptionalism is bolstered by a host of book-length studies of Scalia's judicial philosophy by legal scholars, historians, and biographers of Scalia himself. In *Scalia v. Scalia: Opportunistic Textualism in Constitutional Interpretation*, Catherine Langford argues that Scalia was an "opportunistic textualist" that utilized his textualism to achieve his own desired results. Through a close examination of Scalia's jurisprudence, Langford observes that "When we examine Scalia's actual jurisprudential reasoning, "we witness Scalia twist the meaning of terms beyond their plain meaning into a convoluted historical exploration of a position that supported his thinking."[77] Scalia's flexible and "rhetorical" textualism, therefore, allowed him to argue for his preferred outcome by twisting the meaning of the text to comport with an "original meaning" or "ordinary meaning" supporting his goals. Langford argues that Scalia utilized textualism "when it furthers the results he seeks; he alters reasonable textual constructions or uses other forms of interpretation when it does not."[78] In *The Unexpected Scalia,* David Dorsey similarly concludes that Scalia was a "selective" originalist,[79] applying originalism inconsistently and selectively to some issues not others. American legal historian Gordon S. Wood, in his ultimate assessment of textualism, concluded that, "Textualism, as Justice Scalia defines it, appears to me as permissive and as open to arbitrary judicial discretion and expansion as the use of legislative intent or other interpretive methods, if the text-minded judge is so inclined."[80] In Bruce Allen Murphy's biography, *Scalia: a Court of One*, Murphy traces the development of Scalia's originalism and its proliferation as a popular method of legal interpretation in the legal community. Commenting on the now widespread use of "originalist" methods across the conservative-liberal spectrum, Murphy concludes that, "Like other legal theories, originalism was becoming just another tool to reach whatever ideological results a judge preferred."[81] In *Justice of Contradictions: Antonin Scalia and the Politics of Disruption*, American legal scholar Richard Hasen gives the most critical assessment of Scalia's method, writing:

> The notion that judges can use originalist methods to "find" or "discover" the law, rather than make it, has proven to be an illusion. Instead, originalism looks like a subconscious crutch or, worse, a fig leaf, a pretext justifying a result that lines up with one's ideology. Should it surprise anyone that the originalist analyses of the liberal Justice Stevens in the *Citizens United* and *Heller* cases supported more liberal results than the originalist analyses of Justice Scalia? No doubt Scalia's response would be that Stevens was misusing originalism, while he was not. But with so much malleability to the approach, who could say? It certainly seemed as malleable as other constitutional approaches.[82]

In his book-length examination of Scalia's jurisprudence, Hasen argues that Scalia utilized his textualist-originalist method when he wanted to reach conservative results,[83] and at worst utilized textualism as the pretext to do so. Ultimately, Hasen concludes that

> his doctrines were so flexible that he could reach a range of interpretations and still claim fidelity to his ostensibly neutral methodology. Part of what must have subconsciously attracted him to his theories and methodologies is that they mostly led him where he wanted to go.[84]

Agreeing with Langford's analysis, Hasen argues that Scalia's textualist-originalism allowed him to believe in the "myth" of a pure, objective method of interpreting legal texts. Hasen writes, "Scalia's blind spot was his belief that it is possible to objectively and neutrally determine what the Constitution 'actually commands.'"[85] In a similar way, Langford argues that Scalia's textualism is premised on

> the myth that the law can be interpreted in an unbiased and nonpreferential fashion . . . the method of legal interpretation is a rhetorical maneuver to support judicial legitimacy, for how justices interpret the law creates the *reality* of the law as a social practice.[86]

However, ultimately, Langford argues, Scalia failed to recognize that it is impossible "to separate the judicial from the political. In the end, I conclude that such a division is not possible. The judicial is the political, but the political does not have to be the judicial."[87]

In this way, the "malleability," "flexibility," "opportunist," and "rhetorical" character of Scalia's textualism supports the thesis of the book, namely that textualism thrives on the *performativity* of legal texts and legal speech. Textualist meaning determination depends upon opening up a vast field of possible legal meanings that then *require* a sovereign inclusion/exclusion from the universe of legal meaning. Thus, precisely because of this performativity implied by textualist methods, textualism requires the judge to include/exclude certain social meanings of the text as an exception to the universe of legal meaning. In turn, it is precisely this sovereign exceptionalism that allows textualism to serve as "arbitrary judicial discretion"; "a pretext justifying a result that lines up with one's ideology"; "a rhetorical maneuver to support judicial legitimacy." As a result, textualism should be understood as a *performative* theory of the text which requires the inclusion/exclusion of social meaning through sovereign exception.

Victoria Nourse has argued in a similar vein that textualism itself is a form of power, a kind of *textual power* "by which the interpreter can increase the interpreter's *power* over the text."[88] For Nourse, there are three distinct stages for the exercise of textualist judicial power:

> the first, *isolation* of the text (focusing on the word executive); the second, *reduction* of the text (taking the word out of context from larger constitutional text); and third, *addition* to the constitutional text by pragmatic enrichment (adding meaning to the text).[89]

Viewed in terms of a sovereign exceptionalism, textual power is exercised by the judge by *isolating* the text from its context within a statute or subject matter, *reducing* the text to a dictionary definition or ordinary meaning abstracted from historical context and *adding* to the text by appealing to the unwritten traditions of the people embodied in the what Savigny called the *volkgeist* or spirit of the people. In this way, Nourse's analysis of *textual power* supports the view that textualism *depends* upon a sort of sovereign exceptionalism for making determinations regarding the meaning of any given text. A textualist judge becomes the sovereign decider of any and all exceptions to the legal meaning of any given text.

Dino's case, along with cases such as *Yates v. United States*, is particularly significant for another reason. In addition to demonstrating how textualist methods require a sovereign exceptionalism, we also see that textualism comes in many different "political" colors. As noted earlier, Judge Alvarez has a considerable history of textualist opinions and often clarifies her court's approach as it did in Dino's case: "We apply the plain meaning of the text, absent a different definition provided by the legislature, unless the plain meaning leads to absurd results."[90] Justice Kagan, a liberal bastion of the Supreme Court, has quite openly embraced textualist methods and joined both Scalia and Thomas in opposing a more "purposivist" reading of statutes. Indeed, textualism is utilized across the political spectrum to endorse admittedly unfair, unjust, and often arbitrary outcomes—outcomes that are often admitted as such by textualist judges and courts themselves. On further inspection, however, the "objective interpretation" of the text in fact involves the application of a pretextual rule hidden by the "neutrality" of the text itself. This possibility of the application of a pretextual rule results from the vast field of meanings available to a textualist searching for "ordinary meaning." In this way, unfair, unjust, or arbitrary results may be justified—on a multiplicity of conservative or liberal grounds—by a *performance* of the text that hides the application of a pretextual rule. The sovereign exceptionalism of textualism constitutes one of the main sources of malevolent legality.

However, if the text hides the exceptionalism of the sovereign decision, what legal tools are there to combat or address these forms of undemocratic, sovereign power in judicial decision-making? Here, we descend into the dark, obscure realm of malevolent legality. Recall the technical definition of a legal act performed *mala fide*: a legal speech act that seeks to disguise its own performance as a "bad faith" act. This means that any act performed *mala fide* that is perfectly successful will be a legal speech act that has disguised its own performance as *mala fide*. In other words, such perfectly successful malevolent legalities are those "bad faith" acts that are never discovered. Thus, the difficult task of antidiscrimination law is facing the following question: how does one "discover" or detect malevolent legality?

In what follows, I trace a jurisprudence of textual skepticism grounded in doctrines of antidiscrimination law such as discriminatory purpose dating back to *Yick Wo*. The jurisprudence of textual skepticism reviewed here provides a brief history of how courts have approached the problem of malevolent legality or "bad faith" in the law. This brief history of legal acts performed *mala fide* will in turn serve as the legal ground upon which to build a methodology for analyzing malevolent legalities.

## THE DOMAIN OF MALEVOLENT LEGALITY

In the private law of contracts and property, the term *mala fide* originally referred to "an intention to injure or vex the plaintiff, or with a consciousness of violating right."[91] In 1796, the Supreme Court defined acts performed *mala fide* in contradistinction to acts performed *bona fide*. The court had clarified,

> *Bona fide* is a legal technical expression; and the law of Great Britain and this country has annexed a certain idea to it. It is a term used in statutes in England, and in acts of Assembly of all the States, and signifies a thing done really, with good faith, without fraud, or deceit, or collusion, or trust.[92]

As Markovitz observes, "good faith" is the core value of our modern property regime, where "bad faith" is understood as when "one party exploits a strategic vulnerability of the other" to secure an advantage or defeat the rights of another.[93] This good faith requirement in modern property law is enshrined in the Uniform Commercial Code, where the seller is required to disclose any known defects of property.[94] The problem of bad faith in the private law of contracts and property can be traced to the early development of the Western legal tradition. As Alan Watson notes in his classic study *Legal Change and Legal Origins,* the text of a Aedilician edict of the Roman republic provided that buyers of slaves could demand a refund of their purchase due to an undisclosed disease (*morbus*) or physical defect (*vitium*) of the purchased slave.[95] As Watson observes, Roman jurists recognized the "bad faith" strategies employed by both sellers and buyers in the slave market, and as a result,

"Slave-dealers were notoriously untrustworthy—they were used-car salesmen of the ancient world—and there was a tendency to interpret the Edict against them."[96] Watson notes that in cases where the text of an edict clearly led to unjust manipulation by "bad faith" actors or harm to public interest, "Public utility prevailed over the obvious meaning of the interdict."[97]

The American institution of slavery was also plagued with "bad faith" actors who utilized legal "duties to disclose" to their economic advantage. In the early republic, state statutes on fraud allowed a purchaser to recover damages from an "undisclosed" vice or defect of a purchased slave. In Louisiana, for example, a purchaser could recover damages if a slaveholder violated the statutory requirement "to disclose redhibitory vices and defects not apparent in the things sold, when he knows of their existence"[98] However, since the statute on fraud included a *knowledge* element that requires proof that the seller *knew of the defect* at the time of sale, the only thing a seller must have done to avoid liability is to show that they did not have knowledge of the defect at the time of sale. Therefore, even if a slaveholder sold a slave who had a chronic, fatal illness at the time of sale that led to her death, slaveholders could still be said to act in "good faith" as long as they could convince the court that they did not know of the disease *at the time of sale*. In 1853, the Supreme Court of Louisiana found precisely this, writing about the death of the purchased slave:

> The disease is shown to have existed within the three days which followed the sale, and the presumption is that it existed before the sale; but as there is nothing to show that the defendant was apprised of its existence, he must be held to have acted in good faith.[99]

These cases demonstrate one of the core insights of malevolent legality, namely the historical insight that legal actors often engage in evil acts that are performed and recognized as acting in "good faith." In this way, the legal recognition of good faith is often a *performance* that utilizes the procedures and instruments of the law (text, pretext, rules of evidence, burdens of proof) to "self-confer" good intent or absolve oneself of "bad intent." As the historical example of slavery illustrates, good faith doctrines often served as the malevolent legality that absolved slaveholders of any legal wrongdoing, such that the evil of slavery is perpetuated precisely through the performance of good faith.

Etymologically, the term *malevolent* derives from the Greek term *mal* meaning "bad" or "evil," and *volentis* meaning "will." Therefore, a malevolent act is one performed with *bad* or *evil intent* of the will. However, as in often the case in understanding legal language, there are more than one sense of a malevolent act in the eyes of the law. Take the term *malice*, for example, derived from the same Greek root, *mal.* Black's Law Dictionary distinguishes between two senses of the word malice: first, *express malice*, which involves direct proof of subjective intention to do injury, and second, *implied* or *constructive malice*, which is defined as, "malice inferred from acts; malice imputed by law; malice which is not shown by direct proof of an intention to do injury (express malice), but which is inferentially established by the necessarily injurious results of the acts shown to have been committed."[100] It is this second sense—implied or constructive malice—which constitutes the domain of study in this book. Implied malice suggests that a bad or evil act in the eyes of the law may be performed but where there is a lack of direct proof of the intention behind the act itself. In other words, implied malice refers to a domain of malevolent acts whose bad or evil intentions are "hidden" or concealed and therefore must be inferred through legal reasoning, that is, *a willful act to do harm that conceals its own intentions.*

This sense of malevolent, understood as a concealed intent to harm, is highly problematic and paradoxical. If a *malevolent* speech-act seeks to conceal its own bad intent, then it follows that a "successful" malevolent speech-act will be one in which the bad intent is successfully concealed, one whose evil intent is never discovered. Therefore, the paradoxical nature of a malevolent speech-act is that if it is truly successful, there will not be any proof of its bad intent. Therefore, it is impossible to prove the existence of a successful malevolent speech-act. Strictly speaking, truly malevolent speech-acts that are completely successful will be impossible to discover.

The legal notion of *implied malice* therefore allows us to see why, in American law, courts have gone *beyond* the text in judicial construction interpreting the discriminatory intentions of state legislatures. In 1880, the city of San Francisco enacted an ordinance requiring all laundry businesses to apply for a permit to operate subject to approval by the city Board of Supervisors. Out of a total of 340 laundries in the city, 240 were operated and owned by Chinese immigrants. After the ordinance was enacted, the Board of Supervisors denied all permit requests made by Chinese laundries while granting permits to all non-Chinese laundries except one. As a result, Yick Wo and more than 150 Chinese immigrants were arrested and, in Yick Wo's case, imprisoned for failure to pay the fine for violating the ordinance. Yick Wo brought a challenge to the ordinance claiming that his punishment violated the Equal Protection Clause of the Fourteenth Amendment. However, there was one problem: the ordinance enacted by the city was "facially neutral"— the text of the law did not *say* anything about discriminating on the basis of race, national origin, or alienage (immigration status), and therefore was "fair on its face and impartial in appearance."[101] Indeed, the counsel for the city of San Francisco provided a "race-neutral" reason for its action, arguing that the city retained its constitutional police power to regulate "the use of wooden buildings as laundries . . . with a view to the protection of the public against the dangers of fire."[102] Nonetheless, in one of the most influential and foundational cases in constitutional law, the Supreme Court concluded:

> Though the law itself be fair on its face and impartial in appearance, yet, if it is applied and administered by public authority with an evil eye and an unequal hand, so as practically to make unjust and illegal discriminations between persons in similar circumstances, material to their rights, the denial of equal justice is still within the prohibition of the Constitution.[103]

The court made the important observation that although nothing "on the face" of the text of the ordinance suggested a discriminatory motive, this does not exempt "neutral" laws from the scrutiny of the Equal Protection Clause of the Fourteenth Amendment, which also seeks to ferret out "improper influences and motives easy of concealment and difficult to be detected and exposed."[104] As the court in Yick Wo observed, the "evil eye" of the legislature must sometimes be checked by examining the implied malice that sometimes lies behind the "facially neutral" text.

*Yick Wo* represents a tradition in American law we can call a *jurisprudence of textual skepticism*: a method of legal interpretation that retains a healthy skepticism with regard to the good faith intentions stated on the face of the text. Contrasted with the judicial philosophy of textualist "fidelity," a jurisprudence of textual skepticism retains a hermeneutic of skepticism with regard to the constitutional rationales stated on the face of the text. A jurisprudence of textual skepticism, for example, views the equal protection guarantee of the Constitution as requiring scrutiny into the "improper influences and motives" of discrimination that are easily concealed by the face of the text. Since *Yick Wo*, textual skeptics have observed that legal actors perform acts *mala fide* through enactment of a neutral legal text or speech that covers a hidden motive. As Judge Richard Posner observed, the very nature of discrimination as it covertly operates in the workplace, for example, poses significant hurdles for plaintiffs and courts attempting to get to the bottom of the truth of any discriminatory act:

> Proof of such [intentional] discrimination is always difficult. Defendants of even minimal sophistication will neither admit discriminatory animus nor leave a paper trail demonstrating it...alternative hypotheses (including that of simple mistake) will always be possible and often plausible. . . . The law tries to protect average and even below-average workers . . . but . . . it is so easy to concoct a plausible reason for not hiring, or firing, or failing to promote, or denying a pay raise to, a worker who is not superlative. A plaintiff's ability

to prove discrimination indirectly, circumstantially, must not be crippled by evidentiary rulings that keep out probative evidence because of crabbed notions of relevance or excessive mistrust of juries.[105]

In 1977, the Supreme Court addressed this issue in substance, providing the first constitutional test for determining whether a government law and policy was motivated by discriminatory purpose. In the Supreme Court's analysis in *Arlington Heights* (1977), the court created a five-factor evidentiary test for assessing whether a law or policy was motivated by discriminatory purpose—regardless of the stated intent of the law or policy. The rationale of what came to be known as the *Arlington Heights* framework was a simple yet ambitious effort "to sharpen the inquiry into the elusive factual question of intentional discrimination."[106] By focusing the inquiry away from explicit statements of intent to discriminate and toward a "mosaic" of circumstantial, contextual, historical, legislative, procedural, and temporal factors, the framework was intended as a "nonexhaustive" list of evidentiary factors courts should consider when determining the presence of a discriminatory purpose, rather than simply taking the word of the drafters of the law or policy.

The *Arlington Heights* framework has served as the US Supreme Court's test for discriminatory governmental purpose for over 50 years. This seemingly basic notion of antidiscrimination served as the court's primary tool for attempting to identify improperly discriminatory purposes that might be disguised or concealed behind an "official" stated governmental purpose. The nonexhaustive, five-factor test was first explained by the court as follows: "Determining whether invidious discriminatory purpose was a motivating factor demands a sensitive inquiry into such circumstantial and direct evidence of intent as may be available."[107] The five factors the court identified are: (i) the impact of the official action in its effect on one race compared to another, (ii) the historical background of the decision (i.e., whether there exists a "series" of actions taken for invidious purposes), (iii) the specific sequence of events leading up to the decision, (iv) departures from normal procedural sequence (i.e., whether the decision appears contrary to those normally made by the decisionmaker), and (v) the legislative or administrative history (i.e., congressional record, committee meetings, testimony, etc.). Notably, the court ends the explication of the five-factor test by stating that the list is nonexhaustive but that these five factors are "without purporting to be exhaustive, subjects of proper inquiry in determining whether racially discriminatory intent existed. *Arlington Heights v. Metropolitan Housing Corp.*, 429 U.S. 252, 268 (1977)."

In the outlining of the framework, the court clarified that all that is required of a plaintiff is to show that a discriminatory purpose was *one motivating factor* in the decision, not the dominant or primary one. The rationale of this burden of proof for invalidating a governmental action, according to the court, is that racial discrimination is a much more serious constitutional harm than simply the charge of arbitrariness or irrationality. As the court wrote:

> Rarely can it be said that a legislature or administrative body operating under a broad mandate made a decision motivated solely by a single concern, or even that a particular purpose was the "dominant" or "primary" one. In fact, it is because legislators and administrators are properly concerned with balancing numerous competing considerations that courts refrain from reviewing the merits of their decisions, absent a showing of arbitrariness or irrationality. But racial discrimination is not just another competing consideration. When there is a proof that a discriminatory purpose has been a motivating factor in the decision, this judicial deference is no longer justified.[108]

For the Supreme Court, the judicial deference shown to legislatures in lawmaking is taken away when presented with proof of a discriminatory purpose. Due to the serious nature of the constitutional harm involved, judicial deference to the legislature's stated intentions is not justified even in "mixed-motive" decisions where discriminatory purpose is found to be simply *one* among those motivating factors.

Despite its use in constitutional cases for over 50 years, there is still fundamental disagreement, debate, and confusion over the scope, application, and misapplication of the *Arlington Heights* framework. Legal scholars have called for its demise, and practitioners have lamented its usefulness in identifying "smoking gun" evidence of discrimination. In 2023, the Supreme Court of North Carolina openly rejected the framework altogether as being incompatible with their state constitutions, writing:

> *Arlington Heights*' analytical framework is incompatible with our state Constitution and this Court's precedent as it allows challengers to succeed on such claims by proffering evidence that is by its very nature speculative, subjective, and thus, insufficient to meet the well-established burden of proof. The differing outcomes reached by the Fourth Circuit in *Raymond* and the trial court below highlight the subjective nature of the *Arlington Heights* test. The fact that different results can be reached using the *Arlington Heights* test suggests that personal biases and subjective interpretations concerning presumptively valid legislative acts can greatly influence outcomes in these types of cases. It is the objective application of legal principles that leads to consistent and fair judicial decisions. There, the *Arlington Heights* framework falls short.[109]

Even sitting Supreme Court justices do not utilize the framework consistently, do not apply all five factors, and fail to consistently and seriously engage in the "sensitive inquiry" into direct and circumstantial evidence demanded by the court's own framework in cases concerning claims of discriminatory government purpose. In a 2020 case concerning the government's rescinding of the Deferred Action for Childhood Arrivals program (DACA), Chief Justice John Roberts himself, when introducing the *Arlington Heights* framework, enumerates only three factors: impact, departures from procedure, and "contemporary statements by members of the decisionmaking body."[110] Given this woefully incomplete and misleading characterization of court's own historic framework, Roberts then quickly proceeds to dismiss the challenge of discriminatory purpose.[111] In the DACA case, Roberts not only excludes crucial factors that the court specifically identified to be consulted as evidence but also mischaracterizes and narrowly construes the last factor he does mention, since "contemporary statements" of the decision-makers are merely one source that might be considered in the final fifth factor of legislative *and* administrative history. But the most glaring omission from Roberts's analysis is without a doubt the omission of arguably the two *most important* factors that speak to evidence of discriminatory purpose: historical background and legislative and administrative history. Nowhere in Roberts's opinion appears a mention or discussion of either the historical record or legislative or administrative history of the decision to rescind DACA.

Similarly, in *Abbott v. Perez* (2018), a case alleging discriminatory purpose in racial gerrymandering by the Texas legislature, Justice Samuel Alito (writing for the majority), when citing the *Arlington Heights* framework, mentions only one factor, historical background. In her dissent, Justice Sotomayor—the only justice in the case to do so—enumerates all five *Arlington Heights* factors, addressing each one through precisely the same "sensitive inquiry" instructed by the court in *Arlington Heights*. In her dissent, she accused the majority of "selectively reviewing" the historical record of discrimination *with the intention* to avoid a finding of discriminatory purpose behind the voting scheme.[112]

Justice Sotomayor's dissenting argument directly challenges the conventional way of understanding how judges decide cases in a transparent, democratic system of rule of law. Instead, Sotomayor's suggestion implies that Supreme Court justices make decisions *not* based on precedent, procedure, standards, rules, and evidence but rather on the basis of certain pretextual *strategies* and concealed views about discrimination itself. But if true, this presents a major problem: how do we determine which decisions are the outcomes of "conventional" legal analysis and which are the results of "selective" strategic speech advancing one's views on history, memory, etc.? Is it even possible to know the hidden motives or reasons of judicial (and, for that matter, legislative) decisions that are concealed by the actors themselves? How do we know whether Sotomayor's hypothesis is correct or not?

Are decisions about discriminatory purpose really determined not by rules, precedents, and evidence but by much more strategic, pretextual, and performative factors disguised by legal rules and language? If so, is there a way to anticipate the influence of these factors through an interpretation of the communicative content implied by such strategic actions and decisions? In short: how do we know whether legal actors are *concealing* something by *saying* something? How do we know whether the "legal arguments" presented are not, in Justice Ginsburg's words, merely yet another insidious manifestation of racism or discrimination regenerated in another form? How does one know when the saying of something by legal actors is in fact a strategic performance disguising or evading some ulterior message or motive? How do we know when the text conceals a performance of something left *unstated*? How does one detect legal acts performed *mala fide*?

One answer is that the legal, technical, modern definition of acts performed *mala fide* or in bad faith defies the more conventional understanding of the term malevolent, which imputes an evil or hateful motive animated toward a particular individual or group.[113] As Justice Oliver Wendell Holmes, Jr. observed, an evil or hateful motive is *not* required for describing an act as "malicious" from a legal standpoint. Rather, Holmes wrote, all that is required for a finding of legal *mala fide* is the intent to inflict temporal harm upon a legal adversary. Holmes argued that, from the standpoint of the law, all that is required for a malicious act is an intent to inflict temporal harm on a legal adversary. In *The Path of Law,* Holmes wrote that

> no one doubts that a man may be liable, without any malevolent motive at all, for false statements manifestly calculated to inflict temporal damage. In stating the case in pleading, we still should call the defendant's conduct malicious; but, in my opinion at least, the word means nothing about motives, or even about the defendant's attitude toward the future, but only signifies that the tendency of his conduct under the known circumstances was very plainly to cause the plaintiff temporal harm.[114]

That is, acts performed *mala fide* do not necessarily require an evil motive or hateful *animus*, although in some cases they may coincide. Rather, one's act may be considered *mala fide* if one seeks to take advantage of the good faith presumption of cooperation as a legal strategy to defeat one's adversary. In this sense, the broad domain of malevolent legality can be understood as a set of legal strategies that seeks to take advantage of the benevolent or good faith presumptions of the law and legal communication in order to defeat or inflict temporal damage on one's legal adversary. The broad domain of malevolent legality therefore is first and foremost a study of law as *strategic* legal speech performed *mala fide*.

American legal history demonstrates the ways in which law has often become a vehicle for "facial" discrimination, that is, legal speech that identifies the discriminatory purpose and target on the face of the text itself: Native American tribes are forcibly relocated under the "benevolent policy" of Indian Removal.[115] Blacks and Asians are denied citizenship[116] and women denied the right to vote according to an "originalist" reading of the word *citizens* "at the time of the adoption of the Constitution."[117] Japanese-Americans are ordered into internment camps under the justification of national defense and the constitutional war powers of Congress and the executive branch.[118] To a modern eye, these well-known historical examples might appear at first glance to belong to a by-gone era where the law was brazenly utilized for clearly discriminatory purposes. Such examples are said to be "facially discriminatory" since the text of the law or policy explicitly states the purpose and persons targeted for unjust discrimination: blacks, Asians, women, Native Americans. Much like the era of *de jure* segregation, where discrimination was sanctioned "by law," these examples utilize legal texts whose discriminatory purpose is clearly stated on the face of the text.

In contrast, most discrimination in the post-civil rights era often *cannot* be described as facially discriminatory. Instead, as Justice Ginsburg observed, contemporary forms of discrimination—like in *Yick Wo*—are most often performed in the manner of the mythical Hydra, regenerating discriminatory aims through *performances* of "neutral" legal texts and policies: a city denies a low-income, multiracial housing project under the pretext that the project will decrease surrounding home values.[119] A legal counsel strikes Hispanic jurors by using bilingualism as a proxy for race.[120] A racially motivated employer discharges a black employee under the false pretext of a fabricated work altercation with a superior.[121] A movie theater ejects two black women for "disruptive conduct" after the manager "smirked" when told about white patrons using the "n-word."[122] A state legislature uses politics as a proxy to dilute the voting power of minorities under the pretext of "good faith."[123] The federal government reenacts a statute that has disparate impact on Mexican and Latinx individuals and was historically motivated by racial animus under the pretext of "good faith."[124] The Supreme Court allows a business to refuse service to same-sex couples under the pretext of "free speech."[125] The Supreme Court invalidates affirmative action policies under the pretext of a "color-blind" reading of the text of the Equal Protection Clause of the Fourteenth Amendment.[126]

In these cases, the official reason for action is presented as a "facially neutral" policy, without any textual mention of an explicit targeting of persons based on race, religion, sex, nationality, sexual orientation, or alienage. Rather than being facially discriminatory, defendants in the cases above explicitly *deny* that they are discriminating *at all*. Specifically, they utilize the *prima facie* neutrality of the law as a cover for discrimination. In this sense, they are forms of discrimination performed *mala fide* using the *performativity* of legal texts as a mask or disguise: a text, a "police regulation," a "smirk," a "race-neutral" policy, a "good faith" presumption, a "legitimate business reason," a "colorblind" interpretation. The factor that distinguishes these more recent, subtler forms of malevolent legality examined in the book, therefore, is that such acts cannot be described as facially discriminatory. In contrast to facially discriminatory legal acts, malevolent legalities utilize legal pretexts, proxies, and neutral policies to disguise the "face" of discrimination behind or beneath the text itself. In doing so, they contribute to the construction of a *legal reality* of discrimination that is animated through the neutrality of the text itself, persisting through time in a way that changes our relationship to the law, memory, and to each other as legal subjects sharing a common temporal experience.

Malevolent legal strategies are in no way, however, exclusive to discrimination law. As legal scholars have shown, bad faith strategies are prevalent in virtually all areas of legal practice, from contract, property, negotiation, and mediation to labor law, tax law, criminal law, constitutional law, and many more. In the area of statutory law, legal scholars have highlighted how courts have attempted to address bad faith legislative acts and strategies through the development of "antievasion doctrines" (AEDs), which "operate as standards designed to prevent governmental actors from simply enacting facially neutral laws cleverly drawn to circumvent decision rules."[127] Across many areas of law, courts have utilized such doctrines to combat bad faith, including doctrines of *proxy, pretext*, and *purpose tests*.[128] The basic recognition behind these antievasion doctrines is that employers, legislators, and other parties sometimes seek to take advantage of gaps or indeterminacies in the law to circumvent or undermine the basic purpose or spirit of the law, including even the purpose of constitutional principles.[129] To combat these bad faith strategies, courts have developed doctrines and standards to reduce and discourage these "strategic speech" acts, including doctrines of false pretext, discrimination by proxy and invidious purpose.[130] In this way, the nature and prevalence of bad faith strategies suggests that such cases are not insular or exceptional.

However, in the area where bad faith strategies arguably have the highest stakes—constitutional law—David Pozen has argued that antievasion doctrines are least developed, utilized, or enforced.[131] Discrimination performed in bad faith not only deceives and unjustly deprives plaintiffs of basic rights but destroys the legal and temporal relations that bind us together as a political community responsible for our past, present, and future. When acts performed *mala fide* deprive individuals of constitutional rights against being treated unfairly due to discrimination, the evil perpetuated seems doubly wrong. What I call malevolent legality thus contributes not only to the deception and erosion of trust in law and the deprivation of constitutional rights but also to the destruction of what legal scholar Reva Siegel calls "constitutional memory."[132] Therefore, the domain of malevolent legality will be approached not simply as a set of bad faith legal strategies to defeat a legal adversary but as a philosophical reconfiguration of the way of thinking about time and the meaning of our collective legal subjectivity. In this way, the book argues that malevolent legalities must be understood as a *performative* enactment that also severs the memory of the law, thereby destroying the inhabitation of what Arendt called our "common world," which is necessary for collectively responding to the present.

As I argue in the book, Scalia's textualist methodology explicitly denies that it is a covert "device calculated to produce socially or politically conservative outcomes."[133] Rather, Justice Scalia claims that it is a "science of construing legal texts" that claims to simply "read the text" without respect to the policy consequences or the (in its view) nonexistent policy purposes of legislators embedded in the text. In this respect, then, textualism, in its own estimation, is the worst judicial philosophy for analyzing the judge's malevolent will [*volentis*] or personal intentions in legal interpretation. Therefore, the argument goes, speaking of a judge's *malevolent* intentions would be inappropriate, since according to textualism, a judge's own individual will—that is, what the judge wills to be the case—should play no role whatsoever in the "scientific" adjudication of cases and controversies. The judge should simply apply the meaning of the words of the text, no more, no less. According to a textualist, it is not the judicial branch but the legislative branch that is the proper place for questions of policy, justice, and the will of the people that animates the reason of the law. The will of a judge, however, is not an influence according to a textualist interpretation of legal meaning. For a textualist, the will of a judge, like the intention of a legislature or a committee report, is "extratextual" and plays no role in legal interpretation. That is, a textualist judge (in the eyes of the textualist) *cannot* be malevolent for the simple reason that a textualist judge does not will [*volens*] a certain outcome. Rather, he simply renders a "fair meaning" of the text.

In contrast, as I have argued, malevolent legalities can be seen as an extension of the jurisprudence of *textual skepticism*, developing a framework for understanding the *performance* of law (its theatrical enactment in a specific time and place) in relation to its *performativity* (its practices of citation, recitation, resignification, regeneration, self-reference, and self-conferral). It does so by focusing not on one specific practice of discrimination (e.g., vote dilution or racial profiling) but rather targets the very *performative* character of law that allows it to regenerate or reanimate itself in new forms and thus escape legal scrutiny. From legal doctrines of pretext, proxy, animus, and discriminatory purpose, I examine how discrimination is *performed* over, above, before, and through the text that appears in the language of a written enactment or policy. In this way, the book examines the ways in which textualism facilitates a performance of the text that masks its own *pretextuality*. Just as the Athenian writes in Plato's *Laws*, every legal text contains a pretext, and it is precisely at the intersection between text and pretext where the inquiry into malevolent legality must begin. These modes of discrimination performed *mala fide*, and the judicial philosophies that authorize them as text, are what I refer to as malevolent legality.

## METHODS

Methodologically, my arguments activate a framework for what might be called a *discriminatology*, understood as *the philosophical study of discrimination as a socio-legal reality persisting over time*. The three elements of such a method include the *temporality* of law, the *performativity* of law, and the *pragmatics* of law. These methodological elements of discriminatology provide a theoretical framework for analyzing and reconstructing malevolent legalities. Specifically, these analytic tools illuminate in their own way the fact that discrimination: (1) is performed *through the law*, (2) persists through *time*, and (3) is a product of strategic manipulation of legal speech.

While more narrow, legal studies of "animus" or discriminatory purpose clearly fall under the domain of malevolent legalities,[134] the discriminatology proposed in this book takes a broader, philosophical approach in understanding discrimination as *a web of socio-legal practices regenerating themselves through novel forms of unjust exclusion*. By examining discrimination in a more systematic and functional way as a *regenerating unjust exclusion*, discriminatology takes a more theoretical approach to discrimination than pursued in Sophia Moreau's influential treatment of direct and indirect forms of discrimination in *Faces of Inequality*.[135] Rather than beginning an inquiry into discrimination from legal doctrines and materials themselves, the discriminatology proposed in this book begins from philosophical and theoretical insights about the *temporality of law*. Drawing upon the work of Gerhart Husserl, the book develops an account of law as a "creative juridical performance" (*die rechtsschöpferische Leistung*).[136] This ontology of law applies not only to judicial speech-acts regarding discrimination but also to legal speech-acts more broadly where law is seen as not simply enacted through a written text but *performed* through the text itself by legal actors. This approach to legal speech is also consistent with the definition of *performance*, which Diana Taylor defines as practices and processes in a specific time and place that construct new realities.[137] In such a way, discriminatology approaches the law in terms of a creative performance of legal norms through a contested process of legal interpretation. This framework approaches the study of malevolent legalities through the analysis of law as (i) temporal regime, (ii) a form of legal speech and legal reality, and (iii) as the practice of sovereign exceptionalism, resignification, and self-conferral. These three methodological axes of analysis—legal temporality, legal performativity, legal pragmatics—provide a deeper understanding of how malevolent legalities regenerate and make themselves legible within conventional legal discourse, in turn contributing to the determination and legitimation of legal outcomes.

Thinking about discrimination in terms of its *juridical performances* dramatically reorients our way of thinking about not just the nature of discrimination but also our relationship to law, time, and to each other as legal subjects who share a common temporal frame of experience. In contemporary legal discourse, discrimination is usually understood in one of two ways. First, discrimination is often defined as *an intention to subordinate or demean*.[138] This psychological understanding approaches discrimination in terms of attitudes of *disparate treatment* in which there exists proof of an individual subjective intent to treat someone worse off because of a protected characteristic. However, as I demonstrate in the chapters that follow, malevolent legalities are legal speech-acts that seek to mask precisely that evidence of "direct" discrimination or "disparate treatment." In chapter 5, for example, I show how so-called "voluntarist" or intent-based accounts of discrimination fail to do justice to cases where legal actors *disguise* their intent, leaving only other "nonpsychological" factors or effects on which to evaluate the unlawfulness of the act. In these cases, "even if the discriminator does not discriminate, perhaps because the law forbids it, his discriminatory attitudes may persist. His discriminatory acts merely reveal his attitudes, which could be revealed in countless other ways."[139]

A second proposal for understanding discrimination is that, in addition to *disparate treatment,* other forms of "indirect" discrimination may be defined as *a negligence to consider the harmful effects of a policy*.[140] This *epistemological* understanding defines discrimination in terms of a *cognitive failure* of policymakers to take into account the harmful disparate impact of a policy on insular minorities or protected categories of individuals. This approach can be seen in studies following the virtue epistemology lens of Miranda Fricker's *Epistemic Justice,*[141] where forms of discrimination such as colorblindness are understood primarily as an epistemological problem of *hermeneutical injustice*.[142] Such an epistemological approach is prominent in Sophia Moreau's treatment of "indirect discrimination," where discrimination is understood as a kind of negligence. But again, as the chapters that follow demonstrate, the problem posed by malevolent legalities is *not* that legal actors have neglected to consider the effects of their actions but rather the contrary: "bad faith" actors intentionally seek to *disguise* or "unperform" their actions precisely because they understand their own actions as discriminatory. In chapter 6, for example, I demonstrate that the epistemological lens of epistemic or hermeneutic injustice fails to capture and diagnose a central aspect of malevolent legality, namely the intent to disguise the performance of one's speech-act *as malevolent*. According to existing frameworks, then, discrimination is primarily a problem of *harmful attitudes* (disparate treatment) and/or deficient *cognitive skills* in lawmaking (disparate impact). That is, existing frameworks for understanding discrimination rest on the notion that discrimination is a primarily a *psychological* and/or *epistemological* problem This aspect of malevolent legalities means that, for such speech-acts, (a) evidence of disparate treatment (direct discrimination) will often be disguised or lacking, and (b) the charge of negligence misses the mark, since the acts in question are *intentional*. Thus, current ways of analyzing, diagnosing, and detecting these malevolent forms of discrimination are simply inadequate. The term malevolent legality is therefore an attempt to articulate the ways in which discrimination seeks not only to do harm to individuals through subordinating or demeaning or through a negligent failure to consider the effects of one's actions but also—through the performativity of law—to disguise or cover discrimination by "regenerating" and resignifying past acts of discrimination through the performativity of legal texts itself.

Because discrimination remains largely understood within these either psychological or epistemological frameworks, many have concluded that "real" discrimination is no longer a significant factor as a matter of law today. First, if discrimination is defined as a *subjective, intentional attitude* to subordinate, this kind of overt discrimination (it is argued) simply is no longer expressed in the law. During the era of *de jure* racism, where overt forms of discrimination were mandated by law, such an understanding of discrimination was appropriate. However (the argument goes), since the "rights revolution" of the 1960s, including the civil rights movement, the women's movement, and the LGBTQ movement since the 1980s, such overt forms of *intentional attitudes* of discrimination are no longer expressed in the law. We have finally arrived, as the argument goes in race relations, at a truly "colorblind" society. Alternatively, if discrimination is defined simply as a *nonintentional negligence* to consider the disparate impact of a policy, then it seems to follow that *no one intended* to subordinate, or demean, and therefore, we cannot really speak of a subjective, "discriminatory intent" or motive that many associate with unlawful discrimination. Further, since legislators swear an oath to act constitutionally, and since intentional discrimination is unconstitutional, some argue that we *must* assume that legislators are always acting in "good faith" and therefore never acting with unlawful discriminatory intent. Therefore (the argument goes), defining discrimination as a *nonintentional negligence* to consider disparate impact fails to capture the intuitive notion that discrimination involves *an intent* or *motive* to treat others unequally by subordinating or demeaning them. Thus, the current frameworks for understanding discrimination as a problem of *psychological attitudes* and/or *cognitive negligence* have led many to the conclusion that "real" discrimination today simply no longer exists.

Without denying these aspects of discrimination, I seek to shift our understanding of discrimination as not only a psychological and epistemological problem but also principally an *ontological* and *political* problem. Focusing on the *creative juridical performances* of discrimination shifts our focus to the ways in which "bad faith" legal actors utilize the *text itself* in perpetuating the legal reality of discrimination through time. In this way, the methodology of the book seeks to develop more fully the observation of the Supreme Court in *United States v. Fordice* (1992) that "discriminatory intent does tend to persist through time."[143]

The method of discriminatology also draws upon a jurisprudence of antidiscrimination law that emphasizes what constitutional law scholar Kerrell Murray calls an "institutional realist" approach. For Murray, statutes, laws, and policies acquire meaning as a *continuous policy* of the state and therefore must be understood within the institutional responsibility for harm created by governmental actors. The problem of past government-sponsored discrimination, Murray writes, "raise[s] questions about whether and when responsibility for past government acts constrains modern government behavior. We cannot answer those questions with a view from nowhere. But we can answer them against the backdrop of widespread legal recognition that continuity informs meaning and responsibility, and in light of widely accepted antidiscrimination commitments."[144] Arguing against interpretive accounts that give deference to the "good faith" intentions of the text enacted by policymakers, Murray writes:

> The problems of evasion and lingering effects of past wrongdoing do not disappear simply because multimember bodies have inconstant personnel. An institutional realist approach suggests that institutional continuity helps explain how identity matters, as well as the nature of the responsibility ... [it] recognizes responsibility as connected not just to individual decisionmakers but to the institutions of which they are a part.[145]

Given the realities of institutional continuity and state responsibility for state-created harm resulting in discriminatory effects and disparate impact, Murray's institutional realist approach focuses on addressing disparate impact, directing that "courts first ask whether the state can show that the contemporary policy has eliminated any meaningful disparate impact," and if it cannot, courts must give a legitimate reason why pursuing a non-discriminatory policy outweighs shielding the disparate impact of a tainted policy.[146] On this point, Murray writes:

> Persistent disparate impact does not necessarily doom the policy. But, to purge the taint, governments must offer (1) a legitimate, nondiscriminatory interest that will be substantially impaired absent this policy, (2) direct engagement with the past problematic history, (3) an explanation of why the disparate impact cannot be eliminated, and (4) an explanation of why the legitimate need for this means of pursuing the legitimate interest outweighs the harm of shielding the disparate impact of a tainted rule.[147]

On Murray's account, the fact that a legislature merely "considers" the past discrimination falls well short of a constitutional engagement with the specific elements of disparate impact created or posed by a governmental policy. Instead, Murray's institutional realist model proposes placing the burden of proof upon the state to first demonstrate lack of disparate impact and a demonstration of the state's departure from the discriminatory intent of its past policy. Institutional realism thus approaches the study of discrimination as *an historical-institutional legal reality persisting through time.* In this way, institutional realism suggests that malevolent legalities evolve and persist through the historical action or inaction of government policy.

Methodologically, then, one central aim of the book is to develop a unique theoretical framework for understanding theories of legal interpretation *themselves* as philosophical orientations toward time, memory, and history. By approaching the judicial philosophy of textualism as itself a "temporal regime," I advance the thesis that textualism reconfigures our shared notions of legal subjectivity through a performative regeneration and reconstruction of the historical meaning of discrimination. In what follows, I explore the three elements of discriminatology discussed in the book to understand the judicial philosophy of textualism: first, the *temporality* of law, second, the *performativity* of law, and third, the *pragmatics* of law.

## The Temporality of Law

The first and most important element of the framework of discriminatology is the *temporality of law,* which I define following the work of Gerhart

Husserl as the study of the internal time-structure of legal objects, practices, and theories of interpretation. The lens of temporality is applied in chapters 3, 4, 5, and 6. The methodological justification for utilizing the temporality of law is two-fold. In particular, Gerhart Husserl's analysis of the temporality of law allows us to understand two major methodological insights, namely: (1) the persistence of discrimination over time and (2) the notion that theories of legal interpretation (i.e., "originalism") are *themselves* distinct ways of thinking about time.

On the first point, the temporality of law allows us to see that discrimination cannot be understood as a series of discrete acts but rather as *a socio-legal reality that persists through time*. Secondly, the lens of temporality allows us to see that different theories of legal interpretation are at the same time *temporal regimes*, understood as a set of political rules for ordering the official public time and memory of a society. This definition of temporal regimes draws upon the recent work of scholars examining temporal regimes as *political* systems of thought that guide the implementation of rules for ordering relations of our past, present, and future.[148] As part 2 of the book demonstrates, Scalia's textualist-originalism is a quintessential "temporal regime," billing itself as an activist judicial philosophy seeking to prevent progress by enacting a regime of static law. Scalia's originalism, in particular, seeks to "turn back time" by fixing constitutional rights to a static point in past time. In this way, the lens of temporality allows us to see that legal theories of interpretation are also *temporal narratives* about our common history, shared identity, and public time.

In his most developed work, *Recht und Zeit* (1955), Gerhart Husserl sets out to examine the "inner time-structure of legal things" ("Die innere Zeitstruktur von Dingen des Rechts").[149] For Husserl, legal objects have their own distinct ontology or "time-structure" (*Zeitstruktur*) that reflects both an "objective," legal side and an "historical," social side. On first appearance, "the law" (i.e., criminal codes, health codes, standards of negligence, etc.) appears as an "abstract" body of legal rules, codes and standards that are independent from history and everyday experience. In this sense, "The law creates its own realm of volitional behavior, which leads an existence completely detached from the reality of concrete social action."[150] However, Husserl notes that this "objective" existence of the law in its abstract form always refers to some concrete "life-situation" (*lebensituationen*) or social problem that emerges within the lifeworld of a people: a marriage, an employment contract, a property dispute, a legal claim. In this way, Husserl notes that all legal norms enacted by the legislature have a *historicity*. As he writes, "Every legal norm has a history attributable to it."[151] Therefore, legal norms are not "fixed once and for all by the process of its creation."[152] As a result, every legal norm has a "pre-history" that must be understood to explain its meaning as a social "tool" designed to solve a concrete social problem in a historical context.

In *Recht und Zeit* (1955), Husserl examines the specific "time-perspective" of the judge when engaging in legal interpretation. For Husserl, the judge has a "double" temporal role within a system of separation of powers. On the one hand, the judge serves a conservative function of the legal system in preserving established law through observing *stare decisis,* custom, and tradition. In a system of division of powers, the judge is a functionary who lives in the past and whose principle of action is the *status quo*.[153] Judges, Husserl writes, are a "people of the past" (*Vergangenheitsmenschen*).[154] On the other hand, the judge is a representative of all members of the legal community as equal persons in the society.[155] In this latter respect, a judge's legal interpretation must take into account the *temporality* of law within the historical experience of a certain social problem at the time. From the perspective of legal interpretation, Husserl writes, "The question of the meaning of a legal standard can only be asked in such a way that we ask: What does it mean today—with regard to the concrete life situation of which the standardization is concerned today"[156] Once again, Husserl says, "What ultimately matters when it comes to the interpretation of a legal clause is what it means for us today, who live under this legal order."[157] Thus, even at the "abstract" level of legal codes, rules, and standards, the judge cannot engage in legal interpretation without the background of the will or intent of the legislator to solve a concrete social problem in a particular historical experience of people in a specific context. Husserl concludes by writing:

> In this way, the judge establishes "a living relationship with 'today' and its problems. If a legal standard is interpreted differently today than at the time of its entry into force thirty years ago, this is justified by its historical time-structure. Norms of law develop their effect according to their sense (Sinne), to the extent that they "go with the times," as we say.[158]

What matters for legal interpretation, then, is understanding how to take the problem-solving purpose or "sense" of the law in its historical context and apply it to *today,* to the present-day circumstances. For the judge, therefore, legal interpretation necessary includes a "creative" element in adapting the social purpose of the law to today's "life situation" (*lebenssituationen*). For Husserl, the "abstract" law of rules, codes and standards should not fool us. For the judge, the moment of the legal judgment is a therefore a "creative juridical performance" (*die rechtsschöpferische Leistung*).[159] When we speak of the abstract body of "law," Husserl cautions, "this way of speaking must not lead to a failure to recognize the creative juridical performance that is inherent in every judgment, namely the creation of law through the interpretation of the law in force."¹⁶⁰ In this way, the judge takes the "abstract" law and makes it "temporalized" (*Verzeitung*).

As Husserl notes, the judge therefore has a "double experience" (*doppelte Erfahrung*) as both (a) a conservative, backwards-looking person of the past *and* (b) a representative of the legal community striving to solve social problems *today*, in the present.¹⁶¹ This temporal role conflict, we can call it, is a product of modern legal systems based on division of powers in which socio-historical processes have led to the development of separate institutional roles and personality types for regulating legal norms. Whereas the legislator is "a planner" concerned with creating legal norms governing *future*-oriented policy considerations for the society,¹⁶² and the executive or administrative role is concerned with implementing norms of action in the *present*,¹⁶³ the judge is concerned with establishing legal norms that are uniform and consistent with like cases in *the past*. As Husserl writes, "It is not his task to say what the law should be, but what it is: what the legal situation is in the specific case, in accordance with the legal sentences created *before* his decision,"⁹⁴ which means:

> The decisions made by the judge are not rooted in "today" and are not in favor of "today." For a rational procedure of application of the law, it is essential that equal cases are treated equally. In order to ensure this, the judge must turn his gaze back (*Blick zurückwenden*) from the given case to previous decisions in which the legal problems are equivalent.¹⁶⁴

In order to treat like cases alike, the judge necessarily views each case "as the last in a chain of judgment that preceded him."¹⁶⁵ In this respect, the motivating idea of all the judge's activity is the *status quo*.

In 1988, French jurists Michel van de Kerchove and François Ost took up Husserl's phenomenological investigations into law and time from a systems-theory perspective in their work, *Le système juridique entre ordre et désordre*.¹⁶⁶ For van de Kerchove and Ost, we can distinguish six different configurations or "temporalities" that have emerged in modern legal systems. First, there is a temporality of "founding time," which represents the enactment of law through an "original time" (*d'un temps original*) that is at once both sacred and mythical. In founding time, the constitutional text is seen as at once forming the unity of the nation while establishing the sacred and unchanging original meaning of the law and the constitution.¹⁶⁷ The American Declaration of Independence is exemplary of a document often cited to support legitimacy derived from "founding time." Second, there is the *atemporal* or abstract time of legal doctrines. The abstract time of legal doctrine is exemplified in legal codes, standards, and doctrines, including criminal codes, health codes, standards of "reasonableness," due care, negligence, and the like. These legal codes and doctrines are *atemporal* in the sense that they have a *generality* that allows a standard to be applied regardless of time. For example, in negligence claims, the legal construct of "the reasonable man" serves as an "atemporal" legal standard for judging claims of liability and negligence regardless of the historical or temporal context from which such claims arise. Third, there is *customary time* (*le temps coutimier*), which represents the law in terms of the "backwards-looking" customs, traditions and practices of the "people" accumulated over time. As Ost observes, the German Historical School adopted this temporality, exemplified in the work of Frederick von Savigny and the conception of the *volkgeist*, as the animating customary spirit of German law. In a similar way, some versions of American "originalism" adopt this view, exemplified by Justice Antonin Scalia's argument that long-standing traditions of the "people" acquire constitutional validity. Fourth, there is *Promethean time* (*le temps promethean*), which represents law as a progressive march toward progress using human reason to shape and master the future.[168] Also called "voluntary future time," Promethean time anticipates the future and thereby seeks to constantly actualize the future good of the community in the legal norms and codes of today, in the present. Finally, there is the temporality that van de Kerchove and Ost argue is most characteristic of contemporary legal rationality, namely that of "dialectical time," which is a time perspective that oscillates between past and future, tradition and progress, memory and revision, custom and change. Under this conception of time, law is understood as both a process of cumulative evolution and a process of constant revision and adaptation.[169]

Husserl and Ost's exploration of legal temporality provides a rich analytic framework to understand the practice of legal interpretation. As part 2 of the book argues, textualist-originalism seeks to establish what Scalia called a "static regime of law" that is always backward-looking in its interpretation of the "original meaning" of the text at its time of enactment (i.e., in 1789, or in 1982, etc.). Textualism is staunchly opposed to interpreting the meaning of a text by relying upon its historical policy context or Congressional purpose to solve social problems. For textualism, neither social policy considerations, consequences, or principles of justice are valid to use as guiding posts for interpretation of legal texts. As a result, textualism is a temporal regime that institutes rules for instating the "customary" meaning of law by looking *backwards* toward a static point in time: the "original meaning" embodied in either dictionary definitions, customary practices, or the traditions of the people—a notion inspired by Carl von Savigny's concept of the "spirit" of the people (*volkgeist*). As chapter 1 demonstrates, Scalia's textualism embraces the unwritten law embodied in the traditions of the people, a feature of textualism that requires the textualist judge to become a sovereign exceptionalist in selecting his preferred meaning from the vast array of written, unwritten, customary, "original" or "public" meanings available to him.

In this way, textualist interpretation relies upon two similar but distinct temporal regimes, namely what Ost and Kerchove call "founding time" and "customary time."[170] While textualism allows the interpreter to identify the original meaning of law embodied in the unwritten customs or "traditions" of "the people" (customary time), textualism also allows the interpreter to ground the meaning of law in dictionary definitions or legal practices at the time of enactment (founding time). Thus, textualism opens up a temporal hermeneutic that allows the interpreter a wide universe of meaning in which to select the meaning of law via judicial discretion: the judge may identify the meaning in a certain unwritten "tradition of the people," or in a selective "public meaning" taken from a dictionary definition or contemporaneous "public meaning" such as a popular song or children's rhyme. As Scalia remarked in a speech in 1988, textualism adopts the view of Hayek and Fuller that the "customary practices" of the people constitute an "unwritten law" that judges must enforce as positive law. Scalia writes:

> We undoubtedly have in this country an unwritten complement to our textual constitution, at least in some of the senses that I have described above . . . it is unarguably a reality. Given that it is reality, however, how is it that that system of customary "law" (and I obviously agree with Hayek and Fuller that customary practices as well as statutory rules are at times accurately described as law) is to be enforced?[171]

Finally, as discussed in chapter 4, Scalia's judicial philosophy of "originalism" explicitly takes the position of what Husserl calls an "enemy of progress." Because Scalia openly described the judicial role as one of preventing progress and enforcing a regime of static law, it is illuminating to view this attitude through the lens of Husserl's critique of the judge as a "past-person" who has adopted an "hostility to progress." Methodologically, then, the lens of temporality allows us to analyze and critique judicial philosophies of interpretation as being themselves distinct ways of thinking about time.

## The Performativity of Law

The second methodological element of discriminatology is the theory of performativity and its application to legal speech-acts. In the book, the methodological axis of performativity is applied in chapters 2, 5, and 6. The justification for utilizing the lens of performativity is that such a methodological perspective illuminates the unique ways that textualism itself is a *performative* theory of legal texts. By examining how textualism relies upon textual procedures of sovereign exceptionalism, resignification, and self-conferral, the lens of performativity allows us to see the surprising convergence of textualism with elements of both performativity theory as well as deconstruction. In turn, the performativity of textualism helps explain the often cited "malleability," "flexibility," and "rhetorical" nature of textualist methods in hiding or "masking" its interpretive goals and aims. In this way, the lens of performativity provides an extremely fruitful way of thinking about legal speech-acts that seek to "unperform" themselves. For example, discriminatory speech that seeks to mask its own intentions by "unperforming" itself can be called *performative discrimination*.

In *How to Do Things with Words*, J. L. Austin sets out to study a certain category of utterances that he first describes as "masqueraders"—forms of utterances which "masquerade" as statements of fact or descriptions of states of affairs.[172] Austin is interested in utterances that, in the very saying of something, are *doing something*. In a marriage ceremony, the utterance of "I do" is neither describing a state of affairs nor stating a truth claim but rather "indulging" in the act itself. When I stub my toe and exclaim, "damn!" the utterance has neither a truth value (is neither true nor false) nor describes a state of affairs. Such "masqueraders," for Austin, must be *unmasked* to reveal what he calls their "performative" character:

> What are we to call a sentence or an utterance of this type? I propose to call it a *performative sentence* or performative utterance, or for short, a "performative".... The name is derived, of course, from "perform," the usual verb with the noun "action": it indicates that the issuing of the utterance is the performing of an action—it is not normally thought of as just saying something.[173]

Austin turns to the example of the "promise" as a special kind of performative that implies that the speaker has a certain *intention* to keep his word. Unlike other performatives such as "I bet," or "I declare," promises imply the *good faith* intention of the speaker. When the promise is not fulfilled, "the promise here is not even *void*, though it is given *in bad faith*. His utterance is perhaps misleading, probably deceitful, and doubtless wrong, but it is not a lie or misstatement."[174]

For Austin, "contractual" promises that one finds in law, for example, allow the unique possibility of "false promises": performative utterances that are misleading or deceitful, given in bad faith. Notably for Austin, such utterances cannot be strictly considered a lie or misstatement, since performatives are not truth claims or descriptions of fact, and given that a "promise" separates the *act* of the promise from its subsequent performance. In other words, a promise is a performative act, what Austin calls a kind of "masquerade," that allows the masking of one's intention behind the *performativity* of one's utterance itself. For this reason, Austin says, "we do not speak of a false bet or a false christening; and that we *do* speak of a false promise." The contractual promise one finds at the heart of law, therefore, is a performative utterance that allows "false promises" to be made *in bad faith*.

Judith Butler's *Excitable Speech: a Politics of the Performative* stands as one of the most influential texts of contemporary political theory, feminist philosophy, communication studies, and a host of other disciplines interested in the *political* potentialities of language. In that ground-breaking work, Butler outlines a political theory of the *performative* character of harmful speech that draws upon Austin's theory of speech-acts. As Butler notes, Austin distinguished between two kinds of performativity in language: first, the *perlocutionary* function of speech-acts that refers to the *effects* that *follow* from a speech act *later* in a temporal sequence, and second, the *illocutionary* function of language that refers to the *doing* of a speech that coincides *in the temporal instant* the speech act occurs and is uttered. The speech act of a judge who declares in a court room, "You are hereby sentenced" has illocutionary force since the very *saying* of the act by the judge in that context *actually makes it so*, in that instant, that the defendant is thereby sentenced. However, this illocutionary force can be distinguished from the act's *perlocutionary* force: the sentence uttered by the judge will have predictable effects down the line in a temporal sequence of events on the psychological states of the defendant and the plaintiff, will result in a certain series of actions taken by the court and public officials, etc.

As Butler's work on performativity suggests, legal speech-acts, including discriminatory acts, lack any fixed origin of meaning and are separated from the present by a time interval which in turn allows for the resignification or reinterpretation of the meaning of such utterances.[175] As Butler writes, such speech-acts have

> a kind of discursive performativity that is not a discrete series of speech-acts, but a ritual chain of resignifications whose origin and end remain unfixed and unfixable. In this sense, an "act" is not a momentary happening, but a certain nexus of temporal horizons, the condensation of an iterability that exceeds the moment it occasions. The possibility for a speech act to resignify a prior context depends, in part, upon the gap between the originating context or intention by which an utterance is animated and the effects it produces.[176]

For Butler, the discursive performativity of speech-acts allows an "alternative" to the search for a "legal remedy" for injurious speech-acts. The reason for this, Butler writes, is because of the open temporality of the speech act. That no speech act has to perform injury as its effect means that no simple elaboration of speech-acts will provide a standard by which the injuries of speech might be effectively adjudicated. Such a loosening of the link between act and injury, however, opens up the possibility for a counter-speech, a kind of talking back, that would be foreclosed by the tightening of that link. Thus, the gap that separates the speech act from its future effects has its auspicious implications: it begins a theory of linguistic agency that provides an alternative to the relentless search for legal remedy. The interval between instances of utterance not only makes the repetition and resignification of the utterance possible, but shows how words might, through time, become disjoined from their power to injure and recontextualized in more affirmative modes.[177]

For Butler, the "open temporality" of the speech-act undermines the link between an utterance and its original intention by the speaker or author. Therefore, according to performativity theory, this provides an alternative to the "relentless search for a legal remedy" since no speech act "has to perform injury." In this way, performativity suggests that there is no such thing as an "original intent" that can be anchored to a stable meaning of a prior speech-act.

Butler's performative critique of the notion of an original intent of a sovereign legal subject coincides with Derrida's deconstructive reading of the same notion in Austin's work. In Derrida's chapter on "Signature Event Context" in *Limited Inc.*, we are given a critique of the notion that for any text, there exists a determinate "intention" whose meaning may be rationally reconstructed through its communicative context.[178] For Derrida, as for Butler, we must reject the idea that there exists an "original" intention behind a text or speech-act that anchors its "true" meaning. Here, Derrida takes aim at the "metaphysical origins" of the notion of idea of the sovereign subject behind the text of a writing, namely "the ethical and teleological discourse of consciousness."[179] According to Derrida, Austin's treatment of performatives reveals "the irreducible absence of intention . . . to the performative utterance."[180] For Derrida, the performative reveals itself as a form of speech-act that has been untethered to any determinate, "true" meaning anchored in a subjective intention of a writing subject. For Derrida, this demonstrates that "communication . . . is not the means of transference of meaning, the exchange of intentions and meanings."[181] This means that, according to a deconstructive reading of Austin's performatives, the writing of a text "is not the site, in the last instance, of a hermeneutic deciphering, the decoding of a meaning or truth."[182] Instead, Derrida writes that the performative demonstrates

> the possibility of its functioning being cut off, at a certain point, from its "original" desire-to-say-what-one-means [*vouloir-dire*] and from its participation in a saturable and constraining context. Every sign, linguistic or nonlinguistic, spoken

or written (in the current sense of this opposition), in a small or large unit, can be *cited* put between quotation marks; in so doing it can break with every given context, engendering an infinity of new contexts in a manner which is absolutely illimitable. This does not imply that the mark is valid outside of a context, but on the contrary that there are only contexts without any center or absolute anchoring [*ancrage*]. This citationality, this duplication or duplicity, this iterability of the mark is neither an accident nor an anomaly, it is that (normal/abnormal) without which a mark could not even have a function called "normal." What would a mark be that could not be cited? Or one whose origins would not get lost along the way?[183]

Performativity and deconstruction therefore share the view that it is impossible to rationally reconstruct the original intent of a text that anchors the true meaning of a text. Instead, the temporal distance opened up by the illocutionary nature of speech-acts allows the meaning of texts to be either "resignified" (Butler) or "recited" (Derrida) in subsequent events and utterances that give them new meanings or potentialities.

In a surprisingly similar way to performativity and deconstruction, Scalia's textualism also rejects the notion of a determinate "intention" or purpose that anchors and animates the speech-acts of a sovereign legal subject (individual or collective). Scalia's famous rejection of the notion of legislative intent or purpose, and his consequent rejection of legislative history as a source of legal interpretation, in fact squares nicely with the insights of performativity and deconstruction. As Scalia openly declared in 1986, "I do not believe in legislative intent."[184] But if the meaning of a Congressional statute is untethered from any legislative intent or purpose, then it appears (like Butler's speech-act) that there is no anchoring, original sense of the statute and the meaning of the statute can simply be "resignified" at a later time by the legislature or even a single, unelected judge.

This similarity between Scalia's textualism and performativity raises major issues for addressing discrimination. Butler points out that the performativity of speech-acts raises a major problem for the possibility of addressing, remedying, and *detecting* discriminatory speech. If discriminatory speech is *performative* in the way described by Austin and Butler, then it becomes possible for discriminatory acts of the past to be resignified, reinterpreted, or even "cleansed" or cured by a subsequent legislature or subsequent speech-acts. Thus, if the law is *performative* in the way described by Austin and Butler, does this imply that there is no "fixed" discriminatory intention or "purpose" that makes an act of discrimination wrong? Does this imply that there is no fixed meaning of discriminatory intent or purpose that makes the speech act *objectively* morally harmful? Or alternatively: does this imply that a discriminatory speech-act can simply be "resignified" at a later point in time to "cleanse" the harmful acts of the past? In *Abbott v. Perez* (2018), the Supreme Court ruled that past acts of legislative discrimination were barred as evidence of a legislature's *present* intent and presumption of "good faith."[185] The court's ruling in *Abbot* therefore appears consistent with performativity theory and deconstruction, since the performativity of law makes possible and even facilitates attempts to resignify or make a clean break from the discriminatory motive or intentions of the past. If there is no "fixed," determinate meaning of speech-acts anchored in a subjective intention or "purpose" of the state legislature, then the search for discriminatory purpose or intent is, as Scalia argued, a search for something that does not exist. This problem raises many questions: may a legislature who has engaged in clear instances of discrimination utilize the performativity of speechacts in resignifying the utterance in order to "cleanse" itself from the discriminatory act (chapter 5)? May an employer who has clearly discriminated against an employee simply lie in court and proffer a "nondiscriminatory" reason after the fact in order to defeat the plaintiff (chapter 3)? May courts use the performativity of law to cleanse or make a "clean break" with the past (chapter 6)? May the Supreme Court, as Justice Jackson argued in her dissent in *Students for Fair Admission v. Harvard* (2023), simply redefine or "resignify" the meaning of the Fourteenth Amendment's Equal Protection Clause and thereby "announce colorblindness for all by legal fiat?"[186] Does the deconstruction of the "sovereign legal subject" with a collective purpose imply the death of antidiscrimination law altogether? In other words, is it possible for discriminatory speech-acts to *unperform* themselves?

As the work of political philosopher Peg Birmingham's work suggests, a solely performative approach to law ultimately leads to disastrous results for our understanding of democracy. To understand why we should resist a purely performative reading of the law vis-à-vis Butler or Derrida, Birmingham reminds us of Derrida's claim in *Force of Law*. There, Derrida writes,

> Since the origin of authority, the foundation or ground, the position of the law can't by definition rest on anything but themselves, they are themselves a violence without ground. Which is not to say that they are in themselves unjust, in the sense of "illegal." They are neither legal nor illegal in their founding moment. They exceed the opposition between founded and unfounded, or between any foundationalism or anti-foundationalism. Even if the success of performatives that found law or right (for example, and this is more than an example, of a state as guarantor of a right) presupposes earlier conditions and conventions (for example in the national or international arena), the same "mystical" limit will reappear at the supposed origin of said conditions, rules or conventions, and at the origin of their dominant interpretation.[187]

As Birmingham reminds us, for Derrida, the founding of political authority (i.e., the Declaration of Independence) is an act of *originary violence*. Legal declarations are thus a kind of performative decision, founding the authority of the law in its very declaration. The *logos* of legal writing and legal speech can be understood as a kind of performative declaration, a bringing into existence of political authority itself by legal declaration. According to Derrida, then, the authority of law is grounded in an originary violence, exemplified by the signature, the declaration, and the sovereign subject of all legal writing.

For Birmingham, Derrida's performative analysis of law reproduces Schmitt's sovereign decisionism, resulting in the inability to distinguish *deceptive* or *evil* legal speech-acts. For Birmingham,

> there is at the very heart of Derrida's thinking a residual Schmittean decisionism, even if formulated in terms of the undecidable. For Derrida, the authority of the laws emerges out of an originary decision, an originary violence as it were, that makes Derrida's political thought much closer to Schmitt's than his readers usually admit.[188]

Because Derrida fails to follow Arendt's distinction between ποίησις (*poesis*, or "performance") and πρᾶξις (*praxis*, or action), Birmingham argues that Derrida's deconstruction of law is unable to draw normative distinctions between legal speech-acts that are "true" or "false," faithful or deceptive, good or evil. Noting the critical distinction between "interpretation" and "manipulation," Birmingham notes that for Arendt,

> it is important to distinguish between "interpretation" and "manipulation." As the above passage indicates, for Arendt each generation has the right to its interpretation of the facts; each generation must engage in the hermeneutical task of establishing the meaning of the facts, and in this way factual truth will, for each generation, take on new hues and tones. "Manipulation," on the other hand, is literally a "handling" of the matter itself. In other words, manipulation is not concerned with the meaning of factual truth (hermeneutics) but actively transforms the matter into something else entirely. Manipulation is a ποίησις that handles the factual matter in a manner that produces a new, albeit deceptive, reality. Arendt's distinction between ποίησις and πρᾶξις is helpful in grasping the difference between "manipulation" and "action." While manipulation appears to be an action insofar as it introduces something new, it more closely resembles ποίησις insofar as its real intent is to produce a new (although deceptive) reality, using as its means ideology and image-making.[189]

As Birmingham notes, for Arendt, "interpretation" is the collective act of each new generation to arrange the facts of its historical memory according to its own contemporary perspective. Arendt notes, however, that in interpretation, *the facts themselves* are not redefined or "resignified." Rather, each new generation arranges the facts themselves within a narrative that helps the new generation make sense of their won present. In contrast, "manipulation" is the redefinition or resignification of the facts *themselves*. Manipulation, for Arendt, is therefore the deceptive resignification of *reality itself*. In this way, manipulation presupposes a purely performative understanding of the role of law in not simply crafting a common *narrative* from the facts, but in redefining the political *legal reality* itself.

In contrast to Derrida's Schmittian, performative reading of law, Birmingham argues that Arendt's conception of the political enables us to distinguish the "originary violence" of the sovereign performativity of law from the domain of plural *action* where human beings appear together in their *givenness* or simple act of *being-there* in common. Birmingham writes that, for Arendt,

> the space of the political is not primarily or first of all the realm of logos, with its declarations and manifestos; instead, it is rather first of all the realm of appearance, the exposure or the taking-place of a "commonality of singularities." Before the law and animating the law is the human being, exposed in its very appearance, in its very being-manifest.[190]

According to Birmingham, whereas Derrida's conception of the political remains grounded in the figure of the sovereign as performative founder of originary violence, Arendt's conception of the political is grounded in the figure of the refugee *sans papiers*. As Birmingham elegantly writes:

> Without logos or proper identity papers, nevertheless, the refugee exposes the rightful appearance (*expose de droit*) of the purely human as such. The appearance of the human as such is a principled appearance, and to paraphrase Agamben, who in this case is very close to Arendt, in the coming community this principled appearance of the human as such will be the spirit subtending the law, surrounding it like a halo. This disturbing miracle of givenness is the spirit that animates the law; it is the basis for all political declarations and performance. And this to my mind refutes the notion of originary violence, a coup de force, that constitutes the law. Instead, what animates the law, its spirit, is gratitude for various kinds of givenness—the singularity of human beings, the otherness of living things, the web of appearance, the unfolding of time, the earth itself—accompanied by the pleasure of inhabiting together with a plurality of others a world where the miracle of beginning saves us from ruin.[191]

In this way, the crucial value of Birmingham's work is that it allows us to see why a purely *performative* understanding of the law—whether via Derrida or Butler—merely reinscribes a Schmittian decisionism as the foundation of political authority. If the authority of law is grounded simply in the self-authorizing, performative practices of "petty sovereigns" (Butler), then how is it possible to distinguish "good" from "bad" or "legitimate" versus "illegitimate" uses of the law? If law is performative all the way down, isn't all legal writing and legal practice grounded in a kind of self-authorizing, originary violence? Similarly, if the origin of legal authority lacks any ground except its own performative speech-act (Derrida), how then do we distinguish between "just" and "unjust" laws or "malevolent" versus "benevolent" uses of law? Birmingham writes, "If reality is constituted through a performative event or act, as Derrida claims it is, then by what measure or standard do we judge a deceptive performance? And when is the deception such that it becomes a phenomenon of radical evil?"[192] For this reason, Birmingham has urged the importance of Arendt's conception of the political in the midst of contemporary "crises" of truth, democracy, and various rising antidemocratic and neofascist tendencies across the globe today. As Birmingham writes,

> In conclusion, rather than the Schmittean idea of the law as rooted in the miraculous sovereign decision that violently distinguishes between friend/enemy, included/excluded, and zones of life and death, the Arendtian conception of law is rooted in alliances and treaties in which spheres of power are conjoined. . . . In a slight modification of Arendt, we could say, then, that the political task today, and it is a task that requires that we live and act from the borders, is to transform the sacred violence of the sovereign into political praxis, no longer founded in bloody myths and supreme fictions but, instead, animated by the twin political affectivities of gratitude for givenness and the pleasure of acting in political solidarity.[193]

As Birmingham observes, Arendt urgently calls our attention to the specific relation between totalitarianism and *deception*. For Arendt, as Birmingham explains, the very condition for the emergence of fascist political movements is the fabrication of a "lying world order" in which there is no longer a distinction between facts and fantasy. In this world, the pure performativity of law gives free reign for the sovereign resignification and redefinition of *reality itself*. As Birmingham explains, for Arendt, "the destruction of the facts is the destruction of the world. The destruction of the facts, she argues, occurs through deceptions and lies. Given that these deceptions destroy the world, she argues that they are "criminal."[194] If the authority of law is grounded in nothing other than the performative speech-acts of the sovereign, then it follows that political reality itself may be simply redefined or "resignified" according to the decisions of sovereign authorities. In the terminology of Francois Ost, this configuration would allow sovereign authorities themselves to simply redefine the "public time" or collective memory of the law by an act of revision. And, in the words of constitutional scholars Reva Seigal and Jack Balkin, such a performative reading facilitates the sovereign redefinition and selective erasure of the "constitutional memory" of the law, remaking the history of the nation in its own sovereign image. For Birmingham, Arendt's conception of the political, exemplified by the figure of the refugee *sans papiers,* refutes and opposes this purely performative reading of law. Rather than granting the sovereign the right to manipulate reality according to its own performative speech-acts, Birmingham writes:

> The survival of the public space depends upon those who are able to testify truthfully to the facts of the matter. This is the only authority upon which the democratic contest and debate on issues of power, knowledge and the law can rely.[195]

For this reason, Birmingham's work demonstrates the need to go beyond the lens of performativity by itself toward an understanding of the *temporality* and *legal pragmatics* at work in the shared, collective project of meaning-making fundamental to law and politics.

## Legal Pragmatics and Strategic Speech

The third and final element of discriminatology utilized in the book consists in the insights of legal pragmatics, which are applied in the case studies of chapters 1, 2, and 5. The justification for utilizing legal pragmatics is that such methodological tools illuminate the deficiencies of the textualist theory of legal meaning, while providing a framework for reconstructing and retrieving discriminatory meaning that is "implicit" or hidden behind the neutrality of legal texts. As Lloyd, Marmor, and others have shown, the tools of pragmatics demonstrate the major deficiencies of textualism as an account of meaning.[196] In particular, Marmor's approach to legal pragmatics highlights how "strategic speech" is used to advance political or legislative goals under the "good faith" legal presumption of cooperation. Marmor's notions of "strategic speech" and "manipulative speech" explored in chapter 2 are therefore extremely useful in reconstructing the *performative* practices of legal speech-acts performed *mala fide* or in "bad faith."

In general, pragmatics can best be understood as the study of "mechanisms thought to govern the relation between utterance, context and meaning."[197] Pragmatic interpretation, then, focuses on analyzing cases where meaning is underdetermined by what is said and requires inference based on some set of communicative principles that seek to explain the relation between the variables mentioned. In legal interpretation, pragmatics is of special import for understanding legal phenomena of semantic indeterminacy, indirect and implied meaning, and ambiguity. In modern pragmatics, cases of underdetermined meaning are approached usually through techniques of pragmatic enrichment, whereby disambiguation of all possible senses is conducted until the utterance best fits the occasion and context-specificity of its communicative purpose. When the meaning or intention of a legal utterance is disputed,

> any interpretation must be arrived at by contextual inference, filling out an incomplete, encoded semantic meaning on the basis of pragmatic features such as co-text, accessible background knowledge and relevant purpose. Intention will be central, but an interpretive choice must be made between different kinds of intention, including: the subjective, historical intention of an author or authors; an attributed, objective (or external) assessment of collective and cumulative intent of the legislature; and intention modernised to fit contemporary norms or sense of legal purpose, either of the specific legislation or of principles of law more generally.[198]

A person who has four siblings, when asked if they have two siblings and responds *Yes*, violates a pragmatic maxim because they have said "too little," inviting speculation about the speaker's intention to conceal information.[199] While the asserted content is technically true, pragmatic considerations suggest that the speaker intends something over and above what is asserted. In this way, pragmatics studies the mechanisms by which underdetermined meaning of utterances can be captured or reconstructed in their proper context-specificity.

In one of the most influential works in pragmatics and philosophy of language, *Studies with the Way of Words,* Paul Grice outlines the essential features of all rational, purpose-driven conversation which has as its aim "maximally effective exchange of information."[200] For Grice, all participants in such conversation are assumed to abide by the Cooperative Principle, which states that all participants must "make your conversational contribution such as is required, at the stage at which it occurs, by the accepted purpose or direction of the talk exchange in which are you are engaged."[201] Along with this general principle of cooperation, all participants can be expected to observe the conversational maxims of quantity, quality, relation and manner. The maxim of quantity can be summarized as the maxim, "don't say too little"; the maxim of quality can be summarized as the maxim to not say what you believe to be false or that for which you lack sufficient evidence; the maxim of relevance can be summarized as the maxim to make one's contribution relevant to the conversation; the maxim of manner can be summarized as the maxim to avoid obscurity and ambiguity.[202] For Grice, speech that follows these principles and maxims can be said to be "quasicontractual" in that: (i) the participants share some immediate common aims despite diverging ultimate aims, (ii) the participants' contributions are mutually dependent, and (iii) there is mutual understanding that the transaction should continue unless both parties agree it should be terminated.[203] The "conversational" model of legal interpretation has been challenged most directly by Poggi and Marmor, who both argue that legislative speech-acts in particular do not conform to the Gricean model of conversation.[204] While some commentators have argued that judicial speech and opinions are consistent with the conversational model,[205] there is still considerable debate over the application of the model to the legislative context. In this way, the debate centers around to what extent certain kinds of legal acts and speech can be accurately understood and interpreted through a Gricean conversational model of interpretation.

Like Grice, Andrei Marmor argues that the full communicative content of legal speech-acts often exceeds the semantic and assertive content of speech-acts. Instead, the full communicative content of speech-acts includes *implied content*, understood as any content a *reasonable* hearer would find incredible if the speaker subsequently denied it. For Marmor, the communicative content of legal speech-acts is traditionally understood by reference to semantic content and assertive content. Semantic content refers to the content expressed by the semantic and syntactic structure of the sentence, while assertive content refers to the truth-evaluable propositions of the sentence. What a speaker actually says "often goes beyond what the words and sentences semantically mean, depending on various pragmatical features of the context of the utterance and the speaker's communicative intentions."[206] Marmor gives the following definition of implied content:

> the implied content of the utterance of P in context C can be defined as the content that the speaker, in the specific context of C, is committed to by uttering P, and the hearers are expected to know that the speaker is committed to, and the speaker can be expected to know this.[207]

Further, speakers will be committed to a specific implied content "if and only if an explicit, *ex post* denial of the implied content would strike any *reasonable* hearer under the circumstances as perplexing, disingenuous, or contradictory."[208] For Marmor, the two kinds of implied content are *implicatures* and *presuppositions*, the former being governed by Grice's maxims of ordinary conversation.

For Marmor, the content of a speech-act is implied by a speaker, "if it is not part of what the speaker had actually asserted, but nevertheless is implicated by what he said in the specific speech situation, given the conversational maxims that apply."[209] As Marmor explains, Grice's two essential features of conversational implicatures are *cancelability* and *context-specificity*. Cancelability refers to the fact that a speaker "can always add an explicit clarification to cancel the implication that would otherwise follow from his utterance."[210] By adding a clarification that some specific implication is not intended, a speaker may cancel out any such implication that would be reasonably inferred within the context. Context-specificity refers to the fact that conversational implicatures follow from their situatedness within some background story or context.

However, Marmor observes (correctly) that for Grice, conversational implicatures operate within a certain conversational framework where norms of cooperation obtain. Recall that for Grice, this means that in ordinary conversation, the purpose of the exchange is the efficient exchange of information. However, as Marmor argues, many speech situations are noncooperative or rely upon a mix of both cooperative *and* noncooperative forms of communication. In these situations—for example, a polite remark that is not exactly true—it is clear that the normative framework diverges such that what is literally *said* is not intended to convey what is true but rather to comply with certain social norms and rituals of polite speech, behavior, and so on.[211]

This analysis leads Marmor to the notion of "strategic speech." In many noncooperative situations, "Parties to a strategic conversation may wish to employ conversational maxims in ways that generate implications that act to their advantage, without a real intention to be committed to such implicated content."[212] If a PhD in philosophy, Mr. Smith, visits a hospital and presents himself as "a doctor," the asserted content is true but Smith deliberately implicates something he knows to be false. Marmor calls this "manipulative speech," an extreme example of strategic speech. For Marmor, the "essential feature of a strategic speech . . . is that the speaker strives to implicate more than he would be willing to make explicit."[213] Because of the very nature of strategic interactions, "they allow the parties to make moves within the game, so to speak, without disclosing *ex ante* all their ulterior motives, expectations, or aims."[214] Marmor gives the following example of how strategic speech might be utilized in legislative speech-acts, focusing on the indeterminacy of an antidiscrimination provision:

> As an example, consider two legislators agreeing to the following formula of an antidiscrimination provision: "it is unlawful to discriminate against persons on the basis of gender, race, ethnicity, or nationality." Now suppose that one of the legislators assumed that "to discriminate against a person" clearly implies that discrimination would be unlawful if, and only if, it is intentional. But the other legislator may not have shared this intended implication. After all (she thought), people can engage in discriminatory practices even if they are not aware of the discriminatory effect of their conduct. And similar divergence can be present with respect to the question of whether the list of grounds for discrimination in the legal provision is exhaustive or not; does this law allow discrimination if it is not

based on the listed grounds? (I will say more on this type of implication below.) Once again, it is certainly possible that the collective expression is intended to be indeterminate about these questions (which is typically tantamount to an intention to delegate the decision to the courts). But it is equally possible that legislators simply intend to implicate different content by their collective expression.[215]

Here, Marmor shows how the indeterminacy of an antidiscrimination provision allows different content to be implicated by each party in the legislative context. The issue of whether *intent* is required for a showing of discrimination is left undetermined by the provision. This specific indeterminacy of legislative speech-acts has been studied in linguistic research, where some scholars have argued that such speech "excludes that legislators be able to convey particularized conversational implicatures, as it is impossible for legislators to foresee the variety of settings in which the legislative act will play its function."[216]

In Marmor's example above, then, it is left undetermined whether discrimination requires a showing of subjective, "invidious" intent or not. The likely explanations for this are many: it might be the case that legislators compromised on the language of the provision, while hoping that their own party's implicated content is taken up and recognized by the courts. Alternatively, it could be the case only one legislator or political party has adopted this strategy and has carefully crafted the language and form of the provision in a way that favors their own implicated content. For Marmor, it is entirely plausible that a political party or group of legislators may employ strategic speech in just this way while presenting a cooperative façade. Legal texts, in other words, can be used as a vehicle of "manipulative speech." In this case, one party may be seen to be playing the conversational or "dialectical" game of argumentative, evidence-based reason-giving, while the other party is strategically utilizing the formal parameters of the argumentative legal framework precisely in order to disguise their true motives and strategies, or to circumvent certain legal doctrines or legal scrutiny. In other words, one party may be acting under the assumptions of Gricean conversational maxims and implicatures, while another party is not. In these cases, the use of strategic speech to advance one's disguised strategic goals conflicts with an outward presumption that legislators are acting reciprocally in good faith with respect to their basic shared motivations and communications That is, this use of strategic speech conflicts with basic Gricean principles and maxims of conversation upon which an argumentative, dialectical argumentative framework is based. Therefore, if legal actors explicitly or implicitly reject the applicability of these basic conversational maxims, it follows that the normal, "cooperative" model of legal interpretation cannot apply in such cases of bad faith.

In this way, Marmor's approach to pragmatics is a useful starting point in highlighting how strategic speech is used to advance political or legislative goals under the guise of mutual cooperation. Marmor's pragmatic notions of strategic speech and manipulative speech explored in chapter 2 are therefore extremely useful in reconstructing the *performative* practices of legal speech-acts performed *mala fide* or in bad faith. Recent work in legal pragmatics has examined bad faith strategies in law enforcement interrogation techniques. This research documents how police use coercive interrogation tactics while avoiding violating constitutional using pragmatic implication. By avoiding direct implication in interrogation techniques, interrogators convey constitutionally suspect messages in coercing cooperation while maintaining deniability for violating the letter of the law.[217] In these cases, the formal speech parameters of interrogation are followed but in a way that implicates coercive messages that may later be plausibly denied on the basis that no such explicit messages were conveyed. In this way, implied content is utilized for coercive and unlawful purposes, using implication that is "cancelable" through plausible deniability. This body of work demonstrates the ways in which the pragmatic maxims of ordinary conversation fail to apply and capture the full communicative content of legal speech-acts, since in many speech-acts, the speakers are not committed to the implied content they convey when speaking. In fact, in some cases, speakers *intend* such coercive implicated messages to be cancelable and deniable.[218] They are instances of manipulative speech. This raises the question of whether the conversational model is even appropriate for attempting to understand highly adversarial and strategic forms of legal interactions and speech-acts. Instead, as the book's central argument suggests, many domains of strategic legal speech should be characterized as a kind of malevolent legality pursued in bad faith.

For this reason, legal pragmatics is indispensable for understanding discriminatory speech. In many cases, for example, discrimination contains no linguistic "speech" at all. In such cases, courts are faced with a dilemma: either take the defendant's word "on faith" that their actions were not motivated by discrimination, or try to "unmask the defendant's discrimination that they wish to disguise by putting on a legal performance. Consider the case of *Ezell v. Edwards Theatres, Inc* (2006). In this case, a movie theater ejected two black women from a theater under the pretext of "disruptive conduct" after the manager repeatedly "smirked" when informed about white patrons using the "n-word" directed toward the women during a screening. The undisputed facts of the case are that a white movie patron called the sisters the "n-word" during the movie and that the theater manager, when confronted with the allegation, visibly smirked and then failed to investigate the malicious racial remark. A federal district court found that the theater manager was motivated by discriminatory intent. The court reasoned that while the manager did not utter any explicitly discriminatory speech himself, the smirk—which the manager does not dispute—along with failure to confront the white patron and investigate the racial slur, constituted sufficient evidence that the manager harbored discriminatory intent.[219] In this case, the lack of an explicit linguistic utterance of racial animus did not deter the court from engaging in a careful and pragmatic analysis of the evidence in the context of the historical significance of the racial slur and the communicative content of the manager's smirk. The court, in other words, was able to recognize the face of discrimination where there was no text or utterance to interpret.

In *Ezell,* the court engaged in what the book calls *textual skepticism* by analyzing the ways in which discrimination is *performed* through pretext, proxy, purposes, and policies presented in the "neutral" form of legality. In *Ezell,* discrimination is performed through the legal act of both the smirk and the facially neutral pretext ("disruptive conduct"), which simultaneously acknowledges the malicious racial history of the slur, while both ignoring that history and concealing discriminatory motives that led to the ejection of the sisters and failure to investigate the temporal sequence of events that led to the racial slur. The discrimination was inferred not simply by the negligent failure to act upon the racial slur—rather it was the theater's bad faith strategy of offering a *pretext* for ejecting the sisters ("disruptive conduct") coupled with the performative act of the smirk itself that evinced a hidden "malevolent" motive. The manager's smirk and pretextual justification simultaneously acknowledged the racial history of the slur—literally "on the face" of the manager—while at the same time omitting and severing the very temporal nexus between that racial history and the present responsibility of the theatre to redress the harmful speech.

Here, it is significant that the court read the discriminatory intent literally on the face of the manager's smirk, without the manager *saying* anything. In performance studies, law is understood as not simply a body of rules and texts but as an embodied and often theatrical set of speech-acts delivered by actors directed toward a particular set of audiences. In this sense, viewing law from the perspective of performance, the smirk reveals that which goes *unsaid:* the amusement and enjoyment that itself disguises the hidden endorsement of discriminatory speech. This element also underscores the distinction between *performance* and *performativity*: while performance studies of law enable a grid of analysis for speech which is *unsaid, unstated, and unwritten,* performativity is a grid of analysis for understanding law as the citation and recitation of the written, stated and said. In many cases of malevolent legality, however, both performance and performativity are extremely useful and complementary. Thus, in *Ezell,* the malevolent legality was hidden or disguised by both (a) the performance of the smirk and (b) the pretextual policy proffered as a neutral, nondiscriminatory reason. Only by using *pragmatic* considerations and looking beyond or *behind* the smirk and the facially neutral reasons given by the theater was the court able to recognize the true face of discrimination. In this way, courts have utilized the tools of legal pragmatics in reconstructing the discriminatory meaning of an act. In some cases of discrimination, there will be no text to analyze, only acts that must be interpreted—as in the case of the smirk. Therefore, in cases such as these, legal pragmatics is an indispensable tool for reconstructing and understanding discriminatory speech.

Together, these three methodological elements of discriminatology—temporality, performativity, legal pragmatics—provide a theoretical framework for analyzing and reconstructing malevolent legalities. Namely, these tools allow us to see that discrimination: (1) is performed *through the law*, (2) persists through *time*, and (3) is a product of strategic manipulation of legal speech.

## CHAPTER OUTLINE

The organization of the book consists of two parts, each with three chapters. Part 1 examines Scalia's textualist methodology in three Supreme Court cases in light of his speech on the "Rule of Law." The overall argument of part 1 is as follows: since textualism rejects judicial scrutiny into "extratextual" purposes not made textually explicit, and because injustice is performed by discrimination not made textually explicit, it follows that textualism results in injustice. Part 1 therefore advances the thesis that textualism makes it lawful to perform discrimination through the law. Chapter 1 examines Scalia's rejection of the "purpose" doctrine and analysis in *Edwards* (1987), which undermines the pragmatic reconstruction of discriminatory purpose. By rejecting the legal ontology of purpose or intent for legal interpretation, textualism undermines any attempt to scrutinize discriminatory purposes not made textually explicit. Scalia's rejection of the "Humpty Dumpty" view of purposivism therefore leads textualism to ignore any discriminatory motives that might shed interpretive light upon the meaning of a law. In this way, Scalia's rejection of purposivism in *Edwards* laid the judicial groundwork for the legality of discriminatory practices that seek to sever themselves from the past. Chapter 2 argues that Scalia's pre-Supreme Court opinions regarding Section 1981 of the Civil Rights Act on the US Court of Appeals foreshadowed his majority opinion in *St. Mary's Honor Ctr* (1993) establishing the court's infamous "pretext plus" doctrine. Here, I argue that Scalia's majority in *St. Mary's* established the evidentiary framework for performative lying to be utilized as "bad faith" speech-acts to defeat discrimination claims. Scalia's pretext plus doctrine therefore reflects textualism's rejection of the notion that legal interpretation aims at doing justice. Instead, textualism allows what Marmor calls "manipulative speech," or what Scalia himself called "prudent evil," to flourish through the law. Chapter 3 examines Scalia's dissenting opinion in *Romer v. Evans* (1996) in light of Scalia's argument for an "unwritten constitution." In particular, Scalia found in the work of German jurist Frederick Charles von Savigny's notion of the *volkgeist* a confirmation of his view that the "reason" of law (*ratio*) could be embodied in the "traditions" of "the people," even if discriminatory. According to Scalia, certain kinds of discrimination are lawful if embodied in the "traditions" of the people and are not textually prohibited by the Constitution. In *Romer v. Evans* and *Windsor* (2014), Scalia maintained that certain kinds of "mean-spirited" animus against homosexuals were perfectly constitutional. The forms of malevolent legality explored in part 1, as I argue, established the philosophical and judicial foundations for *performative discrimination*—the performing of discrimination through legal text.

Part 2 of the book examines the temporal aspect of Scalia's self-described "activist" judicial philosophy of originalism, whose goal is to "prevent progress" by enacting a "regime of static law." Taking up the methodological lens of temporality, each chapter in part 2 examines the temporal regime involved in textualist-originalist methods of interpretation. Chapter 4 analyzes Scalia's opposition to the Voting Rights Act through his opinions in *Reno v. Bossier* (2000) and *Shelby County v. Holder* (2013), showing how Scalia's opposition to the "progressive" Congressional purpose of the Voting Rights Act was an extension of Scalia's "originalist" approach to thinking about constitutional time and constitutional rights. It also argues that Scalia's originalist position was first accurately critiqued by Gerhart Husserl in *Recht und Zeit* (1954) as a judicial "enemy of progress." Chapter 5 shows how the Supreme Court's majority in *Abbott v. Perez* (2018) recycles Scalia's arguments in *Edwards* explored in chapter 1. Drawing upon Justice Sotomayor's dissent, Chapter 5 shows how the court's sovereign exceptionalism in *Abbott v. Perez* allows state legislatures to performatively "resignify" their own discriminatory actions of the past through a performance of good faith—precisely what occurred in *Alexander v. South Carolina State Conference of the NAACP* (2024). After examining the case study of *Abbott v. Perez* and *Alexander*, I review the various temporal solutions to the problem of "discriminatory taint" that have been proposed in various jurisdictions and in constitutional scholarship. I argue that an *institutional realist* approach to discrimination ensures that the history and memory of discrimination is not severed, as in *Abbott,* but brought into a hermeneutic reading of the present. Chapter 6 analyzes the court's opinion in *Students for Fair Admission v. Harvard* (2023) invalidating affirmative action based on its textualist reading of a "race-neutral" Fourteenth Amendment. The chapter shows how the court's conclusion in this case was in many respects the culmination of Scalia's textualist-originalism in action. The chapter also addresses the argument that "colorblindness" should be considered a form of *hermeneutical injustice,* concluding that the framework of epistemic injustice fails to apply to cases of malevolent legality such as the court's race-neutral textualist philosophy. In contrast, as Justices Ketanji Brown Jackson and Sotomayor have argued, the court's colorblindness should be understood as a selective, sovereign decision to sever the historical memory from the text of the law: that is, "by legal fiat." The invalidation of affirmative action therefore represents the culmination of the temporal regime of textualist-originalism that both abstracts law away from its historical ground while exercising a sovereign exceptionalism in excluding from history the very memory of discrimination. As a result, I argue, the lens of epistemic injustice fails to capture both the political and ontological stakes of the court's colorblind jurisprudence.

The malevolent legalities examined in the chapters that follow each share the common goal of disguising their own intentions through textual procedures, strategies, tactics, and methods of "manipulation" that are performative in nature. It is for this reason that I have developed in this book a novel methodology of discriminatology for understanding the unique mode of speech-acts involved in the performance of malevolent legality. The second axis of discriminatology, the theory of performativity, is applied in chapters 2, 5, and 6. Here, the book examines case studies that demonstrate the ways in which textualism is *itself* a performative theory of the law. Chapter 2 examines the ways that Scalia's pretext plus doctrine in *St. Mary's* facilitates performative lying by defendants to defeat discrimination claims. Chapter 5 examines the "strategic speech" of the Texas legislature in *Abbott v. Perez* and the court's "good faith" doctrine allowing legal actors to "resignify" their past acts of discrimination. Chapter 6 examines the court's decision in *Students v. Harvard* performing a "race-neutral" reading of the text by resignifying the social meanings of the Fourteenth Amendment. The revealed performativity of textualism allows us to understand the often cited "malleability" or "flexibility" of textualist methods in disguising or "masking" one's ideological or political goals or preferences. The axis of performativity is therefore the methodological perspective that activates a new way of thinking about legal speech-acts whose aim is to "unperform" themselves—namely what the book refers to as *performative discrimination*.

The first axis of the method of discriminatology, the lens of temporality, is applied in chapters 3, 4, 5, and 6. The lens of temporality pursued in these chapters shows that (1) discrimination should not be understood as a series of discrete acts, but rather as persisting through time and (2) legal theories of interpretation are themselves distinct ways of thinking about time. In this way, temporality illuminates the ways in which discrimination regenerates itself through novel forms of legal reality—what Justice Ginsburg had referred to as the "Hydra" of discrimination." Chapter 3 examines the temporal aspect of Scalia's originalist argument that there is an "unwritten" constitution embodied in the "traditions" of the people. Chapter 4 examines Scalia's quest to "prevent progress" on the Voting Rights Act by enacting a backwards-looking "regime of static law." Chapter 5 examines the temporality of the court's ruling in *Abbott v. Perez* severing the evidence of past discrimination from the present. This chapter analyzes the problem of "discriminatory taint" from a temporal perspective, showing how the textualist solutions to this problem constitute a sovereign exclusion of the past altogether from the legal universe of meaning, and the creation of a "good faith" presumption that severs the past from the present. Chapter 6 examines the court's "race-neutral" erasure of the "constitutional memory" of the Fourteenth Amendment in *Students v. Harvard* announcing "colorblindness for all by legal fiat." The lens of temporality thus illuminates the fact that textualist-originalism is a specific *temporal regime* or certain way of thinking time through law. Only when we acknowledge that textualist-originalism is a temporal regime can we properly understand Scalia's remarks that textualism is an activist judicial philosophy which seeks to prevent progress by enacting a "regime of static law." In this way, we see that textualism is much more than a theory of legal interpretation—it is a philosophical theory presupposing certain conceptions of time, memory, history, and national identity.

The third axis of discriminatology, legal pragmatics, is applied in chapters 1, 2, and 5. In these chapters, the methods of legal pragmatics allow us to demonstrate the deficiencies inherent in the textualist theory of legal meaning, while also providing a framework for reconstructing and retrieving discriminatory meaning that is "implicit" or hidden behind the neutrality of legal texts and "bad faith" legal actors. Chapter 1 examines Scalia's dissenting opinion in *Edwards v. Aguillard* attacking the court's doctrines of "purpose" and demonstrating the pragmatic deficiencies of the textualist theory of legal meaning. Chapter 2 examines the pragmatics of the court's evidentiary framework in *St. Mary's*, showing how the court's framework facilitates the "strategic speech" of bad faith legal actors seeking to disguise discrimination. Chapter 5 examines the pragmatics of discriminatory speech in *Abbott v.*

*Perez*, showing how the court neglected pragmatic canons (i.e., *in pari materia*) in rejecting past discrimination as evidence of present discriminatory intent. In this way, the axis of legal pragmatics contributes to a much fuller understanding of discrimination as it is practiced in reality and provides real tools for analyzing and detecting forms of discriminatory speech I've called malevolent legalities.

In total, the methodology advanced in the book seeks to contribute both to the theoretical and practical legal understanding and analysis of discriminatory speech. In particular, I hope that the arguments and methodology advanced in the book may be of use for practitioners, scholars, and theorists of discrimination alike in understanding modes of legal speech-acts that seek to "un-perform" themselves or disguise their intent behind the neutrality of legal texts or speech. In this way, the book has consciously followed the path of a long tradition of what I've called *textual skepticism* in antidiscrimination law dating back to *Yick Wo*. Pursuant to these ends, I also hope that the book will advance the core aspirations of justice when interpreting "neutral" legal texts and policies—an aspiration that was first set out so clearly by the court in *Yick Wo*:

> Though the law itself be fair on its face and impartial in appearance, yet, if it is applied and administered by public authority with an evil eye and an unequal hand, so as practically to make unjust and illegal discriminations between persons in similar circumstances, material to their rights, the denial of equal justice is still within the prohibition of the Constitution.[220]

## NOTES

1. Glenn Elmers, "'Conservatism' Is No Longer Enough," *The American Mind*, September 24, 2021, https://americanmind.org/salvo/why-the-claremont-institute-is-not-conservative-and-you-shouldnt-be-either/.

2. Mike Sabo, "Christian Nationalism Isn't Going Away," *The American Mind*, February 27, 2024, https://americanmind.org/salvo/christian-nationalism-isnt-going-away/.

3. *Students for Fair Admissions, Inc. v. President & Fellows of Harv. Coll.*, 143 S. Ct. 2141, 2177 (U.S. June 29, 2023).

4. *Shelby Cnty. v. Holder*, 570 U.S. 529, 560 (2013).

5. Duncan Kennedy, *A Critique of Adjudication (Fin de siècle)* (Cambridge, MA: Harvard University Press, 1997), 4.

6. Antonin Scalia, "Response," in *A Matter of Interpretation: Federal Courts and the Law*, ed. Amy Gutman (Princeton, NJ: Princeton University Press, 1997), 132.

7. Kennedy, *A Critique of Adjudication*, 14.

8. Kennedy, *A Critique of Adjudication*, 14.

9. William Baude, "The 2023 Scalia Lecture: Beyond Textualism?" *Harvard Journal of Law and Public Policy* 46 (2023): 1332.

10. Steve Karnowski, "Justice Barrett expresses support for a formal US Supreme Court Ethics Code in Minnesota Speech," Associated Press, October 16, 2023, https://apnews.com/article/supreme-court-justice-amy-coney-barrett-ethics-9088cbf33256ff6995b740087f78c698.

11. *New York Times*, "Full Transcript: Read Judge Amy Coney Barrett's Remarks." September 26, 2020, Available at https://www.nytimes.com/2020/09/26/us/politics/full-transcript-amy-coney-barrett.html?smid=url-share.

12. Antonin Scalia and Bryan A. Garner, *Reading Law* (St. Paul: West Publishing 2012), xxvii.

13. *Dobbs v. Jackson Women's Health Org.*, 142 S. Ct. 2228, 2283 (2022).

14. *Students for Fair Admissions, Inc. v. President & Fellows of Harv. Coll.*, 143 S. Ct. 2141, 2177 (2023).

15. *Students for Fair Admissions, Inc. v. President & Fellows of Harv. Coll.*, 143 S. Ct. 2141, 2182 (2023).

16. Brian Slodysko and Eric Tucker, "Supreme Court Justices and donors mingle at campus visits. These documents show the ethical dilemmas," Associated Press, July 11, 2023, https://apnews.com/article/supreme-court-ethics-donors-politics-4b6dc4ae23aac75d4fccb1bcff0b7e0b.

17. *Students for Fair Admissions, Inc. v. President & Fellows of Harv. Coll.*, 143 S. Ct. 2141, 2277 (2023).

18. *Students for Fair Admissions, Inc. v. President & Fellows of Harv. Coll.*, 143 S. Ct. 2141, 2279 (2023).

19. *Students for Fair Admissions, Inc. v. President & Fellows of Harv. Coll.*, 143 S. Ct. 2141, 2279 (2023).

20. Allen R. Kamp, "The Counter-Revolutionary Nature of Justice Scalia's 'Traditionalism,'" 27 *Pac. L. J.* 99 (1995).

21. Bruce Allen Murphy, *Scalia: A Court of One* (New York: Simon & Schuster, 2014), 172.

22. Paul Smith, *Justice Kennedy: The linchpin of the transformation of civil rights for the LGBTQ community*, SCOTUSblog (June 28, 2018, 5:02 PM), https://www.scotusblog.com/2018/06/justice-kennedy-the-linchpin-of-the-transformation-of-civil-rights-for-the-lgbtq-community/.

23. *Bostock v. Clayton Cty.*, 140 S. Ct. 1731, 1751 (2020).

24. Scalia and Garner, *Reading Law*, 101.

25. *Bostock v. Clayton Cty.*, 140 S. Ct. 1731, 1737 (2020).

26. Harry Litman, "Originalism Divided" *The Atlantic*, May 25, 2021, https://www.theatlantic.com/ideas/archive/2021/05/originalism-meaning/618953/?utm_source=copy-link&utm_medium=social&utm_campaign=share; Cass R. Sunstein, "Originalism for Liberals," *The New Republic*, September 28, 1998, https://newrepublic.com/article/64084/originalism-liberals.

27. *Pereira v. Sessions*, 138 S. Ct. 2105, 2114 (2018).

28. *Me. Cmty. Health Options v. United States*, 140 S. Ct. 1308, 1320 (2020).

29. Harvard Law School, The Antonin Scalia Lecture Series: A Dialogue with Justice Elena Kagan on the Reading of Statutes, YouTube (November 25, 2015), https://www.youtube.com/watch?v=dpEtszFT0Tg.

30. *Ross v. Blake*, 578 U.S. 632, 638 (2016).

31. William Eskridge, Brian Slocum, and Kevin Tobia, "Textualism's Defining Moment," *Columbia Law Review* 123, no. 6 (2023): 1611-698.

32. Andrew Chung and John Kruzel, "Supreme Court to Hear Trump Appeal on Colorado Ballot," Reuters, January 6, 2024, https://www.reuters.com/legal/us-supreme-court-hear-trump-appeal-colorado-ballot-disqualification-2024-01-05/.

33. Section Three of the Fourteenth Amendment states, "No person shall be a Senator or Representative in Congress, or elector of President and Vice-President, or hold any office, civil or military, under the United States, or under any State, who, having previously taken an oath, as a member of Congress, or as an officer of the United States, or as a member of any State legislature, or as an executive or judicial officer of any State, to support the Constitution of the United States, shall have engaged in insurrection or rebellion against the same, or given aid or comfort to the enemies thereof. But Congress may by a vote of two-thirds of each House, remove such disability." USCS Const. Amend. 14.

34. The Supreme Court of Colorado begins their constitutional interpretation by stating, "we begin with Section Three's plain language, giving its terms their ordinary and popular meanings." *Anderson v. Griswold*, 2023 CO 63, ¶ 27.

35. *Trump v. Anderson*, No. 23-719, 601 U.S. 100 (2024).

36. Scalia and Garner, *Reading Law*, xxiv.

37. Scalia and Garner, *Reading Law*, xxv.

38. Antonin Scalia, speech on "Realism and the Religion Clauses," Federalism speech, 1982, Antonin Scalia papers, LAW, MMC, 291, Series III, Box: 73, Folder: 2, Harvard Law School Library, Historical & Special Collections, 1.

39. Scalia and Garner, *Reading Law*, xxv.

40. In re Sandoval, No. 04-15-00244-CV, 2016 Tex. App. LEXIS 754, at 3 (Tex. App. Jan. 27, 2016).

41. Tex. Fam. Code § 160.602.

42. In re Sandoval, No. 04-15-00244-CV, 2016 Tex. App. LEXIS 754, at 8 (Tex. App. Jan. 27, 2016).

43. In re Sandoval, No. 04-15-00244-CV, 2016 Tex. App. LEXIS 754, at 13-14 (Tex. App. Jan. 27, 2016).

44. In re Sandoval, No. 04-15-00244-CV, 2016 Tex. App. LEXIS 754, at *14 (Tex. App. Jan. 27, 2016).

45. In re N.I.V.S., No. 04-14-00108-CV, 2015 Tex. App. LEXIS 2282, at *7 (Tex. App. Mar. 11, 2015).

46. In re Sandoval, No. 04-15-00244-CV, 2016 Tex. App. LEXIS 754, at *9 (Tex. App. Jan. 27, 2016).

47. Michel Foucault, *Security, Territory, Population: Lectures at the College de France, 1977-1978* (New York: Palgrave Macmillan 2007), 103.

48. Michel Foucault, *The History of Sexuality: Volume 1: an Introduction* (New York: Random House, 1991), 136.

49. Foucault, *The History of Sexuality: Volume 1: an Introduction*, 144.
50. Foucault, *The History of Sexuality: Volume 1: an Introduction*, 144.
51. Foucault, *Security, Territory, Population*, 109.
52. Foucault, *Security, Territory, Population*, 99.
53. Foucault, *Security, Territory, Population*, 106.
54. Foucault, *Security, Territory, Population*, 107.
55. Judith Butler, "Indefinite Detention," in *Precarious Life: the Powers of Mourning and Violence* (New York: Verso Books, 2004), 50–100.
56. Giorgio Agamben, *State of Exception*, trans. Kevin Attell (Chicago: University of Chicago Press 2005), 4.
57. Agamben, *State of Exception*, 21, 35; Carl Schmitt, *Political Theology: Four Chapters on the Concept of Sovereignty*, trans. George Schwab (Chicago: University of Chicago Press, 2005), 5.
58. Schmitt, *Political Theology*, 7.
59. Agamben, *State of Exception*, 7.
60. Schmitt, *Political Theology*, 5.
61. Butler, "Indefinite Detention," 54.
62. Butler, "Indefinite Detention," 55.
63. Butler, "Indefinite Detention," 55.
64. Butler, "Indefinite Detention," 56.
65. Scalia and Garner, *Reading Law*, 408.
66. Antonin Scalia, "Common-Law Courts in a Civil-Law System: The Role of United States Federal Courts in Interpreting the Constitution and Laws, in *A Matter of Interpretation: Federal Courts and the Law*, Amy Gutmann ed. (Princeton, NJ: Princeton University Press, 1997), 22.
67. Scalia and Garner, *Reading Law*, 51.
68. Antonin Scalia, speech to Federalist Society, January 30, 1987, Antonin Scalia papers, LAW, MMC, 291, Series III, Box: 77, Folder: 14, Harvard Law School Library, Historical & Special Collections, 72.
69. Scalia, Common Law Court in a Civil Law System, 132.
70. *Yates v. United States*, 574 U.S. 528, 537, 135 S. Ct. 1074, 1081 (2015).
71. *Yates v. United States*, 574 U.S. 528, 557 (U.S. February 25, 2015).
72. *Yates v. United States*, 574 U.S. 528, 553-54, 135 S. Ct. 1074, 1091 (2015).
73. Shel Silverstein, "Fish?" in *So Many Heads, So Many Wits: An Anthology of English Proverb Poetry*, ed. Janet Sobieski (Burlington: University of Vermont Press, 2005), 208.
74. Scalia, Common Law Court in a Civil Law System, 132.
75. Scalia and Garner, *Reading Law*, 89.
76. Schmitt, *Political Theology*, 13.
77. Catherine L. Langford, *Scalia v. Scalia: Opportunistic Textualism in Constitutional Interpretation* (Tuscaloosa: University of Alabama Press, 2017), 50.
78. Langford, *Scalia v. Scalia*, 121.
79. David Dorsen, *The Unexpected Scalia: A Conservative Justice's Liberal Opinions* (Cambridge: Cambridge University Press, 2017), 12.

80. Gordon S. Wood, "Comment," in *A Matter of Interpretation: Federal Courts and the Law*, ed. Amy Gutman (Princeton, NJ: Princeton University Press, 1997), 63.

81. Bruce Allen Murphy, *Scalia: A Court of One*. (London: Simon & Schuster, 2014), 398.

82. Richard Hasen, *The Justice of Contradictions: Antonin Scalia and the Politics of Disruption* (London: Yale University Press, 2018), 63.

83. Hasen, *The Justice of Contradictions*, 172.

84. Hasen, *The Justice of Contradictions*, 174.

85. Hasen, *The Justice of Contradictions*, 178.

86. Langford, *Scalia v. Scalia*, 9.

87. Langford, *Scalia v. Scalia*, 127.

88. Victoria Nourse, "Power," in Brian G. Slocum and Franics J. Mootz, *Justice Scalia: Rhetoric and the Rule of Law* (Chicago: University of Chicago Press, 2019), 35.

89. Nourse, "Power," 35.

90. *Rivera v. Garcia,* 589 S.W.3d 242, 245 (Tex. App. 2019).

91. *Heath v. M'Inroy*, 6 Johns. 277, 278 (N.Y. Sup. Ct. August 1, 1810).

92. *Ware v. Hylton*, 3 U.S. 199, 241 (U.S. March 7, 1796).

93. Daniel Markovits, "Good Faith as Contract's Core Value," *Michigan State Law Review*. 1 (2021).

94. U.C.C. § 2-314 cmt. 4.

95. Alan Watson, *Legal Change and Legal Origins* (London: Hambledon Press 1991), 15.

96. Watson, *Legal Change and Legal Origins*, 15.

97. Watson, *Legal Change and Legal Origins*, 15.

98. *Huntington v. Brown*, 17 La. Ann. 48, 49 (1865).

99. *Simon v. Burnett*, 8 La. Ann. 84, 84 (1853).

100. Henry Campbell Black, Joseph R Nolan, Michael J Connolly, *Black's Law Dictionary: Definitions of the Terms and Phrases of American and English Jurisprudence, Ancient and Modern* (St. Paul: West Publishing Co. 1990), 957.

101. *Yick Wo v. Hopkins*, 118 U.S. 356, 373-74 (1886).

102. *Yick Wo v. Hopkins*, 118 U.S. 356, 366 (1886).

103. *Yick Wo v. Hopkins*, 118 U.S. 356, 373-74 (1886).

104. *Yick Wo v. Hopkins*, 118 U.S. 356, 373 (1886).

105. *Riordan v. Kempiners*, 831 F.2d 690, 697-98 (7th Cir. 1987).

106. *Tex. Dept. of Cmty. Affairs v. Burdine*, 450 U.S. 248, 256 n.8 (1981).

107. *Arlington Heights v. Metropolitan Housing Corp.*, 429 U.S. 252, 266 (1977).

108. *Arlington Heights v. Metropolitan Housing Corp.*, 429 U.S. 252, 265-66 (1977).

109. *Holmes v. Moore*, 384 N.C. 426, 440-41, 886 S.E.2d 120, 132 (2023).

110. *Department of Homeland Security v. Regents of Univ. of Cal.*, 140 S. Ct. 1891, 1915 (2020).

111. Roberts's only discussion of the Arlington Heights factors is the following: "To plead animus, a plaintiff must raise a plausible inference that an "invidious discriminatory purpose was a motivating factor" in the relevant decision. *Arlington Heights v. Metropolitan Housing Development Corp.*, 429 U.S. 252, 266, 97 S.Ct.

555, 50 L.Ed.2d 450 (1977). Possible evidence includes disparate impact on a particular group, '[d]epartures from the normal procedural sequence,' and 'contemporary statements by members of the decisionmaking body.' *Department of Homeland Security v. Regents of Univ. of Cal.*, 140 S. Ct. 1891, 1915 (2020)."

112. *Abbott v. Perez*, 138 S. Ct. 2305, 2354 (U.S. June 25, 2018).

113. William Araiza, *Animus: A Brief Introduction to Bias in the Law* (New York: NYU Press, 2017).

114. Oliver Wendell Holmes, "The Path of the *Law*," 10 *Harvard Law Review* 457 (1897), 463.

115. President Andrew Jackson's Message to Congress, "On Indian Removal"; 12/6/1830; Presidential Messages, 1789–1875; Records of the U.S. Senate, Record Group 46; National Archives Building, Washington, DC, accessed October 23, 2023, https://www.archives.gov/milestone-documents/jacksons-message-to-congress-on-indian-removal.

116. *Scott v. Sandford*, 60 U.S. (19 How.) 393 (1857).

117. *Minor v. Happersett*, 88 U.S. (21 Wall.) 162, 167 (1874).

118. *Korematsu v. United States*, 323 U.S. 214, 216 (1944).

119. *Arlington Heights v. Metropolitan Housing Corp.*, 429 U.S. 252, 266 (1977).

120. *Hernandez v. New York*, 500 U.S. 352, 111 S. Ct. 1859, 1864 (1991).

121. *Hicks v. St. Mary's Honor Center*, 756 F. Supp. 1244, 1250 (E.D. Mo. 1991).

122. *Ezell v. Edwards Theatres, Inc.*, No. 1:04-CV-6533-SMS, 2006 U.S. Dist. LEXIS 92413 (E.D. Cal. Dec. 21, 2006).

123. *Abbott v. Perez*, 138 S. Ct. 2305 (2018).

124. *United States v. Carrillo-Lopez*, 555 F. Supp. 3d 996 (D. Nev. 2021).

125. *303 Creative LLC v. Elenis,* 143 S. Ct. 2298 (2023).

126. *Students for Fair Admissions, Inc. v. President & Fellows of Harv. Coll.*, 143 S. Ct. 2141 (2023).

127. Michael B. Kent Jr. and Brannon P. Denning, "*Anti-Evasion Doctrines in Constitutional Law*," Utah L. Rev. 1773 (2012): 1796.

128. Kent Jr. and Denning, "*Anti-Evasion Doctrines in Constitutional Law*."

129. See David E. Pozen, "*Constitutional Bad Faith,*" 129 *Harvard Law Review* 885 (2016).

130. See Brannon P. Denning & Michael B. Kent, Jr., "*Anti-Anti-Evasion in Constitutional Law*," 41 *Florida State University Law Review* 397 (2014).

131. Pozen, "*Constitutional Bad Faith*."

132. Reva Siegel, "The Politics of Constitutional Memory," 20 *Georgetown Journal of Law & Public Policy* 19 (2022).

133. Scalia and Garner, *Reading Law*, 16.

134. William Araiza, *Animus: A Short Introduction to Bias in the Law* (New York: NYU Press, 2017).

135. Sophia Moreau, *Faces of Inequality: A Theory of Wrongful Discrimination* (Oxford: Oxford University Press, 2020).

136. Gerhart Husserl, *Recht und Welt* (Halle: Max Niemeyer Verlag, 1929), 21.

137. Diana Taylor, *Performance* (Chapel Hill: Duke University Press, 2016).

138. Deborah Hellman, *When Is Discrimination Wrong?* (Cambridge, MA: Harvard University Press, 2008); Moreau, *Faces of Inequality: A Theory of Wrongful Discrimination*).

139. Larry Alexander, Deborah Hellman, and Sophia Moreau, eds., *Philosophical Foundations of Discrimination Law* (Oxford: Oxford University Press, 2013), 283.

140. Sophia Moreau, "Discrimination as Negligence," in *Justice and Equality*, ed. Colin Murry Macleod (Calgary: University of Calgary Press), 123–49; Sophia Moreau, "Discrimination as Negligence," *Canadian Journal of Philosophy Supplementary Volume* 36 (2010): 123–49, doi:10.1080/00455091.2010.10717657.

141. Miranda Fricker, *Epistemic Injustice: Power and the Ethics of Knowing* (Oxford: Oxford University Press, 2007).

142. Josué Piñeiro, "Colorblindness, Hermeneutical Marginalization and Hermeneutical Injustice," *Southwest Philosophy Review* 38, no. 1 (2022): 115–22.

143. *United States v. Fordice*, 505 U.S. 717, 747 (1992).

144. Kerrel Murray, "Discriminatory Taint," 135 *Harvard Law Review* 1190, 1226 (2022).

145. Murray, "Discriminatory Taint," 1221.

146. Murray, "Discriminatory Taint," 1197.

147. Murray, "Discriminatory Taint," 1241.

148. See Felipe Torres, *Temporal Regimes: Materiality, Politics, Technology* (New York: NYU Press, 2022); Collin Bjork and Frida Buhre, "Resisting Temporal Regimes, Imagining Just Temporalities," *Rhetoric Society Quarterly* 51:3 (2021):177–81; François Ost, *Le Temps du Droit* (Paris: Odile Jacob, 1999).

149. Gerhart Husserl, *Recht und Zeit: fünf rechtsphilosophische Essays* (Vittorio Klostermann, Frankfurt am Main, 1955), 10.

150. Husserl, *Recht und Welt*, 13.

151. Husserl, *Recht und Zeit*, 23.

152. Husserl, *Recht und Zeit*, 23.

153. Husserl, *Recht und Zeit*, 51.

154. Husserl, *Recht und Zeit*, 58.

155. Husserl, *Recht und Zeit*, 86.

156. Husserl, *Recht und Zeit*, 86.

157. Husserl, *Recht und Zeit*, 26.

158. Husserl, *Recht und Zeit*, 26.

159. Husserl, *Recht und Welt*, 21.

160. Husserl, *Recht und Welt*, 21.

161. Husserl, *Recht und Zeit*, 86.

162. Husserl, *Recht und Zeit*, 55.

163. Husserl, *Recht und Zeit*, 54.

164. Husserl, *Recht und Zeit*, 61.

165. Husserl, *Recht und Zeit*, 62.

166. Michel van de Kerchove and François Ost, *Le système juridique entre ordre et désordre* (Presses Universitaires de France: Paris 1988).

167. van de Kerchove and Ost, *Le système juridique entre ordre et désordre*, 224.

168. van de Kerchove and Ost, *Le système juridique entre ordre et désordre*, 226.
169. van de Kerchove and Ost, *Le système juridique entre ordre et désordre*, 227–28.
170. van de Kerchove and Ost, *Le système juridique entre ordre et désordre*, 226.
171. Antonin Scalia, "U.V.A. Federalist Society Introduction," Federalist Society Symposium, Charlottesville, March 4, 1988, Antonin Scalia papers, LAW, MMC, 291, Series III, Box: 79, Folder: 1, Harvard Law School Library, Historical & Special Collections, 6–7.
172. J. L. Austin, *How to Do Things with Words* (Oxford: Clarendon Press, 1962), 4.
173. Austin, *How to Do Things with Words*, 6–7.
174. Austin, *How to Do Things with Words*, 11.
175. Judith Butler, *Excitable Speech*: a Politics of the Performative (New York: Routledge 1997), 14.
176. Butler, *Excitable Speech*, 14.
177. Butler, *Excitable Speech*, 16.
178. Jacques Derrida, "Signature Event Context," in *Limited Inc* (Evanston: Northwestern University Press, 1988).
179. Derrida, "Signature Event Context," 18.
180. Derrida, "Signature Event Context," 18–19.
181. Derrida, "Signature Event Context," 20.
182. Derrida, "Signature Event Context," 21.
183. Derrida, "Signature Event Context," 12.
184. Antonin Scalia, "John M. Olin Lecture Series on Political Economy Lecture of Judge Antonin Scalia," April 25, 1986, Philadelphia, PA, Wharton School, University of Pennsylvania, Antonin Scalia papers, LAW, MMC, 291, Series III, Box: 76, Folder: 28, Harvard Law School Library, Historical & Special Collections, 17.
185. *Abbott v. Perez*, 138 S. Ct. 2305, 201 L. Ed. 2d 714 (2018).
186. *Students for Fair Admissions, Inc. v. President & Fellows of Harvard Coll.*, No. 20-1199, at 233 (June 29, 2023).
187. Jacques Derrida, "Force of Law: The 'Mystical Foundation of Authority," in *Deconstruction and the Possibility of Justice*, ed. Drucilla Cornell, Michael Rosenfield, and David G. Carlson (New York: Routledge, 1992), 14.
188. Peg Birmingham, "On Violence, Politics, and the Law," *The Journal of Speculative Philosophy* 24, no. 1 (2010): 13–14.
189. Peg Birmingham, "Elated Citizenry: Deception and the Democratic Task of Bearing Witness," *Research in Phenomenology* 38, no. 2 (2008): 206.
190. Birmingham, "On Violence, Politics, and the Law," 14.
191. Birmingham, "On Violence, Politics, and the Law," 14.
192. Peg Birmingham, "On Deception: Radical Evil and the Destruction of the Archive," in *Difficulties of Ethical Life*, ed. Shannon Sullivan and Dennis J. Schmidt (New York: Fordham University Press, 2008), 198.
193. Birmingham, "On Violence, Politics, and the Law," 18.
194. Birmingham, "Elated Citizenry: Deception and the Democratic Task of Bearing Witness," 205.

195. Birmingham, "Elated Citizenry: Deception and the Democratic Task of Bearing Witness," 205.

196. Harold Anthony Lloyd, "Law's 'Way of Words': Pragmatics and Textualist Error," *Creighton Law Review* 49, no. 2 (2016); Andrei Marmor, "Textualism in Context," in *The Language of Law* (Oxford: Oxford University Press, 2014).

197. Alan Durant and Janny H. C. Leung. "Pragmatics in Legal Interpretation," in*The Routledge Handbook of Pragmatics*, ed. Anne Barron, Peter Grundy and Gu Yueguo (New York: Routledge, 2017), 538.

198. Durant and Leung, "Pragmatics in Legal Interpretation," 536.

199. Durant and Leung, "Pragmatics in Legal Interpretation," 539.

200. Paul Grice, *Studies in the Way of Words* (Cambridge, MA: Harvard University Press, 1991), 24.

201. Grice, *Studies in the Way of Words*, 24.

202. Andrei Marmor, "Can the Law Imply More than It Says? On Some Pragmatic Aspects of Strategic Speech," in *Philosophical Foundations of Language in the Law*, ed. Andrei Marmor and Scott Soames (Oxford: Oxford University Press, 2011), 85.

203. Grice, *Studies in the Way of Words*, 29.

204. See Francesca Poggi, "Against the conversational model of legal interpretation," *Revus* (Ljubljana) issue 40 (2020) str. 9–26, 127; Marmor, "Can the Law Imply More than It Says? On Some Pragmatic Aspects of Strategic Speech," 83–104.

205. Marat Shardimgaliev, "Implicatures in Judicial Opinions," *Int J Semiot Law* 32 (2019): 391–415.

206. Marmor, "Can the Law Imply More than It Says? On Some Pragmatic Aspects of Strategic Speech," 84.

207. Marmor, "Can the Law Imply More than It Says? On Some Pragmatic Aspects of Strategic Speech," 84.

208. Marmor, "Can the Law Imply More than It Says? On Some Pragmatic Aspects of Strategic Speech," 84.

209. Marmor, "Can the Law Imply More than It Says? On Some Pragmatic Aspects of Strategic Speech," 86.

210. Marmor, "Can the Law Imply More than It Says? On Some Pragmatic Aspects of Strategic Speech," 86.

211. Marmor, "Can the Law Imply More than It Says? On Some Pragmatic Aspects of Strategic Speech," 92.

212. Marmor, "Can the Law Imply More than It Says? On Some Pragmatic Aspects of Strategic Speech," 92–93.

213. Marmor, "Can the Law Imply More than It Says? On Some Pragmatic Aspects of Strategic Speech," 93.

214. Marmor, "Can the Law Imply More than It Says? On Some Pragmatic Aspects of Strategic Speech," 93.

215. Marmor, "Can the Law Imply More than It Says? On Some Pragmatic Aspects of Strategic Speech," 97.

216. Roberta Colonna Dahlman, "Conveying meaning in legal language – Why the language of legislation needs to be more explicit than ordinary language," *Journal of Pragmatics* 198 (2022): 43–53, 51.

217. Deborah Davis and Richard A. Leo, "Interrogation Through Pragmatic Implication: Sticking to the Letter of the Law While Violating its Intent," in *The Oxford Handbook of Language and Law*, ed. Lawrence M. Solan and Peter M. Tiersma *(Oxford: Oxford University Press 2*012), 354–68.

218. See L.W. Hunt, "Legal Speech and Implicit Content in the Law," *Ratio Juris* 29 (2016): 3–22.

219. *Ezell v. Edwards Theatres*, Inc., 2006 U.S. Dist. LEXIS 92413, 2006 WL 3782698 (United States District Court for the Eastern District of California December 21, 2006, Filed), https://advance.lexis.com/api/document?collection=cases&id=urn:contentItem:4MMP-YRW0-TVSH-338W-00000-00&context=1516831.

220. *Yick Wo v. Hopkins*, 118 U.S. 356, 373-74 (1886).

*Part 1*

# "PRUDENT EVIL"

In an unpublished speech entitled "The Rule of Law," written before his nomination to the Supreme Court, Scalia proposed "to trace the Rule of Law's gradual conquest of private associations and institutions."[1] In this speech, Scalia advanced the argument that the expansion of rule of law principles in American law—what Scalia called after Lon Fuller "galloping legalism"—had a "deleterious" effect on the "shared commitments" of associations such as the family, church, and traditional values. With this expansion of rule of law principles into civil litigation and federal due process and equal protection jurisprudence, the United States had become, in Scalia's words, a

> law-ridden county. There has been a veritable explosion of laws, of all sorts and at all levels. . . . And finally, there are the courts, which have long since cast aside the shackles of stare decisis, have expanded the scope of their business through virtual elimination of such self-limiting doctrines as standing, ripeness, and the "political question" doctrine. They are now a continual and fertile source of new law.[2]

For Scalia, the creation of "new law" by courts and expansion of the rule of law were symptoms of the same malaise, namely the deterioration of traditional associations and the premise that all social ills have a legal remedy. For Scalia, the unauthorized expansion of rule of law into all aspects of society was therefore the result of the broader social acceptance of the idea that social injustices should be remedied by the law. This mistaken notion, Scalia writes, is exemplified by the common-law maxim, "No wrong without a remedy."[3] This galloping legalism, Scalia argued, was a reminder of the evil of man, since "left to his own he would not wish aright."[4] According to Scalia, the "conquest" of the rule of law in all areas of society signals the level of selfishness and evil of mankind because society had, in his view, replaced the "glue" of traditional voluntary associations (family, church, etc.) with a "legalism" that seeks a remedy for all social ills. Scalia writes:

The law is, after all, not a vindication of the nobility of man, but a constant reminder of his selfishness and frailty. It is a restraint against his acting the way he wishes, because left to his own he would not wish aright. During the Middle Ages apocalyptic religious sects, both Chrisitan and Hebrew, would, on what they believed was the last day and coming of the millennium, engage in veritable orgies of self-indulgence—because the Law had been lifted. That is what heaven was—the absence of any constraints, so that what one wanted was right. More traditional religion also does not give the Law good marks. As St. Paul put it—[saying perhaps the same thing as Lon Fuller]—"the written law killeth, but the Spirit giveth life." In our most intimate association, in the context of our deepest commitments, we eschew the law. It is indeed a kinky bride and broom that sit down before their wedding to write out a detailed formal statement of their agreed rights and responsibilities. One may indeed go so far as to say that the more law a society has need of, the weaker the internal cohesion of the society is.[5]

Scalia's attack on the expansion of legalism as a remedy for all social ills was consistent with his endorsement of the Augustinian view of the sinfulness and frailty of man's existence in the earthly cities of man, as opposed to the perfect justice in the "kingdom of God."[6] For Scalia, while it may be true that the mortal lawyer or judge in her everyday practice sees "prudent evil flourish,"[7] the task of achieving justice and righting moral wrongs ultimately belongs to God, not to lawyers, much less to an unelected body of nine justices on the Supreme Court. As Scalia would write in his treatise *Reading Law* that mature and responsible judges reject "the false notion that the quest in statutory interpretation is to do justice."[8]

If the goal of textualism is *not* to do justice, then what is the political function of textualism—that is, what is the relation of textualism to the "the people?" For Scalia, the answer to this question can again be found in his speech on "The Rule of Law" in his reference to St. Paul: "the written law killeth, but the spirit giveth life." The shocking irony of Scalia's textualism is that, despite Scalia's insistence on sticking to the explicit written words of "the text," he acknowledged in his opinions and speeches that there existed an "unwritten law" of the Constitution and that textualist judges could identify this "unwritten law" in the customary "traditions of the people" by diving into the hermeneutic depths of the interpretive communities of the distant past. As chapter 1 demonstrates, Scalia rejected the notion of legislative intent in favor of the *ratio legis*, or abstract "reason" of law embodied in the unwritten traditions of the people. As his speeches and course materials on statutory interpretation show, Scalia endorsed the unwritten law embodied in the traditions and customs of the people, a notion inspired in part from von Savigny's conception of the *volkgeist*, or "spirit of the people."

The three cases examined in part 1 should thus be seen in the light of Scalia's speech "The Rule of Law." Specifically, the cases examined demonstrate Scalia's contention that textualism allows injustice or "prudent evil" to be performed through the law. First, in chapter 1, I analyze Scalia's rejection of purposivism in *Edwards* (1987). Textualism's rejection of the "Humpty Dumpty" view of purposivism therefore leads textualism to ignore any discriminatory motives that might shed interpretive light upon the meaning of a law. In this way, Scalia laid the judicial groundwork for the legality of discriminatory practices that seek to sever themselves from the past.

In chapter 2, I show how the pretext plus doctrine established by Scalia's majority in *St. Mary's* (1993) facilitates *malevolent legalities* by providing the framework within which "strategic speech" is used to defeat discrimination claims. In *St. Mary's*, Scalia argues that employers do lie about their motives in discrimination cases but that judges are responsible for enforcing legal *process*, not searching for the "true" motives to achieve justice.

Finally, in chapter 3, I examine Scalia's dissenting opinion in *Romer v. Evans* (1996) in light of his speeches and opinions arguing for an "unwritten constitution." The chapter argues that Scalia's originalist views on an unwritten constitution reflect the direct influence of Frederick Charles von Savigny's German historicist school. Scalia found in von Savigny's notion of the *volkgeist* a confirmation of his view that the "reason" of law (*ratio*) could be embodied in the "traditions" of "the people," even if discriminatory. In this way, we can better appreciate the citation of St. Paul in Scalia's speech.

Scalia's opinions and speeches through this period (1982–1993) demonstrate his consistent view that while "prudent evil" may flourish through the law, the role of the judge is to apply the technical instruments of *process* and not the substance of law in importing one's own conceptions of justice, fairness, "sympathy and the like." For Scalia, it is *not* the role of the judge to do justice by searching the "hearts" of legislators discern their intentions in a "quest" to provide a legal remedy for all social "wrongs." As a result, although Scalia admitted that "injustice is the game" in many legal cases, the textualist judge must allow such prudent evil to flourish. In this way, the argument presented in chapter 2 serves as the heart of part 1 of the book, which can be outlined as follows: (1) Since textualism rejects legal meaning derived from "extratextual" sources of interpretation, and (2) since injustice occurs when discriminatory meaning is *not* made textually explicit, it follows that (3) textualism results in injustice. In sum, textualism makes it lawful for the injustice of discrimination to be performed through the law. I refer to this argument as "Scalia's Argument for Textualist Injustice."

## NOTES

1. Antonin Scalia, speech on "The Rule of Law," 1970–1982, Antonin Scalia papers, LAW, MMC, 291, Series I, Sub-Series I, Box: 8, Folder: 7, Harvard Law School Library, Historical & Special Collections, 12.
2. Scalia, speech on "The Rule of Law," 7–8.
3. Scalia, speech on "The Rule of Law," 12.
4. Scalia, speech on "The Rule of Law," 13.
5. Scalia, speech on "The Rule of Law," 13.
6. Antonin Scalia, speech on nature of being a lawyer [submitted as part of nomination questionnaire], 1984, Antonin Scalia papers, LAW, MMC, 291, Series I, Box: 26, Folder: 7, Harvard Law School Library, Historical & Special Collections.
7. Scalia, speech on nature of being a lawyer [submitted as part of nomination questionnaire], 5.
8. Antonin Scalia and Bryan A. Garner, *Reading Law: The Interpretation of Legal Texts* (St. Paul: Thomson/West, 2012), 347.

# 1

## *Edwards v. Aguillard* (1987)
## Humpty Dumpty Had a Fall

In this chapter, I argue that Scalia's rejection of the "purpose" doctrine and analysis in *Edwards* (1987) undermines the basic notion of discriminatory purpose in antidiscrimination jurisprudence. Scalia's textualist rejection of the "Humpty Dumpty" view of purposivism therefore leads textualists to ignore any discriminatory motives that might shed interpretive light upon the meaning of a law. In this way, Scalia's rejection of purposivism in *Edwards* laid the judicial groundwork for the legality of discriminatory practices that seek to disguise themselves through the "neutrality" of legal texts and the performance of "good faith." These forms of malevolent legality, as I argue, seek to perform discrimination through legal texts that have been stripped of pragmatic meaning gained from an understanding of the history, temporality, and memory of the law.

In a speech to the Federalist Society in January 1987, Scalia described his method of legal interpretation as that of the "reasonable import" method, which questions what the words of a text mean: "regardless of what the offeror intended, what would the words convey to a reasonable person."[1] In a series of cases and lectures throughout 1986 and 1987, Scalia had laid out the basis of his judicial philosophy of "textualism": since legislative "purpose" likely did not exist and collective "intent" is a "pure fiction,"[2] the only authoritative source of interpretation are the explicit words of text itself. Just one year after Scalia's nomination by President Reagan in October 1986, Scalia mounted an aggressive assault on what he derisively called the "Humpty Dumpty" method of the Supreme Court's legal interpretation, namely the idea that the meaning of law or policy could be understood by reconstructing its purpose as intended by the lawmakers who enacted it. Scalia thus contrasted his textualist model with the "subjective intent" model, which holds that "even if the words reasonably convey X, if both of the parties to the agreement in fact intend them to mean Y, Y it is."[3] Scalia sharply criticized this subjective intent model, especially when applied to the interpretation of statutes enacted by legislatures:

> Well, who is the other party to legislation, or is not legislation more of a unilateral act like a contract offer, for which, as I have noted earlier, we ordinarily disregard subjective intent, and we ask what is the import upon the people to whom it is addressed. Would it be not somewhat disturbing to endorse the principle that a statute means—never mind its plain language—precisely whatever the legislature intended it to mean. I don't think it was the Queen of hearts in Alice in Wonderland that said that. I guess it was the Cheshire Car, but it could as well have been the Queen of hearts. Who was it? . . . It was Humpty Dumpty.[4]

In a speech criticizing what he referred to as "fictitious legislative intent," Scalia writes that textualism rejects examining statutes in terms of their legislative purpose:

> We do not allow such a counter-textual intent to prevail, I think, because we are, as the Constitution of Massachusetts describes it, a government of laws, not of men—which means government by legislated text, not by legislators' intentions.[5]

Scalia's brand of textualism was therefore committed to the principle that judges ought to give effect to the written text as enacted by the legislature, regardless of alleged unlawful motives or even if lawmakers were "fall-down drunk" when they wrote and voted for the bill. In the same speech on fictitious legislative intent, Scalia writes:

> A statute, on the other hand, has a claim to our attention simply because Article I, section 7 of the Constitution provides that since it has been passed by the prescribed majority (*with or without adequate understanding*—indeed, even if they are all fall-down drunk) it is law.[6]

Just prior to his nomination to the Supreme Court, Scalia made his textualist attack on the notion of legislative purpose entirely clear. In a speech delivered at the Attorney General's Conference on Economic Liberties in 1986, Scalia argued that "Statutes should be interpreted, it seems to me, not on the basis of the unpromulgated intentions of those who enact them . . . but rather on the basis of what is the most probable meaning of the words of the enactment."[7] Indeed, in a speech at the University of Pennsylvania in April of 1986, Scalia had openly declared, "I do not believe in legislative intent."[8]

Scalia's chance to advance his attack on notion of legislative intent or purpose came in *Edwards v. Aguillard* (1987) and *INS v. Cardoza-Fonseca*

(1987). In these cases, Scalia argued forcefully that what he had previously called the "Humpty Dumpty" view of subjective intent should be rejected in favor of the brand of textualism he advocated. Judges, according to Scalia, must stick to the "reasonable import" of the explicit words of the text as understood at the time of its enactment and reject "extratextual" sources of interpretation that are unreliable and manipulable, such as congressional history, historical record, committee reports, and the judges own conception of justice. As Scalia would argue a quarter-century later in his treatise *Reading Law,* textualism held that judges must "reject judicial speculation about both the drafters' extratextually derived purposes and the desirability of the fair reading's anticipated consequences."[9] This was allegedly a very narrow, limited view of the judge, since the claim to "stick to the text" was grounded in the idea that judges ought not to "import" either their own values, policy concerns, or justice considerations into the text nor the "unenacted intentions" or purposes of lawmakers that one can pick out in the legislative history or congressional record. Whether the "anticipated consequences" were desirable, good or bad, just or unjust, they were all extratextual concerns for the judge.

Likewise, the intended purpose of lawmakers, if not made explicit in the text, was also extratextual. This position implied that laws did not, strictly speaking, have a clear purpose that can be faithfully understood or hermeneutically retrieved by examining the motives or intentions of lawmakers to enact good policy or to do justice. As Scalia argued in *Reading Law,* "collective intent is pure fiction because dozens if not hundreds of legislators have their own subjective views on the minutiae of bills they are voting on—or perhaps no views at all because they are wholly unaware of the minutiae."[10] For Scalia, the idea that a judge's role in legal interpretation is one of "doing justice" or making social policy are both "false notions."

In December 1986, one month before Scalia's speech to the Federalist Society attacking the "Humpty Dumpty" view of purposivism, the Supreme Court had heard arguments in *Edwards v. Aguillard.* This case concerned the Louisiana Creation Act, a statute requiring public schools to teach the biblical account of creationism alongside Darwinian evolution. Plaintiffs challenged the constitutionality of the statute on the grounds that the true purpose of the statute was religious, not secular, in nature and thus violated the Establishment Clause of the Constitution separating church and state. According to section 4 of the statute, "When creation or evolution is taught, each shall be taught as a theory, rather than as proven scientific fact."[11] The central claim at issue in *Edwards* was the statute's explicitly stated purpose in section 2, which stated that the statute "is enacted for the purposes of protecting academic freedom."[12] Skeptical of this stated purpose, the Supreme Court employed its *Lemon* test for examining the true purpose of governmental acts concerning religion to determine compliance with the Establishment Clause. Under this constitutional doctrine, the purpose prong of the *Lemon* test directs courts to examine legislative history to interpret the motivations and intentions of legislators in passing a law, thereby examining its "true" intended purpose. Justice William J. Brennan, the leading purposivist on the court, explained its legal interpretation of unlawful purpose:

> A court's finding of improper purpose behind a statute is appropriately determined by the statute on its face, its legislative history, or its interpretation by a responsible administrative agency. . . . The plain meaning of the statute's words, enlightened by their context and the contemporaneous legislative history, can control the determination of legislative purpose. . . . Moreover, in determining the legislative purpose of a statute, the Court has also considered the historical context of the statute, *e. g., Epperson* v. *Arkansas, supra*, and the specific sequence of events leading to passage of the statute.[13]

Justice Brennan's purposivist approach to interpretation represented a contemporary extension of the purposivism advocated by the "legal process" school of Henry M. Hart Jr. and Albert Sacks. As Hart and Sacks had argued in their 1958 college teaching materials,

> Law is a doing of something, a purposive activity, a continuous striving to solve the basic problems of social living. . . . Underlying every rule and standard, in other words, is at the least a policy and in most cases a principle. This principle or policy is always available to guide judgment in resolving uncertainties about the arrangement's meaning. The uncertainties cannot be intelligently resolved . . . without reference to it. If the policy is in doubt in relevant respects, that doubt must be cleared up. Always the question must be faced: What purpose—what policy or objective or underlying principle—should be attributed to the arrangement in question?[14]

For Brennan and like-minded judges, the *Lemon* test was one way that courts could scrutinize whether statutes harbored an "improper" purpose. Writing for the majority, Justice Brennan concluded:

> True, the Act's stated purpose is to protect academic freedom. . . . While the Court is normally deferential to a State's articulation of a secular purpose, it is required that the statement of such purpose be sincere and not a sham. . . . It is equally clear that requiring schools to teach creation science with evolution does not advance academic freedom.[15]

Brennan's method of interpretation, however, also provided the groundwork for various other Supreme Court doctrines for examining the lawfulness of a law or policy's stated purpose. Among them were the *Arlington Heights* (1977) discriminatory purpose test, the *animus* doctrine, the pretext doctrine, "good faith" covenants in contract law, and others. Such doctrines relied upon a jurisprudential tradition of textual skepticism dating back to *Yick Wo* (1897) that adopted a healthy sense of skepticism regarding "neutral" texts being utilized for discriminatory purposes. Just as in *Yick Wo*, where a "facially neutral" ordinance was used for discriminatory purposes, Brennan's majority opinion in *Edwards* concluded that the "neutral" reason proffered by the text of the Louisiana statute was a "sham" that was, in fact, hiding a discriminatory purpose. The explicit words of the text, in other words, were a mask for the underlying discriminatory purpose. Therefore, the role of the judiciary, according to the court's purpose doctrines, was to look beyond the text itself to scrutinize the true, underlying purpose.

In this way, *Edwards* was an historic moment in the history of the struggle over constitutional interpretation that continues today. On one side, Brennan's purposivism argued that judges sometimes are required to look beyond the explicit words of the text and examine the true purpose of a legal text that is hidden by the text itself. On the other side, Scalia's textualism argued that such an intangible purpose did not exist and that legislative "intent" was pure fiction that allowed judges to speculate about the motives of individuals not made explicit in the text itself. In 2018, a congressional report on statutory interpretation contrasted textualism with the other theory of interpretation, purposivism.[16] As already noted, purposivism in statutory interpretation developed out of the legal process school of Hart and Sacks.[17] For them, purposivism begins with the recognition that the political life of human beings is characterized by "interdependence with other human beings and the community of interest which grows out of it."[18] Within the political society, human being form often exclusive groups, clubs, and private associations as expressions of this community of interest. However, as Hart and Sacks write:

> There is, in addition, an invariably felt need for an overriding, general purpose group to protect and further the overriding, basic interests which the members of a community have in common and which must be protected and furthered if they are to survive and to prosper and if their various special-purpose groups are to be able to exist and to function.... People who are living together under conditions of interdependence must obviously have a set of understandings or arrangements of some kind about the terms upon which they are doing so. This necessarily follows from the fact that interdependent living is collaborative, cooperative living. People need understandings about the kinds of conduct which must be avoided if cooperation is to be maintained. Even more importantly, they need understandings about the kinds of affirmative conduct which

is required if each member of the community is to make his due contribution to the common interest.[19]

For Hart and Sacks, the common understandings of the community required mutual cooperation to give rise to the *institutional* procedures of law, writing that,

> substantive understandings or arrangements about how the members of an interdependent community are to conduct themselves in relation to each other and to the community necessarily imply the existence of what may be called constitutive or procedural understandings or arrangements about how questions in connection with arrangements of both types are to be settled. The constitutive arrangements serve to establish and to govern the operation of regularly working—that is, institutionalized—procedures for the settlement of questions of group concern.[20]

In this way, then, the institutional arrangements of law reflect the substantive understandings of the community required for mutual cooperation and resolution of disputes. Purposivism, therefore, is simply the consequent thesis that the meaning of a legislative statute should be interpreted according to the substantive purposes that motivated the underling policy or principle of its enactment by the political community. Instead of rejecting extratextual sources of meaning not contained in "the text itself," purposivism *relies* upon the extratextual legislative background and development of the statute through the legal process to inform what the policy purpose of the statute is. As the US Supreme Court said in 1980:

> We have recognized consistently that statutes are to be interpreted not only by a consideration of the words themselves, but by considering, as well, the context, the purposes of the law, and the circumstances under which the words were employed.[21]

Earlier, in *Richards v. United States* (1962), a case involving environmental regulations, the Supreme Court had clarified that the purpose of legislative acts should be read in concert with its broader policy purpose or rationale. This basic principle of legal interpretation, which we revisit in chapter 5, is the principle of *in pari materia*. According to this principle, the purpose of a law should be considered within its broader policy context within the subject-matter jurisdiction in which it exists. Guided by this principle, the meaning of an environmental statute, for example, should be considered within the specific policy goals of the broader legislative act. The meaning of a health care statute should be considered in the policy context of the broader policy goals of the health care legislation in which it exists. The court wrote:

We believe it fundamental that a section of a statute should not be read in isolation from the context of the whole Act, and that in fulfilling our responsibility in interpreting legislation, "we must not be guided by a single sentence or member of a sentence, but [should] look to the provisions of the whole law, and to its object and policy." We should not assume that Congress intended to set the courts completely adrift from state law with regard to questions for which it has not provided a specific and definite answer in an act such as the one before us which, as we have indicated, is so intimately related to state law. Thus, we conclude that a reading of the statute as a whole, with due regard to its purpose, requires application of the whole law of the State where the act or omission occurred.[22]

For purposivists such as Justice Brennan, legal meaning is thus informed by examining not simply the linguistic or semantic meaning of the text, but rather the *teleological meaning* of a law, which Lawrence Solum has usefully distinguished as the purpose or end goal for which a law is enacted.[23] Justice Brennan again illustrated his purposivist method in *United Steelworkers v. Weber* (1979). In this case, a white steelworker (Weber) argued that his employer's collectively bargained affirmative action plan unlawfully discriminated against him on the basis of race. To support his claim, Weber cited Title VII of the Civil Rights Act, which prohibits employment discrimination on the basis of race. Therefore, the question in *Weber* was whether Title VII should be given a more "literal" construction or whether it should be read in historical context according to Congress's intended purpose pursuant to the Civil Rights Act. Writing for the majority opinion, Justice Brennan concluded:

Weber's reliance upon a literal construction of the statutory provisions and upon *McDonald* v. *Santa Fe Trail Transp. Co.*, 427 U.S. 273, which held, in a case not involving affirmative action, that Title VII protects whites as well as blacks from certain forms of racial discrimination, is misplaced, since the Kaiser-USWA plan is an affirmative action plan voluntarily adopted by private parties to eliminate traditional patterns of racial segregation. "A thing may be within the letter of the statute and yet not within the statute, because not within its spirit, nor within the intention of its makers," *Holy Trinity Church* v. *United States*, 143 U.S. 457, 459, and, thus, the prohibition against racial discrimination in §§ 703 (a) and (d) must be read against the background of the legislative history of Title VII and the historical context from which the Act arose.[24]

In this way, Brennan rejected a literal and strict textualist construction by adopting instead a teleological meaning of the law in historical context, that is, examining the legislative history of a law's enactment, including committee reports, congressional debates, historical record, etc. Examining a law's legislative history gives essential insight into *why* a law was enacted and an understanding of its intended, substantive purpose within a political community.

One major advantage of purposivism looking beyond the explicit words of the text is precisely because unlawful purposes often hide behind neutral texts and therefore must be exposed as a "sham," as Brennan suggested in *Edwards*. Indeed in 1954, the same year the Supreme Court ended *de jure* segregation in public schools in *Brown v. Board of Education* (1954), a New York court of appeals, in reference to a state antidiscrimination law prohibiting employment discrimination on the basis of race, religion, color, and national origin, observed:

> One intent on violating the Law Against Discrimination cannot be expected to declare or announce his purpose. Far more likely is it that he will pursue his discriminatory practices in ways that are devious, by methods subtle and elusive—for we deal with an area in which 'subtleties of conduct . . . play no small part.[25]

With the historic passage of the 1964 Civil Rights Act, courts were faced with the problem of combating covert discrimination by employers, recognizing that actors who discriminate "do not openly admit such discrimination, but rather try to conceal it."[26] One of the most common areas where covert discrimination occurs is housing. As the Department of Justice observes, often "housing providers try to disguise their discrimination by giving false information about availability of housing, either saying that nothing was available or steering homeseekers to certain areas based on race. Individuals who receive such false information or misdirection may have no knowledge that they have been victims of discrimination."[27] In 1968, Congress enacted Title VIII of the Civil Rights Act, the Fair Housing Act, "designed to provide fair housing throughout the nation and is a valid exercise of congressional power under the Thirteenth Amendment to eliminate badges and incidents of slavery."[28] That same year, the Supreme Court held that the legislative purpose of the Fair Housing Act prohibited racial discrimination in both public and private housing. Clarifying the historical purpose of the Fair Housing Act, the court wrote:

> Just as the Black Codes, enacted after the Civil War to restrict the free exercise of those rights, were substitutes for the slave system, so the exclusion of Negroes from white communities became a substitute for the Black Codes. And when racial discrimination herds men into ghettos and makes their ability to buy property turn on the color of their skin, then it too is a relic of slavery.[29]

Pursuant to this legislative purpose, courts recognized that discrimination in housing also extended to housing policies exhibiting a "pattern or practice" that uses a facially neutral reason as a hidden excuse to discriminate. As a federal court of appeals found in 1971,

> the facially neutral deposit requirement served yet another function—an excuse not to process the applications of many blacks. Appellee's assertion that the deposit requirement was not conceived out of racial discrimination is of no avail, since the requirement was administered in a discriminatory manner. Failure to advise these applicants of the deposit requirement was a disingenuous scheme or device to exclude blacks from the apartments and is additional evidence of a post-Act pattern or practice of racial discrimination.[30]

However, other disguised practices of discrimination were not so easily identified. By 1977, the Supreme Court faced such a situation in *Arlington Heights*. In this case, the board members of a village denied rezoning for the creation of a racially integrated, low-income housing development. The official reason given by the village for denying the rezoning request was to protect property values, since according to the board, the creation of low to middle-income multifamily units would decrease the property values of the single-family units in the village. Low-income residents brought suit against the village, claiming the denial of the housing constituted a violation of equal protection under the Fourteenth Amendment.

Unlike claims under the Fair Housing Act, the court had decided in 1976 that an equal protection claim requires plaintiffs to show not only a disparate impact on a protected class but also a discriminatory *purpose*.[31] The court therefore had to clarify what constitutes "discriminatory purpose." In *Arlington Heights*, it ruled in the village's favor, finding no discriminatory purpose behind the village's action and dismissing the equal protection challenge. One year later, however, plaintiffs brought suit again under the Fair Housing Act,[32] which does *not* require a showing of discriminatory purpose, only disparate impact. In that case, the plaintiffs were successful.[33] In its enforcement ruling of the consent decree establishing low-income housing, a federal district court clarified that Congress, in enacting the Fair Housing Act, "established a strong and unquestionable congressional intent to use every available means to limit public and private conduct which prevents racial minorities from escaping urban ghettoes and obtaining housing in the suburbs."[34] Pursuant to this purpose, the Fair Housing Act prohibits zoning policies that have discriminatory impact, regardless of intent. In this way, the court's discriminatory purpose test originally developed in *Arlington Heights* aimed to provide criteria for making context-informed inferences about discriminatory motives in cases where evidence of clear, subjective intent to discriminate is difficult to identify. As Judge Richard Posner pointed out, most defendants will neither openly admit discrimination nor leave any direct proof of discrimination. On the contrary, defendants will predictably "concoct a plausible reason" as a legal justification for excusing discrimination.

Thus, in *Edwards*, Justice Brennan had advanced the purposivist reading of the Louisiana statute in accordance with the Supreme Court's "discriminatory purpose" test first outlined in *Arlington Heights*. By examining the legislative history and historical context (among other factors) of a statute, judges may scrutinize an unlawful intent or discriminatory motives that lurks behind the facially neutral text of the law. Grounded in a tradition of antidiscrimination jurisprudence dating back to *Yick Wo*'s test of facially neutral but discriminatory laws, then, the court utilized legislative history and historical context in examining the purpose of a law to ensure that "the statement of such purpose be sincere and not a sham."[35]

## SCALIA'S DISSENT

In a lengthy dissent in *Edwards*, Justice Scalia attacked the fundamental basis of the court's purpose doctrine and analysis, arguing that the court should defer to the explicitly stated purpose of the statute's text instead of "impugning the motives of its supporters." Scalia argued that the majority, by scrutinizing the unstated and implicit motives of the legislature, were declaring

> that the members of the Louisiana Legislature knowingly violated their oaths and then lied about it. I dissent. Had requirements of the Balanced Treatment Act that are not apparent on its face been clarified by an interpretation of the Louisiana Supreme Court, or by the manner of its implementation, the Act might well be found unconstitutional; but the question of its constitutionality cannot rightly be disposed of on the gallop, by impugning the motives of its supporters.[36]

Scalia argued that the court should believe the "sincerity" of the purpose as explicitly stated in the section 3 of the text that the purpose was to advance academic freedom rather than endorse a discriminatory preference for biblical Christian creation science. For Scalia, a law *requiring* teachers to teach biblical Christian creation science alongside evolution did not exhibit a discriminatory preference for or governmental endorsement of Christian religious beliefs. Instead, the discriminatory motives of the legislature should not be impugned, and the explicit text should be taken in "sincerity."

Scalia's argument in *Edwards* was grounded in a novel legal ontology. For Scalia, it was not simply that the statute lacked a discriminatory purpose.

Rather, according to Scalia, the *Lemon* test was constitutionally suspect precisely because the very notion of "purpose" was itself philosophically flawed. Scalia argued:

> The difficulty of knowing what vitiating purpose one is looking for is as nothing compared with the difficulty of knowing how or where to find it. For while it is possible to discern the objective "purpose" of a statute (i.e., the public good at which its provisions appear to be directed), or even the formal motivation for a statute where that is explicitly set forth (as it was, to no avail, here), discerning the subjective motivation of those enacting the statute is, to be honest, almost always an impossible task. The number of possible motivations, to begin with, is not binary, or indeed even finite. In the present case, for example, a particular legislator need not have voted for the Act either because he wanted to foster religion or because he wanted to improve education. He may have thought the bill would provide jobs for his district, or may have wanted to make amends with a faction of his party he had alienated on another vote, or he may have been a close friend of the bill's sponsor, or he may have been repaying a favor he owed the Majority Leader, or he may have hoped the Governor would appreciate his vote and make a fundraising appearance for him, or he may have been pressured to vote for a bill he disliked by a wealthy contributor or by a flood of constituent mail, or he may have been seeking favorable publicity, or he may have been reluctant to hurt the feelings of a loyal staff member who worked on the bill, or he may have been settling an old score with a legislator who opposed the bill, or he may have been mad at his wife who opposed the bill, or he may have been intoxicated and utterly unmotivated when the vote was called, or he may have accidentally voted "yes" instead of "no," or, of course, he may have had (and very likely did have) a combination of some of the above and many other motivations. To look for the sole purpose of even a single legislator is probably to look for something that does not exist.[37]

In this breathtaking deconstruction of the Supreme Court's doctrines of purpose inquiry, Scalia had launched at attack on the very rationale of the court's antidiscrimination jurisprudence. Indeed, Scalia rejected the very premise on which antidiscrimination jurisprudence rested: namely, the idea that the role or duty of judges is to examine the constitutionality of "facially neutral" laws and policies that are enacted with an unlawful, discriminatory motive or intent. In *K Mart Corp. v. Carter* (1988) just one year later, Scalia would continue his assault on the purposivist inquiry, writing that Justice Brennan's purposivist theory

> requires judges to rewrite the United States Code to accord with the unenacted purposes of Congresses long since called home. (The reality, I fear, may be even worse than the theory. In practice, the rewriting is less likely to accord with the legislative purposes of yester-year than the judicial predelictions of today.)[38]

Once again, Scalia's judicial opinions were a direct translation of his arguments attacking the notion of "unenacted intentions" made in speeches and writings just years prior to his nomination. In 1986, Scalia had similarly argued, "Statutes should be interpreted, it seems to me, not on the basis of the unpromulgated intentions of those who enact them . . . but rather on the basis of what is the most probable meaning of the words of the enactment."[39] These judicial outcomes rejecting the purpose of law in interpretation, therefore, were a direct reflection of Scalia's brand of textualism. As Scalia would articulate clearly in his 2012 treatise *Reading Law*:

> In the interpretation of legislation, we aspire to be "a nation of laws, not of men." This means (1) giving effect to the text that lawmakers have adopted and that the people are entitled to rely on, and (2) giving no effect to lawmakers' unenacted desires.

In this way, Scalia's textualist rejection of the purpose inquiry into the meaning of law undermined not only the fundamental premise of purposivism as a theory of interpretation but also, by extension, the notion that judges can identify an unlawful discriminatory purpose behind a statute. If legislative purpose and intent are "pure fictions," then it seemed to follow that "discriminatory purpose" is also "pure fiction." If judges are supposed to exclude from interpretation any source of meaning not made explicit on the face of the text, how do judges address "bad faith" legal actors who seek to disguise their purposes through the law? In this way, Scalia's position sharply conflicted with the court's traditional antidiscrimination jurisprudence since at least *Yick Wo*, which focused precisely on laws which are "facially neutral" but which are motivated by discriminatory intent.

Scalia's rejection of the very notion of legislative intent or purpose thus dismissed the entire tradition of *textual skepticism* in antidiscrimination jurisprudence that had led to the development of the *discriminatory purpose* doctrine developed in *Arlington Heights* (1977). The historical legal experience of the Chinese Exclusions Acts, Japanese internment during WWII, Jim Crow, the Voting Rights Act, and many others had demonstrated that "minimally sophisticated" defendants could disguise discriminatory motives through facially neutral policies and legal texts. This led to the court's many purpose doctrines, including its five-factor test in *Arlington Heights* to examine through contextual, historical, and pragmatic factors the likelihood of discrimination in enacting a law or policy. Textualism, however, rejected as a matter of interpretation the very existence of such hidden motives if not made explicit on the face of the text itself. But if textualism for Scalia rejected the very existence of these factors, how did Scalia's textualism propose to address these kinds of cases and claims?

One answer to this question came in the Supreme Court's decision in *Richmond v. Croson* (1989). In *Richmond*, the city council of Richmond, Virginia, passed a resolution requiring that 30 percent of the dollar amount of city subcontractors be awarded to minority business enterprises as a remedial measure for the city's history of racial discrimination in business contracting.[40] A contractor plaintiff challenged the resolution, claiming that the requirement violated the Equal Protection Clause of the Fourteenth Amendment. In a 6–3 decision, the court ruled in favor of the contractor, holding that evidence of past discrimination cannot justify racial preferences in city contracting regardless of a "remedial purpose." In his concurring opinion, Scalia argued that there was only *one* instance where race could be used by state governments, namely in cases like *Brown v. Board of Education* (1954) where a state uses race to dismantle dual admissions policies explicitly based on race. Outside of that specific context, however, Scalia argued that race may never be used by state governments, even for "remedial" purposes to correct injustice. From Scalia's textualist point of view, therefore, what is required by the Equal Protection Clause is a "race-neutral" policy. Scalia's consistent view, seen again in *Schuette v. Coalition to Defend Affirmative Action* (2014), was that any race-neutral policy *cannot* violate the Equal Protection Clause, full stop.[41] For him, the Equal Protection Clause prohibits any state from enacting a law whose text *explicitly* utilizes racial preferences. Conversely, however, the Equal Protection Clause does *not* prohibit states from enacting a law whose text *implicitly* utilizes racial preferences. This is for the simple reason that, from the standpoint of the textualist judge, such "implicit" content does not exist, since according to Scalia, individual and collective "intent" is pure fiction. Legal texts must be interpreted to mean what they *say,* and not according to what they *do not say.* Therefore, legal texts should *not* be interpreted according to some allegedly illicit motive not made explicit on the face of the text itself. Reiterating this point in *Schuette*, Scalia wrote:

> In my view, any law expressly requiring state actors to afford all persons equal protection of the laws . . . does not—cannot—deny "to any person . . . equal protection of the laws," U.S. Const., Amdt. 14, §1, regardless of whatever evidence of seemingly foul purposes plaintiffs may cook up in the trial court.[42]

Therefore, according to Scalia, a facially neutral, constitutional law enacted by a legislature cannot be invalidated on the basis of judicial scrutiny into its alleged "discriminatory purpose." As Scalia had intimated years earlier in his "The Rule of Law" speech, the "galloping legalism" that has run rampant in

American society has allowed plaintiffs to "cook up" foul purposes in the trial court in order to pursue a "remedy for every wrong."[43]

However, there was one glaring problem with Scalia's argument. In *Richmond*, Scalia had openly acknowledged that race-neutral policies of the past had been vehicles for discrimination. Remarking on racial discrimination in American history, Scalia surprisingly writes:

> The same thing has no doubt happened before in other cities (though the racial basis of the preference has rarely been made textually explicit)—and blacks have often been on the receiving end of the injustice. Where injustice is the game, however, turnabout is not fair play.[44]

Here, Scalia openly acknowledged that African Americans had suffered injustice through laws in which racial preferences were not made textually explicit. That is, Scalia acknowledged that discrimination could be performed through implicit textual means. However, Scalia was still a steadfast textualist. Even though a law had been utilized for injustice by hiding racial preferences from the explicit content of the text, Scalia then argued that that the correction of this injustice through any sort of racial preferences was not "fair play." But if blacks have been on the receiving end of injustice as a result of laws in which discrimination was not made textually explicit, and the Equal Protection Clause *requires* laws in which race is not textually explicit (race-neutral), then it follows from Scalia's own view that the Equal Protection Clause *requires* laws that have historically been used to unjustly discriminate against blacks. Because of this, Scalia's view is that it would be *unfair* for a legislature to use the Equal Protection Clause to remedy the past effects of implicit discrimination by using race at all (unless within the specific context of school desegregation).

But where does this leave textualism on the question of addressing injustice that is perpetuated through the law? If Scalia acknowledged in *Richmond* that "race-neutral" texts have historically been used to perpetuate injustice, then what tools does Scalia offer to address these forms of injustice? To answer to this question, we need to be reminded that Scalia's textualism explicitly states that doing justice or correcting injustice are *not* goals of statutory interpretation. In his treatise *Reading Law*, Scalia made it explicit that, according to textualism, judges must reject "the false notion that the quest in statutory interpretation is to do justice."[45] In his concurrence in *Richmond*, Scalia argued that racial discrimination was in fact a practice that was prevalent at the local and state levels that can be traced to the very founding of the nation. Although injustice had been, since the founding of the nation, advanced by discrimination that was *implicit* in the text, the Constitution prohibited only the *explicit* use of race to remedy such injustice. For Scalia, the Fourteenth

Amendment established the will of the people that "equal protection" guaranteed that race shall not be used by state governments in decision-making. Therefore, according to Scalia, a law guaranteeing "equal protection" simply means that no state could make a law that explicitly used race in government decision-making. Conversely, however, Congress has *never* enacted a statute prohibiting the enactment of neutral laws based on illicit motives *implied* by the text. For Scalia, legal interpretation must stick to the meaning of what the texts explicitly says and must reject the search for implied meaning or importing one's own views about justice. As Scalia would write in a speech on "Realism and the Religion Clause," "The Constitution says what it says, and does not say what it does not say."[46] So, according to Scalia's textualism, if the Constitution does *not* explicitly prohibit a legislature from passing a law that *implicitly* discriminates against blacks, then judges cannot invalidate laws on the basis of implicit discrimination not evidenced on the "face" of the text itself. After all, as Scalia wrote in *Reading Law*, the idea that statutory interpretation is about doing justice or preventing injustice is simply a "false notion."[47]

The consequences of rejecting the notion of legislative purpose and by extension discriminatory purpose therefore had more dramatic effects. In *Chisom v. Roemer*, Scalia argued that the Voting Rights Act should be read *not* as a purposive mechanism for addressing discrimination but rather as a narrow text whose "ordinary meaning" was fixed in 1982 by the congressional amendments to the statute. Therefore, according to Scalia, even if a judicial election scheme had resulted in unfair vote dilution for African Americans, this unfair result did *not*, strictly speaking, violate the Voting Rights Act because *judges* were not considered "representatives" in its 1982 ordinary dictionary meaning. Scalia wrote:

> Section 2 of the Voting Rights Act of 1965 is not some all-purpose weapon for well-intentioned judges to wield as they please in the battle against discrimination. It is a statute. I thought we had adopted a regular method for interpreting the meaning of language in a statute: first, find the ordinary meaning of the language in its textual context; and second, using established canons of construction, ask whether there is any clear indication that some permissible meaning other than the ordinary one applies. If not—and especially if a good reason for the ordinary meaning appears plain—we apply that ordinary meaning.[48]

Scalia once again firmly rejected a purposivist reading of the Voting Rights Act as a remedy to combat discrimination in voting. Instead, he adopted a narrow textualist reading of the text itself, declaring, "We are here to apply the statute, not legislative history, and certainly not the absence of legislative history. Statutes are the law though sleeping dogs lie."[49]

Just as in the case of Dino analyzed in the introduction, in *Chisom v. Roemer*, Scalia engaged in a narrow, textual reading of the definition of a word based on the "ordinary meaning." In Dino's case, the textualist reading of the word *male* allowed the court discretion to exclude any dictionary definitions it might disfavor (Black's Law) without further justification by presenting its preferred definition (Webster's Dictionary) as "the ordinary meaning." In *Chisom*, Scalia performed a similar maneuver, arguing, "There is little doubt that the ordinary meaning of 'representatives' does not include judges, see Webster's Second New International Dictionary 2114 (1950)."[50] Even though judges in *Chisom* were elected officials, and the election scheme without dispute resulted in vote dilution for African Americans, Scalia argued that the text of the statute was not violated since judges were not considered "representatives" by Webster's Dictionary in 1982. Crucially, because Scalia argued that judges ought not engage in the "Humpty Dumpty" method of purposivist interpretation, the Voting Rights Act cannot be understood in terms of the "well-intentioned" purposes of Congress to combat discrimination. Instead of applying the *purpose* of the Voting Rights Act to addressing this clear case of racial vote dilution, therefore, Scalia appealed to the dictionary definition of "representative" and concluded that the election scheme was not unconstitutional according to the act.

## THE PRAGMATICS OF TEXTUALISM

Scalia's rejection of the purpose doctrine and analysis in *Edwards* insisted that judges should *not* go searching for "unenacted intentions" or "hidden" purposes or motivations that might be inferred or implied from words not made explicit on the face of the text itself. For Scalia, judges must identify the original meaning of the text, not infer "pretext" or purposes that might "be cooked up" from legislative history or materials. This raises a major interpretive question: since laws are enacted by politicians, legislators, and public officials with a wide variety of intentions and motives, how should textualist judges take these intentions and motives into account when interpreting "the text?" What is the relationship between *what* a law says (its semantic meaning), *why* it exists, and *for* what purpose (its *teleological* meaning)? As Lawrence Solum has helpfully articulated:

> When we ask the question, "What does this provision mean?" we might refer to the linguistic meaning or semantic content. Call this first sense of meaning the semantic sense. But the term "meaning" can also be used to refer to implications, consequences, or applications. Call this second sense of meaning the implicative sense.

We might also use the term meaning to refer to the purpose or function of a given constitutional provision. Call this third sense of meaning the teleological sense.[51]

According to Solum's helpful elucidation, Scalia's textualism denies the existence of a law's *teleological* sense to interpret its meaning. Because textualism is a judicial philosophy that eschews using extratextual methods for reading text, such a method therefore rejects the inquiry into "hidden" motives of pretext as a legitimate means of reading the text. As Justice Scalia decisively declared in a 2012 interview, "A textualist is someone who believes that the meaning of a statute is to be derived exclusively, exclusively from the text enacted by Congress and signed by the President, or else re-passed over his veto. The text is the sole source that the judge ought to be using in making his judgment."[52]

For this reason, I argue that the phrase "fidelity to the text" takes on a philosophical, ontological meaning. Justice Scalia's argument in *Edwards* that legislative intent does not exist laid the groundwork of his judicial philosophy, which denies outright the Athenian stranger's thesis in Plato's *The Laws* mentioned in the preface: namely, that the meaning of every text implies a pretext or purpose behind it. But Scalia's thesis goes even further. According to Scalia's textualist view, *there is no such thing* as an invidious, unlawful, or discriminatory motive that is *pretextual*. Since textualism eschews "extratextual" methods of inquiry and denies the existence of a coherent, prior legislative intent behind the text, it follows that textualism denies the existence of such a thing as a hidden malevolent or "discriminatory intent" that lurks behind the text. Unenacted intentions are therefore irrelevant to legal interpretation. Instead, as Scalia writes in *Edwards*, the judiciary should assume that legislators are acting in good faith pursuant to the oath of fidelity they take as part of their oath of office.[53] According to textualism, then, a legal text cannot possibly have a "discriminatory purpose" or intent for the simple reason that, according to Scalia, to look for the "purpose" of a statute is "to look for something that does not exist."[54]

Scalia's textualism has been widely criticized within the field of legal pragmatics. Harold Lloyd has argued that textualism ignores the entire pragmatic field of context within which any good interpreter considers the meaning of a text. For Lloyd, pragmatic reconstruction of meaning begins with the assumption that the speaker has a purpose in producing the message.[55] Because any legal text is a purposive work, any good interpreter, according to Lloyd, begins with the following question:

> If we think of a text as a work woven together for some purpose, we can ask ourselves what defining characteristics might exist for a text. Since the parts of something woven are intertwined, interrelatedness or internal cohesion provides

a good first textual characteristic to examine. That can be followed by examining in more detail the notion of purpose that work and weaving suggest.[56]

For Lloyd, any good interpreter of a text will apply sensible principles of pragmatics, including principles of cohesion, background knowledge, and context as part of the reconstruction or retrieval of a textual meaning. The goal of interpretation, therefore, is to "search for any cohesion of intent, reference, relation, form, context, other background, and purpose that might indicate the existence of a text."[57] For this reason, any decent interpreter cannot simply begin with "the text," taking it on faith that the meaning of the text is obvious from the words of the text as they appear. According to legal pragmatics, therefore, the task of the judge seeking to understand legal meaning should be the following:

> We use intent, reference, relation, form context, other background, and purpose to define text; we therefore cannot simply begin with "the text" unless we just take it as a m atter of faith or dogma that we have "the text." We cannot, for example, determine that a particular contract comprises only four pages unless we have already to some degree interpreted the text by looking at any intent, reference, relation, form, context, other background, and purpose that make it a text. Any such "text" handed to us may comprise four pages but review might well show that one page is an unrelated invoice or that a number of pages are actually missing. Not only must interpretation involve more than text: text itself cannot be determined unless we look beyond the words for the necessary cohesion.[58]

Lloyd's analysis of legal pragmatics provides a comprehensive account of the various principles any good interpreter will apply. One of the most fundamental principles is *context*, which includes examination of cognitive context, temporal context, sociocultural context, discourse context, internal context, purpose context and policy context. For Lloyd, temporal context of a statute includes legislative history and the historical record of governmental decision made concerning the statute.[59] Pragmatic reconstruction of legal meaning therefore will take into account not only the congressional record of the statute but also the historical context of the legislation, which "also provides invaluable context. Since history of legislation would include the way courts have interpreted that legislation, again, how could we possibly understand the meaning of such legislation without looking at its history?"[60] In addition, sociocultural context includes the context of power relations that structure the relationship between the parties. In this regard, legal meaning should be interpreted according to the political or legislative strategies employed by the parties involved. Discourse context, according to Lloyd, concerns the *type* of discursive norms that apply to a particular subject-matter of area of law. Here, one may observe that the discursive norms one finds in property law or tort law will differ from discrimination law or employment law. As a result, the norms of cooperation and truth-telling, for example, might be more consistently observed in one area of law compared to another.

In discrimination law, the discursive norms that obtain are different than otherwise might be the case precisely because defendants attempt to mask their own discrimination resulting in antidiscrimination doctrine that does *not* presuppose discursive norms of cooperation that obtain in other domains. Internal or textual context, for Lloyd, concerns the surrounding context of the statutory language. Purpose context, according to Lloyd, concerns examination of "the author's objective, goal, or end or 'general rationale' for the text."[61] Finally, Lloyd emphasizes the policy context, which focuses on the role of the state's policy goals in interpreting the meaning of a text.[62] Together, Lloyd summarizes the task of legal interpretation using legal pragmatics:

> After determining a relevant text, good interpreters examine the applicable cognitive, physical, temporal, social, cultural, discursive, textual, purposive, and policy contexts of the text. They consider this evidence in addition to the evidence of the text.[63]

Given these principles of legal pragmatics, Llyod sharply criticizes textualist methods of "plain meaning" or "ordinary meaning" of the text, writing that, "Since virtually every word has multiple meanings, how could it make practical sense to hold that the text itself provides sufficient context for a "plain" reading?"[64] Lloyd concludes that from the perspective of legal pragmatics, textualism as a theory of interpretation is woefully inadequate and ignores how language works in the real world. Lloyd writes:

> Seekers of the truth do not advance interpretive theories that ignore pragmatics, that ignore how language works in the real world. Nor do they advance interpretive theories that lack relevance to the real world. As seekers of the truth, lawyers should not delude themselves or judges with a textualism "that requires the judge to rely on the text to the exclusion of other interpretive criteria, if the meaning is plain." As we have seen, meaning of text is never truly "plain" in itself because it always depends upon its context.[65]

In this way, Scalia's rejection of the purpose doctrine and analysis in *Edwards* undermines any feasible pragmatic reconstruction of meaning. By rejecting the policy and purpose context of law for understanding meaning, textualism undermines any attempt to retrieve contextual meaning in any fully pragmatic sense. Textualism's rejection of the "Humpty Dumpty" view of purposivism therefore leads it to ignore any discriminatory motives that might shed interpretive light upon the meaning of a law. In this way, Scalia's rejection of purposivism in *Edwards* laid the judicial groundwork for the legality of discriminatory practices that seek to disguise themselves in the neutrality of legal texts themselves.

## *HERNANDEZ V. NEW YORK* (1991)

Scalia's rejection of the "purpose" inquiry into the meaning of law had immediate and dramatic consequences for antidiscrimination law. The "unenacted" intentions of policymakers were not a valid object of judicial scrutiny, according to Scalia, and therefore, judges should not go searching for unacted desires to discriminate that are not explicit in the stated reasons offered in the words of legal texts. However, if Scalia's court rejected any scrutiny into the "unenacted desires" or intentions behind the law, then it followed that any "race-neutral" reason offered in an official legal text could not be unlawful due to some alleged "discriminatory purpose" lurking behind the desires of policymakers. Scalia's rejection of the "purpose" inquiry into the meaning the law took center stage in *Hernandez v. New York* (1991). In this case, a prosecutor used peremptory strikes to dismiss bilingual Latino jurors from a jury based on an allegedly race-neutral reason of language. This action was challenged as a violation of the Equal Protection Clause on the basis of race. In *Hernandez*,

> the prosecutor here offered a race-neutral basis for these peremptory strikes. As explained by the prosecutor, the challenges rested neither on the intention to exclude Latino or bilingual jurors, nor on stereotypical assumptions about Latinos or bilinguals. The prosecutor's articulated basis for these challenges divided potential jurors into two classes: those whose conduct during *voir dire* would persuade him they might have difficulty in accepting the translator's rendition of Spanish-language testimony and those potential jurors who gave no such reason for doubt. Each category would include both Latinos and non-Latinos. While the prosecutor's criterion might well result in the disproportionate removal of prospective Latino jurors, that disproportionate impact does not turn the prosecutor's actions into a *per se* violation of the Equal Protection Clause.[66]

In a majority opinion joined by Scalia, the court argued that the plaintiffs failed to demonstrate that the dismissal of the jurors was *racially* motivated given the race-neutral reason offered by the defendants. The court wrote, "Absent intentional discrimination violative of the Equal Protection Clause, parties should be free to exercise their peremptory strikes for any reason, or no reason at all."[67] Although the court admitted that dismissing bilingual Spanish-speaking jurors had a clearly disparate impact upon Hispanics, the court concluded that,

> An argument relating to the impact of a classification does not alone show its purpose. . . . Equal protection analysis turns on the intended consequences of government classifications. Unless the government actor adopted a criterion with the intent of causing the impact asserted, that impact itself does not violate the principle of race neutrality.[68]

In a concurrence joined by Justice Scalia, Justice O'Connor argued:

> Disproportionate effect may, of course, constitute evidence of intentional discrimination. . . . But if, as in this case, the trial court believes the prosecutor's nonracial justification, and that finding is not clearly erroneous, that is the end of the matter.[69]

In a dissenting opinion, Justice John Paul Stevens criticized the majority's rejection of the *Arlington Heights* factors for objectively determining "discriminatory purpose," writing:

> The Court overlooks, however, the fact that the "discriminatory purpose" which characterizes violations of the Equal Protection Clause can sometimes be established by objective evidence that is consistent with a decisionmaker's honest belief that his motive was entirely benign. "Frequently the most probative evidence of intent will be objective evidence of what actually happened," . . . The line between discriminatory purpose and discriminatory impact is neither as bright nor as critical as the Court appears to believe.[70]

As Stevens argued, Scalia's majority rejected judicial scrutiny into discriminatory intent provided by the *Arlington Heights* framework. For Stevens, this test was the court's evidentiary framework for determining what counts as an objectively impermissible reason for action under equal protection. Instead, Scalia's majority simply rejected scrutiny into the "unenacted desires" or intentions behind the race-neutral reason proffered in court. According to Scalia's textualism, it followed that any race neutral reason offered in an official legal text could not be unlawful due to some alleged discriminatory purpose lurking behind the desires of policymakers. Consequently, the unenacted intentions of policymakers were not an object of judicial scrutiny because judges, according to Scalia, should not go searching for such unenacted desires to discriminate that are not made explicit in the stated reasons offered in the words of legal texts. Only the enacted text rules.

## CONCLUSION

In this chapter, I've argued that Scalia's attack on the court's purpose doctrine in *Edwards* undermines the pragmatic reconstruction of legal meaning and thus rejects reading the text in its historical, policy, and purpose contexts. By doing so, textualism undermines the attempt to retrieve contextual meaning of law in its purpose and policy goals, and its rejection of the "Humpty Dumpty" view of purposivism therefore leads textualism to ignore any discriminatory motives that might shed interpretive light upon the meaning of a law. In this way, Scalia's rejection of purposivism in *Edwards* laid the judicial groundwork for the legality of discriminatory practices that seek to disguise themselves through the "neutrality" of legal texts themselves.

Scalia's argument rejecting the search for unlawful purpose in *Edwards* would mirror his rejection of the search for discriminatory purpose in employment discrimination dating back to his service on the district court as far back as 1982, when he rejected the idea that a court could discover discriminatory purpose on the basis of race because there exists an "infinite variety" of factors for which an employer may lawfully discharge an individual. Because of these innumerable valid reasons, Scalia argued, we cannot know the true reason behind the motives of the employer. As a result, the standard of proof required for a plaintiff to show that the true reason was because of race is extremely high. Therefore, as Scalia openly declared in *Edwards*, to look for discriminatory purpose on the basis of race is to look for something that probably does not exist.

Scalia's textualism, by excluding any inquiry into the purpose of a law to understand its meaning, produced dramatic consequences in antidiscrimination jurisprudence. By rejecting judicial scrutiny into the "unenacted desires" or intentions behind the stated reasons of a law or policy, Scalia had effectively undermined the court's "discriminatory purpose" jurisprudence established in *Arlington Heights* and dating back to *Yick Wo*. Following his attack on "purposivism" in his speeches and opinions from 1986–987, Scalia argued in *Chisom v. Roemer* that the Voting Rights Act was not an "all-purpose weapon for well-intentioned judges to wield as they please in the battle against discrimination."[71] In *Hernandez*, the court ruled that the dismissal of bilingual Latino jurors because of their language was *not* unlawful since a "race-neutral" reason prevails over alleged "unenacted desires" or intentions to discriminate. In *St. Mary's Honor Ctr v. Hicks* (1993), examined in chapter 3, Scalia's majority established the "pretext plus" doctrine, which allowed defendants to proffer false reasons in court to defeat discrimination claims. In this, Scalia began to pave the way for what Marmor calls "strategic" and "manipulative speech" to flourish through the law itself.

## NOTES

1. Antonin Scalia, speech to Federalist Society, January 30, 1987, Antonin Scalia papers, LAW, MMC, 291, Series III, Box: 77, Folder: 14, Harvard Law School Library, Historical & Special Collections, 67.
2. Antonin Scalia and Bryan A. Garner, *Reading Law: The Interpretation of Legal Texts* (St. Paul: Thomson/West, 2012), 392.
3. Scalia and Garner, *Reading Law*, 392.
4. Scalia, speech to Federalist Society, 69.
5. Antonin Scalia, "Use of Legislative History: Judicial Abdication to Fictitious Legislative Intent," Antonin Scalia papers, LAW, MMC, 291, Series VIII, Box: MISC-4, Folder: 2, Harvard Law School Library, Historical & Special Collections, 6.
6. Scalia, "Use of Legislative History," 18.
7. Antonin Scalia, speech on original intent [submitted as part of nomination questionnaire], delivered at the Attorney General's Conference on Economic Liberties, June 14, 1986, Antonin Scalia papers, LAW, MMC, 291, Series I, Box: 26, Folder: 11, Harvard Law School Library, Historical & Special Collections, 2.
8. Antonin Scalia, John M. Olin Lecture Series on Political Economy, Wharton School, University of Pennsylvania, April 25, 1986, Antonin Scalia papers, LAW, MMC, 291, Series III, Box: 76, Folder: 28, Harvard Law School Library, Historical & Special Collections, 17.
9. Scalia and Garner, *Reading Law*, xxvii.
10. Scalia and Garner, *Reading Law*, 392.
11. La. Rev. Stat. Ann. § 17:286.4 (LexisNexis).
12. La. Rev. Stat. Ann. § 17:286.2 (LexisNexis).
13. *Edwards v. Aguillard*, 482 U.S. 578, 594 (U.S. June 19, 1987).
14. Henry M. Hart, Jr. and Albert M. Sacks, *The Legal Process: Basic Problems in the Making and Application of Law* (Westbury, NY: Foundation Press, 1994), 148.
15. *Edwards v. Aguillard*, 482 U.S. 578, 586-587 (U.S. June 19, 1987).
16. CRS Report R45153, "Statutory Interpretation: Theories, Tools, and Trends," by Valerie C. Brannon (2023).
17. Henry M. Hart, Jr. and Albert M. Sacks, "The Legal Process: Basic Problems in the Making and Application of Law, Problem No. 1, in *The Canon of American Legal Thought,* ed. David Kennedy and William W. Fisher (Princeton, NJ: Princeton University Press, 2007), 241–310, https://doi.org/10.1515/9780691186429-010.
18. Hart and Sacks, "The Legal Process," 256.
19. Hart and Sacks, "The Legal Process," 256.
20. Hart and Sacks, "The Legal Process," 257.
21. *Maine v. Thiboutot*, 448 U.S. 1, 13-14 (1980).
22. *Richards v. United States*, 369 U.S. 1, 11 (1962).
23. Lawrence B. Solum, "The Unity of Interpretation," 90 B.U. L. Rev. 551-578 (2010), 561.
24. *United Steelworkers v. Weber*, 443 U.S. 193, 197 (1979).
25. *Matter of Holland v. Edwards*, 307 N.Y. 38, 45 (N.Y. 1954).
26. *Murphy v. Am. Home Prods Corp.*, 159 A.D.2d 46, 49 (N.Y. App. Div. 1990).

27. US Department of Justice, "The Fair Housing Act," Civil Rights Division, accessed May 31, 2024, https://www.justice.gov/crt/fair-housing-act-1.
28. *United States v. Hunter*, 459 F.2d 205, 214 (4th Cir. 1972).
29. *Jones v. Alfred H. Mayer Co.*, 392 U.S. 409, 441-43 (1968).
30. *United States v. W. Peachtree Tenth Corp.*, 437 F.2d 221, 228 (5th Cir. 1971).
31. *Washington v. Davis (*1976).
32. *Metro. Hous. Dev. Corp. v. Vill. of Arlington Heights*, 558 F.2d 1283 (7th Cir. 1977), cert denied, 434 U.S. 1025 (1978).
33. Henry Rose, "Arlington Heights Won in the Supreme Court but the Fair Housing Act's Goal of Promoting Racial Integration Saved the Low-Income Housing," *Touro Law Review* 35, no. 2 (2019), Article 8.
34. *Metro. Hous. Dev. Corp. v. Vill. of Arlington Heights*, 469 F. Supp. 836, 845 (N.D. Ill. 1979).
35. *Edwards v. Aguillard*, 482 U.S. 578, 587 (U.S. June 19, 1987).
36. *Edwards v. Aguillard*, 482 U.S. 578, 610-611 (U.S. June 19, 1987).
37. *Edwards v. Aguillard*, 482 U.S. 578, 636-637 (U.S. June 19, 1987).
38. *K Mart Corp. v. Cartier*, 486 U.S. 281, 325 (1988).
39. Scalia, speech on original intent [submitted as part of nomination questionnaire], 2.
40. *Richmond v. J. A. Croson Co.*, 488 U.S. 469.
41. *Schuette v. Coalition to Defend Affirmative Action*, 572 U.S. 291, 318 (U.S. April 22, 2014).
42. *Schuette v. Coalition to Defend Affirmative Action*, 572 U.S. 291, 318 (U.S. April 22, 2014), 331–32.
43. Antonin Scalia, speech on "The Rule of Law," Antonin Scalia papers, LAW, MMC, 291, Series I, Sub-Series I, Box: 8, Folder: 7, Harvard Law School Library, Historical & Special Collections, 12.
44. *Richmond v. J. A. Croson Co.*, 488 U.S. 469, 524 (U.S. January 23, 1989).
45. Scalia and Garner, *Reading Law*, 347.
46. Antonin Scalia, speech on "Realism and the Religion Clauses," Antonin Scalia papers, LAW, MMC, 291, Series III, Box: 73, Folder: 19, Harvard Law School Library, Historical & Special Collections, 1.
47. Scalia and Garner, *Reading Law*, 347.
48. *Chisom v. Roemer*, 501 U.S. 380, 404 (1991).
49. *Chisom v. Roemer*, 501 U.S. 380, 406 (1991).
50. *Chisom v. Roemer*, 501 U.S. 380, 410 (1991).
51. Lawrence B. Solum, "The Unity of Interpretation," 90 B.U. L. Rev. 551-578 (2010): 561.
52. Antonin Scalia, interview, "Q&A with Justice Antonin Scalia" at 00:27:51, Washington, DC, July 29, 2012, C-SPAN, https://www.c-span.org/video/?307035-1/qa-justice-antonin-scalia.
53. *Edwards v. Aguillard*, 482 U.S. 578, 618-19 (1987).
54. *Edwards v. Aguillard*, 482 U.S. 578, 637 (1987).
55. Harold Anthony Lloyd, "Law's 'Way of Words': Pragmatics and Textualist Error," *Creighton Law Review* 49, no. 2 (2016): 223.

56. Lloyd, "Law's "Way of Words," 243.
57. Lloyd, "Law's "Way of Words," 249.
58. Lloyd, "Law's "Way of Words," 247.
59. Lloyd, "Law's "Way of Words," 256.
60. Lloyd, "Law's "Way of Words," 257.
61. Lloyd, "Law's "Way of Words," 261.
62. Lloyd, "Law's "Way of Words," 261–62.
63. Lloyd, "Law's "Way of Words," 283.
64. Lloyd, "Law's "Way of Words," 269.
65. Lloyd, "Law's "Way of Words," 284.
66. *Hernandez v. New York*, 500 U.S. 352, 361 (U.S. May 28, 1991).
67. *Hernandez v. New York*, 500 U.S. 352, 374 (U.S. May 28, 1991).
68. *Hernandez v. New York,* 500 U.S. 352, 362 (U.S. May 28, 1991).
69. *Hernandez v. New York*, 500 U.S. 352, 375 (U.S. May 28, 1991).
70. *Hernandez v. New York,* 500 U.S. 352, 377-378 (U.S. May 28, 1991).
71. *Chisom v. Roemer*, 501 U.S. 380, 404 (1991).

# 2

## *St. Mary's Honor Ctr. v. Hicks* (1993)
"Injustice is the Game"

In this chapter, I argue that the "pretext plus" doctrine introduced by Scalia's Supreme Court majority in *St. Mary's* (1993) established the lawfulness of lying as a performative act of "strategic speech" to defeat discrimination claims, or what Andrei Marmor calls "manipulative speech." I further argue that Scalia's textualism rejects any judicial scrutiny into "strategic" or "manipulative speech" because of a sovereign decision to exclude discriminatory meaning from the interpretation of the law. Furthermore, this demonstrates that legal communications within discrimination law should be understood not as a cooperative form of "conversational" speech but rather as a form of "strategic speech" that can nonetheless be rationally reconstructed with the tools of discriminatology.

## "INJUSTICE IS THE GAME"

In his 1984 commencement speech to Daytona University Law School, Justice Scalia argued that the nature of being a lawyer consists of the development of the legal habits and practices of *precision* and *process*. As Scalia gracefully wrote:

> The entire of parade of life comes before the lawyer, and must be described precisely in the instruments, the opinions and the statutes with which he or she deals. So that describing a thing—<u>any</u>thing—precisely becomes a habit, a compulsion that tends to spread into all aspects of a lawyer's life.[1]

Most significantly, Scalia juxtaposed these habitual practices of precision and process in the law with the policy-oriented engagement with the *substance* of the law. A lawyer, Scalia had argued, has no interest or expertise in what the substance of our laws is or should be, and therefore is not qualified nor authorized to import any substantive views on social policy or justice into their legal interpretation, such as considerations of economic deregulation or criminal sentencing. Scalia argued, "Lawyers really have no more interest than anyone else—and no more expertise than anyone else—in what the substance of our laws should be."[2] This speech previewed Scalia's view over a quarter-century later in his 2012 treatise *Reading Law* that "doing justice" is *not* one of the goals of legal interpretation. As Scalia argued, "It is doubtless true, as a descriptive matter, that judges will often strain to avoid what they consider an unjust result. But we decline to elevate that human tendency to an approved principle of interpretation."[3] The principle of justice, therefore, is not an approved principle for judges to use in interpreting the law. Instead,

> The soundest, most defensible position is one that requires discipline and self-abnegation. If judges think no further ahead than achieving justice in the dispute now at hand, the law becomes subject to personal preferences and hence shrouded in doubt. It is age-old wisdom among mature, experienced legal thinkers that procedure matters most: how things should be done, as opposed to what should be done. And for judges the "how" is fidelity to law. But it is a hard lesson to learn, and harder to follow.[4]

One reason why such discipline was so difficult for lawyers to sustain, Scalia observed, is that this "human tendency" to do justice and avoid injustice is because lawyers are always confronted by the "evil" that appears in the case reports that they must describe with such detached *precision*. As Scalia said in his 1984 commencement address:

> And we have not just learned about life, we have learned about people. People at their worst. By and large, human fault and human perfidy are what the cases are about. We have seen the careless, the avaricious, the criminal, the profligate, the foolhardy, parade across the pages of the case reports. We have seen evil punished and virtue rewarded. But we have also seen prudent evil flourish and foolish virtue fall. We have seen partners become antagonists, brothers and sisters become contesting claimants, lovers become enemies.[5]

The problem of "prudent evil" flourishing in the law, therefore, points to the fundamental tension that exists in Scalia's notion of a lawyer. The difficult task of being a lawyer, Scalia suggests, consists in the notion that we are governed by legislated text, *not* the good intentions, motivations, or mindsets of judges or Congress to do justice or prevent evil. In Scalia's view, then, lawyering consists of a science of precision and process, not the quest for justice and substantive policy issues. Even if prudent evil flourishes in the "legalisms" of the day, it is not, strictly speaking, the duty or role of a judge to correct or remedy the evil by using the principles of justice as a source of interpretation. Instead, as Scalia said in 2012:

> We are governed by text enacted by the Members of Congress, not by their purposes. Since we can't know what's in the minds of 436 legislators (counting the President), all we can know is that they voted for a text that they presumably thought would be read the same way any reasonable English speaker would read it. In fact, it does not matter whether they were fall-down drunk when they voted for it. So long as they voted for it, that text is the law.[6]

Even if Congress were "fall-down drunk" when enacting a text, a judge is required to follow process and procedure in giving effect to the text rather than attempt to correct the injustice or evils that result. The law, therefore, is just what the *text* says and never what the judge thinks is "just" or what "should" have been done. For Scalia, therefore, the difficult nature of being a lawyer consists of developing the technical habits of precision using legal instruments and the engagement with the process rather than the justice of the laws themselves. Despite the flourishing of prudent evil within the law, the lawyer or judge must remain disciplined in giving effect to the text enacted, not the unenacted motives or principles of justice. In *Reading Law*, for example, Scalia had argued forcefully against "the false notion that the quest in statutory interpretation is to do justice."[7]

It is within this context of Justice Scalia's insistence on the *process* over *substance* of the law that his opinions on pretext in employment discrimination should be understood. According to Justice Scalia, textualism prohibits a judge from interpreting laws according to sources that are "extratextual," that is, sources not derived from the explicit words of the text itself. As Scalia wrote in *Reading Law*, textualism "rejects judicial speculation about both the drafters' extratextually derived purposes and the desirability of the fair reading's anticipated consequences."[8] However, in *Richmond v. Croson* (1989), Scalia had openly acknowledged that historically, injustice has been perpetuated against African Americans through discriminatory preferences that have *not* been made textually explicit. Speaking about the history of racial discrimination, Scalia wrote, "the racial basis of the preference has rarely been made textually explicit . . . and blacks have often been on the receiving end of the injustice. Where injustice is the game, however, turnabout is not fair play."[9] Here, Scalia acknowledged that unjust discrimination occurs when racial preferences are extratextual but that judges *must* disregard precisely these extratextual sources in interpreting the meaning of a law. Therefore, according to Scalia's own premises, we can derive what I call Scalia's Argument for Textualist Injustice:

(1) Textualism rejects meaning derived from "extratextual" sources of interpretation.[10]
(2) Injustice occurs when discriminatory meaning is *not* made textually explicit.[11]
(3) *Textualism rejects the use of discriminatory meaning (from 1 and 2).*
∴ Textualism results in injustice

The valid argument above that textualism results in injustice is, perhaps, not surprising when we recall Scalia's consistent view, from his 1984 commencement speech to his 2012 treatise *Reading Law*, that the nature of being a lawyer or judge does *not* have anything to do with substantive issues of law and justice. Rather, Scalia's consistent view was that, despite the prudent evil that often flourishes through the law, the judge must retain fidelity to the law by a "discipline and self-abnegation" to enforce the process of law but not utilize the principle of justice as a guide. In this way, the conclusion that textualism results in injustice is less surprising viewed from Scalia's own remarks on the relationship between the law and justice.

## PRETEXT AS MALEVOLENT LEGALITY

That textualism predictably results in injustice can be illustrated in the establishment of the Supreme Court's pretext plus doctrine in *St. Mary's Honor Ctr. v. Hicks*, in which Scalia's majority ruled that a defendant may still defeat a Title VII discrimination claim by proffering "non-discriminatory" reasons that were false and given in "bad faith" (*mala fide*). According to the pretext plus doctrine, plaintiffs in employment discrimination cases must not only demonstrate that the employer is lying about the reasons for termination, but must also themselves provide proof by "clear and convincing evidence" that the true reason was unlawful. This evidentiary framework placed a heavy burden on plaintiffs, since all a defendant must do is proffer a plausible "nondiscriminatory" reason that the plaintiff could not disprove. In short, the framework established by Scalia's majority in *St. Mary's* allowed defendants to lie and thereby defeat the plaintiff. However, these kinds of "unjust" results, according to textualism, are not the concern of the judge. Instead, textualism enforces the process and not the substance or justice of law. As a result, the pretext plus doctrine sanctioned an evidentiary framework in which discrimination could be performed *mala fide*.

Scalia's permissive attitude toward "bad faith" actors performing discrimination *mala fide* can be traced throughout his career. Prior to his nomination to the Supreme Court, Scalia had served on the US Court of Appeals for the

District of Columbia. During his tenure, Scalia's court confronted several employment discrimination cases based on Section 1981 of the Civil Rights Act. In specific terms, the purpose of Section 1981 as enacted by Congress is "to provide appropriate remedies for intentional discrimination and unlawful harassment in the workplace."[12] In broader, more purposivist terms, a federal district court in 1974 clarified:

> As originally designed in 1866, Section 1981 was intended to uproot the institution of slavery and to eradicate its badges and incidents. . . . When an employer, public or private, places more stringent requirements on employees because of their race, Section 1981 is violated. The purpose for which the Section was enacted—to afford equal opportunities to secure the benefits of American life regardless of race—requires that a court adopt a broad outlook in enforcing Section 1981. Schemes of discrimination, whether blatant or subtle, are forbidden.[13]

Accordingly, courts were authorized to scrutinize schemes of discrimination in employment that were either blatant or subtle. However, cases of subtle discrimination in employment proved difficult to adjudicate, as courts were increasingly acknowledging in cases involving collective bargaining pursuant to the National Labor Relations Act. In these cases, an employer defendant often claimed to be acting in "good faith" by proffering nondiscriminatory reasons for their action. Therefore, the central question in such cases came down to the credibility of the defendant as to whether he was "disguising" a discriminatory motive behind a "neutral" reason proffered to the court. Because the National Labor Relations Act guaranteed unions the statutory enforcement of their employers' obligation to bargain with them in good faith, courts increasingly recognized the importance of scrutinizing the bad faith of employers who engaged in "service bargaining" in order to avoid making concessions to unions in negotiations. Since employers were becoming increasingly sophisticated in disguising their legal strategies, courts soon reacted to this fact. As the US Court of Appeals for the 7th Circuit wrote in 1979:

> Sometimes, especially if the parties are sophisticated, the only indicia of bad faith may be the proposals advanced and adhered to. . . . The fact that it may be difficult to distinguish bad faith bargaining from hard bargaining cannot excuse our obligation to do so.[14]

In this way, antidiscrimination doctrines in employment law in the 1970s and 1980s increasingly scrutinized the "bad faith" of defendants to disguise their motives through "neutral" texts. Courts across the country had begun to realize the various ways that defendants in discrimination cases may, in the words of Judge Richard Posner, "concoct a plausible reason" that the plaintiff could not disprove and thereby defeat the plaintiff's burden of proof. For this reason, antidiscrimination jurisprudence reflected by the Civil Rights Act, the Supreme Court's *Arlington Heights* (1977) discriminatory purpose test, the *Lemon* test, and other good faith covenants recognized the basic notion that discrimination often hides behind legal claims, reasons, and texts that are nonetheless "facially neutral."

Despite these developments in antidiscrimination law, in *Carter v. Duncan-Higgins* (1984), Scalia argued that despite sympathy for the plaintiff who had suffered disfavored treatment by an employer, a racial slur by an employee combined with circumstantial evidence of differential treatment was *not* sufficient to establish a violation of intentional discrimination because of race under the Civil Rights Act. 42 U.S.C.S. § 1981. Writing for the dissent, Scalia argued that the text of §1981 required proof not only of discriminatory treatment but also "clear and convincing" evidence that the true reason the employer treated the plaintiff differently was *race*. As Scalia argued, while the company may have "disfavored" the plaintiff compared to other similarly situated employees, the possible reasons for this disfavor were "infinite" and could not be attributable specifically to race. As Scalia wrote, "The 'numerous other pieces of circumstantial evidence' the majority refers to—the "many discrete instances of disparate treatment and broken promises"—are not circumstantial evidence of racial motivation, but only . . . of an intent to disfavor Carter. That is not against the law."[15] Scalia wrote:

> I fully acknowledge that the fact of discrimination suggests an intent to discriminate. But that intent may be based upon an infinite variety of factors. In the present case, for example, the company may have decided to save money on Carter because she was the least assertive of the employees, and thus the most likely to take it. Or Perez may have picked her out for unfavorable treatment because she was the *most* assertive, and thus the most obnoxious. I am willing, in other words, to accept discriminatory treatment as circumstantial evidence of discriminatory animus, but only race-related treatment as circumstantial evidence of racial animus. By treating the one as evidence of the other, the majority effectively eliminates the second element necessary to establish a §1981 case.[16]

Scalia's reasoning here mirrored his reasoning in *Edwards* just three years later as a newly minted Supreme Court Justice when he argued against the notion that a judge could rationally determine the one true motive or intention of the legislature. In *Edwards*, Scalia argued that since there was an "infinite" variety of possible intentions motivating legislators to pass a law, the notion of finding the one true legislative intent or purpose was "pure fiction." In *Carter*, Scalia had used a similar argument: because there are "an infinite variety of factors" that may be present for an employer to disfavor an employee, a plaintiff shoulders the heavy burden of proving that the one true reason that motivated the employer was race. Because this is such a high burden of proof, and a judge's role is to observe the process of legal argument that allows each side to present reasons and evidence, the plaintiff is simply at a relative disadvantage. Importantly, it is *not,* Scalia argued, the role of the judge to determine the justice or injustice of this process but rather to enforce the rules of the process itself. Furthermore, since a judge's role is *not* to go ferreting out the motives of individuals that are not made explicit in legal texts themselves, Scalia had additional reasons to rule in favor of a defendant who offered a "nondiscriminatory" reason that was not disproved by the plaintiff.

As Scalia further wrote in *Carter*:

> The majority's fallacy lies in using the word "discrimination" as a synonym for "discrimination on the basis of race." Such usage may suffice in common parlance, but for purposes of analyzing the proof in a §1981 suit it is, if I may not be misunderstood in so expressing it, too undiscriminating. Even assuming she had established discrimination (a subject discussed in part I of this opinion), the plaintiff had further to establish that the reason for that discrimination was her race. She offered nothing to support that point—neither direct evidence, nor circumstantial evidence, statistical or otherwise—except the single racial slur.[17]

Scalia' reasoning in *Carter* echoed his reasoning in a previous employment discrimination case his court had heard just two years prior in *Toney v. Block* (1983), when Scalia took the position that even if a plaintiff demonstrates that the defendant lied about the initial reason for termination, the defendant may still proffer a "nondiscriminatory" reason and defeat the plaintiff, again reflecting Scalia's view that it is *not* the role of judges to search the motives or intentions of the defendant but only to give effect to the legal process sanctioned by the text of the statute. Scalia wrote that,

> demonstration of discrimination at large constitutes, for purposes of individual relief, no more than the *prima facie* case that shifts the burden to the defendant to produce some nondiscriminatory justification—which, when done (as it was done here), shifts the burden back to the plaintiff "to prove by a preponderance of the evidence that the legitimate reasons offered by the defendant were not its true reasons, but were a pretext for discrimination. . . . The existence of generalized discrimination within the employment unit, or of discrimination against the plaintiff in other employment contexts, may of course be taken into account . . . in the factfinder's determination of whether the proof of pretext

has adequately been made. But it is the plaintiff's task to prove it, rather than the defendant's to prove, by "clear and convincing evidence," the opposite.[18]

Thus, in *Carter*, while Scalia argued that discrimination evidenced by disfavored treatment and a racial slur might elicit sympathy for a defendant, the statute's text requires the plaintiff to demonstrate that *race* was the reason out of the "infinite variety" of factors possible. As a result, he argued, judges cannot base their interpretation of the facts based on "factors as sympathy and the like."[19] For Scalia, judicial sympathy for a plaintiff's discriminatory treatment does not by itself warrant a finding for the plaintiff in a §1981 race discrimination lawsuit. As Scalia wrote,

> without careful and conscientious fact-finding the antidiscrimination laws can either be frustrated by, or be converted into instruments of, the very evil they are designed to prevent. The court's decision facilitates the latter development, permitting juries to render awards where no solid evidence exists, leaving them to decide "on the basis of sheer speculation, ultimately tipped, in view of the impossibility of choosing rationally between mere 'possibilities,' by impermissible but understandable resort to such factors as sympathy and the like.[20]

As Scalia had argued in his 1984 commencement address, the judge must show discipline in preventing any sympathy for one receiving discriminatory treatment from "tipping" the scales in favor of what the *judge* believes is right or just. Rather, the text of the statute required the plaintiff to shoulder the burden of proving that the real true reason for the discrimination was *racial*. Here, Scalia defines discriminatory treatment as being treated differently from others who were, for the relevant purposes, similarly situated."[21] However, as Scalia had argued, §1981 required a showing of discrimination *intended because of race*. Since the employer proffered nonracial reasons for their actions that the plaintiff could not disprove, Scalia ruled for the employer.

For Scalia, the real reason why unstated motives or intentions should not be sources for making determinations about public antidiscrimination law is that, according to textualism, it was not the court's job to determine social policy:

> Of course, equal treatment need not be accorded when there is a good reason to making a distinction: government employees performing different jobs may be given different salaries. But if it were up to the courts to determine in each case whether the reason for different treatment was a *good enough* reason, judges would become the ultimate arbiters of vast numbers of social policies.[22]

Instead, the role of a judge is to observe the process and procedures of law, including rules of evidence and presumptions, without inserting one's own view of justice, fairness, or "sympathy and the like." By making broad rulings on the unconstitutionality of certain kinds of unlawful discrimination, Scalia thought, judges were engaging in social policy. For Scalia, an employer who lies about the reasons for terminating an employee does not by that fact alone commit unlawful discrimination. Rather, the burden of proof lies on the plaintiff to show on the basis of clear and convincing evidence that the defendant violated all necessary elements of a statute, not on the basis of "possibility or speculation" regarding the "hidden" motives of the defendant, nor on the basis of sympathy or a judge's sense of justice and fairness. For courts to adjudicate whether or not a defendant's motives or reasons were "pure of heart" would, in Scalia's view, make the courts "the ultimate arbiters of vast numbers of social policies." Since judges, according to Scalia, are not arbiters of the substance of the law and should *not* be legislating their views on justice from the bench, engaging in speculation about the unstated, discriminatory motives of a defendant is by extension the creation of "judge-made" law that amounts to making social policy. Antidiscrimination law pursued in this way, therefore, was to Scalia a form of "galloping legalism" that seeks a remedy for every wrong by impugning the motives and intentions of the accused.

## ST. MARY'S HONOR CTR V. HICKS (1993)

Scalia's opinions in *Toney v. Block* and *Carter v. Duncan-Higgins* therefore foreshadowed his majority opinion in the Supreme Court's holding in *St. Mary's Honor Ctr v. Hicks*. Melvin Hicks was a correctional officer employed by St. Mary's Honor Center, a halfway house operated under the Missouri Department of Corrections in the United States. After an alleged altercation, Hicks was discharged and subsequently filed a claim under Title VII of the Civil Rights Act for unlawful intentional discrimination on the basis of race.[23] Since 1973, Title VII claims have been evaluated according to the Supreme Court's model established in *McDonnell Douglass*, which clarified a step-by-step argumentative framework for evaluating the nature and order of proof for all Title VII discrimination claims.[24] According the argumentative, burden-shifting framework established under *McDonnell Douglass*, a Title VII claim must proceed in the following steps:

(1) Plaintiff must show *prima facie* case of discrimination.
(2) Employer must articulate a legitimate, nondiscriminatory reason for discharge.
(3) Plaintiff has opportunity to show that proffered reason (2) is *pretextual.*
   a. If pretext is shown, judgment is rendered for plaintiff.
   b. If pretext is not shown, plaintiffs claim fails.

Under the doctrine of pretext established under the *McDonnell Douglass* framework, a plaintiff successfully shows pretext by demonstrating that a stated reason for firing is not truthful and instead conceals the true reason.[25] The doctrine of pretext is thus part of a larger category of "bad faith" doctrines found throughout the legal system that address the problem of evasion in contract law, property law, tax law, labor law, constitutional law, and others.[26] The purpose of bad faith doctrines generally is to discourage legal actors from utilizing the formal parameters of the legal system to engage in dishonest, deceptive, or opportunistic strategies that aim to evade or subvert the purpose or spirit of the law.[27] Thus, in order for any Title VII discrimination claim to succeed, a plaintiff must show a *prima facie* case of discrimination, coupled with a showing that the proffered reason given by the defendant was false. The basic rationale of this framework, according to the court, lies in the common experience that "it is 'more likely than not' that the employer who lies is simply trying to cover up the illegality alleged by the plaintiff."[28]

In *St Mary's*, Hicks had already proved the undisputed facts: "(1) that he is black, (2) that he was qualified for the job of shift commander, (3) that he was demoted from that position and ultimately discharged, and (4) that the position remained open and was ultimately filled by a white man."[29] In employment discrimination, this constituted a *prima facie* case for racial discrimination. In response, St. Mary's claimed that the reason was *not* race and argued that the termination was due to Hicks's repeated violation of rules. Hicks' supervisor, John Powell, claimed that he had a verbal confrontation with Hicks. However, during trial, the district court

> found that the reasons petitioners gave were not the real reasons for respondent's demotion and discharge. It found that respondent was the only supervisor disciplined for violations committed by his subordinates; that similar and even more serious violations committed by respondent's co-workers were either disregarded or treated more leniently; and that Powell manufactured the final verbal confrontation in order to provoke respondent into threatening him.[30]

Nonetheless, the district court found that even though Hicks had proved that the employer lied by giving a pretextual reason that was false, Hicks must *also* provide clear proof that the crusade to terminate him was racially motivated. Therefore, the district court ruled in the employer's favor. On appeal, the US Court of Appeals for the Eighth Circuit reversed the decision, ruling that all that is required for Hicks to prevail on a discrimination claim is to show that the employer lied by giving a pretextual reason for terminating him. Since Hicks already provided undisputed *prima facie* evidence of racial discrimination, the court wrote:

Because all of defendants' proffered reasons were discredited, defendants were in a position of having offered no legitimate reason for their actions. In other words, defendants were in no better position than if they had remained silent, offering no rebuttal to an established inference that they had unlawfully discriminated against plaintiff on the basis of his race.[31]

As the undisputed facts showed, the stated reasons given by St. Mary's (company violations of conduct and an alleged altercation with a supervisor) were fabricated, and numerous other non-black employees with similar or worse violations were not so disciplined or discharged. Therefore, according to the court of appeals, Hicks was entitled to judgment as a matter of law.

However, Justice Scalia penned a majority opinion holding that a plaintiff's showing of false pretext was *not* sufficient for a successful Title VII discrimination claim. Instead, Scalia's majority developed what has been called the "pretext plus" doctrine, which modifies the framework by requiring the plaintiff to demonstrate Scalia's clear and convincing evidence standard in addition to showing that the employer was lying. According to the pretext plus doctrine, the judicial inquiry does *not* end when the plaintiff successfully shows the stated reasons for discharge are false. Rather, after their legal reasons have been shown to be false, the employer is then given an opportunity to proffer nondiscriminatory reasons for its actions that the plaintiff must then rebut. Under this framework, plaintiffs must show not only a *prima facie* case of discrimination, along with showing that the stated reasons for discharge were false pretext, but *also* demonstrate through clear and convincing evidence that race was a motivating factor. The steps of this framework are the following:

(1) Plaintiff must show *prima facie* case of discrimination.
(2) Employer must articulate a legitimate, nondiscriminatory reason for discharge.
(3) Plaintiff has opportunity to show that proffered reason (2) is pretextual.
   a. If showing of pretext fails, judgement is rendered for defendant.
   b. If showing of pretext is successful, then process advances to (4).
(4) Plaintiff must show by clear and convincing evidence that race was motivating factor in reasons given by defendant.

Thus, under this pretext plus doctrine, the plaintiff must not only show a *prima facie* case of discrimination and negate the defendant's proffered reason but must then also affirmatively demonstrate that the real reason was discriminatory intent based on race.[32] As Scalia writes in the majority opinion, the plaintiff does not win by showing a *prima facie* case of discrimination *and* showing that the defendant lied about the termination. Rather, as Scalia stated, "That the employer's proffered reason is unpersuasive, or even obviously contrived, does not necessarily establish that the plaintiff's proffered reason of race is correct."[33]

The dissent in *St. Mary's* argued at length that the court's modified burden-shifting framework constitutes "a scheme that will be unfair to plaintiffs, unworkable in practice, and inexplicable in forgiving employers who present false evidence in court."[34] Since common experience tells us that it is more likely than not that discrimination explains (1) an employer lying about the reasons for discharging an employee, and that there is (2) a *prima facie* case of discrimination, the dissent argued that the traditional pretext framework was sufficient for Title VII claims of discrimination. It argued that the pretext plus doctrine establishes an argumentative, burden-shifting framework that unduly places upon the plaintiff "the amorphous requirement of disproving all possible nondiscriminatory reasons that a factfinder might find lurking in the record."[35] As the dissent and some legal scholars have argued, this framework, in short, allows the defendant to lie as a strategy to make the plaintiff lose.[36] In the majority opinion, Scalia openly acknowledged that some employers will, of course, lie about their unlawful discrimination but that the Civil Rights Act is not to be used for remedying these kinds of acts. Scalia writes:

> Undoubtedly some employers (or at least their employees) will be lying. But even if we could readily identify these perjurers, what an extraordinary notion, that we "exempt them from responsibility for their lies" unless we enter Title VII judgments for the plaintiffs! Title VII is not a cause of action for perjury; we have other civil and criminal remedies for that.[37]

That is, according to Scalia, the Title VII Civil Rights prohibition against racial discrimination should not be used to remedy racial discrimination in employment when the employer lies about the reasons for unlawfully terminating employees on the basis of race. His pretext plus doctrine, therefore, allows employers to use lying to defend themselves against a Title VII discrimination claim. In this way, Scalia's pretext plus doctrine sanctioned an evidentiary framework in which discrimination could be performed *mala fide*.

## PRETEXT AS PERFORMATIVITY

Under pretext plus doctrine, discriminators are afforded the opportunity to proffer multiple deceitful reasons for their actions that the plaintiff then must attempt to disprove. In this way, an employer's speech act of lying can be seen as a kind of performative resignification of their discriminatory actions. In *Excitable Speech*, Judith Butler writes that one of the textual practices of performativity consists in, "the restaging and resignifying of offensive utterance, deployments of linguistic power that seek at once to expose and counter the offensive exercise of speech."[38] She argues that

> terms are subject to resignification. Such a redoubling of injurious speech takes place not only in rap music and in various forms of political parody and satire, but in the political and social critique of such speech, where "mentioning" those very terms is crucial to the arguments at hand, and even in the legal arguments that make the call for censorship, in which the rhetoric that is deplored is invariably proliferated within the context of legal speech. Paradoxically, the explicit legal and political arguments that seek to tie such speech to certain contexts fail to note that even in their own discourse, such speech has become citational, breaking with the prior contexts of its utterance and acquiring new contexts for which it was not intended.[39]

Because of a speech act's performative power to resignify itself, Butler argues that the search for a legal remedy for injurious speech acts becomes elusive, since all speech acts exists within a "ritual chain of resignifications whose origin and end remain unfixed and unfixable."[40] This leads Butler to the following crucial passage, arguing that

> no speech act has to perform injury as its effect means that no simple elaboration of speech acts will provide a standard by which the injuries of speech might be effectively adjudicated. Such a loosening of the link between act and injury, however, opens up the possibility for a counter-speech, a kind of talking back, that would be foreclosed by the tightening of that link. Thus, the gap that separates the speech act from its future effects has its auspicious implications: it begins a theory of linguistic agency that provides an alternative to the relentless search for legal remedy. The interval between instances of utterance not only makes the repetition and resignification of the utterance possible, but shows how words might, through time, become disjoined from their power to injure and recontextualized in more affirmative modes.[41]

Applied to the pretext plus doctrine established by *St. Mary's*, we can see that the employer utilizes the performativity of legal speech acts that is sanctioned by Scalia's majority, allowing the employer to resignify the meaning of their originally discriminatory actions in court. Crucially, this performative resignification is strategic, aiming to defeat the plaintiff by concocting a plausible reason that the plaintiff will not be able to disprove. As Judge Posner observed:

> Defendants of even minimal sophistication will neither admit discriminatory animus nor leave a paper trail demonstrating it . . . alternative hypotheses

(including that of simple mistake) will always be possible and often plausible ... it is so easy to concoct a plausible reason for not hiring, or firing, or failing to promote, or denying a pay raise to, a worker who is not superlative.[42]

In this way, Scalia's majority provides the judicial framework within which Butler's theory of performativity can be utilized by defendants by allowing them to resignify their own legal speech acts and thereby severing them from any "fixed" origin point of meaning. By utilizing the performativity of legal speech acts sanctioned by the court, defendants may engage in a kind of *performative discrimination*.

For Butler, the thesis of performativity stems from the argument that injurious speech acts lack a determinate, fixed origin of meaning. Discursive performativity refers to the fact that speech acts exist within "a ritual chain of resignifications whose origin and end remain unfixed and unfixable."[43] In a recent work,[44] Butler argues that performativity can be used by those unjustly excluded by legal authorities as a way of exposing injustice and calling for more inclusive legal norms. Here, Butler gives the example of undocumented citizens asserting that, despite lacking legal papers, they are citizens who belong. Butler writes, "Such claims are not strictly legal or, rather, not yet legal, but they operate within the imaginary of possible law or, rather, their power consists in opening up that imaginary."[45] However, Butler fails to consider the implications of performativity in legal speech and doctrine. If legal speech and doctrine operates as a performance in the way Butler describes, then it follows that *all actors* within the legal community may utilize the performativity of the law, including "bad faith" actors, discriminators, politicians, legislators, and the state for a variety of malicious or malevolent purposes. In this way, legal assertions and claims are made by both the powerful and the marginalized, the benevolent and the malevolent. Butler describes the performative assertion of a legal claim as a form of "self-conferral." For her, a legal claim or assertion can be described as a *not-yet* legal statement of right:

> So the speech act can be described as self-conferral. As much as such a claim asserts something, it also shows something: it enacts the very speech act in public that the law should be enacting. So, it exposes that failure and calls for its rectification and prescribes a course for the future, and both the critical and prescriptive operations take place through the form of an assertion. The exposure and the calling for are implied by the performance of the assertion. Performance thus takes on a double meaning: something is said, but something is also done.[46]

In this passage, Butler describes the performative practice of self-conferral as a speech act that is challenged by those unjustly excluded from the legal order or by legal authorities. Once again, however, Butler does not address the myriad of ways in which the state or "bad faith" legal actors can also utilize the performative practice of self-conferral to resignify the past, or self-confer upon themselves "good faith" intentions, or to simply deny that there is a "fixed" origin of discriminatory meaning altogether. As she writes, "The performative is thus, in such instances, self-authorizing. . . . It may not [be] legal . . . but it could, in principle, become both, or one without the other. It is that open-ended becoming that is asserted and shown by the citational practice."[47]

## PERFORMATIVE LYING AND THE LAW

In this way, the pretext plus doctrine draws upon the already tenuous relationship between the law and truth. If one agrees with Butler's account of the performativity of law, we may say that the law has a distinctly permissive attitude toward the *performance* of lying. Indeed, the law's relationship to truth is a strained and complex one. In *Bronson v. United States* (1973), the Supreme Court ruled that witnesses who give intentionally misleading answers are not subject to prosecution under the federal perjury statute so long as answers are "literally true."[48] Witnesses therefore are allowed by law to give answers that are "literally true, but unresponsive, even assuming the witness intends to mislead his questioner by the answer, and even assuming the answer is arguably "false by negative implication.'"[49] As Alexander and Sherwin (2002) observe, in the private law of contracts and torts, even statements of intention are not to be reasonably believed to be true if the formal terms of the relationship allows deception. As for lawyers advocating for clients, effective advocacy often "requires the lawyer to disguise to some extent his adversary posture."[50] While legal discourse broadly condemns deception, as seen in the ABA's Model Rules of Professional Conduct, legal doctrine and practice demonstrates a high degree of toleration and mutual *benefit* from deception and ambiguity. They write:

> Much of what lawyers do in representing clients can be viewed as deceptive. Judges traditionally have endorsed legal fictions as means of adjusting rules of law to new circumstances. The body of law at times seems designed to mislead ordinary citizens about the content of legal duties and the consequences that follow from their breach. Finally, there is a sense in which any determinate legal rule of conduct deceives its audience about what action they should take.[51]

As Alexander suggests, the "real" world of legal practice and doctrine (as opposed to public perceptions) reflects the assumption that in many cases, it is far more efficient to *assume* truthfulness than to pursue claims of deception, fraud, or bad faith. For this reason, strategic uses of the law *mala fide* reflect "the law's own willingness to use or endorse deceptive practices in furtherance of systemic ends."[52] As Alexander and Sherwin conclude, the law "is an exercise in institutionalized collective self-deception."[53]

It is for this reason that it is often said that politics is simply war continued by other means. In some areas of law, such a slogan has become a tautology. As one US district court remarked in 2019, "At bottom, litigation is war."[54] In the context of employment discrimination law, this observation has increasingly become a common refrain. As one US court of appeals said in 2005, the competitive nature of equal protection discrimination cases provides "incentive to turn litigation, to paraphrase Clausewitz, into a continuation of politics by other means."[55] One way this insight has been pursued by philosophers of language is the observation that law has taken a "pragmatic" turn. In this content, forms of speech delivered through legal texts have been studied as not simply "conversational" but what Marmor calls "strategic speech."

The justifications for analyzing legal texts as not simply textual artefacts but as a performance of a legal strategy are many. First, within the American legal system, law operates within the "adversarial" system. When doing legal research, one is encouraged to "get to know your opponent" *and* your judge through legal analytics as a way to increase your likelihood of success based on a prediction of what legal moves they will make. This model exhibits characteristics of a complex game-theory situation, whereas in legal decision-making, "it is typically the case that individuals must choose and act under the assumption that others are choosing and acting in reaction to one's decisions or in anticipation of them, where those reactions can be either benevolent or malevolent."[56]

Second, game theory perspectives in legal communication therefore argue that because law exhibits highly noncooperative, competitive features of interaction, it should be understood as a game-theory situation in which each participant has at least some foreknowledge of their adversary's past legal behavior and possible strategic legal moves. This game-theory model is especially applicable in the areas of "litigation wars," forced mediation, negotiation, "cause lawyering," and, as Marmor argues, the highly political context of legislative speech. In these domains of legal speech,

> you must be concerned that, since they know you are aware of their past behaviors, they might try to confound your calculations by defecting in some way from whatever patterns their earlier decisions exhibit. And there is, moreover, an additional complication. Since in a game theoretic analysis we can also assume that they know you know their past history, they also know you know they might have an incentive to thwart your calculations by not changing past patterns of

behavior at all. But, since you also know that they know that you know they might consider sticking to past patterns . . . and so on, ad infinitum once again.⁵⁷

As one defendant's cocounsel explained during a criminal defense trial in 2023:

> There's a quote by Sun Tzu, the Chinese general, strategist, tactician, who says that . . . an attack everywhere is an attack nowhere. So I think when you're talking about military strategy or trial strategy, the concept of concentrating your forces on the opposition's weakest point is well settled to be the best way to win that battle.⁵⁸

In the litigation and mediation context, the language of strategy is pervasive. As one district court observed in 2014:

> Litigation is sometimes analogized to war, and it seems as though the parties and their counsel are following at least one of the teachings of Sun Tzu (544–496 BC), the famous Chinese military general, strategist, and philosopher: "The quality of decision is like the well-timed swoop of a falcon which enables it to strike and destroy its victim."⁵⁹

And in yet another separate case involving environmental litigation, a court of appeals candidly wrote in 1996:

> We are not fooled by what is going on in this case. Wearing down the enemy by making it cover many fronts is a classic tactic of warfare . . . and it is obvious that the lesson has not been lost on the shipowner. We are fully aware that the present appeal simply represents a new tactical theater of operations designed to inflict collateral damage on an enemy through a costly diversion. As a policy matter, it is unthinkable that state agencies statutorily charged with recovering costs of cleaning up pollution should be deterred from their purpose because they can be outmanned in a paper war.⁶⁰

In this way, the pretext plus doctrine doubles down on the law's often permissive attitude toward the performance of "bad faith" actors in disguising discriminatory speech acts. Since employers under the doctrine may utilize lying as a performative act of resignification or self-conferral, discriminatory actions may be successfully disguised behind the nondiscriminatory reasons proffered subsequently in court.

## MANIPULATIVE SPEECH

In what follows, I argue that we can use the insights of legal pragmatics to see that Scalia's pretext plus framework also facilitates the use of what philosopher of language Andrei Marmor has called "strategic speech." In this way, such speech should be seen as one of the judicial hallmarks of Scalia's textualist insistence on the *process* rather than *substance* of law. Rather than understanding legal communications within discrimination cases as a cooperative form of "conversational" speech (i.e., Grice), such speech acts should be understood as "strategic" or "manipulative speech" that can nonetheless be rationally reconstructed with the tools of discriminatology outlined in this book.

For Marmor, a conversational model of legal language presupposes certain "cooperative" Gricean principles, where each party assumes that the other party is at minimum sharing the goal of facilitating maximally effective and nondeceptive communication of information. In contrast, Marmor writes,

> Some types of speech are strategic. Parties to a strategic conversation may wish to employ conversational maxims in ways which generate implications that act to their advantage, without a real intention to be committed to such implicated content. The extreme example is manipulative speech: these are cases in which a speaker asserts something true while deliberately implicating something that he knows to be false. As an example, consider this case: Mr. Smith goes to a hospital, and in making some medical enquiries with one of the nurses, he presents himself as "Dr Smith." As it happens, Smith's doctorate is in philosophy. Wouldn't the nurse be rather surprised, and quite rightly annoyed, in learning this little detail later? True, Mr. Smith did not assert that he is a medical doctor, but given the circumstances, it is an implication that would naturally follow. In other words, the asserted content here is true; it is only the implicature that is false.[61]

For Marmor, manipulative speech is an extreme form of strategic legal speech in which "the abuse or manipulation is made possible precisely because the hearer wrongly assumes that the speaker adheres to the ordinary Gricean conversational maxims."[62]

The surprising takeaway from Marmor's legal pragmatics is therefore the following insight: strategic or manipulative speech thrives within a legal framework that forces all parties to follow "cooperative" Gricean principles, even when one party has incentive to be strategic. For Marmor, "Manipulative implications are possible only because the hearers are led to assume that the speaker follows the ordinary conversational maxims."[63] This means that strategic or manipulative speech thrives best within an evidentiary framework that forces all parties to "cooperate" by accepting one another's stated reasons while *not* enforcing a prohibition against lying. However, this is precisely what Scalia's pretext plus doctrine had established—an evidentiary framework *acknowledging* that defendants may lie, while enforcing the plaintiff to "cooperate." As Scalia writes in *St. Mary's*:

Undoubtedly some employers (or at least their employees) will be lying. But even if we could readily identify these perjurers, what an extraordinary notion, that we "exempt them from responsibility for their lies" unless we enter Title VII judgments for the plaintiffs! Title VII is not a cause of action for perjury; we have other civil and criminal remedies for that.[64]

By acknowledging that the pretext plus framework allows performative lying but rejects any cause of action for such lying, Scalia's majority therefore quite literally made manipulative speech lawful.

Some philosophers, however, have argued that the basic argumentative framework utilized by Scalia's majority in *St. Mary's* can nonetheless be used as a model for legal interpretation that may be applied in computational models of argumentation.[65] Under this account, Walton, Macagno and Sartor argue that "interpretation is essentially a matter of arguments,"[66] where competing interpretations are identified and assessed using tools of pragmatics to determine the best interpretation within a dialectical, evidence-based framework of the best explanation. In this literature, the argument is made that the "conversational" approach or framework can still be used even in "strategic" legal contexts. Since the goal of the model is to demonstrate how legal interpretation can be adequately modeled primarily an argumentative task, one major presupposition of the model is that legal disputes—even strategic ones—are a type of argumentative activity.[67] Building on models of computational argumentation, a "normative dialectical model" of interpretation is developed that provides an abstract structure of argumentation to help determine and predict how arguments may be defeated within a burden-shifting framework of rational, evidence-based exchange of reasons.

As the authors state, one major presupposition of the model is that it is possible to identify a "common mechanism" or structure of arguments that is shared by *both* legal interpretation and the field of pragmatics, which in turn makes it possible to reduce the complexity of legal disputes into ".simplified and schematic representations of conflicting arguments."[68] Under such an account, therefore, legal interpretation may be modeled on basic Gricean conversational principles and maxims, whereby participants within the framework each accept the cooperative aim of maximally efficient exchange of information. By utilizing an argumentative, burden-shifting framework as a model of retrieving a speaker's legal meaning, Gricean maxims and legal canons of construction are used to guide and evaluate the presumptions that favor or disfavor each interpretation. Under this framework, "generic Gricean maxims can be used for describing the reasoning underlying legal interpretation."[69]

Using the cooperative conversational maxims and their analogous legal canons of construction as a guide, Walton, Macagno, and Sartor outline a step-by-step procedure for the dialogic adjudication of the best legal interpretation. They write:

> the arguments of legal interpretation and the conversational maxims represent distinct levels of analysis of the reasoning underlying an interpretive dispute. The legal arguments can be used to point out the various perspectives on the subject matter that can be used pro and con a viewpoint, while the maxims can show the general strategies (relying on absent context, or the most natural reading, or the existing context, or the contextual and co-textual effects and consequences). What emerges from this picture is that these two dimensions of interpretation can be integrated within an argumentative model. This model can represent the presumptive grounds on which such maxims and arguments are based. On this view, the reconstruction of the speaker's meaning can be analyzed through the categories of presumptions that can be used to support it.[70]

Given this argumentative structure of reason-giving and assessment, the best interpretation can be identified as an inference to the best explanation of the interpretation. According to the model, the best explanation under this framework will be the explanation that fits best with the shared background assumptions of the actors and the communicative intent of the speakers given what is said.[71]

In cases where noncooperative interaction exists, Walton, Macagno, and Sartor argue that Gricean maxims of conversation may be adapted such that they "are more adequate to the purpose of the dialogue, aimed at providing the strongest reasons in favor or against a controversial interpretation."[72] While some legal contexts exhibit transitory features of noncooperation, they write that, "The apparent failure to adhere to the cooperative maxim in some cases does not mean that cooperation is excluded from legal discussion."[73] Because the model assumes that legal interpretation and conversational pragmatics share a common argumentative scheme, such noncooperative behavior (in this view) may also be interpreted within the model itself. For this reason, the model above will be referred to as the "conversational-argumentative-dialectical" (CAD) model of legal interpretation, since it proposes to utilize Gricean principles and maxims of conversation, coupled with the tools of argumentation theory, to construct an abstract theory of legal interpretation based on the dialectical reconstruction of meaning through pragmatic argumentation.

To simplify and illustrate the CAD model of legal interpretation, let us suppose an employer (A) demotes and discharges an employee (B) for presumably work-related violations of policy. The employer's (A) stated reasons (R) for the discharge of employee (B) are:

*R: Employee (B) violated work policies.*

Now let us suppose that employee (B) believes her discharge was in fact due to her race, and that the proffered reasons given (R) were "pretextual," that is, "a statement that does not describe the actual reasons for the decision."[74] Let us suppose that employee (B) brings a discrimination claim against the employer under the Civil Rights Act, which prohibits employers from discharging employees due to race.[75] In such a case, then, employee (B) is disputing the asserted meaning or content of employer's (A) stated legal reasons. In such a case, the need for legal interpretation is raised, since the claim turns on the legal interpretation of whether the employer's stated legal reasons are lawful or not. Let us suppose that employee (B) then makes a *prima facie* case supporting the true reason of discrimination on the basis of race, creating a *prima facie* inference of discrimination against the employer. Employee (B) then offers the alternative reason (R2) for unlawful discharge:

*R2: Employee (B) was discharged on account of her race.*

However, once a *prima facie* case has been made by employee (B) for R2, then the employer (A) has an opportunity to respond, and the dialogue continues. If the employer provides a satisfactory description of another (nondiscriminatory) reason, then this "shifts a burden of proof onto the respondent. The respondent has to show that an alternative interpretation is better, and provide arguments and evidence supporting it."[76] Under Walton, Macagno, and Sartor's dialectic framework, each of these competing interpretations of the meaning or content of the employer's reason will be

> compared with the possible alternatives, and the default conditions of each interpretation are evaluated. The one that is the least subject to attack and that is better supported by the evidence that can be marshaled on both sides of the disputed issue is chosen as the best one. The competing hypotheses are eliminated by this procedure.[77]

According to the framework, less credible explanations and interpretations are eliminated in the process of evidence assessment and reason giving, such that "the best interpretation is the one that is less controversial, namely less subject to defeat based on conflicting propositions contained in the common ground."[78]

However, as the case of Mr. Hicks shows in *St. Mary's*, the CAD model for legal interpretation is highly vulnerable to strategic manipulation by "bad faith" defendants who seek to defeat discrimination claims by insulating and disguising pretextual reasons. The reason for this, I argue, is that Scalia's pretext doctrine framework openly *acknowledges* that defendants may lie while rejecting any enforcement against such lying. For this reason, discriminatory speech in such cases is best understood as a special kind of strategic speech that *cannot* be captured by the Gricean, cooperative framework that is *enforced* by Scalia's pretext plus framework. In chapter 5, I will show how this burden-shifting framework has also been utilized in the legislative context to circumvent antidiscrimination doctrine and insulate plans for racial gerrymandering. Consequently, as these cases show, discriminatory speech cannot be understood or interpreted according to the conversational model of legal interpretation and should instead be considered as a form of strategic speech that can nonetheless be rationally reconstructed with the tools of discriminatology outlined in this book. In this way, Marmor's approach to pragmatics is a useful starting point in highlighting how strategic speech is used to advance political or legislative goals under the guise of cooperation.

According to Marmor, textualism *accepts* the thesis that legal speech, and particularly legislative speech, is *strategic*. However, the problem for Marmor is that textualism completely fails to offer any useful tools for interpreting or reconstructing meaning out of this strategic field of communication. In *The Language of Law,* Marmor writes that

> textualism has no resources to deal with interpretative questions stemming from vagueness; it has no resources to deal with conflict between different laws, especially when the asserted content of each is in no serious doubt; and, though this is an issue I have not dealt with here, textualism's record on dealing with cases where what the law actually says yields absurd results is uneven, at best. In short, textualism turns out to be a very minimal interpretative tool, one that is simply not going to help judges solve most of the actual problems they face in statutory interpretation.[79]

Marmor's conclusion from his analysis of textualism is that it fails to offer "anything useful" for interpreting strategic speech in law.[80] In this respect, Marmor is correct about textualism: it is clear that Scalia acknowledges the use of strategic speech in the law. In highly "strategic" contexts such as discrimination law, in particular, Scalia often openly acknowledges that defendants may lie in court to avoid liability.

By the same token, Marmor's analysis of textualism is partly incomplete. The reason *why* textualism fails to offer anything useful for addressing or interpreting strategic speech is because this feature of textualism is *by design*. As chapter 1 demonstrated, Scalia rejects *any* scrutiny into the alleged motives or unlawful purposes behind the stated legal reasons or texts given in court. For Scalia, textualism prohibits judges from scrutinizing or ferreting out the discriminatory motives of a speaker. Therefore, textualism does not offer anything useful for interpreting strategic or manipulative speech precisely because textualism simply chooses not to. In other words, textualism rejects any judicial scrutiny into strategic or manipulative speech because of a sovereign decision to exclude this from the meaning of the law.

Under the original pretext doctrine established under the *McDonnell Douglass* framework, a *mala fide* presumption of bad faith is sufficient for a discrimination claim, since this presumption shows that the formal, argumentative, burden-shifting framework has been strategically manipulated by the employer to disguise pretextual motives. According to this view, the argumentative, burden-shifting framework is no longer applicable once a *mala fide* presumption is created against a defendant in a discrimination suit who has been shown to have proffered a false reason in court for discharging an employee. On this view, this bad faith showing coupled with *prima facie* discrimination ends and limits the interpretive task. That is, the argumentative, burden-shifting framework has done its job and the inquiry into reconstructing meaning has been sufficiently adjudicated. This means that the argumentative, burden-shifting framework for reconstructing the meaning of the reasons given is no longer applicable. The inquiry is complete. To continue utilizing the argumentative, burden-shifting framework despite a showing of bad faith by the defendant would, under this view, permit the defendant to further manipulate the reason-giving framework by proffering *post hoc* rationalizations and create an undue burden on the plaintiff to rebut any new, elusive reasons given by the defendant and demonstrate an intent based on subjective, contextual factors that may not be available to the plaintiff. In short, the pretext plus doctrine provides the evidentiary framework that allows defendants to perform discrimination by lying and thereby defeat the plaintiff.

Instead, the pretext doctrine originally established under *McDonnell Douglas* recognizes that there are important limitations and weaknesses of an argumentative, burden-shifting framework in certain cases of legal interpretation of discriminatory speech. When a plaintiff shows that a defendant lied about the legal reasons given for discharging an employee, the pretext doctrine understands the situation as if the defendant has disclaimed the basic Gricean principles of cooperation and maxims of conversation. The pretext doctrine views the defendant, by officially submitting to a court a false reason for unlawfully discharging an employee, as implicitly rejecting of the cooperation principle and basic maxims of conversation, thereby forfeiting the reciprocal consideration and recognition of defendant's arguments and evidence. In other words, once a *mala fide* presumption is created against a plaintiff, a pretext court views the defendant as implicitly rejecting the basic cooperative purpose of the argumentative, evidence-based framework. Any attempt to continue to utilize the argumentative framework, the defendant is not engaging in a cooperative, good faith conversational exchange of reasons and evidence but rather utilizing the formal parameters of the framework precisely to undermine its purpose for unlawful ends. Therefore, common experience tells us that such actions imply the rejection of a good faith procedure of argument evaluation and evidence-giving that results in the best interpretation given the truth of the matter.

The case study of *St. Mary's* illustrates several points in favor of viewing these kinds of discriminatory speech using the strategic model proposed by Andrei Marmor. First, the fields of legal pragmatics and speech-act theory are both particularly helpful for illuminating communicative content in a noncooperative, complex language game. From this perspective, the legal communications of legislative acts will often exhibit features of deception and "double-speak" whereby "Legislators may wish to create the impression that they are doing one thing. . . while actually trying to do the opposite."[81] As was the case in *St. Mary's* and *Abbott v. Perez*, games of implicature and double-speak are employed in competitive legislative strategies for strategic ends. And, in some cases, such ends are unlawful and discriminatory. In such cases, it is reasonable to understand the actions of legislators as fundamentally strategic or "manipulative" by disguising their intentions and evading any mechanisms to reconstruct the meaning of their act. Crucially, this point cannot be understood properly assuming Gricean cooperative norms of a conversational model of speech acts for the simple reason that tactics of double-speak and masking of one's motives are inconsistent with the basic premise of Grice's "cooperative principle" and the maxims of quantity, quality, and the corresponding legal canons of construction.

As a result, the legal speech examined in this chapter cannot be understood as purely conversational or dialectical. Instead, as the case studies of *St. Mary's* and *Abbott* show, bad faith legal contexts demonstrate that legal actors often intend to subvert the purpose of antidiscrimination doctrine by disguising the very intentions that the court is attempting to reconstruct and bring to light. For this reason, courts utilize "antievasion" doctrines as a recognition of the evasive and manipulative tactics of defendants, routinely and sometimes explicitly describing the arguments or testimony of defendants as "incredible," as "pretext," as "proxy," and in some cases, outright "lies."[82] The way that participants and courts *themselves* describe the kinds of speech-acts being used in this context reflects the use of the law as strategic or "manipulative" speech rather than a cooperative model of conversation.

## CONCLUSION

In this chapter, I've argued that the pretext plus framework established by Scalia's majority allows performative lying but rejects any cause of action for such lying. As a result, Scalia's majority made lawful what Marmor calls manipulative speech.

Using the insights of both performativity theory and legal pragmatics, we can see that the forms of strategic speech sanctioned by Scalia's pretext plus doctrine are the result of the evidentiary process of performance that textualism enforces and facilitates, while rejecting any substantive engagement with the justice or injustice of the results that occur due to bad faith actors lying to defeat discrimination claims. Rather than understanding the legal communications within discrimination law as a purely cooperative form of conversational speech, such speech acts should be understood as strategic speech that can nonetheless be rationally reconstructed with the tools of discriminatology outlined in this book. Textualism, however (as Marmor has argued) does not provide such tools and predictably results in injustice. As I've shown, Scalia's pretext plus doctrine facilitates *malevolent legalities* by providing the framework within which strategic or manipulative speech can defeat discrimination claims.

Nonetheless, several objections might be raised against the argument that discriminatory speech is better understood on the strategic and not conversational model. The first possible objection is that, according to the conversational model, conflict between the aims of participants is expected and accounted for. Walton, Macagno, and Sartor address this concern when they argue that specific instances of noncooperative interactions does not preclude the application and usefulness of the CAD model. In particular, they argue that in the legislative context, evidence is available that allows the epistemological task of reconstruction of meaning. However, as I've shown, in cases of bad faith, the presupposition that there exists such available evidence is undermined. This is because legal actors implicitly reject the assumption that the purpose of the interaction is to subject the available evidence to scrutiny. Since bad faith legal actors reject this baseline condition, it is not reasonable to expect either that there is such evidence available or that legal actors are providing arguments that are transparent, truthful, and nonpretextual in nature. Instead, as the jurisprudences of *textual skepticism* suggest, we can reconstruct these forms of "strategic speech" using the tools of discriminatology I've outlined.

A second possible objection is that the specific kinds of speech acts examined in his chapter are an exception from the more general rule of cooperative or near-cooperative discourse that obtains in legal speech more broadly. Some legal scholars, for example, have argued that specific areas of legal speech acts more closely exhibit features of the conversational model, such as judicial opinions.[83] However, it is abundantly clear that bad-faith strategies are quite prevalent in many areas of law, including contract, property, negotiation, mediation, labor, tax, criminal, and constitutional law, and many more. Legal scholars have highlighted how courts have attempted to address bad faith legislative acts through the development of "antievasion doctrines" (AEDs) that "operate as standards designed to prevent governmental actors from simply enacting facially neutral laws cleverly drawn to circumvent decision rules."[84] Across many areas of law, courts have utilized such doctrines to combat bad faith, including doctrines of *proxy, pretext*, and *purpose tests*. In each case, an antievasion doctrine is developed in response to a party disguising their motives, using a false reason to discriminate, or being motivated by an impermissible or invidious purpose. The basic recognition behind these antievasion doctrines is that employers, legislators, and other parties sometimes seek to take advantage of gaps or indeterminacies in the law to circumvent or undermine the basic purpose or spirit of the law, including even the purpose of constitutional principles.[85] To combat these bad faith strategies, courts have developed doctrines and standards to reduce and discourage these strategic speech acts, including doctrines of false pretext, discrimination by proxy, and invidious purpose.[86] In this way, the nature and prevalence of bad-faith strategies suggests that such cases are not insular or exceptional. The framework for studying *malevolent legalities* proposed in this book is a crucial tool for addressing such legal strategies prevalent in the law.

A third possible objection to the argument made in this chapter is that lawmakers, judges, and legal decision-makers do not view or interpret legislation as strategic speech. Rather, the objection goes, interpretations of legal content and meaning as strategic speech are mostly of academic or legal scholarly interest but do not reflect how legal decision-makers understand and interpret legislation, or legal speech more broadly. Rather, the dominant way legal actors understand legal speech and actions is primarily conversational or dialectical in the way that Walton, Macagno, and Sartor describe. On this point, research on the subject to date has demonstrated only that legal actors widely attribute pragmatic meaning to legal texts,[87] although this research tells us little about whether and to what extent participants are themselves *acting strategically* when planning, drafting, enacting, and interpreting legal texts. An obvious difficulty in this research, however, goes directly back to the initial problem of strategic speech in masking intent: how does one find reliable evidence of strategic speech when actors intend that such evidence not be found? Once again, textualism does not provide the tools to answer these questions. On the contrary, textualism facilitates the use of strategic forms of speech in the law to disguise *malevolent legalities*. As a remedial tool, the framework of discriminatology proposed here seeks to provide a rational method of reconstructing the discriminatory meaning that is lost or covered up by the performative practices of legal actors in the arena of discrimination law.

As a transition to the following chapter, let us take stock of the *performative* character of law in facilitating *malevolent legalities*. This chapter has investigated pretext as a source of *malevolent legalities,* showing that the pretext plus doctrine established the lawfulness of lying as a performative speech-act in discrimination claims. The performative role of "strategic discriminatory speech" as seen in *St. Mary's* facilitates the use of pretext in hiding or masking discrimination. Here, the pretextual strategies utilized by the employer proved successful through utilizing the performance of good faith facilitated by manipulative speech. The doctrine of pretext plus announced by the court allows employers to effectively resignify their discriminatory actions *after* the plaintiff has brought a successful *prima facie* case of discrimination against the employer. Notably, the plaintiff does not win under pretext plus *even when showing the employer's initial reason was false.* Scalia's framework, in fact, acknowledges that defendants may lie while rejecting any enforcement against such lying. Thus, in *St Mary's*, the majority of the Supreme Court establishes the lawfulness of lying as a performative speech-act to defeat discrimination claims.

## NOTES

1. Antonin Scalia, speech on nature of being a lawyer [submitted as part of nomination questionnaire], 1984, Antonin Scalia papers, LAW, MMC, 291, Series I, Box: 26, Folder: 7, Harvard Law School Library, Historical & Special Collections, 3.
2. Scalia, speech on nature of being a lawyer, 6.
3. Antonin Scalia and Bryan A. Garner, *Reading Law: The Interpretation of Legal Texts* (St. Paul: Thomson/West, 2012), 348.
4. Scalia and Garner, *Reading Law,* 348.
5. Scalia, speech on nature of being a lawyer, 5.
6. The Honorable Antonin Scalia and John F. Manning, "A Dialogue on Constitutional and Statutory Interpretation," 80 *Geo. Wash. L. Rev.* 1610 (2012): 1613.
7. Scalia and Garner, *Reading Law*, 347.
8. Scalia and Garner, *Reading Law*, xxvii.
9. *Richmond v. J. A. Croson Co.*, 488 U.S. 469, 524 (1989).
10. Scalia and Garner, *Reading Law*, xxvii.
11. *Richmond v. J. A. Croson Co.*, 488 U.S. 469, 524 (1989).
12. CIVIL RIGHTS ACT OF 1991, 1991 Enacted S. 1745, 102 Enacted S. 1745, 105 Stat. 1071, 1072.
13. *Long v. Ford Motor Co.*, 496 F.2d 500, 504-05 (6th Cir. 1974).
14. *NLRB v. Wright Motors, Inc.*, 603 F.2d 604, 609-10 (7th Cir. 1979).

15. *Carter v. Duncan-Huggins, Ltd.*, 234 U.S. App. D.C. 126, 727 F.2d 1225, 1246 (1984).
16. *Carter v. Duncan-Huggins, Ltd.*, 234 U.S. App. D.C. 126, 727 F.2d 1225, 1247 (1984).
17. *Carter v. Duncan-Huggins, Ltd.*, 234 U.S. App. D.C. 126, 727 F.2d 1225, 1247 (1984).
18. *Toney v. Block*, 227 U.S. App. D.C. 273, 705 F.2d 1364, 1367-68 (1983).
19. *Carter v. Duncan-Huggins, Ltd.*, 234 U.S. App. D.C. 126, 727 F.2d 1225, 1247 (1984).
20. *Carter v. Duncan-Huggins*, Ltd., 234 U.S. App. D.C. 126, 727 F.2d 1225, 1247 (1984).
21. *Carter v. Duncan-Huggins, Ltd.*, 234 U.S. App. D.C. 126, 727 F.2d 1225, 1239 (1984).
22. Antonin Scalia, "Federal Constitution Guarantees of Individual Rights in the United States of America," July 28, 1993, Antonin Scalia papers, LAW, MMC, 291, Series III, Box: 73, Folder: 9, Harvard Law School Library, Historical & Special Collections, 36.
23. *St. Mary's Honor Ctr. v. Hicks*, 509 U.S. 502 (1993).
24. *McDonnell Douglas Corp. v. Green*, 411 U.S. 792 (1973).
25. See Laina R. Reinsmith, "Proving an Employer's Intent: Disparate Treatment Discrimination and the Stray Remarks Doctrine After *Reeves v. Sanderson Plumbing Products*," *Vanderbilt Law Review* 55 (2002): 219.
26. Samuel W. Buell, "Good Faith and Law Evasion," *UCLA Law Review* 58 (2011): 61166.
27. See David E. *Pozen*, "Constitutional Bad Faith," *Harvard Law Review* 885 (2016): 129.
28. *St. Mary's Honor Ctr. v. Hicks*, 509 U.S. 502, 536 (1993).
29. *St. Mary's Honor Ctr. v. Hicks*, 509 U.S. 502, 506 (1993).
30. *St. Mary's Honor Ctr. v. Hicks*, 509 U.S. 502, 508 (1993).
31. *Hicks v. St. Mary's Honor Ctr., Div. of Adult Insts. of Dep't of Corr. & Human Res.*, 970 F.2d 487, 492 (8th Cir. 1992).
32. See Catherine J. Lanctot, "The Defendant Lies and the Plaintiff Loses: The Fallacy of the Pretext-Plus Rule in Employment Discrimination Cases," *Hastings Law Journal* 43 (1991): 57.
33. *St. Mary's Honor Ctr. v. Hicks*, 509 U.S. 502, 524 (1993).
34. *St. Mary's Honor Ctr. v. Hicks*, 509 U.S. 502, 533 (1993).
35. *St. Mary's Honor Ctr. v. Hicks*, 509 U.S. 502, 535 (1993).
36. See Lanctot, "The Defendant Lies and the Plaintiff Loses."
37. *St. Mary's Honor Ctr. v. Hicks*, 509 U.S. 502, 521 (1993).
38. Judith Butler, *Excitable Speech: A Politics of the Performative* (New York: Routledge, 2021), 13.
39. Butler, *Excitable Speech*, 14.
40. Butler, *Excitable Speech*, 14.
41. Butler, *Excitable Speech*, 15.
42. *Riordan v. Kempiners*, 831 F.2d 690, 697-98 (7th Cir. 1987).

43. Butler, *Excitable Speech*, 14.
44. Judith Butler, "Categories by which we try to live," *European Journal of Philosophy* 31, no. 1 (2023): 28388.
45. Butler, "Categories by which we try to live," 285.
46. Butler, "Categories by which we try to live," 285.
47. Butler, "Categories by which we try to live," 285.
48. *Bronston v. United States*, 409 U.S. 352 (1973).
49. *Bronston v. United States*, 409 U.S. 352 (1973).
50. Larry Alexander and Emily Sherwin, "Deception in Morality and Law," *Law and Philosophy* 22 (2003): 418.
51. Alexander and Sherwin, "Deception in Morality and Law," 417.
52. Alexander and Sherwin, "Deception in Morality and Law," 431.
53. Alexander and Sherwin, "Deception in Morality and Law," 450.
54. *Olguin v. Florida's Ultimate Heavy Hauling*, 2019 U.S. Dist. LEXIS 95284 at 1 (S.D. Fla. June 5, 2019).
55. *Parents Involved in Cmty. Sch. v. Seattle Sch. Dist.*, No. 1, 426 F.3d 1162, 1196, 2005 U.S. App. LEXIS 22515, *92 (9th Cir. Wash. October 20, 2005).
56. E. M. S. Niou and P. C. Ordeshook, *Strategy and Politics: An Introduction to Game Theory* (New York: Routledge, 2015), 2.
57. Niou and Ordeshook, *Strategy and Politics: An Introduction to Game Theory*, 3.
58. *Campbell v. Gittere*, 3:19-cv-00576-MMD-CSD, at 19 (D. Nev. June 16, 2023).
59. *ProCaps S.A. v. Patheon Inc.*, No. 12-24356-CIV-GOODMAN, at 5 (S.D. Fla. Jan. 30, 2014).
60. *People ex rel. Dept. of Fish & Game v. Attransco, Inc.*, 50 Cal.App.4th 1926, 1937-38 (Cal. Ct. App. 1996).
61. Andrei Marmor, "Can the Law Imply More than It Says? On Some Pragmatic Aspects of Strategic Speech," in *Philosophical Foundations of Language in the Law*, ed. Andrai Marmor and Scott Soames (Oxford: Oxford University Press, 2011), 92–93.
62. Marmor, "Can the Law Imply More than It Says?" 93.
63. Marmor, "Can the Law Imply More than It Says?" 93.
64. *St. Mary's Honor Ctr. v. Hicks*, 509 U.S. 502, 521 (1993).
65. See Douglas Walton, Fabrizio Macagno, and Giovanni Sartor, *Statutory Interpretation: Pragmatics and Argumentation* (Cambridge: Cambridge University Press, 2022); Douglas Walton, Fabrizio Macagno, and Giovanni Sartor, "Pragmatic Maxims and Presumptions in Legal Interpretation," *Law and Philosophy* 37 (2018): 69–115.
66. Walton, Macagno, and Sartor, *Statutory Interpretation*, 3.
67. Walton, Macagno, and Sartor, *Statutory Interpretation*, 2–3.
68. Walton, Macagno, and Sartor, *Statutory Interpretation*, 6.
69. Walton, Macagno, and Sartor, "Pragmatic Maxims and Presumptions in Legal Interpretation," 87.
70. Walton, Macagno, and Sartor, "Pragmatic Maxims and Presumptions in Legal Interpretation," 99.

71. Walton, Macagno, and Sartor, "Pragmatic Maxims and Presumptions in Legal Interpretation," 74.

72. Walton, Macagno, and Sartor, "Pragmatic Maxims and Presumptions in Legal Interpretation," 74.

73. Walton, Macagno, and Sartor, "Pragmatic Maxims and Presumptions in Legal Interpretation," 86.

74. *Hicks v. St. Mary's Honor Center*, 756 F. Supp. 1244, 1250 (E.D. Mo. 1991).

75. 42 U.S.C. § 2000e-2.

76. Walton, Macagno, and Sartor, "Pragmatic Maxims and Presumptions in Legal Interpretation," 84.

77. Walton, Macagno, and Sartor, "Pragmatic Maxims and Presumptions in Legal Interpretation," 84.

78. Walton, Macagno, and Sartor, "Pragmatic Maxims and Presumptions in Legal Interpretation," 83.

79. Andrei Marmor, "Textualism in Context" in *The Language of Law* (Oxford: Oxford University Press, 2014), 107–28.

80. Marmor, "Textualism in Context," 107–30.

81. Andrei Marmor, "The Pragmatics of Legal Language," USC Law Legal Studies Paper No. 08-11 (May 2008), 23, https://ssrn.com/abstract=1130863.

82. The dissenting US Supreme Court justices in *St. Mary's Honor Ctr* (1993) repeatedly lamented that the court's decision allows employers to conceal discriminatory motives "by exempting them from responsibility for lies." See *St. Mary's Honor Ctr. v. Hicks*, 509 U.S. 502, 537 (1993).

83. M. Shardimgaliev, "Implicatures in Judicial Opinions," *International Journal of Semiot Law* 32 (2019): 391–415, https://doi.org/10.1007/s11196-018-09601-4.

84. Brannon P. Denning and Michael B. Kent, Jr., "Anti-Evasion Doctrines in Constitutional Law," *Utah Law Review* 1773 (2012): 1796.

85. See David E. *Pozen, "Constitutional Bad Faith," Harvard Law Review* 885 (2016): 129.

86. See Brannon P. Denning and Michael B. Kent, Jr., "*Anti-Anti-Evasion in* Constitutional Law," *Fla. St. University Law Review* 397 (2014): 41.

87. See Filippo Domaneschi, Francesca Poggi, and Eleonora Marocchini, "Why Lawyers are More Logical Than Ordinary Speakers and When They are Not," *International Journal of Language & Law* 11 (2022): 121–41.

# 3

## *Romer v. Evans* (1996)
## "The Written Law Killeth, but the Spirit Giveth Life"

In this chapter, I examine Scalia's dissenting opinion in *Romer v. Evans* (1996) in light of Scalia's speeches and opinions arguing for an "unwritten constitution." I argue that Scalia's originalist views on an "unwritten" constitution should be seen as evidence of the influence of Frederick Charles von Savigny's German historicist school. Scalia found in von Savigny's notion of the *volkgeist* a confirmation of his view that the "reason" of law (*ratio*) could be embodied in the customs or "traditions" of "the people," *even if discriminatory*. Like von Savigny, Scalia's textualism grounded legal interpretation in the notion of an unwritten constitution that could be given lawful expression only by judges such as himself. The consequence of this view was that certain kinds of discriminatory "animus" could be found perfectly constitutional by originalist judges. As Scalia argued in *Romer v. Evans* and *Windsor* (2013), the text of the Constitution does not prohibit "mean-spirited" laws enacted by the people against certain groups such as homosexuals. Unwritten textualism, therefore, could sanction certain kinds of discrimination as long as they were not explicitly prohibited by the text of such laws. The explanation for this, I argue, is Scalia's affinity with and citation of von Savigny as one of "the most pertinent sources" consulted in developing his theory of interpretation. In this way, we can better appreciate the citation of St. Paul in Scalia's speech on "The Rule of Law" that "the written law killeth, but the Spirit giveth life."

### SCALIA'S *VOLKGEIST*

From 1977 to 1982, Scalia taught courses at the University of Chicago School of Law, with a one-year visiting professorship at Stanford University. During this period, Scalia developed a course on "Statutory Interpretation" that covered major legal and philosophical treatises and readings on law and legal interpretation.¹ Scalia's course materials included Aristotle, Cicero, Aquinas and the Scholastics, Justinian's Code, and numerous commentaries on Roman law, including H. F. Jolowicz's *Roman Foundations of Modern Law*.² His selection of passages from Jolowicz's work included the chapter on "The Construction of Statutes" in which Jolowicz articulates the historical distinction between the *reason* of the law (*ratio*), which is backward-looking, as opposed to the *purpose* of the law, which is forward-looking. In a series of passages, Jolowicz approvingly cites Pufendorf and German Romantic jurist Frederick Charles von Savigny's distinction between

> the *mens legis*, which is nothing other than the true intention of the law, and the "ratio legis". . . . which is a help towards finding it. . . . Savigny, *System* I, 217, puts the same idea in a yet more abstract way when he contrasts the reason (*Grund*), which looks backward to an existing higher principle with the *purpose* (*Zweck* or *Abischt*), which looks forward.³

Here, Scalia endorses the distinction between the *intention* of the legislator as opposed to the reason of the law itself, which acquires a life of its own apart from the policy intentions of the legislator. In a passage again underlined with Scalia's affirmative margin notes ("Yes!"), Jolowicz, again referencing von Savigny, writes that,

> There are even some theorists who hold that the text of a statute once promulgated "lives a life of its own," and that the intention with which the interpreter is concerned is not that of the legislator, but that of the law itself.⁴

It is clear, therefore, that Scalia endorsed von Savigny's ideas that the reason of law acquires a "life of its own" and should be distinguished from the legislative intent *(mens legis)* of the law.

The influence of von Savigny on Scalia, however, was even more direct. In their 2012 treatise *Reading Law*, Scalia and Garner cite von Savigny's 1831 treatise *Of the Vocation of Our Age for Legislation and Jurisprudence*,⁵ and describe it as one of "the most pertinent sources"⁶ that they directly consulted in developing their theory of legal interpretation. In it, von Savigny inquired into "how law has actually developed itself amongst nations of the nobler races."⁷ He writes:

> In the earliest times to which authentic history extends, the law will be found to have already attained a fixed character, peculiar to the people, like their language, manners and constitution. Nay, these phenomena have no separate existence, they are but the particular faculties and tendencies of an individual people, inseparably united in nature, and only wearing the semblance of distinct attributes

to our view. That which binds them into one whole is the common conviction of the people, the kindred consciousness of an inward necessity.[8]

For von Savigny, the reason of the law is actually found in the "fixed character" peculiar to the customs and tradition of a people. As a result, the law simply meant the expression of the consciousness of the German *Volk* in their customary traditions: the "spirit of the people" (*volkgeist*). As explored more in part 2, this way of thinking about the "time" of law is what Francois Ost calls "customary time" (*le temps coutimier*), which gives interpretive priority to the past—namely, the "backwards-looking" customs, traditions, and practices of the "people."[9]

As Frederick Beiser explains, von Savigny's concept of the *volkgeist* suffers from obvious vagueness and mystical associations that lend itself to a wide variety of possible meanings.[10] The notion of the spirit of the people was clearly not to be found in a set of written texts. For the same reason, one of Scalia's favorite objects of criticism was the court's decision in *Church of the Holy Trinity* (1892). In this case, a church contracted with a pastor from England to be an employee in violation of a federal statute that prohibited employers from hiring foreign workers.[11] As a defense, the church argued that the statute does not apply to churches. In its ruling, the Supreme Court agreed with the church, appealing to the notion of the "spirit" of the law, writing that "It is a familiar rule, that a thing may be within the letter of the statute and yet not within the statute, because not within its spirit, nor within the intention of its makers."[12] For Scalia, *Holy Trinity* (1892) represents all that is wrong with legal interpretation when it departs from the text and appeals to "extratextual" sources to pursue its own policy agenda.[13] According to Scalia, the court's appeal to the spirit of the law was a "foolish" enterprise in "judicial lawmaking."[14]

On further inspection, however, the court's reasoning in *Holy Trinity* had also appealed to the textualist notion of "ordinary meaning," writing:

> The common understanding of the terms labor and laborers does not include preaching and preachers; and it is to be assumed that words and phrases are used in their ordinary meaning. So whatever of light is thrown upon the statute by the language of the title indicates an exclusion from its penal provisions of all contracts for the employment of ministers, rectors and pastors.[15]

According to the court, the spirit of the statute could be understood in terms of its "ordinary meaning"—precisely the same metric that Scalia advocated to illuminate the meaning of a law at its time of enactment. Nonetheless, Scalia rejected this interpretation of "ordinary meaning," concluding that the notion of the spirit of the law was simply an appeal to extratextual sources in order to legislate from the bench.

Given the above, it is perhaps surprising that Scalia—the architect of modern textualism—would endorse any conception of law as vague and "mystical" as an unwritten law of "the people" like von Savigny's conception of the *volkgeist* as the unwritten "spirit of the law." However, this is precisely what Scalia had argued in a series of speeches in 1988 and in later Supreme Court opinions. In a speech given to the Federalist Society at the University of Virginia in 1988, Scalia addressed four different senses of the meaning of an "unwritten constitution." The first sense refers to

> a system of customary and traditional laws or understanding either about how a government is to function or additionally about the rights and privileges of its citizens. The most famous unwritten constitution, that of Great Britain, represents just such a web of traditional expectations. . . . the British tradition, dating back as it does to Magna Carta, is especially striking and is often juxtaposed to our own supposed tradition of exclusively written constitutionalism. It is often said, and there may be some truth in this, that reliance on an unwritten web of custom and tradition is more feasible in a relatively homogeneous and insular country as Britain than it would be in the United States.[16]

Second, Scalia writes that the term can also refer to "the web of private law understandings that underlie and inform the meaning of many of the textual provisions in our written constitution," for example, the understanding of "property" in the Due Process Clause.[17] Third, an unwritten constitution may refer to the idea of a "living constitution" in which certain constitutional provisions or clauses "were intended to have and do have an evolving and unwritten meaning."[18] Here, Scalia cites the example of the Supreme Court's debate over the Eighth Amendment's Cruel and Unusual Punishments Clause and unreasonable searches and seizures. Finally, Scalia writes that an unwritten constitution can refer to

> the body of case law that has grown up around all the various constitutional clauses. Obviously, some of those cases have changed the understanding of many constitutional provisions in directions that were not necessarily preordained when the textual provisions were written. The judiciary's constitution, reinforce as it is by the doctrine of stare decisis, can arguably be described as an unwritten American Constitution, although throughout our history there has been disagreement as to whether judge-made fundamental law is a good thing.[19]

After surveying these four distinct meanings of an unwritten constitution, Scalia concludes:

> We undoubtedly have in this country an unwritten complement to our textual constitution, at least in some of the senses that I have described above . . . it is

unarguably a reality. Given that it is reality, however, how is it that that system of customary "law" (and I obviously agree with Hayek and Fuller that customary practices as well as statutory rules are at times accurately described as law) is to be enforced? It seems to me that the answer may well differ depending on the different meanings of the term unwritten constitution. Obviously, some unwritten social contractarian traditions, perhaps particularly those concerning structural expectations, are enforced by public opinion. . . . The unwritten constitution in other senses, however, is sometimes argued also to require judicial enforcement. It is at this point that debate often ensues. As Chief Justice John Marshall pointed out in *Marbury v. Madison*, judges are empowered under our Constitution to refuse to enforce laws when they contravene the constitutional text because that text is also law, is binding on the judges, and is a higher law than any other.[20]

In this remarkable speech, Scalia makes two strong claims. First, agreeing with Lon Fuller and Friedrich Hayek, Scalia argues that there is un "unwritten law" in the form of "customary practices" of the people. Second, in a more familiar textualist argument, Scalia argues that the text itself is also law, and judges are empowered to enforce the constitutional text as the highest law above all others.

Therefore, according to Scalia, the law may refer to *either* the explicit words of the text, *or* to the *unwritten* traditions or customs of a people. Scalia would openly argue for the *latter* conception of unwritten law in his dissenting opinion in *United States v. Virginia* (1996) in which the Supreme Court majority ruled that the Virginia Military Institute's policy of all-male admissions violated the Equal Protection Clause. In a lengthy dissent, Scalia presented an argument for the unwritten constitution, writing that

> But in my view the function of this Court is to preserve our society's values regarding (among other things) equal protection, not to revise them; to prevent backsliding from the degree of restriction the Constitution imposed upon democratic government, not to prescribe, on our own authority, progressively higher degrees. For that reason it is my view that, whatever abstract tests we may choose to devise, they cannot supersede—and indeed ought to be crafted so as to reflect—those constant and unbroken national traditions that embody the people's understanding of ambiguous constitutional texts. More specifically, it is my view that when a practice not expressly prohibited by the text of the Bill of Rights bears the endorsement of a long tradition of open, widespread, and unchallenged use that dates back to the beginning of the Republic, we have no proper basis for striking it down.[21]

In this way, Scalia adopted a view of an unwritten constitution strikingly similar to von Savigny's conception of the *volksrecht*—law as embodied in the traditional practices of the people. Interestingly, as Beiser explains, for von Savigny, the *volksrecht* had "a double life: in its fundaments it lives in the common consciousness of the people; but in it its more exact formulation and development it belongs to professional jurists."[22] As a consequence, for von Savigny's, this means that "jurisprudence itself becomes one form of the creation of law."[23] This more active role of the jurist in advancing the "spirit of the people" would seem to fly in the face of Scalia's textualism, which railed against the "activist" judges who took policy considerations into their own hands. However, in his early speeches, Scalia openly acknowledged himself as a self-proclaimed "activist" of sorts. Indeed, when it came to advancing the textualist-originalist views on legal interpretation, Scalia was open about his position, declaring:

> My views on statutory construction may similarly contravene what is the perceived conservative and hence the perceived federalist society view on such matters, because my views allow a role for judges that is seemingly at least, more—dare I use the word—activist.[24]

In a 1982 speech on "The Two Faces of Federalism," Scalia would argue that textualism is an activist, not a passive, force for judicial change. Commenting on the activist nature of textualism, Scalia writes:

> "We" (Conservatives) have been out-gunned at the federal level for 50 years. It has been the case that any federal intervention since the 1930s has tended to be intervention in a direction that we do not consider particularly desirable. The result, whatever the reasons, has been that we have ended up fighting a two-front war on only one front, or at least fighting it only defensively on one of the two fronts. When the statists are in power at the federal level, those who would impose regulation and controls, they do it. They have no embarrassment at the use of a federal structure that has been established by the people for the goals which they consider sound governmental goals. On the other hand, when conservatives are in power, the most they hope to do is to stop anything from happening. In the current administration, there are, I understand, in some offices, witty little signs on the wall that read, "Don't just stand there; undo something." That is good as far as it goes, but is it really far enough? Why should conservatives be limited to that kind of an approach to the federal government?[25]

In this way, Scalia openly advanced a kind of textualist judicial activism in rejecting the legislative purposes and intentions of the lawmakers and instead seizing upon the more elusive *unwritten* traditions of a people. This aspect of Scalia's textualism has not been sufficiently examined, as it stands at odds with Scalia's disparaging remarks toward both the notion of the "spirit of the law" and "activist" judges pursuing social policy through the law. According to most accounts, Scalia's textualism says that only the text rules, that we are a "government of text and not of unenacted intentions" and that judges must reject the "spirit of the law" as an interpretive guide for understanding the meaning of written text. However, in an early speech on "The Rule of Law," Scalia had advanced an argument in favor of the spirit of the law against the expansion of "legalism" into more areas of society, writing:

> The law is, after all, not a vindication of the nobility of man, but a constant reminder of his selfishness and frailty. It is a restraint against his acting the way he wishes, because left to his own he would not wish aright. . . . As St. Paul put it,—saying, perhaps the same thing as Lon Fuller—"the written law killeth, but the Spirit giveth life." In our most intimate association, in the context of our deepest commitments, we eschew the law. It is indeed a kinky bride and broom that sit down before their wedding to write out a detailed formal statement of their agreed rights and responsibilities. One may indeed go so far as to say that the more law a society has need of, the weaker the internal cohesion of the society is.[26]

Even in this early speech, Scalia made clear that the more written law a society has need for, the weaker that society's cohesion. Instead, the more "spirit" that exists in a society that binds together the community in the form of family, church, and private associations, the less a society has need for written laws. Again, this rather pessimistic view of written law might come as a surprise to observers of Scalia, since it stands at odds with the vision of Scalia as a strict reader of "the text itself" against the much-aligned "spirit of the law."

This relatively marginalized aspect of Scalia's "unwritten" textualism, I argue, reflects a crucial aspect of my argument, specifically, that it reflects the *sovereign exceptionalism* upon which the method of textualism is grounded. As Agamben defined the term via Schmitt, the sovereign refers to the power to decide on the exception.[27] As a practice of juridical interpretation, sovereign exceptionalism then refers to the authoritative selection of a single, determinate legal meaning by making arbitrary exceptions to a certain universe of legal meaning. For Scalia, a textualist judge may appeal to *any* of: (a) a dictionary definition of the explicit words of a text, (2) the "ordinary meaning" of a word using a variety of "public meanings" at the time, or (3) the unwritten "traditions" of the people. This textualist-originalist toolbox of legal meaning opens up a vast field of possible meanings that may be selected by sovereign decision to include by exclusion. As a result, *any* one of these selected meanings may be presented by the judge as the "neutral, objective" meaning of the text, without further justification for excluding other legal meanings. The decision to include the selected legal meaning is therefore simultaneously *exclusive* of those legal meanings the judge disfavors. In this way, the sovereign textualist makes determinations about legal meaning precisely by making exceptions to the universe of legal meaning. The textualist method of interpretation, therefore, *requires* the textualist judge to become a sovereign exceptionalist by selecting one "objective" meaning to the exclusion of others, without providing further legal justification.

## *ROMER V. EVANS* (1996)

Scalia's unwritten textualism played a major role in the Supreme Court's debate over a Colorado statewide ban on antidiscrimination policies protecting homosexuals. In 1992, Colorado voters approved "Amendment 2" to the state constitution that "prohibits all legislative, executive or judicial action at any level of state or local government designed to protect the named class, a class we shall refer to as homosexual persons or gays and lesbians."[28] Overnight, the entire bedrock of both private and public antidiscrimination statutes and provisions of Colorado law protecting homosexuals from discriminatory treatment were invalidated. The amendment was challenged on the basis that it violated the Equal Protection Clause of the Fourteenth Amendment. In a 6–3 opinion, Justice Anthony Kennedy concluded for the majority that "Amendment 2 classifies homosexuals not to further a proper legislative end but to make them unequal to everyone else. This Colorado cannot do. A State cannot so deem a class of persons a stranger to its laws. Amendment 2 violates the Equal Protection Clause."[29]

In a "vigorous" dissent, Justice Scalia advanced the textualist argument that since the original Constitutional text is silent on this issue, Coloradans are free to enact laws preserving traditional sexual mores or even expressing "animus" against homosexual conduct. Scalia wrote:

> Since the Constitution of the United States says nothing about this subject, it is left to be resolved by normal democratic means, including the democratic adoption of provisions in state constitutions. This Court has no business imposing upon all Americans the resolution favored by the elite class from which the Members of this institution are selected, pronouncing that "animosity" toward homosexuality . . . is evil. I vigorously dissent.[30]

Defending the "tolerance" of Coloradans and the animosity toward homosexuals, Scalia wrote:

> The Court has mistaken a Kulturkampf for a fit of spite. The constitutional amendment before us here is not the manifestation of a "bare . . . desire to harm"

homosexuals . . . but is rather a modest attempt by seemingly tolerant Coloradans to preserve traditional sexual mores against the efforts of a politically powerful minority to revise those mores through use of the laws.[31]

Because the text of the federal Constitution does not explicitly prohibit a state from enforcing traditional customs of sexuality, family, and marriage (as Scalia would argue in *Windsor*), the "people" of a state may constitutionally enact laws expressing "animus" and "hostility" toward certain kinds of conduct. As Scalia wrote:

> Of course it is our moral heritage that one should not hate any human being or class of human beings. But I had thought that one could consider certain conduct reprehensible—murder, for example, or polygamy, or cruelty to animals—and could exhibit even "animus" toward such conduct. Surely that is the only sort of "animus" at issue here: moral disapproval of homosexual conduct, the same sort of moral disapproval that produced the centuries-old criminal laws that we held constitutional in Bowers.[32]

Thus, Scalia concludes, the US Constitution allows states to enact laws expressing animus against homosexuals even though this legal form of animus or hostility did not rise to the level of harming an "insular minority": "But though Coloradans are, as I say, entitled to be hostile toward homosexual conduct, the fact is that the degree of hostility reflected by Amendment 2 is the smallest conceivable."[33]

In the aftermath of the Supreme Court's landmark ruling in *Lawrence v. Texas* (2003) invalidating a Texas statute criminalizing same-sex intimacy, Scalia would double down on his *Romer* dissent. In *Romer*, Scalia had cited the *Bowers v. Hardwick* (1986) precedent that had ruled constitutional a Georgia statute criminalizing consensual same-sex intimacy in the privacy of one's home. However, in *Lawrence v. Texas*, Justice Kennedy—another Reagan appointment—wrote a majority opinion overturning *Bowers* and invalidating state laws criminalizing such private conduct. In another strong dissent, Scalia advanced the argument that discriminatory laws targeting homosexuals should not be described as "discrimination," writing:

> Many Americans do not want persons who openly engage in homosexual conduct as partners in their business, as scoutmasters for their children, as teachers in their children's schools, or as boarders in their home. They view this as protecting themselves and their families from a lifestyle that they believe to be immoral and destructive. The Court views it as "discrimination" which it is the function of our judgments to deter. So imbued is the Court with the law profession's anti-anti-homosexual culture, that it is seemingly unaware that the attitudes of that culture

are not obviously "mainstream"; that in most States what the Court calls "discrimination" against those who engage in homosexual acts is perfectly legal.[34]

Lamenting the American Bar Association's acceptance of "the so-called homosexual agenda," Scalia defended state laws criminalizing such conduct by appealing once again to the traditional customs and mores of "the people" and "the moral opprobrium that has traditionally attached to homosexual conduct."[35]

Scalia continued to advance this position that animus against certain classes was not discrimination in his dissent in *United States v. Windsor*. In this landmark case, the Supreme Court struck down the Defense of Marriage Act (DOMA), which denied federal recognition to same-sex spouses. In this case, a surviving spouse in the State of New York was denied marital benefits of tax exemption, "which excludes from taxation 'any interest in property which passes or has passed from the decedent to his surviving spouse.'"[36] Once again writing for the majority, Kennedy explained why DOMA was unconstitutional:

> DOMA's history of enactment and its own text demonstrate that interference with the equal dignity of same-sex marriages, conferred by the States in the exercise of their sovereign power, was more than an incidental effect of the federal statute. It was its essence. . . . It frustrates New York's objective of eliminating inequality by writing inequality into the entire United States Code. . . . DOMA's principal effect is to identify and make unequal a subset of state-sanctioned marriages. It contrives to deprive some couples married under the laws of their State, but not others, of both rights and responsibilities, creating two contradictory marriage regimes within the same State.[37]

The seemingly straightforward application of the Fifth Amendment's Equal Protection and Due Process Clauses, according to the majority, prohibited the federal government from creating two "contradictory marriage regimes" granting different rights and privileges to different classes of individuals without a compelling government interest. However, once again writing a lengthy dissent, Scalia argue that "the Constitution does not forbid the government to enforce traditional moral and sexual norms."[38] For Scalia, excluding homosexuals from the government institution of marriage was not animus. Even though this time it was the *federal* government enforcing "tradition" or custom, the text of the federal constitution did not prohibit such a sweeping law. For Scalia, "That is not animus—just stabilizing prudence."[39] Once again relying upon the "unwritten" traditions of "the people," Scalia argued that DOMA "did no more than codify an aspect of marriage that had been unquestioned in our society for most of its existence—indeed, had been unquestioned in virtually all societies for virtually all of human history."[40] As Scalia had consistently argued since *Romer*, then, state *and* federal governments were constitutionally allowed to enact laws expressing "animus" against certain classes of individuals, and these legal measures were *not* "discrimination" but rather a kind of legal animus grounded in "tradition" and "customs" of the people.

## ORIGINALISM AS DISCRIMINATORY JUSTIFICATION

The legal history of originalism reveals that originalist arguments have been utilized to deny citizenship to Blacks and Asians,[41] and to deny women the right to vote under the pretext of an originalist reading of the word "citizens" "at the time of the adoption of the Constitution."[42] Professor Cass Sunstein, Christopher Eisgruber, and others have noted originalism's historical connection to the American history of discrimination. In *Dred Scott v. Sanford* (1857), Justice Taney explicitly utilized an originalist argument to exclude Scott from citizenship on the basis that the "original meaning" of "citizen" in the text of the constitution did not include slaves and went into excruciating detail in defending the exclusion of slaves from citizenship based on it. As Eisgruber writes, in *Dred Scott*, "Taney's application of originalism to the word 'property' was the engine of Scott's pro-slavery doctrine."[43] In this way, Justice Taney "premised his interpretation on the assumption that the Framers could not have intended the Constitution to incorporate a standard of conduct higher than the one they met."[44] Eisenbruber points out Abraham Lincoln's criticism of *Dred Scott,* observing that rather than objecting to the *Dred Scott* decision because it lacked "fidelity to the text" or the "original" understanding of the framers, "Lincoln's criticism of Scott emphasized the importance of construing the Constitution in a way consistent with moral principle."[45] He proceeds to compare Taney's originalist reasoning to Scalia's retooled originalism as outlined in his treatise *Reading Law* and in his published opinions. Eisenbruber concludes that, at best, Scalia shares with Justice Taney's pro-slavery doctrine an originalist dogma that exhibits a clear "indifference to injustice."[46] Eisenbruber writes:

> Originalism does not cease to be originalism when done badly. People who recommend originalism do so knowing that it, like any other approach, will have incompetent as well as competent disciples. Indeed, if originalism is a particularly difficult strategy to carry out (because, for example, the historical record is ambiguous), so that poor originalist arguments dominate good ones, that might be a reason to discount originalism's value as an interpretive strategy.[47]

However, Eisengruber also leaves open the real possibility that Taney and Scalia both found originalism attractive precisely because it allowed the interpreter to arrive at results they preferred, writing:

> Taney might have been lying: he might have invoked originalist arguments, knowing them to be wrong, in order to cover up an illegitimate conclusion that he reached on other grounds . . . if Taney fabricated his originalism as a disguise, he must have believed that originalism provided an especially fertile set of arguments to legitimate illegitimate conclusions.[48]

In a similar fashion, Professor Cass Sunstein describes Taney's use of originalism to justify slavery a case where "a supposed past historical judgment, itself not clearly embodied in the constitutional text, is used to foreclose democratic experimentation."[49] Sunstein compares the originalism used in *Dred Scott* to the originalist analysis that is currently used against affirmative action. Critiquing the "hubris" of using originalism to invalidate affirmative action, Sunstein writes that *Dred Scott* exhibited the same hubris:

> the Court purported to make the original intentions of the framers binding, even though those intentions were murky, did not compel the Court's conclusion, and were not in the Constitution itself. Perhaps worst of all, the Court deliberately reached out to decide nationally crucial issues that deserved and would ultimately receive an answer from the people rather than the judiciary.[50]

In this way, the legal history of originalism demonstrates that originalist arguments have often provided an appealing legal ground for denying expansion of rights and legal status to disfavored groups and minorities. By utilizing the backward-looking temporal framework of originalist methods, interpreters fix the package of rights for *all* individuals to a static point in time.

Scalia's justification for sanctioning discrimination against same-sex individuals was therefore grounded on the *temporal* regime specific to his originalism. He would later refer to this temporal function of originalism as enacting a "regime of static law."[51] In *Time and Law*, Francois Ost and Michel van de Kerchove identify distinct "temporalities" of law, understood as specific "rationalities" or configurations of time coded by the law. For Ost and Kerchove, "founding time" refers to the way in which law is thought in terms of a mythical, sacred origin that fixes a common identity of a nation, such as the Declaration of Independence.[52] "Timeless time" for them refers to legal rules and doctrines that are thought of as a kind of "static law" that is fixed and constant. As Mark van Hoecke observes, the specific method of originalism developed by Robert Bork and Justice Scalia can be aptly described as a regime of "timeless time,"[53] but for Scalia, originalism at times appeals to both "timeless time" and "founding time." Indeed, for Scalia, the original Constitution is precisely *the* founding document that unifies "the people" and without which there can be no "people." Scalia wrote:

> If one wishes to evoke the deep and enduring symbol of our nationhood and our unity as a people, it seems to me the toast ought to be, "Ladies and Gentlemen the Constitution of the United States." For that is the equivalent of the royal armies that brought forth one nation out of a diversity of states; and not only the token but indeed the substance of what continues to bind us together as a people.[54]

For Scalia, then, the constitution perfectly embodies a kind of founding time, but in its founding moment, the specific rules and provisions of the constitution are also *static*. Scalia argues that,

> until relatively recently the meaning of laws, including fundamental laws or constitution, was thought to be static. What vague provisions such as a right to "respect for . . . private life" or a right to "equal protection" meant at the time of the constitution's enactment could readily be determined (in most controversial areas) from the accepted and unchallenged practices that existed at the time. And what the constitution permitted at the time of its enactment it permitted forever; only the people could bring about change, by amending the constitution.[55]

Describing in detail the temporally "static" aspect of his textualist-originalism, Scalia writes that,

> under a regime of static law, it was not difficult to decide whether, under the American Constitution, there was a right to abortion, or to homosexual conduct, or to assisted suicide. When the constitution was adopted, all those acts were criminal throughout the United States, and remained so for several centuries; there was no credible argument that the Constitution made those laws invalid. Of course, society remained free to decriminalize those acts, as some States have; but under a static Constitution *judges* could not do so.[56]

However, according to Scalia, this notion of a static regime of law grounded in an unchanging, original constitution was eventually upended with the emergence of the notion of the "living constitution." Scalia laments:

> A change occurred in the last half of the 20th century, and I am sorry to say my Court was responsible for it. It was my Court that invented the notion of a "living Constitution." Beginning with the Cruel and Unusual Punishments Clause of our Eighth Amendment, we developed the doctrine that the meaning of Constitution could change over time, to comport with "the evolving standards of decency that mark the progress of a maturing society."[57]

According to Scalia's account, then, the rise of this notion of the living constitution ushered in all manner of novel legal rights and entitlements that were not found in the original text. Scalia writes, "On the basis of this theory, all sorts of entirely novel constitutional requirements were imposed, from the obligation to give a prior hearing before terminating welfare payments to the obligation to have law libraries in prison."[58] Therefore, according to Scalia, the best defense against the imposition of these novel constitutional requirements was precisely to enforce a regime of static law by reading the law in terms of its founding, timeless meaning, *not* in terms of the intentions of the legislators or purposes of Congress. Clarifying his own approach as distinct from the doctrine of "original intent," Scalia said in a speech in 1986:

> Statutes should be interpreted, it seems to me, not on the basis of the unpromulgated intentions of those who enact them . . . but rather on the basis of what is the most probable meaning of the *words* of the enactment. . . . In the interest of precision, however, I suppose I ought to campaign to change the label from the Doctrine of Original Intent to the Doctrine of Original Meaning. As I often tell my law clerks, terminology is destiny.[59]

Thus, the temporal function of textualist-originalism for Scalia was precisely its backwards-looking interpretation of law in both its founding and timeless aspects—a regime of static law. For him, this was the most defensible method for preventing progress and defending against the novel constitutional rights that were not originally in the text and that were beginning to emerge in the 1960s and 1970s.

## CONCLUSION

Scalia's dissent in *Windsor* appealed to a constant textualist principle dating back to his dissent in *Edwards v. Aguillard* examined in chapter 1. Scalia had consistently argued against the idea that judges should go "ferreting" after the hidden motives or discriminatory purposes behind a law. In *Windsor*, as in *Edwards,* Scalia argued once again that facially constitutional laws passed by a state legislature may not be invalidated due to an "alleged illicit motive," declaring that

> the contents of the legislators' hearts [are] quite irrelevant: "It is a familiar principle of constitutional law that this Court will not strike down an otherwise constitutional statute on the basis of an alleged illicit legislative motive. . . . Or at least it *was* a familiar principle. By holding to the contrary, the majority has

declared open season on any law that (in the opinion of the law's opponents and any panel of like-minded federal judges) can be characterized as mean-spirited.[60]

As Scalia argued, just because DOMA sought to preserve the traditional values and customs of the people, judges ought *not* to subject a facially constitutional text to a test for "discriminatory purpose" that motivated legislators. As Scalia had argued in *Edwards*, legislators take an oath of fidelity to the constitution, and their acts should be considered in good faith. Therefore, to go ferreting after the illicit motives behind a law was, for Scalia, not within the purview of nine unelected justices. Indeed, Scalia's selection of materials thus reflected his view that legal interpretation is concerned with the original reason or "rationality" (*ratio*) of the law embodied in the traditions of the people at its time of enactment, *not* the intentions or purposes of legislators.

Crucially, however, Scalia's originalism also entailed that "mean-spirited" laws expressing animus against certain classes of individuals were perfectly constitutional as long as it was not explicitly prohibited by the Constitution. Indeed, under a "regime of static law," the people were allowed to enact laws that expressed animus if that animus was part of the customs and traditions of the people and not textually prohibited. Therefore, the role of the judge for Scalia was to enforce the tradition, mores, and customs of the people through the law, and this, according to Scalia, was not discrimination so much as "prudent stability."

As I have argued, Scalia's originalist views on an "unwritten" constitution should be seen in light of the direct influence of von Savigny's German historicist school, in particular, his notion of the *volkgeist* as a confirmation of his view that the "reason" of law (*ratio*) could be embodied in the traditions of the people even if those traditions were "discriminatory." In this way, Scalia's critique of the "Humpty Dumpty" view of purposivist legal interpretation explored in chapter 1 can also be viewed in light of the philosophical distinction Scalia saw in the writings of von Savigny on the spirit of the people as embodied in traditional customs, values, and mores. Scalia's unwritten textualism can therefore be considered a kind of "customary time" (*le temps coutimier*)—a form of temporality Francois Ost identifies as prioritizing the "backwards-looking" customs, traditions, and practices of the people.[61] Scalia's originalism could claim that there is an "unwritten law" of the US Constitution,[62] a kind of "static regime of law." By exploring the influence of von Savigny on Scalia's unwritten textualist-originalism, we can better appreciate Scalia's endorsement of St. Paul's remarks that "the written law killeth, but the Spirit giveth life."[63]

As part 2 of the book explores in more detail, the temporality of Scalia's textualist-originalism can be accurately diagnosed as what Gerhart Husserl as an attitude of "hostility to progress," which manifested itself in Justice Scalia's opinions concerning the Voting Rights Act (chapters 4 and 5) and affirmative action (chapter 6).

## NOTES

1. Antonin Scalia, Statutory Interpretation [course material], circa 1980-1986. Antonin Scalia papers, LAW, MMC, 291, Series I, Sub-Series I, Box: 19, Folder: 4, Harvard Law School Library, Historical & Special Collections.
2. H. F. Jolowicz, *Roman Foundations of Modern Law* (Oxford: Clarendon Press; Oxford University Press, 1957).
3. Jolowicz, *Roman Foundations of Modern Law*, 15.
4. Jolowicz, *Roman Foundations of Modern Law*, 16.
5. Antonin Scalia and Bryan A. Garner, *Reading Law* (St. Paul: West Publishing 2012), 477.
6. Scalia and Garner, *Reading Law*, 465, 477.
7. Friedrick Charles von Savigny, *Of the Vocation of Our Age for Legislation and Jurisprudence*, trans. Abraham Hayward (London: Littlewood & Co. Old Bailey, 1831), 24.
8. von Savigny, *Of the Vocation of Our Age for Legislation and Jurisprudence*, 24.
9. Michel van de Kerchove and François Ost, *Le système juridique entre ordre et désordre* (Presses Universitaires de France: Paris 1988), 226.
10. Frederick C. Beiser, *The German Historicist Tradition* (Oxford: Oxford University Press, 2011), 250.
11. *Church of the Holy Trinity v. United States*, 143 U.S. 457.
12. *Church of the Holy Trinity v. United States*, 143 U.S. 457, 459 (1892).
13. Scalia, Common Law Courts in a Civil Law System, 19.
14. Scalia, Common Law Courts in a Civil Law System, 19.
15. *Church of the Holy Trinity v. United States*, 143 U.S. 457, 463 (1892).
16. Antonin Scalia, "U.V.A. Federalist Society Introduction," Federalist Society Symposium, Charlottesville, March 4, 1988, Antonin Scalia papers, LAW, MMC, 291, Series III, Box: 79, Folder: 1, Harvard Law School Library, Historical & Special Collections, 4.
17. Scalia, "U.V.A. Federalist Society Introduction," 5.
18. Scalia, "U.V.A. Federalist Society Introduction," 5.
19. Scalia, "U.V.A. Federalist Society Introduction," 5–6.
20. Scalia, "U.V.A. Federalist Society Introduction," 6–7.
21. *United States v. Virginia*, 518 U.S. 515, 568, 116 S. Ct. 2264, 2292 (1996).
22. Beiser, *The German Historicist Tradition*, 247.
23. Beiser, *The German Historicist Tradition*, 247.

24. Antonin Scalia, speech to the Federalist Society, January 30, 1987, Antonin Scalia papers, LAW, MMC, 291, Series III, Box: 77, Folder: 14, Harvard Law School Library, Historical & Special Collections, 66.

25. Antonin Scalia, "The Two Faces of Federalism," April student seminar - New Haven [Federalist Society], 1982, Antonin Scalia papers, LAW, MMC, 291, Series I, Sub-Series I, Box: 18, Folder: 19, Harvard Law School Library, Historical & Special Collections, 3–4.

26. Antonin Scalia, speech on "Rule of Law," 1970–1982, Antonin Scalia papers, LAW, MMC, 291, Series I, Sub-Series I, Box: 8, Folder: 7, Harvard Law School Library, Historical & Special Collections, 13.

27. Agamben, *State of Exception*, 21, 35.

28. *Romer v. Evans*, 517 U.S. 620, 624 (1996).

29. *Romer v. Evans*, 517 U.S. 620, 635 (1996).

30. *Romer v. Evans*, 517 U.S. 620, 636 (1996).

31. *Romer v. Evans*, 517 U.S. 620, 636 (1996).

32. *Romer v. Evans*, 517 U.S. 620, 644 (1996).

33. *Romer v. Evans*, 517 U.S. 620, 644 (1996).

34. *Lawrence v. Texas*, 539 U.S. 558, 602-03 (2003).

35. *Lawrence v. Texas*, 539 U.S. 558, 602 (2003).

36. *United States v. Windsor*, 570 U.S. 744, 753 (2013).

37. *United States v. Windsor*, 570 U.S. 744, 746-47 (2013).

38. *United States v. Windsor*, 570 U.S. 744, 795 (2013).

39. *United States v. Windsor*, 570 U.S. 744, 797 (2013).

40. *United States v. Windsor*, 570 U.S. 744, 797-98 2013).

41. *Scott v. Sandford*, 60 U.S. (19 How.) 393 (1857); *Ozawa v. United States*, 260 U.S. 178.

42. *Minor v. Happersett*, 88 U.S. (21 Wall.) 162, 167 (1874).

43. Christopher L. Eisgruber, "Dred Again: Originalism's Forgotten Past," *Constitutional Commentary* 141 (1993): 62.

44. Eisgruber, "Dred Again: Originalism's Forgotten Past," 47.

45. Eisgruber, "Dred Again: Originalism's Forgotten Past," 62.

46. Eisgruber, "Dred Again: Originalism's Forgotten Past," 62.

47. Eisgruber, "Dred Again: Originalism's Forgotten Past," 48.

48. Eisgruber, "Dred Again: Originalism's Forgotten Past," 48n.

49. Cass R. Sunstein, "Constitutional Myth-Making: Lessons from the Dred Scott Case," University of Chicago Law Occasional Paper, No. 37 (1996): 16.

50. Sunstein, "Constitutional Myth-Making," 23.

51. Antonin Scalia, "Judges as Propounders of Transcendent Moral Law," 2005, Antonin Scalia papers, LAW, MMC, 291, Series III, Box: 73, Folder: 3, Harvard Law School Library, Historical & Special Collections.

52. François Ost, *L'instantané ou l'institué? L'institué ou l'instituant? Le droit a-t-il pour vocation de durer?* in Sous la direction de François Ost et Mark Van Hoecke, *Temps et droit. Le droit a-t-il pour vocation de durer?* (Bruxelles: Bruylant, 1998), 7–14.

53. Mark van Hoecke, "Time & Law - Is It the Nature of Law to Last? A Conclusion," in *Time and Law (Le Temps et Le Droit)*, ed. F. Ost (Brussel: Bruylant, 1998), 451–69.

54. Antonin Scalia, "Reflections on the Constitution," University of Kentucky Law Lecture, September 14, 1988, Antonin Scalia papers, LAW, MMC, 291, Series III, Box: 79, Folder: 22, Harvard Law School Library, Historical & Special Collections, 1.

55. Scalia, "Judges as Propounders of Transcendent Moral Law," 9.

56. Scalia, "Judges as Propounders of Transcendent Moral Law," 10.

57. Scalia, "Judges as Propounders of Transcendent Moral Law," 10.

58. Scalia, "Judges as Propounders of Transcendent Moral Law," 10.

59. Antonin Scalia, speech on original intent [submitted as part of nomination questionnaire], 1986, delivered at the Attorney General's Conference on Economic Liberties, June 14, 1986, Antonin Scalia papers, LAW, MMC, 291, Series I, Box: 26, Folder: 11, Harvard Law School Library, Historical & Special Collections, 2, 6.

60. *United States v. Windsor*, 570 U.S. 744, 795 (2013).

61. van de Kerchove and Ost, *Le système juridique entre ordre et désordre*, 226.

62. Scalia, "U.V.A. Federalist Society Introduction," 6–7.

63. Antonin Scalia, speech on "The Rule of Law," 1970–1982, Antonin Scalia papers, LAW, MMC, 291, Series I, Sub-Series I, Box: 8, Folder: 7, Harvard Law School Library, Historical & Special Collections, 13.

## Part II

# "A REGIME OF STATIC LAW"

In the John M. Olin Lecture on Political Economy at the Wharton School at the University of Pennsylvania, on April 25, 1986, Scalia argued that judges have a specific temporal role to play in the development of law. For Scalia, textualist judges eschew future-oriented policy questions in interpreting legal meaning and also serve a more active temporal function, namely that of *preventing progress*. For Scalia,

> anyone who looks to the judges for leadership into new terrain is bound to be disappointed. If not universal, it is both the nature and the assigned role of judges to prevent progress. To the extent that their role is expanded, "progress" or perhaps not to be judgmental, change will be slight rather than accelerated.[1]

For Scalia, the judge should never consider the question of whether the law would be more just for the future of the community. Instead, the backwards-looking "objective manifestation" of the law at its time of enactment was always controlling. As Scalia writes, "As a judge you are reacting, you do not initiate policies."[2] Rather than interpreting law in terms of its *present* or *future* policy purpose, Scalia writes, the judge must instead interpret the meaning of law in terms of "what society at the time believed. What was its objective manifestation to that society?"[3] For Scalia, therefore, the judge's temporal role was to recover the "original meaning" of the law at a previous point in time according to the "traditional practices" of the people. As Scalia clarified in an unpublished speech, "I favor an approach called originalism, the basic tenets of which are twofold: (1) adhere to the text, and (2) Give text the meaning it bore when it was adopted."[4] In this way, Scalia argued, judges are in a very real sense *bound* to "prevent progress" by preserving the "original meaning" of the law against attempts to "update" the meaning according to the evolving views of society or judges themselves. In a speech titled "Judges as Propounders of Transcendent Moral Law," Scalia criticized what he saw as the "activist" agenda of judges that sought to update the meaning of the Constitution according to the evolving views of society. Instead, Scalia advocated a temporal role of the originalist judge as enacting a "regime of static law."[5]

For Scalia, however, the court's jurisprudence on rights since the 1960s had departed from this originalist position to prevent progress. Instead, the court had "liberated" itself from the text and the "traditions of the people," establishing novel constitutional rights grounded in "meaningless mumbo-jumbo." Specifically, Scalia had argued that the court's "substantive due process" jurisprudence beginning in *Griswold v. Connecticut* (1967) was responsible for the creation of new constitutional rights that were at odds with the "historical practices of the American people." In an unpublished speech, Scalia wrote:

> It is no exaggeration to say that, under the Supreme Court's current jurisprudence, the United States Constitution contains whatever unenumerated rights the Supreme Court believes it ought to contain. Insofar as the creation of new rights is concerned, the Justices are entirely liberated from the text of the Constitution, and even from the historical practices of the American people.[6]

These novel constitutional rights created by the court's substantive due process cases included the right to contraceptives, the right to marry a person of another race, the right to abortion, and the right to marry another person of the same sex. None of these rights, for Scalia, were grounded in the "original meaning" of the Constitution or the "traditional practices of the American people." According to Justice Scalia, the very term "substantive due process" was a term "so self-congratulatory that it invites ridicule . . . and so mindless that it could only be used by a lawyerly caste inured to meaningless mumbo-jumbo."[7] For Scalia, this was judicial "progress" run amok. Rather than upholding the judicial duty to "prevent progress" and enact a regime of "static law," the court was doing just the opposite—pursuing progress by updating the meaning of the law according to prevailing social conditions and views of society.

Part 2 of the book demonstrates that Scalia's view of legal interpretation and the role of the judiciary adopts a very specific way of thinking about time. The overall argument is that Scalia's textualist-originalism is a judicial philosophy with a specific temporal objective: to prevent progress by enforcing a regime of static law. As chapter 4 documents, the temporality of this judicial attitude was first described by Gerhart Husserl in his analysis of the purely past-oriented judge as an "enemy of progress." Textualist-originalism operates according to the temporal regimes of what Ost and van der Kerchove call "founding time" and "customary time." For them, "founding time" refers to a backwards-looking temporal regime that fixes the static meaning of law to a sacred, "original meaning" embodied in traditional practices of "the people." A temporal regime of sacred, founding time, therefore, also allows the judge to search for and fix the meaning of law to the historical practices of the people—a central premise of "customary time" that fixes legal meaning to the past customs of the people. Crucially, under Scalia's self-described method of textualist-originalism, a text may be interpreted in terms of a contemporaneous dictionary definition or "original public meanings" of the term ("founding time"), and/or an "unwritten" law embodied in the traditions of the people ("customary time"). Together, Scalia's textualist-originalism couples two alternating temporal regimes, allowing a judge a wide hermeneutic universe of meaning within which to interpret a variety of written *or* unwritten texts, dictionary definitions, customs, traditions, and practices might be selected as the "controlling" point of fixed, "founding time." As a result, the textualist-originalist necessarily becomes a *sovereign exceptionalist* who determines unilaterally what the "objective" meaning of legal texts and rules are, simply by his sovereign exclusion. The argument of part 2, therefore, supports the thesis of part 1 of the book, namely that textualist-originalism uses a kind of sovereign exceptionalism in making unilateral, arbitrary exclusions from the meaning of the law. Every textualist is, by definition, a sovereign exceptionalist.

By illuminating the temporal aspect of textualist-originalism, we can better appreciate the effect Scalia's judicial philosophy has had on antidiscrimination jurisprudence on the Supreme Court. As chapter 3 showed, Scalia's originalism rejects the notion of an historical, legislative purpose of law in favor of the reason (*ratio*) of static law embodied in either text or traditions of the people. Therefore, originalism rejects the ferreting out of discriminatory motives in the process of legal interpretation. Chapter 4 continues this theme by examining Scalia's dissenting opinion in *Reno v. Bossier* (2000) and his attack on the "purpose" of the Voting Rights Act (VRA), which led to the court's invalidation of Section 5 of the VRA in *Shelby County v. Holder* (2013). Chapter 5 then shows how Scalia's attack on the VRA provided precedent for the court's decision in *Abbott v. Perez* (2018) barring the past discrimination of a legislature as evidence of a *present* legislative intent. Chapter 6 examines the court's decision in *Students for Fair Admission v. Harvard* (2023) invalidating affirmative action, demonstrating how the court's "race-neutral" reading of the text severs the constitutional memory of the law. The court's decision in that case represents the culmination of the success of Scalia's textualist-originalist methods in rejecting and severing the "memory" of discrimination from the meaning of the text—precisely the conditions necessary for *malevolent legalities*. In this regard, textualist-originalism constitutes a temporal regime that, in Scalia's own words, "prevents progress" by enacting a "static regime of law." This is the argument I call "Scalia's Argument for Preventing Progress."

## NOTES

1. Antonin Scalia, John M. Olin Lecture Series on Political Economy, Wharton School, University of Pennsylvania, John M. Olin series, April 25 1986, Antonin Scalia papers, LAW, MMC, 291, Series III, Box: 76, Folder: 28, Harvard Law School Library, Historical & Special Collections, 3.
2. Scalia, John M. Olin Lecture Series on Political Economy, 5.
3. Scalia, John M. Olin Lecture Series on Political Economy, 17–18.
4. Antonin Scalia, Speech "55" [Speeches, unidentified], circa 1975–2016, Antonin Scalia papers, LAW, MMC, 291, Series III, Box: 73, Folder: 4, Harvard Law School Library, Historical & Special Collections, 1.
5. Antonin Scalia, "Judges as Propounders of Transcendent Moral Law," 2005, Antonin Scalia papers, LAW, MMC, 291, Series III, Box: 73, Folder: 3, Harvard Law School Library, Historical & Special Collections.
6. Scalia, Speech "55" [Speeches, unidentified], 5.
7. Scalia, Speech "55" [Speeches, unidentified], 3.

# 4

## *Reno v. Bossier Parish* (2000)

"Preventing Progress"

In this chapter, I argue that Scalia's textualist opposition to the progressive congressional purpose of the Voting Rights Act was an extension of Scalia's originalist approach to constitutional rights—a judicial position Gerhart Husserl first accurately described in *Recht und Zeit* (1955) as an "enemy of progress." In what follows, I review Scalia's majority opinion in *Reno v. Bossier Parish* (2000) and his court's invalidation of Section 5 of the VRA in *Shelby County v. Holder* (2013). By examining the confrontation between Scalia's court and Congress, we see how Scalia's textualist-originalism explicitly seeks to "prevent progress" and therefore exhibits what Husserl called a judicial attitude of hostility to progress [*Fortschrittsfeindlichkeit*].

In a speech delivered in 1986 just prior to his nomination to the Supreme Court, Scalia had argued that judges, in his view, served a specific temporal function in the development of law. For Scalia, advancing social progress through policy was the domain of the legislature and not the judiciary. However, Scalia went further than this. Speaking about the role of law in advancing social change, Scalia wrote that "it is both the nature and the assigned role of judges to prevent progress."[1] For Scalia, a textualist judges are well aware of the progressive social purposes of many congressional acts, but textualism requires such judges restrain themselves from pursuing those purposes. Scalia writes:

> To be a textualist in good standing, one need not be too dull to perceive the broader social purposes that a statute is designed, or could be designed, to serve. . . . One need only hold the belief that judges have no authority to pursue those broader purposes or write those new laws.[2]

Here, Scalia's rejection of "purposivism," explored in chapter 1, became crucial. Scalia had ardently rejected the "legal process" doctrine of Hart and Sacks, who had argued that

> Law is . . . a purposive activity, a continuous striving to solve the basic problems of social living. . . . Underlying every rule and standard, in other words, is at the least a policy and in most cases a principle. This principle or policy is always available to guide judgment in resolving uncertainties about the arrangement's meaning.[3]

However, Scalia's rejection of purposivism appeared to go well beyond just a theory about the meaning of legal texts. In remarks as early as 1986, Scalia was taking antipurposivism a step further. In Scalia's view, a judge should not only refrain from using legislative purpose to understand the meaning of a text but also actively work *against* progress. The role of the judge is to slow things down and prevent progress, not advance social policy. This more "activist" position held that judges *ought* to be preventing progress by enforcing the "original" meaning that Scalia would later refer to as a "regime of static law."[4]

Scalia's "activist" originalism therefore clashed directly with congressional acts that explicitly sought to make progress on racial discrimination in voting, education, housing, and many other areas. This led to an intractable confrontation: whereas Congress had sought since the 1965 for the Voting Rights Act to make progressive changes addressing racial discrimination in voting,[5] according to Scalia, judges ought to prevent such progress as required by their role in a system of checks and balances. Scalia's activist antipurposivism had a deleterious effect on one particular social policy: voting rights. In *Shelby County v. Holder*, Scalia joined a majority in invalidating Section 5 of the Voting Rights Act. As authorized by Congress, Section 5 of the VRA required many former Confederate states in the South with a discriminatory history to submit any changes to their voting redistricting plans to the federal government for "preclearance" to ensure compliance with the nondiscrimination provisions of the Fourteenth Amendment. In a dissenting opinion in *Shelby County v. Holder*, Justice Ginsburg had pointed out the court's invalidation of Section 5 directly frustrated Congress's progressive purposes. Ginsburg writes:

> In the Court's view, the very success of §5 of the Voting Rights Act demands its dormancy. Congress was of another mind. Recognizing that large progress has been made, Congress determined, based on a voluminous record, that the scourge of discrimination was not yet extirpated.[6]

Indeed, just years prior in its reauthorization of the VRA in 2006, Congress had openly chastised the Supreme Court's previous rulings that had directly frustrated its intent in advancing the historical purpose of the VRA. As Congress has repeatedly clarified in its reauthorizations of the bill since 1965, the purpose of the VRA is directly tied to the Fourteenth and Fifteenth

Amendments' aim of removing the historical vestiges of slavery. However, dating back to *Chisom v. Roemer* (1991), Scalia's textualist method openly rejected interpreting laws according to their legislative purpose or intent. For Scalia, the VRA was not an "all-purpose weapon for well-intentioned judges to wield as they please in the battle against discrimination."[7] Therefore, according to Scalia's textualist judicial philosophy, the meaning of the VRA should *not* be understood by reference to the extensive legislative history that informs the purpose of its antidiscrimination provisions grounded in the Fourteenth and Fifteenth Amendments. As Scalia made perfectly clear in *Chisom v. Roemer*, "We are here to apply the statute, not legislative history, and certainly not the absence of legislative history. Statutes are the law though sleeping dogs lie."[8]

This confrontation between Congress and a Scalia-led majority on the court therefore stemmed from Scalia's activist originalism that sought to prevent progress by enforcing a temporal regime of "static law." In what follows, I review Scalia's majority opinion in *Reno v. Bossier Parish* and the congressional response, which ended with the invalidation of Section 5 of the VRA in *Shelby County v. Holder*.

## *RENO V. BOSSIER PARISH* (2000)

Bossier Parish is a jurisdiction in Louisiana that was covered by Section 5 of the VRA, a provision enacted by Congress requiring certain state voting schemes to be precleared by the federal government. In 2011, the US District Court of the District of Columbia explained the origins and rationale of Section 5:

> Section 5 constituted a direct response to the "common practice in some jurisdictions of staying one step ahead of the federal courts by passing new discriminatory voting laws as soon as the old ones had been struck down.". . . Prior to 1965, such novel methods of minority disenfranchisement would continue to operate "until the Justice Department or private plaintiffs were able to sustain the burden of proving that the new law, too, was discriminatory." But with the passage of Section 5, Congress "shift[ed] the advantage of time and inertia from the perpetrators of the evil to its victim," (*Katzenbach*, 383 U.S. at 328). Rather than requiring minority voters to sue to challenge discriminatory voting practices after their implementation, Section 5 places the burden on covered jurisdictions to show their voting changes are nondiscriminatory before those changes can be put into effect.[9]

Section 2 of the VRA claims of discrimination may be raised only after a discriminatory voting scheme has been implemented and done harm. In contrast, Congress enacted Section 5 so that challenges could be raised to voting schemes *before* they could be implemented by discriminatory actors seeking to disenfranchise voters. Under the VRA, a districting scheme is unconstitutional if it "discriminates by abridging the rights of minority voters to participate in the political process and elect candidates of their choice."[10] As Justice Scalia noted in the majority opinion of *Reno*, under the rules of Section 5, districts are

> prohibited from enacting any change in "voting qualification or prerequisite to voting, or standard, practice, or procedure with respect to voting," without first obtaining either administrative preclearance from the Attorney General or judicial preclearance from the United States District Court for the District of Columbia.[11]

According to the VRA, a vote dilution claim may arise from "cracking" (dividing neighborhoods up by race to avoid creating a racial majority district), or "packing" (concentrating households in a district by race to weaken voting power in other districts). As the court explained, "the benchmark of dilution pure and simple is thus a system in which every minority voter has as good a chance at political participation and voting effectiveness as any other voter."[12] Thus, practices of packing or cracking reduce the voting effectiveness of the targeted group and result in a violation of the VRA.

In 1991, the Bossier Parish School Board submitted a voting redistricting plan that diluted the voting power of the 20 percent African American minority living in the district. In *Bossier II,* the Bossier Parish School Board's voting scheme had been previously shown to have

> diluted black votes by dividing neighboring black communities with common interests in and around at least two of the Parish's municipalities, thereby avoiding the creation of a black-majority district. . . . Even the Board's own cartographer conceded that one of these instances "appeared" to constitute "fracturing," . . . which he defined as "dividing a 'population that has a traditional cohesiveness, lives in the same general area, [and] has a lot of commonalties' . . . with '[the] intent to . . . fracture that population into adjoining white districts,'" *id.,* at 189a-190a (Stipulation 133).[13]

As the court noted, the school board itself conceded the impact of their voting scheme "falling 'more heavily on blacks than on whites,'. . . and in diluting 'black voting strength,' *id.*, at 21. Even without the stipulated history, the conceded dilution would be evidence of a correspondingly discriminatory intent."[14]

However, writing for the majority, Justice Scalia argued that unlawful discrimination under a VRA vote dilution claim must be "retrogressive"— that is, the discriminatory scheme must be *worse* than the previous voting scheme. As a result, if the voting scheme merely perpetuates the same level of discriminatory effect as the previous scheme, there can be no finding of "present" discriminatory intent. Scalia writes:

> Our cases have also recognized retrogression as a subspecies of dilution, the consequence of a scheme that not only gives a minority voter a lesser practical chance to participate and elect than a majority voter enjoys, but even reduces the minority voter's practical power what a preceding scheme of electoral law provided.[15]

According to Scalia's majority, there was not enough evidence that the new voting scheme was enacted with discriminatory intent and that "the Board had legitimate, nondiscriminatory reasons for approving the plan."[16] Rather, the court argued that Section 5 of the VRA only prevents "backsliding," that is, a voting scheme that makes things *worse*. For the court, this means that Section 5 does *not* prohibit a voting scheme that merely maintains the *status quo*. Writing for the majority, Scalia concludes, "§5 does not prohibit preclearance of a redistricting plan enacted with a discriminatory but nonretrogressive purpose."[17]

In a series of dissenting opinions, Justices Stevens, Ginsburg, Breyer, and Souter argued that the court's ruling would lead to the preclearance of voting schemes intentionally designed by bad faith actors to perpetuate status quo discrimination. By allowing voting schemes that perpetuate the status quo, the court was effectively sanctioning discrimination in voting by the very same bad faith actors that have sought to evade the Voting Rights Act since its enactment in 1965. As the dissent documented in detail, Bossier Parish "had applied its energies for decades in an effort to 'limit or evade' its obligation to desegregate the Parish schools."[18] In a joint dissent, Souter, Ginsburg, and Bryer argued that there was more than enough evidence of a "present" discriminatory intent, documenting the parish's history of resistance to remedying discrimination and the events leading up to the adoption of the new voting scheme. Arguing for the dissent, the justices write,

> for decades the School Board manifested sedulous resistance to the constitutional obligation to desegregate parish schools, which have never attained unitary status and are still subject to court order. When faced with the need to act alone in redrawing its voting districts, the Board showed no interest in the Police Jury plan, which made no sense for school purposes and was at odds with normal districting principles applied by the Board. The Board hired

a cartographer in anticipation of drawing district lines significantly different from the Policy Jury lines, and the Attorney General's preclearance of the Police Jury plan for the Jury's use produced no apparent Board interest in adopting that same plan. When minority leaders sought a role in proposing a plan, the Board ignored them and when they produced concrete proposals prepared by the NAACP, the Board sidestepped with successive technical reasons culminating in a patently pretextual objection. It was only then, as its pretexts for resisting the NAACP were wearing thin, that the Board evidently scrapped its intention to obtain an original plan tailored to school district concerns and acted with unwonted haste on the year-old proposal to adopt the manifestly unsuitable Police Jury plan. The proposal received no public hearing support and nothing but objection from minority voters, who pointed out what the Board now agrees, that the Police Jury plan dilutes minority voting strength. The objections were unavailing and the Board adopted the dilutive plan.[19]

After a careful review of the historical record, the dissent concludes that

the behavior of Bossier Parish is a plain effort to deny the voting equality that the Constitution just as plainly guarantees. The point of § 5 is to thwart the ingenuity of the School Board's effort to stay ahead of challenges under § 2. Its object is to bring the country closer to transcending a history of intransigence to enforcement of the Fifteenth Amendment. Now, however, the promise of § 5 is substantially diminished. Now executive and judicial officers of the United States will be forced to preclear illegal and unconstitutional voting schemes patently intended to perpetuate discrimination. The appeal to federalism is no excuse.[20]

Therefore, according to the dissent, Scalia's majority in *Bossier II* had effectively allowed discriminatory voting schemes to be enacted by the very states and districts that had sought to perpetuate discrimination and led to Congress's enactment of the VRA in the first place.

## THE CONGRESSIONAL RESPONSE

The congressional response to *Reno v. Bossier* was dramatic. In 2006, Congress was forced to intervene to correct the court's misinterpretation of the purpose of Voting Rights Act. In its reauthorization of the VRA, Congress chastised the court's interpretation of the congressional purpose of the VRA, noting that Scalia's majority had opened the door for discriminatory voting schemes as long as those schemes did not "make things worse." Taking aim at the court's weakening of the VRA in *Bossier*, Congress observed that

The effectiveness of the Voting Rights Act of 1965 has been significantly weakened by the United States Supreme Court decisions in *Reno v. Bossier Parish II* and *Georgia v. Ashcroft*, which have misconstrued Congress' original intent in enacting the Voting Rights Act of 1965 and narrowed the protections afforded by section 5 of such Act.[21]

In its accompanying congressional report to the reauthorization bill, the Senate Judiciary Committee also criticized the actions of the court, observing:

The Supreme Court's decision in *Bossier Parish II* has created a strange loophole in the law: it is possible that the Justice Department or federal court could be required to approve an unconstitutional voting practice "taken with the purpose of racial discrimination." Testimony of Nina Perales, Renewing the Temporary Provisions of the Voting Rights Act: Legislative Options after *LULAC v. Perry*, Hrg. before the Subcommittee on the Constitution, Civil Rights, and Property Rights of the Senate Judiciary Committee (July 13, 2006). "After Bossier Parish II, the Supreme Court has directed preclearance authorities to permit changes that have an unconstitutional, racially discriminatory purpose as long as the purpose is simply to perpetuate unconstitutional conditions and not to make them actually worse." Pamela S. Karlan, Responses to Written Questions from Sen. Kennedy (submitted for May 16, 2006 hearing). The federal government should not be giving its seal of approval to practices that violate the Constitution. Under this amendment, which forbids voting changes motivated by "any discriminatory purpose," it will not do so.[22]

Because of the Supreme Court's misreading of the purpose of the VRA, Congress clarified that the Congress's intent in enacting the VRA was to prohibit "any discriminatory purpose" that abridges the voting power and rights of minorities. In its own report, the House Judiciary Committee explained that the Supreme Court's weakening of the "purpose" test of the VRA "had been inconsistent with Congress's intent that Section 5 prevent not only purposefully retrogressive discriminatory voting changes, but also those voting changes that 'purposefully' keep minority groups 'in their place.'"[23]

The court's woeful "misconstruing" of Congress's intent violated several fundamental "textualist" principles of statutory interpretation outlined in Scalia and Garner's treatise on *Reading Law*. To start with, the court had completely ignored Scalia's own "Constitutional-Doubt Canon," which states, "The statute should be interpreted in a way that avoids placing its constitutionality in doubt."[24] Rather than affording the text of the VRA an interpretation that avoided placing its constitutionality in doubt, the court invalidated an act of Congress by misconstruing its stated purpose. Second, the court violated the Scalia's canon of construction known as the "Presumption Against Ineffectiveness," which states that "A textually permissible interpretation that furthers rather that obstructs the document's purpose should be favored."[25] According to Scalia, this canon of interpretation "ensures that a text's manifest purpose is furthered, not hindered."[26] This canon of interpretation was not only brazenly violated by Scalia's majority in *Bossier* but turned on its head: instead of examining and preserving Congress's stated purpose of the VRA in the extensive legislative history, Scalia's majority ensured that the stated legislative purpose of the VRA was hindered. As Congress declared in its reauthorization bill of 2006, the *Bossier* court "misconstrued Congress' original intent in enacting the Voting Rights Act of 1965 and narrowed the protections afforded by section 5 of such Act."[27] Finally, by subverting this canon of interpretation, the court was also violating Scalia's canon known as the "Presumption of Validity," which states that "An interpretation that validates outweighs one that invalidates."[28] Rather than giving the text of the Voting Rights Act an interpretation that validates, Scalia's majority gave one that "would nullify the provision or the entire instrument."[29]

While Congress corrected the court's misreading in its VRA reauthorization in 2006, Section 5 of the VRA would be challenged again and found unconstitutional just several years later in *Shelby County v. Holder*. In this way, Scalia's attack on the VRA's notion of "discriminatory purpose" in *Reno v. Bossier* returned in 2013, further weakening the antidiscrimination provisions of the VRA.

## SHELBY COUNTY V. HOLDER (2013)

Within days of Congress's reauthorization of the VRA in 2006, a district in Texas filed a challenge to the constitutionality of Section 5.[30] After a district court ruled against it, Shelby County in Alabama filed an identical challenge. In its 2011 ruling, a federal appeals court ruled against the district by giving deference to Congress's intent in enacting the VRA, but in 2013, the Supreme Court granted certiori in *Shelby County v. Holder*. In 2012, the US Court of Appeals for the District of Columbia had documented the voluminous record of discrimination that Congress had accumulated to justify Section 5. Ruling in favor of maintaining Section 5 as Congress intended, the district court had pointed out just a small sample of the voluminous record Congress had gathered: a Mississippi city canceling their 2001 election when "an unprecedented number" of African Americans ran for office; a Georgia county's 1998 proposal "to reduce the black population in three of the education board's five single-member districts after the school district elected a majority black school board for the first time"; Mississippi's attempt in 1995 to revive a dual registration system enacted originally in 1892 to disenfranchise black voters; a Louisiana Parish's 1993 attempt to reduce the voting power of African Americans by "immediately creat[ing] a new at-large seat to ensure that no white incumbent would lose his seat"; a Texas County's 2004 attempt to reduce early voting in polling locations surrounding a historically black university coupled with threats to prosecute and dissuade black students from running.[31] During its sampling of the congressional record of voting discrimination by local municipalities in the South, the court noted some other egregious examples:

> In Mississippi, for instance, state legislators opposed an early 1990s redistricting plan that would have increased the number of black majority districts, referring to the plan publicly as the "black plan" and privately as the "nigger plan". . . . In Georgia, the state House Reapportionment Committee Chairman "told his colleagues on numerous occasions, 'I don't want to draw nigger districts,'" H.R. Rep. No. 109-478, at 67 (quoting *Busbee v. Smith*, 549 F. Supp. 494, 501 (D.D.C. 1982)). The district court pointed to numerous additional examples of intentional discrimination in the legislative record.[32]

As a result of this congressional record of persistent voting discrimination, the district court had ruled that these findings "support Congress's conclusion that intentional racial discrimination in voting remains so serious and widespread in covered jurisdictions that section 5 preclearance is still needed."[33] Further, in *Shelby County*, Justice Ginsburg had conducted an even more extensive review of the congressional record documented in its 2006 reauthorization of Section 5. Ginsburg summarized the revealing findings of Congress:

> All told, between 1982 and 2006, DOJ objections blocked over 700 voting changes based on a determination that the changes were discriminatory. H. R. Rep. No. 109-478, at 21. Congress found that the majority of DOJ objections included findings of discriminatory intent, see 679 F. 3d, at 867, and that the changes blocked by preclearance were "calculated decisions to keep minority voters from fully participating in the political process." H. R. Rep. No. 109-478, at 21. On top of that, over the same time period DOJ and private plaintiffs succeeded in more than 100 actions to enforce the §5 preclearance requirements.[34]

In her dissent, Ginsburg noted that the sheer number of discriminatory voting schemes that were blocked by Section 5 "suggests that the state of voting rights in the covered jurisdictions would have been significantly different absent this remedy."[35] Ginsburg once reviewed the laundry list of discriminatory voting practices pursued by local municipalities in the South by adding to the list that the district court had reviewed in 2012. Ginsburg noted again the examples Congress had gathered to justify Section 5 challenges to discrimination in voting: a Georgia city's 2000 redistricting plan that reduced the black voting strength in the city as a whole; Texas's 2006 attempt to redraw a congressional district to reduce the voting power of Latinos; a South Carolina county's plan to reintroduce an unconstitutional voting scheme after African Americans had just won a majority of seats on the school board for the first time in its history; a Georgia city's 1993 plan to delay elections in a majority-black district by two years and to move polling locations from black neighborhoods to inaccessible locations in a predominantly white neighborhood outside city limits; and an Alabama county's 1990 plan to purge its voter rolls of black voters for simply failing to pick up a voter update form.[36] After documenting the additional examples of Congress's record of discriminatory voting schemes, Ginsburg concluded, "These examples, and scores more like them, fill the pages of the legislative record. The evidence was indeed sufficient to support Congress's conclusion that "racial discrimination in voting in covered jurisdictions [remained] serious and pervasive."[37]

With respect to the Alabama district at issue in *Shelby County*, Ginsburg noted that between 1982 and 2005, Alabama and its neighbor Mississippi had the two highest rates of Section 2 VRA violations of voting rights. Ginsburg observed the startling fact that even though Alabama was already subject to VRA preclearance requirements, "Alabama was found to have "deni[ed] or abridge[d]" voting rights "on account of race or color" more frequently than nearly all other States in the Union."[38] As a result, Ginsburg concluded that "Alabama's sorry history of §2 violations alone provides sufficient justification for Congress' determination in 2006 that the State should remain subject to §5's preclearance requirement."[39]

However, in a majority opinion joined by Scalia, the court invalidated Section 5 of the VRA as unconstitutional. Writing for the majority, Chief Justice Roberts argued that voting discrimination was a thing of the past, and thus Congress's coverage formula for requiring voting schemes to be precleared "had no logical relation" to "present conditions," writing:

> The Fifteenth Amendment is not designed to punish for the past; its purpose is to ensure a better future. To serve that purpose, Congress—if it is to divide the States—must identify those jurisdictions to be singled out on a basis that makes sense in light of current conditions.[40]

As to the voluminous record of voting discrimination Congress had compiled, the court wrote:

> Respondents also rely heavily on data from the record compiled by Congress before reauthorizing the Act. Regardless of how one looks at that record, no one

can fairly say that it shows anything approaching the "pervasive," "flagrant," "widespread," and "rampant" discrimination that clearly distinguished the covered jurisdictions from the rest of the Nation in 1965. . . . But a more fundamental problem remains: Congress did not use that record to fashion a coverage formula grounded in current conditions. It instead reenacted a formula based on 40-year-old facts having no logical relation to the present day.[41]

In the eyes of the majority, the voting discrimination Congress addressed in the past through the VRA "has no logical relation" to present voting discrimination.

In her dissent, Justice Ginsburg sharply criticized the majority's ironic dismissal of Section 5. For Ginsburg, the court was invalidating one of the very *causes* of preventing discrimination in voting that the majority fails to see in "present conditions." Ginsburg writes:

the Court strikes §4(b)'s coverage provision because, in its view, the provision is not based on "current conditions.". . . It discounts, however, that one such condition was the preclearance remedy in place in the covered jurisdictions, a remedy Congress designed both to catch discrimination before it causes harm, and to guard against return to old ways. 2006 Reauthorization §§2(b)(3), (9). Volumes of evidence supported Congress' determination that the prospect of retrogression was real. Throwing out preclearance when it has worked and is continuing to work to stop discriminatory changes is like throwing away your umbrella in a rainstorm because you are not getting wet.[42]

Here, the majority was arguing that a perfectly valid enactment of Congress was unconstitutional because *social conditions* had changed over time. For Scalia, this was quite an odd argument to make. First, textualism had always maintained that the role of the court was *not* to question Congress's legislative findings or policy judgments. But here, the court overturned a major congressional statutory provision relating to policy governing democratic voting procedures—clearly an issue for "the people," not the courts. Perhaps more striking was the court's argument that a congressional law should be invalidated because *social conditions* had changed, but according to Scalia's textualist-originalism, the meaning of the law does *not* change simply because of changing social conditions. For Scalia, this was the argument given by the "living constitutionalists"—the view that the Constitution changes meaning with the evolving of social conditions over time. Furthermore, even if social conditions *had* drastically changed, as the court asserted, Scalia's textualism would dictate that it is *Congress*'s role to adjust its own policy, *not* the court's. Thus, why would Scalia vote to overturn a valid congressional provision based on the *judiciary's* own policy judgment that social conditions had changed?

One plausible explanation is that Scalia's textualist-originalist "methods" were simply crafted to arrive at different results when it came to certain topics such as race. As Michael Ramsey, Richard S. Wood, Richad Hasen, Catherine Langford, and a host of legal scholars have suggested, Scalia's use of textualism and originalism was strategic, selective, and, at worst, pretextual. In particular, the consistency of Scalia's textualist-originalist methods begins to break down when we examine Scalia's opinions on race. As Ramsey observes:

> In contrast to Justice Scalia's extensive use of founding-era materials, his use of historical materials surrounding the enactment of the post-Civil War amendments may seem thin. To take one example for which he was sharply criticized, Scalia concluded unequivocally that the Equal Protection Clause banned preferential treatment of racial minorities. However, he appeared to base this conclusion (so far as his opinions went) chiefly on the text of the Clause, with little examination of the Clause's enactment or linguistic context.[43]

Catherine Langford, for example, concludes that Scalia was an "opportunistic textualist" who used textualist (or originalist) methods "when it furthers the results he seeks; he alters reasonable textual constructions or uses other forms of interpretation when it does not."[44] Similarly, Richard Hasen observes that Scalia's faithful application of "originalism" in some cases (e.g., the Second Amendment) but not others (e.g., the Voting Rights Act) demonstrates that, "Instead, originalism looks like a subconscious crutch or, worse, a fig leaf, a pretext justifying a result that lines up with one's ideology."[45] The legal historian Gordon S. Wood similarly argued that Scalia's textualism, in practice, was "as permissive and as open to arbitrary judicial discretion and expansion as the use of legislative intent or other interpretive methods, if the text-minded judge is so inclined."[46]

Indeed, specifically on the issue of race, Scalia's textualism provided an even broader flexibility to exercise judicial discretion. In *Shelby County*, the court simply ignored the voluminous record of discrimination in voting upon which Congress based its enactment of Section 5 of the VRA. Instead of examining the "original meaning" of the Voting Rights Act as authorized according to the purpose of the Fifteenth Amendment, or through Congress's explicitly stated purpose in its 2006 reauthorization, Scalia's majority simply refused to engage in an "original meaning" interpretation of Section 5. Instead, contrary to the fact-findings of Congress, the court asserted that society has drastically changed since 1965 and therefore the wisdom of Congress's policy was no longer valid. Indeed, this was a shocking and contradictory result for a textualist judicial philosophy that ardently claimed, "The court's job is to carry out the legislative project, not to change it in conformity with the judge's view of sound policy."[47]

By joining the majority's invalidation of Section 5 in *Shelby County*, Scalia seemed to be inconsistent and even contradictory with the textualist view that a congressional provision enacted "by the people" should be upheld if not clearly unconstitutional. It seemed as if Scalia and the majority were clearly changing congressional policy according to their own judicial vision of "sound policy." Wasn't this legislating from the bench, the very evil that textualism decried? What then was the explanation of this apparent contradiction?

## ORIGINALISM AS ANTIPROGRESSIVISM

The inconsistency of Scalia's view in *Shelby County* seems at first glance perplexing. However, on closer inspection, we are reminded that Scalia's textualism was explicitly antiprogressivist. For Scalia, textualism meant that the judge's role was, quite literally, to prevent progress. In this sense, Scalia's textualist opposition to the "progressive" congressional purpose of the Voting Rights Act was an extension of Scalia's activist judicial philosophy to enforce a *static* regime of law. This position came through in Scalia's opinions on the Voting Rights Act, in which Scalia adamantly held that antidiscrimination provisions such as those contained in the VRA could *not* be used or interpreted by judges to *advance* the voting power of blacks. The most that antidiscrimination provisions could compel judges to do constitutionally, according to Scalia, was to ensure that the voting power of minorities did not *regress*. Scalia maintained this view of the VRA, for example, writing in 2006 that, "Section 5 forbids a State to take action that would worsen minorities' electoral opportunities; it does not require action that would improve them."[48] As Scalia had said over a decade earlier in *Chisom v. Roemer*, "Section 2 of the Voting Rights Act of 1965 is not some all-purpose weapon for well-intentioned judges to wield as they please in the battle against discrimination."[49] For Scalia, then, judges should interpret the congressional provisions narrowly as authorizing the status quo, *not* to pursue social progress.

The antiprogressivism of Scalia's textualist method was of course connected to his originalist philosophy of the constitution itself. As Scalia wrote in a 2005 speech,

> until relatively recently the meaning of laws, including fundamental laws or constitution, was thought to be static. What vague provisions such as a right to "respect for . . . private life," or a right to "equal protection" meant at the time of the constitution's enactment could readily be determined (inmost controversial

areas) from the accepted and unchallenged practices that existed at the time. And what the constitution permitted at the time of its enactment it permitted forever; only the people could bring about change, by amending the constitution."[50]

For Scalia's originalism, this meant that federal Constitutional rights cannot be changed or "updated" with the evolution of social conditions and morality. For Scalia, the Constitution was *not* a "living constitution" whose meaning could change or be revised according to the prevailing society at the time. Instead, as Scalia writes,

under a regime of static law, it was not difficult to decide whether, under the American Constitution, there was a right to abortion, or to homosexual conduct, or to assisted suicide. When the constitution was adopted, all those acts were criminal throughout the United States, and remained so for several centuries; there was no credible argument that the Constitution made those laws invalid. Of course society remained free to decriminalize those acts, as some States have; but under a static Constitution *judges* could not do so.[51]

According to Scalia, this originalist "regime of static law" was the norm until the rise of the Warren Court of the 1950s and 1960s, writing:

A change occurred in the last half of the 20th century, and I am sorry to say my Court was responsible for it. It was my Court that invented the notion of a "living Constitution." Beginning with the Cruel and Unusual Punishments Clause of our Eighth Amendment, we developed the doctrine that the meaning of Constitution could change over time, to comport with "the evolving standards of decency that mark the progress of a maturing society."[52]

As a result of the rise of the living constitutionalist view, Scalia argued, "all sorts of entirely novel constitutional requirements were imposed, from the obligation to give a prior hearing before terminating welfare payments to the obligation to have law libraries in prison."[53]

Constitutional scholars have noted that when it comes to the issue of race, originalist philosophy has a historical record of providing justification for maintaining the status quo of racism rather than confronting it. As Eisengruber has observed, what originalism allows is for an interpreter to justify one's legal conclusions through the "disguise" of a legitimate historical judgment. Noting Justice Taney's famous originalist argument in *Dred Scott,* Eisengruber reminds us of the real possibility that originalist judges of the past have

invoked originalist arguments, knowing them to be wrong, in order to cover up an illegitimate conclusion that [they] reached on other grounds . . . if Taney fabricated his originalism as a disguise, he must have believed that originalism provided an especially fertile set of arguments to legitimate illegitimate conclusions.[54]

As noted in chapter 3, Cass Sunstein has compared the originalist argument against affirmative action to the originalist argument against granting citizenship to slaves, writing that

> the Court purported to make the original intentions of the framers binding, even though those intentions were murky, did not compel the Court's conclusion, and were not in the Constitution itself. Perhaps worst of all, the Court deliberately reached out to decide nationally crucial issues that deserved and would ultimately receive an answer from the people rather than the judiciary.[55]

In the same way that originalism can be utilized to sanction slavery, it has also been utilized to reject policies of affirmative action and voting protections that are viewed as "novel constitutional requirements" imposed by "living constitutionalists" bent on changing the "original" meaning of the Constitution. As David Dorsen has pointed out, Justice Scalia's originalism was matched perhaps only by Justice Clarence Thomas. As Dorsen writes, the "pure" form of originalism championed by Clarence Thomas

> would not only reverse *Roe v. Wade* and *Casey*, special restrictions on capital punishment, affirmative action, the *Miranda* warning, and the exclusionary rule applied to state courts, but it could eviscerate Social Security, Medicare, Medicaid, federal securities laws, child labor laws, environmental laws, the federal minimum wage, laws regulating the manufacture and sale of food and drugs, the nationwide right to counsel in state felony cases, affirmative action, laws against discrimination of women and gays, federal limits on unequal state and congressional election districts, and the virtual incorporation of the Bill of Rights to the State. That is judicial activism of an extreme sort.[56]

As Dorsen observes, Scalia's activist judicial philosophy of originalism is shared and continues to be aggressively enforced by Justice Thomas. Consequently, the "specters" of Scalia continue to thrive through the court's textualist-originalist philosophy, backward-looking and actively resistant to temporal progress, especially on the issue of the Voting Rights Act.

## "ENEMY OF PROGRESS"

The general judicial attitude of Justice Scalia's originalist antiprogressivism had first been addressed in Gerhart Husserl's *Recht und Zeit* (1955), over three decades before Scalia himself began his tenure on the Supreme Court. For Husserl, all modern legal systems based on the separation of powers operate according to distinct institutional roles and "time-perspectives" of the judge, legislator, and executive. As Husserl observes, "The doctrine of the division of powers has temporal aspects that have received little attention."[57] In modern systems of limited representative democracy, the political system is composed of three coordinate branches, each of which however functions according to very different "time modes" or "time dimensions" [*Zeitdimensionen*] for regulating legal norms within a state.

Within a system of separation of powers, Husserl affirms, the legislator is a "future-person" [*Zukunftsmenschen*] responsible for using reason in attempting to master the future [*"Der Gesetzgeber glaubt an die Kraft menschlicher Vernunft, die Zukunkft innerhalb gewiser Grenzen zu meistern"*].[58] In this way, "The legislator is a planner" [*"Der Gesetzgerber ist ein Planender"*].[59] The executive or administrative role, in contrast, is a "present-person" [*Gegenwartsmenschen*] responsible for implementing norms governing decisions that must be made "today": emergency measures, executive orders, administrative decisions, etc. The judge, on the other hand, is a "past-person" [*Vergangenheitmenschen*]. For Husserl, this means that a judge is required to exercise judgment using applicable legal norms that are necessarily rooted in the past. The judge must, for example, observe *stare decisis*—he is required to let binding precedent stand. Temporally, the judge is an exponent of tradition.[60] The judge fails in her task, Husserl notes, to the extent that the judge evaluates cases according to what seems fair and right to him *today*.[61] As Husserl writes, "It is not his task to say what the law should be, but what it is: what the legal situation is in the specific case, in accordance with the legal sentences created *before* his decision."[62] In this regard, Husserl observes that the judge—institutionally speaking—is a person who lives in the past [*in der Vergangenheit lebt*][63] and whose motivating principle is the *status quo* [*"die Idee des status quo als leitendes Motiv seines Handelns"*].[64] In this respect, Husserl writes, the institutional role of the judge requires:

> The decisions made by the judge are not rooted in "today" and are not in favor of "today." For a rational procedure of application of the law, it is essential that equal cases are treated equally. In order to ensure this, the judge must turn his gaze back [*Blick zurückwenden*] from the given case to previous decisions in which the legal problems are equivalent.[65]

In order to treat like cases alike, the judge necessarily views each case "as the last in a chain of judgment that preceded him."[66] In this respect, the motivating idea of all the judge's activity is the status quo.

For Husserl, this institutional role as a "past-person" creates a role conflict in the inner experience of the judge since the judge is also responsible for interpreting the law in its concrete application to social problems of today. Law is not a static body of rules, Husserl notes, but a "life practice of the people [*Lebenspraxis*] who, in this historical reality, strive to solve social problems."[67] However, the very notion of law as "binding" implies for Husserl that the judge is bound to a certain "time-path" [*Zeitweg*] in his interpretation of law. As Husserl notes, "The time path that the judge takes in the process of applying the law leads back in a direction to the historical situation from which the legal norm . . . has arisen. This course into the past is necessary for a proper interpretation of the law."[68] And even though the judge's time-path must lead him back to the concrete social problem of today, her institutional role within a system of separation of powers dictates that the judge lacks the legislative authority to design, revise, or execute plans to direct the future.

This means that, for Husserl, the institutional time perspective of the judge is limited by "a certain narrowness of the future perspective."[69] The danger posed by the judicial role, therefore, is that the judge focuses so narrowly and intensely on the past that the judge's relationship to the future and/or present becomes severed. Rather than pursuing legal interpretation by what Husserl calls a "living relationship" with the present, the distinct danger of the judicial role is that the judge neglects this living relationship with the present and instead narrowly focuses on preserving the status quo. When this occurs, Husserl writes, judges can become so thoroughly institutionalized as a "past person" that the judge

> lacks the idea of an open future. The worldview of the past-person [*Vergangenheitmenschen*] is that of a "finished" world in which there is no real progress. It follows from this basic attitude that the person of the past is fundamentally skeptical about all innovations. He is inclined to see misunderstandings or signs of decay in them. Such a criticism may be an expression of a radical rejection of "today": the inner return to the past has reached such a degree of intensity that things of the present can no longer be understood for what they are. This is the situation in which a person says, "The world has become foreign to me; I no longer understand it." The drawing-back from the present into the past has caused not only the future to lie in the emotional shadow of "strangeness"—as this also applies to the "present-man"—but the present itself is now in the "shadow of foreignness." For the one to whom the present has become foreign, there can be no longer a life of activity: he is close to death.[70]

Husserl notes that in a system of separation of powers, the attitude of the judge above is best described as one who has become an "enemy of progress." Husserl writes, "In the case of 'people of the past,' there is the danger that a persistence in the path of thought of the past will sink him into an attitude of passivity; that hostility to progress [*Fortschrittsfeindlichkeit*] hardens him into an obstruction of any development that affects the *status quo*."

## CONCLUSION

Justice Scalia's view of the judicial role as one of preventing progress is accurately diagnosed by Husserl's critique of the judicial "past-man" as enemy of progress. Husserl's observation that the law for such a "past-man" is close to death calls to mind Scalia's remark that the Constitution is "not a living document. It's dead, dead, dead."[71] For Scalia, an originalist judge *must* prevent progress because there is no such thing as the Constitution's "living relationship with the present." The drastic consequences of such a temporal perspective, Husserl observed, is that the judge's reasoning becomes severed from any conception of an open future. For a textualist such as Scalia, the law is for all practical purposes "dead."

In this way, the confrontation between Congress and Scalia's majority over the VRA should be viewed in light of Scalia's originalist project to enforce a temporal regime of static law. When viewed from Husserl's analysis of the temporality of the judge, Scalia's textualist-originalism exemplifies what Husserl criticized as the attitude of the judge as an "enemy of progress." For Scalia, this hostility to progress on voting discrimination would continue in *Shelby County v. Holder*, in which his court invalidated Section 5 of the VRA. As the following chapter shows, Scalia's continued "hostility to progress" provided the precedent for the court's later decision in *Abbott v. Perez* (2018) giving legislatures a "good faith presumption" allowing them to make a clean break from their past discriminatory record. *Abbott's* new rule would thus allow state legislatures with a discriminatory record the ability to discriminate through the performance of "good faith," as occurred in *Alexander v. South Carolina State Conference of the NAACP* (2024).

## NOTES

1. Antonin Scalia, John M. Olin Lecture Series on Political Economy, Wharton School, University of Pennsylvania, John M. Olin series, April 25, 1986, Antonin Scalia papers, LAW, MMC, 291, Series III, Box: 76, Folder: 28, Harvard Law School Library, Historical & Special Collections, 3.

2. Antonin Scalia, "Common Law Courts in a Civil-Law System," in *A Matter of Interpretation: Federal Courts and the Law*, ed. Amy Gutmann (Princeton, NJ: Princeton University Press, 1997), 23.

3. Henry M. Hart, Jr. and Albert M. Sacks, *The Legal Process: Basic Problems in the Making and Application of Law* (Westbury, NY: Foundation Press, 1994), 148.

4. Antonin Scalia, "Judges as Propounders of Transcendent Moral Law," 2005, Antonin Scalia papers, LAW, MMC, 291, Series III, Box: 73, Folder: 3, Harvard Law School Library, Historical & Special Collections, 10.

5. 89 P.L. 110, 79 Stat. 437.
6. *Shelby Cty. v. Holder*, 133 S. Ct. 2612, 2632 (2013).
7. Chisom v. Roemer, 501 U.S. 380, 404 (1991).
8. Chisom v. Roemer, 501 U.S. 380, 406 (1991).
9. *Shelby Cty. v. Holder*, 811 F. Supp. 2d 424, 431 (D.D.C. 2011).
10. *Reno v. Bossier Par. Sch. Bd.*, 528 U.S. 320, 344 (2000).
11. *Reno v. Bossier Par. Sch. Bd.*, 528 U.S. 320, 323 (2000).
12. *Reno v. Bossier Par. Sch. Bd.,* 528 U.S. 320, 359 (2000).
13. *Reno v. Bossier Par. Sch. Bd.*, 528 U.S. 320, 351 (2000).
14. *Reno v. Bossier Par. Sch. Bd.*, 528 U.S. 320, 349-50 (2000).
15. *Reno v. Bossier Par. Sch. Bd.,* 528 U.S. 320, 359 (2000).
16. *Reno v. Bossier Par. Sch. Bd.,* 528 U.S. 320, 355 (2000).
17. *Reno v. Bossier Par. Sch. Bd.*, 528 U.S. 320, 341 (2000).
18. *Reno v. Bossier Par. Sch. Bd.*, 528 U.S. 320, 344 (2000).
19. *Reno v. Bossier Par. Sch. Bd.,* 528 U.S. 320, 356 (2000).
20. *Reno v. Bossier Par. Sch. Bd.,* 528 U.S. 320, 372 (2000).
21. H.R.9 - Fannie Lou Hamer, Rosa Parks, and Coretta Scott King Voting Rights Act Reauthorization and Amendments Act of 2006, 109 P.L. 246, 120 Stat. 577, 578.
22. S. Rep. No. 109-295, at 16 (2006), https://www.govinfo.gov/app/details/CRPT-109srpt295/CRPT-109srpt295.
23. *LaRoque v. Holder,* 831 F. Supp. 2d 183, 190-91 (D.D.C. 2011).
24. Antonin Scalia and Bryan A. Garner, *Reading Law: The Interpretation of Legal Texts* (St. Paul: Thomson/West, 2012), 247.
25. Scalia and Garner, *Reading Law*, 63.
26. Scalia and Garner, *Reading Law*, 63.
27. H.R.9 - Fannie Lou Hamer, Rosa Parks, and Coretta Scott King Voting Rights Act Reauthorization and Amendments Act of 2006, 578.
28. Scalia and Garner, *Reading Law*, 66.
29. Scalia and Garner, *Reading Law*, 66.
30. *Nw. Austin Mun. Util. Dist. No. One v. Mukasey*, 573 F. Supp. 2d 221, 229 (D.D.C. 2008).
31. *Shelby Cty. v. Holder*, 400 U.S. App. D.C. 367, 385 (2012).
32. *Shelby Cty. v. Holder*, 400 U.S. App. D.C. 367, 385 (2012).
33. *Shelby Cty. v. Holder*, 400 U.S. App. D.C. 367, 385, 679 F.3d 848, 866 (2012).
34. *Shelby Cty. v. Holder*, 570 U.S. 529, 571 (2013).
35. *Shelby Cty. v. Holder*, 570 U.S. 529, 573 (2013).
36. *Shelby Cty. v. Holder*, 570 U.S. 529, 573-75 (2013).
37. *Shelby Cty. v. Holder*, 570 U.S. 529, 575 (2013).
38. *Shelby Cty. v. Holder*, 570 U.S. 529, 590 (2013).
39. *Shelby Cty. v. Holder*, 570 U.S. 529, 582 (2013).

40. *Shelby Cty. v. Holder*, 570 U.S. 529, 532, 133 S. Ct. 2612, 2617 (2013).
41. *Shelby Cty. v. Holder*, 570 U.S. 529, 532, 133 S. Ct. 2612, 2617 (2013).
42. *Shelby Cty. v. Holder*, 570 U.S. 529, 590 (2013).
43. Michael D. Ramsey, "Beyond the Text: Justice Scalia's Originalism in Practice," *Notre Dame Law Review* 92 (2017): 1945.
44. Catherine L. Langford, *Scalia v. Scalia: Opportunistic Textualism in Constitutional Interpretation* (Tuscaloosa: The University of Alabama Press, 2017), 50.
45. Richard Hasen, *The Justice of Contradictions.: Antonin Scalia and the Politics of Disruption* (London: Yale University Press, 2018), 63.
46. Gordon S. Wood, "Comment" in *A Matter of Interpretation: Federal Courts and the Law*, ed. Amy Gutman (Princeton, NJ: Princeton University Press, 1997), 63.
47. Scalia and Garner, *Reading Law*, xxi.
48. *League of United Latin Am. Citizens v. Perry*, 548 U.S. 399, 519 (U.S. June 28, 2006).
49. *Chisom v. Roemer*, 501 U.S. 380, 404 (U.S. June 20, 1991).
50. Scalia, "Judges as Propounders of Transcendent Moral Law," 9
51. Scalia, "Judges as Propounders of Transcendent Moral Law," 10.
52. Scalia, "Judges as Propounders of Transcendent Moral Law," 10.
53. Scalia, "Judges as Propounders of Transcendent Moral Law," 10.
54. Eisgruber, "Dred Again: Originalism's Forgotten Past," 48n.
55. Sunstein, "Constitutional Myth-Making," 23.
56. David Dorsen, *The Unexpected Scalia: A Conservative Justice's Liberal Opinions* (Cambridge: Cambridge University Press, 2017), 149.
57. Husserl, *Recht und Zeit*, 52.
58. Husserl, *Recht und Zeit*, 55.
59. Husserl, *Recht und Zeit*, 55.
60. Husserl, *Recht und Zeit*, 50.
61. Husserl, *Recht und Zeit*, 59.
62. Husserl, *Recht und Zeit*, 59.
63. Husserl, *Recht und Zeit*, 59.
64. Husserl, *Recht und Zeit*, 62.
65. Husserl, *Recht und Zeit*, 61–62.
66. Husserl, *Recht und Zeit*, 62.
67. Husserl, *Recht und Zeit*, 41.
68. Husserl, *Recht und Zeit*, 60.
69. Husserl, *Recht und Zeit*, 60.
70. Husserl, *Recht und Zeit*, 49.
71. Tasha Tsiaperas, "Constitution a 'Dead, Dead, Dead' Document, Scalia Tells SMU Audience," *Dallas Morning News,* January 28. 2013.

# 5

## *Abbott v. Perez* (2018)
### Severing the Memory of Discrimination

In this chapter, I show how Scalia's opinions provided the precedent for the court's decision in *Abbott v. Perez* (2018) and *Alexander v. South Carolina State Conference of the NAACP* (2024). In these cases, the Supreme Court recycled Scalia's textualist argument against discriminatory purpose in *Edwards v. Aguillard* (1987) and cited Scalia's attack on the Voting Rights Act, providing precedent for the court's decision in *Alexander v. South Carolina State Conference of the NAACP*. Drawing upon Justice Sotomayor's dissent in *Abbott v. Perez*, I argue that the Supreme Court's "good faith presumption" in *Abbott* exercises a *sovereign exceptionalism* by "selectively" severing the memory of discrimination from the meaning of the law. After examining the case study of *Abbott v. Perez* and its culmination in *Alexander*, I review the various temporal solutions to the problem of "discriminatory taint" that have been proposed in various jurisdictions and in constitutional scholarship, arguing that Murray's *institutional realist* approach to discrimination provides a remedy to the *malevolent legality* enacted by the court in *Abbott v. Perez*. An institutional realist approach to discrimination, I argue, ensures that memory of discrimination is not forgotten or severed from the law, as in *Abbot* and *Alexander*, but recovered and brought into a hermeneutic reading of the present.

### ABBOTT V. PEREZ (2018)

In 2011, Texas was still a covered district under Section 5 of the Voting Rights Act (VRA). As the previous chapter explained, Section 5 of the VRA required certain states with a history of racial discrimination to submit any changes in their voting schemes to the federal government for "preclearance," which was authorized by Congress to ensure that any voting changes would not have the "purpose nor will have the effect of denying or abridging the right to vote on account of race or color."[1] Due to population growth, the Texas legislature redrew their electoral maps after the 2010 census, which showed an increase of over four million new residents. Since 2010, approximately three-quarters of population growth in Texas was accounted for by Hispanics and African Americans.[2] In creating its new 2011 electoral maps, the Texas legislature used "RedAppl," a software program that had been previously used by the legislature for unlawful racial gerrymandering since 1990.[3] In 1996, the US Supreme Court had found that RedAppl was used by the Texas legislature to create unconstitutional electoral maps in violation of the VRA. By utilizing "the critical impact of the block-by-block racial data available on the REDAPPL program,"[4] the RedAppl software allowed redistricters to create bizarrely shaped districts that "are ultimately unexplainable on grounds other than the racial quotas established for those districts, they are the product of [presumptively] unconstitutional racial gerrymandering."[5]

Despite that history of racial gerrymandering using the same software program, RedAppl was utilized once again to create the 2011 maps, which were challenged in *Perry v. Perez* (2012). In 2012, a federal D.C. court found that the Texas legislature's redistricting maps intentionally redrew districts along racial lines to dilute the Hispanic voting population to favor Anglo Republican candidates,[6] thereby violating the VRA and Fourteenth Amendment. The court found that the legislature had engaged in a deliberate, race-conscious method to manipulate not simply the Democratic vote but, more specifically, the Hispanic vote. In doing so, it had attempted to disguise its discriminatory intentions for racial gerrymandering in order to circumvent two antidiscrimination provisions: the Voting Rights Act and Equal Protection Clause,[7] masking both its discriminatory intent *and* disparate impact.[8]

Texas appealed the ruling, and in 2013, new plans were enacted by the legislature that were modeled on and replicated several of the same districting lines from the unlawful 2011 plans. Once again, these 2013 plans were challenged, and in 2017, a US district court found that

> the racially discriminatory intent and effects that it previously found in the 2011 plans carry over into the 2013 plans where those district lines remain unchanged. The discriminatory taint was not removed by the Legislature's enactment of the Court's interim plans, because the Legislature engaged in no deliberative process to remove any such taint, and in fact intended any such taint to be maintained but be safe from remedy. The Legislature in 2013 intentionally furthered and continued the existing discrimination in the plans.[9]

The district court identified what it saw as the political strategy of the Republican-controlled legislature and executive to insulate its recycled, racially gerrymandered maps from 2011 being defeated in 2013. The strategy was simple and two-pronged: (1) because the 2011 plans were found unconstitutional, argue that the plans never went into effect and therefore had no discriminatory effect, and (2) because the new 2013 plans had no discriminatory intent, they also could not be discriminatory. The clever strategy, the court observed, was that "By arguing that there may have been intent but no effect in 2011 and there may have been effect but no intent in 2013, despite the fact that there is unquestionably both intent and ongoing effect, Defendants' actions in 2013 were attempting to prevent Plaintiffs from obtaining relief for purposeful racial discrimination."[10]

In its ruling, the court documented the great lengths the legislature went to disguise its discriminatory intent. The 2012 court had observed that during testimony, the mapmaker responsible for creating the discriminatory maps ("Mr. Interiano") feigned ignorance of the full gerrymandering capabilities of the infamous software ("RedAppl") used to create the maps, which had, of course, been used earlier by the legislature for racial gerrymandering purposes. The D.C. court had written:

> RedAppl has a function that shades a map to indicate the percentage of ethnic (Hispanic) or racial (Black) voting age population in a certain voter tabulation district ("VTD"). As relevant here, RedAppl further disaggregates this data to allow a user to view the variations of voting age population or total population by race or ethnicity at the census block level through color shading. . . . Similarly, election information, *i.e.*, the percentage of population that voted for a certain candidate in a prior election, is only available at the level of a VTD.[11]

The mapmaker, who had spent over a thousand hours of training and attended conferences on the capabilities of the software, testified that he was unaware of these capabilities, even though all parties agreed that the 2011 maps violated the Voting Rights Act through an improper method of drawing districts along racial lines. The D.C. court had observed that

> it is clear Mr. Interiano knew that using census block data to identify the demographics of voters could advance the goal of maximizing Republican electoral strength by suppressing the minority vote. As previously discussed, in early December 2010, Eric Opiela, counsel to Speaker Straus, suggested to Mr. Interiano that voting and population data might permit distinctions between minorities who turn out heavily to vote and those who do not; with such information, he suggested, districts could be drawn that would retain a large minority population but actually include a much smaller number of minority voters.[12]

Taking this evidence into account, the 2017 district court concurred with the D.C. court in finding this testimony "incredible" and agreed that "the

Legislature engaged in no deliberative process to remove any such taint, and in fact intended any such taint to be maintained but be safe from remedy. The Legislature in 2013 intentionally furthered and continued the existing discrimination in the plans."[13] The court concluded, "This strategy is discriminatory at its heart and should not insulate either plan from review."[14]

However, as explored in the previous chapter, the Supreme Court ruled in *Shelby County v. Holder* (2013) that Section 5 of the VRA was unconstitutional. In a majority opinion joined by Justice Scalia, the court had said that Congress's Section 5 preclearance requirement for states with a discriminatory record in voting (like Texas) was "based on 40-year-old facts having no logical relation to the present day."[15] In the thinking of the court, "things have changed dramatically" since the 1950s and 1960s,[16] and therefore the discriminatory history of a state legislature's record, such as in Texas, is irrelevant to the question of whether there exists smoking-gun evidence of a *current* state legislature's subjective intent to discriminate. In this way, *Shelby County's* invalidation of the VRA's Section 5 was at the same time an exclusion of the history of discrimination from legal interpretation *of the present*. As the court in *Abbott v. Perez* explained:

> After *Shelby County* v. *Holder* . . . was decided, Texas, no longer covered by §5, obtained a vacatur of the D.C. court's preclearance order. But the Texas court did not dismiss the case against the 2011 plans as moot. Instead, it allowed the plaintiffs to amend their complaint to challenge the 2013 plans and held that their challenges to the 2011 plans were live. Texas conducted its 2014 and 2016 elections under the 2013 plans. In 2017, the Texas court found defects in several of the districts in the 2011 federal congressional and State House plans (the State Senate plan is not at issue here). Subsequently, it also invalidated multiple Congressional (CD) and House (HD) Districts in the 2013 plans, holding that the Legislature failed to "cure" the "taint" of discriminatory intent allegedly harbored by the 2011 Legislature. And the court relied on that finding to invalidate several challenged 2013 districts. The court also held that three districts—CD27, HD32, and HD34—were invalid under §2 of the VRA because they had the *effect* of depriving Latinos of the equal opportunity to elect their candidates of choice. And it found that HD90 was a racial gerrymander based on changes made by the 2013 Legislature. It gave the state attorney general three days to tell the court whether the Legislature would remedy the violations; and if the Legislature did not intend to adopt new plans, the court would hold remedial hearings.[17]

For the court, however, *Shelby County* stood for the proposition that a state legislature's *past* history of discrimination in voting was irrelevant for deciding whether a *current* legislature was discriminating. In the court's eyes, "discriminatory taint" was no longer a problem in voting and therefore Section 5 should be invalidated. Therefore, the court found precedent in *Shelby County* or what it would later conclude in *Abbott v. Perez* —namely, that the history of discrimination may be excluded from legal interpretation altogether.

In 2018, the US Supreme Court issued a 5–4 judgment in *Abbott v. Perez* (2018) overturning the district court's decision and ruling that Texas's 2013 plans were not motivated by discriminatory intent.[18] Whereas the 2012 federal D.C. court held that "it is settled law that Texas bears the burden of proving lack of discriminatory intent,"[19] the majority rejected this view and instead held that the challenger bears the burden proof because the legislature enjoys a "good faith presumption" despite its history of discrimination in voting. In a startling reversal, Justice Alito wrote the majority opinion, stating:

> In redistricting cases, the "good faith of [the] state legislature must be presumed." *Miller* v. *Johnson*, 515 U. S. 900, 915, 115 S. Ct. 2475, 132 L. Ed. 2d 762. The allocation of the burden of proof and the presumption of legislative good faith are not changed by a finding of past discrimination, which is but "one evidentiary source" relevant to the question of intent.[20]

Despite the clear discriminatory intent of the 2011 plans, the court held, "The 2013 Legislature was not obligated to show that it had 'cured' the unlawful intent that the court attributed to the 2011 Legislature."[21] As a result, the Supreme Court rejected the core idea of the Voting Rights Act that the state has the burden of showing that its discriminatory electoral maps do not violate the VRA. Instead, the court ruled, past discrimination cannot invalidate valid state action in remaking its voting schemes since legislatures are to be given a "good faith presumption."

In a particularly shocking portion of the ruling, Justice Alito supported the majority's position by citing *Mobile v. Bolden* (1980), in which the Supreme Court held that "past discrimination cannot, in the manner of original sin, condemn governmental action that is not itself unlawful."[22] The only problem with the majority's citation of *Mobile*, however, was that it had been overwhelmingly repudiated by civil rights reforms and overturned by Congress in 1982 through amendments to the Voting Rights Act in direct response to the court's ruling in *Mobile*.[23] In *Mobile*, black plaintiffs challenged a city's election system for a three-seat panel of city commissioners. While black voters comprised one-third of the city's population, no black-preferred candidate had ever won election. Thus, black plaintiffs charged that the election system was discriminatory. However, the *Mobile* court ruled against the plaintiffs, arguing that the Voting Rights Act only prohibits *intentional* discrimination but does *not* prohibit unintentional *effects* that are discriminatory. In response, Congress amended the Voting Rights Act in 1982 to clearly establish once and for all that the VRA prohibits not just intentional discrimination but also *discriminatory effects* of a voting scheme. Remarking on the *Mobile* court's interpretation of the VRA as prohibiting only *intentional* discrimination, one federal appeals court in 2009 observed:

> Overturning a Supreme Court case that held that the original Act contained such a requirement, *see Mobile v. Bolden*, 446 U.S. 55, 61, 100 S. Ct. 1490, 64 L. Ed. 2d 47 (1980), Congress, through the 1982 amendments, made clear that a violation of § 2 could be established by proof of discriminatory *results. See Thornburg*, 478 U.S. at 43-44 (emphasis added) (reading the 1982 Amendment to the VRA as effectively overturning the *Bolden* requirement of showing purposeful discrimination . . . noting that the purpose of the Amendments was to repeal *Bolden* and to focus the judicial inquiry only into whether there exists equal access to electoral opportunity). Congress did so because it recognized the difficulty of proving deliberate and purposeful discrimination, and sought to ensure that "in the context of all the circumstances in the jurisdiction in question," any disparate racial impact of facially neutral voting requirements did not result from racial discrimination. . . . This "results test" was intended "to serve as a prophylactic against voting practices—such as felon disenfranchisement . . . adopted or retained due to intentional discrimination that would be difficult to prove in court."[24]

In this way, *Mobile* was overturned by the 1982 VRA amendments establishing the unlawfulness of discriminatory effects of a voting scheme. In June 1982, the *New York Times* reported the overwhelming passage of the amendment in a Senate vote of 85–8, with four "No" votes coming from representatives from former Confederate states in the South.[25] As a result of Congress's actions, the amended US Code invalidated *Mobile*, stating:

> A violation of subsection (a) is established if, based on the totality of circumstances, it is shown that the political processes leading to nomination or election in the State or political subdivision are not equally open to participation by members of a class of citizens.[26]

This language eliminated the requisite showing of intentional discrimination and instead made it easier for plaintiffs to show discrimination through a "totality of circumstances" test, as Congress expressly intended.

Thus, by the time the Justice Alito cited *Mobile* in *Abbott*, the court's ruling in *Mobile* had been repudiated and overturned by Congress for well over three decades. The *Abbott* court cites for its position the infamous quote from *Mobile* that "past discrimination cannot, in the manner of original sin, condemn governmental action that is not itself unlawful,"[27] but *Mobile* had narrowly defined discrimination as intentional, and had said that the VRA did not prohibit discriminatory effects. However, Congress had amended the US

Code to clarify precisely this "confusion" about what the VRA prohibits, saying that past discrimination *may* condemn subsequent governmental action based on an "effects" test. If a voting scheme had the purpose *"or effect"* of denying individuals the right to vote, then government policy or action was unlawful. Thus, *Abbott*'s citation of *Mobile* was based on bad, invalid law and an understanding of discrimination that Congress had explicitly rejected and amended in the law.

Despite all this, the 5–4 majority in *Abbott* found that the legislature's new maps were not motivated by discrimination. As noted by the 2017 federal district court, the Texas legislature's political strategy successfully circumvented the VRA and antidiscrimination doctrine by (1) relying upon a "good faith" presumption doctrine that shifted the burden of proof, and (2) by disguising their intentions for racial gerrymandering. By doing so, the legislature avoided both the charge of discriminatory intent *and* disparate impact.[28]

## SOTOMAYOR'S DISSENT

In her dissenting opinion in *Abbott v. Perez*, Justice Sotomayor laid bare what she saw as the majority's interpretive strategy in discriminatory purpose tests. In a lengthy dissent—once again conducting a full analysis of the five-factor *Arlington Heights* framework—Sotomayor wrote:

> In selectively reviewing the record below, the majority attempts to shield itself from the otherwise unavoidable conclusion that the district court did not err. If forced to acknowledge the true scope of the legal analysis in the orders below, the majority would find itself without support for its insistence that the district court was singularly focused on whether the Legislature "removed" past taint. And then the majority would have to contend with the thorough analysis of the *Arlington Heights* factors, Part II-B, *supra*, that led the District Court to conclude that the 2013 Legislature acted with invidious intent.[29]

Here, Sotomayor goes well beyond describing the majority's opinion as merely wrong. Instead, her argument is that the majority is "selectively reviewing the record" *in order* to shield itself from agreeing with the lower court that previously found Texas's redistricting maps *were* in fact motivated by unlawful discriminatory purpose or "invidious intent." Sotomayor observes that the court's ruling effectively ignores the *Arlington Heights* test for discriminatory purpose, explicitly excluding evidence of discrimination.

The significance of Justice Sotomayor's argument—namely that the majority "selectively reviews" the evidence of discriminatory purpose set out by *Arlington Heights* because it wishes to avoid finding discriminatory purpose—cannot be overstated. If Justice Sotomayor is correct, this implies that the majority simply ignores its own framework for evaluating evidence of discrimination *because* it disagrees with the conclusions that would follow if they were to actually follow the *Arlington Heights* framework. If this is true, then we are forced to conclude that, at least in these cases, the Supreme Court majority above began with their conclusions and worked backwards, discarding or ignoring evidence, precedent, standards, and burdens of proof that supported a finding of discriminatory purpose. This would suggest, furthermore, that Supreme Court justices select their arguments and premises *strategically* in a way that only supports their conclusions regarding the outcomes of such cases. In sum, this would suggest that the outcomes of Supreme Court decisions (at least in these cases) are based *not* on the application of rules, precedents, and evidentiary frameworks but rather on the preferred results of the majority disguised in post-hoc legal rationalizations not grounded in a carefully reasoned legal analysis proceeding logically from evidence and premises to sound legal conclusions. Rather, Justice Sotomayor argues in *Abbott* that her colleagues in the majority were strategically excluding factors of legislative history and historical record *because* such evidentiary sources are especially probative of discriminatory purpose—the judicial conclusion they wish to avoid.

This observation is important since it reveals the particular methods and strategies employed by the majority—namely, strategies to limit or exclude any temporal nexus of discriminatory intent that might be probative of unlawful voting schemes by the present legislature. Thus, Sotomayor suggests that the majority is engaging in a kind of *sovereign exceptionalism* in making determinations regarding the meaning of a legislative act. As I continue to use the term, in judicial interpretation, sovereign exceptionalism refers to the inclusion/exclusion of legal meaning by making arbitrary exceptions in the law. In this sense, Sotomayor argued that the *Abbott* majority *selectively excludes* evidence of discrimination to reach the conclusion they prefer. According to the court's own discriminatory purpose test established in *Arlington Heights*, the five factors the court is instructed to take into account include: (i) the discriminatory impact of the legislative action upon a protected race, (ii) the historical background of the decision (i.e., whether there is a record of discriminatory decisions), (iii) the specific sequence of events leading up to the decision, (iv) departures from normal procedural sequence, and (v) the legislative or administrative history (i.e., congressional record, committee meetings, testimony, etc.). As the court initially clarified in 1977, this is a nonexhaustive list of "subjects of proper inquiry in determining whether racially discriminatory intent existed."[30] Instead of utilizing the *Arlington Heights* framework for examining the (recent) historical background of the Texas legislature's actions or examining the testimony and legislative history of Texas's political strategy to insulate itself from scrutiny, the *Abbott* court simply excluded these factors from its analysis altogether. Therefore, as Sotomayor suggests, only by *excluding* these factors from its analysis of the legislature's *present* intent does it conclude that "the presumption of legislative good faith [is] not changed by a finding of past discrimination."[31] Therefore, as Sotomayor suggests, the court engages in a sovereign exceptionalism by excluding evidence of past discrimination in order to reach its decision.

As Sotomayor had argued, however, the majority's selection of arguments and evidence is not only strategic or "exceptional" but *performative*, since the court grants the legislature a presumption of "good faith," allowing them to "re-signify their discriminatory actions. In this way, the Supreme Court in *Abbott* discards the *Arlington Heights* framework for Butler's theory of performativity by "loosening of the link between act and injury" and thereby concluding that discriminatory acts may "become disjoined from their power to injure and recontextualized in more affirmative modes."[32] Just as Butler argues in *Excitable Speech*, the *Abbott* court appears to embrace the notion that legal speech acts exist within a "ritual chain of resignifications whose origin and end remain unfixed and unfixable."[33] As a result, the Texas legislature's discriminatory 2011 voting maps had no necessary relationship to the "good faith presumption" of its 2013 voting maps. As a result, the Texas legislature was free to "re-signify" its actions and make a clean break from the temporal nexus of past discrimination. As the court concludes, "the presumption of legislative good faith [is] not changed by a finding of past discrimination."[34] In *Excitable Speech*, Butler writes the following passage, which could have just as easily been written by the *Abbott* court:

> That no speech act has to perform injury as its effect means that no simple elaboration of speech acts will provide a standard by which the injuries of speech might be effectively adjudicated. . . . Thus, the gap that separates the speech act from its future effects has its auspicious implications: it begins a theory of linguistic agency that provides an alternative to the relentless search for legal remedy. The interval between instances of utterance not only makes the repetition and resignification of the utterance possible, but shows how words might, through time, become disjoined from their power to injure and recontextualized in more affirmative modes.[35]

Butler's description of performativity above mirrors the *Abbott* court's use of the good faith presumption. By asserting a good faith presumption in favor of a legislature with a discriminatory history, the *Abbott* court was able to abandon a "relentless search of legal remedy." Since the legislature's new voting maps should be given a good faith presumption regardless of its recent unlawful behavior, the *Abbott* court asserted that the law is purely performative and can simply be re-signified in a way that has no temporal or historical relation with the past. In this way, the court severed the memory of discrimination itself from the interpretation of the law.

## S.C. STATE CONFERENCE OF THE NAACP V. ALEXANDER (2024)

The Supreme Court's severance of discrimination from legal interpretation predictably enabled a new line of defense against voting discrimination claims: the legislature always acts in good faith, even when the evidence suggests that it does not. This line of defense was used in the NAACP's challenge to a racially gerrymandered map drew by Republican legislators in South Carolina. Following a similar playbook to the Texas legislature, legislators in South Carolina sought to redraw voting districts after census data revealed significant population increases. In 2023, a district court examined the plans of the legislature and wrote that, "The Court finds that to achieve a target of 17 percent African American population in Congressional District No. 1, Charleston County, was racially gerrymandered and over 30,000 African Americans were removed from their home district."[36] In its findings, the district court observed that the mapmaker hired by the legislators aggressively used racial data to sort populations in order to weaken the voting strength of African Americans who disproportionately were registered Democrats. The court found:

> The strategies he employed ultimately exiled over 30,000 African American citizens from their previous district and created a stark racial gerrymander of Charleston County and the City of Charleston. As Mr. Roberts admitted under the Court's questioning, the changes he implemented in Charleston County were "dramatic" and "created tremendous disparity" in the placement of African Americans within Congressional Districts Nos. 1 and 6 in Charleston County.[37]

However, in May 2024, the Supreme Court granted certiori and took up the case. In a 6–3 "textualist" majority opinion, the court ruled in favor of the legislature, concluding that the legislature should be given a "good faith" presumption that politics and not race was the motivating factor in redrawing electoral districts. Citing *Abbott,* the court wrote, "This presumption of legislative good faith directs district courts to draw the inference that cuts in the legislature's favor when confronted with evidence that could plausibly support multiple conclusions. See, *e.g.*, *Abbott* v. *Perez*, 585 U. S. 579, 610-612, 138 S. Ct. 2305, 201 L. Ed. 2d 714 (2018)."[38] Justifying their conclusion through the "good faith presumption," the court explained:

> First, this presumption reflects the Federal Judiciary's due respect for the judgment of state legislators, who are similarly bound by an oath to follow the Constitution. Second, when a federal court finds that race drove a legislature's districting decisions, it is declaring that the legislature engaged in "offensive and demeaning" conduct, *Miller*, 515 U. S., at 912, 115 S. Ct. 2475, 132 L. Ed. 2d 762, that "bears an uncomfortable resemblance to political apartheid," *Shaw I*, 509 U. S., at 647, 113 S. Ct. 2816, 125 L. Ed. 2d 511. We should not be quick to hurl such accusations at the political branches. Third, we must be wary of plaintiffs who seek to transform federal courts into "weapons of political warfare" that will deliver victories that eluded them "in the political arena." *Cooper*, 581 U. S., at 335, 137 S. Ct. 1455, 197 L. Ed. 2d 837 (Alito, J., concurring in judgment in part and dissenting in part). The presumption of good faith furthers each of these constitutional interests. It also explains why we have held that the plaintiff's evidentiary burden in these cases is especially stringent.[39]

In a lengthy dissent, Justice Elena Kagan sharply criticized the opinion and accused the majority of giving legislatures a new license to discriminate in voting by covering their tracks in using politics as a proxy for race. Kagan writes bluntly, "This Court is not supposed to be so fearful of telling discriminators, including States, to stop discriminating."[40] Speaking about the effect of *Abbott* (2018) on voting discrimination claims, Kagan observes:

> State legislatures "will often have an incentive to use race as a proxy to achieve partisan ends. See *supra*, at 20-22. And occasionally they might want to straight-up suppress the electoral influence of minority voters. See *Cooper*, 581 U. S., at 319, n. 15, 137 S. Ct. 1455, 197 L. Ed. 2d 837. Go right ahead, this Court says to States today. Go ahead, though you have no recognized justification for using race, such as to comply with statutes ensuring equal voting rights. Go ahead, though you are (at best) using race as a short-cut to bring about partisan gains—to elect more Republicans in one case, more Democrats in another. It will be easy enough to cover your tracks in the end: Just raise a "possibility" of non-race-based decision-making, and it will be "dispositive." *Ante*, at 16. And so this "odious" practice of sorting citizens, built on racial generalizations and exploiting racial divisions, will continue. *Shaw*, 509 U. S., at 643, 113 S. Ct. 2816, 125 L. Ed. 2d 511. In the electoral sphere especially, where "ugly patterns of pervasive racial discrimination" have so long governed, we should demand better—of ourselves, of our political representatives, and most of all of this Court. *Id.*, at 639, 113 S. Ct. 2816, 125 L. Ed. 2d 511. Respectfully, I dissent."[41]

Justices Sotomayor and Jackson joined the dissent, writing of the court's good faith presumption rule established in *Abbott* that, "The principal effect of that novel rule will be to defeat valid voting-discrimination claims."[42] As the dissent pointedly concludes, "The majority's new evidentiary rule is meant to scuttle gerrymandering cases."[43]

## TEMPORALITY AND DISCRIMINATORY TAINT

In this way, the textualist majority in *Abbott* and *Alexander* laid out its solution to dealing with a law's discriminatory legislative history. For the textualist majority, the temporal solution to a law's history of past discrimination is to simply exclude the past as evidence of present discrimination, no matter how recent. In this way, they sought to enact a temporal regime that makes a clean break with the past, conferring "good faith" on any legislature that wishes to "re-signify" the tainted actions of its own speech-acts in a more "affirmative" mode. By doing so, the textualist majority's temporal severance of the past can be described as a form of *malevolent legality* itself, since (as Sotomayor argued) the majority enacts a rule that selectively excludes evidence of discrimination to reach its conclusion.

The malevolent legality established in *Abbott* sought to pacify the problem of "discriminatory taint" (DT), defined as cases where a present law considered for enactment has a temporal predecessor that has historically been found to be unlawfully discriminatory. Whereas the *Abbott* court simply severs the past from an understanding of present discrimination, other jurisdictions and legal scholars have argued that removing discriminatory taint from laws or policies requires taking into account the historical purpose and policy context of law—what Solum has called its *teleological intent*.[44] Addressing the malevolent legality evidenced in *Abbott v. Perez*, therefore, requires taking into account a law's teleological intent or meaning. In this way, addressing *the temporality of discrimination* requires what Francois Ost calls a *dialectical* relationship of law that emerges within the horizon of both past and the future-oriented considerations. While *Abbott* severs the past from the "good faith" of the present, a dialectical relationship of law and time takes into account the purpose and policy context of our shared legal order.

Seen in this way, *Abbott's* purely performative solution to a law's discriminatory history is one among many proposed solutions for dealing with the problem of discriminatory taint. In what follows, I address cases and jurisdictions that have addressed this problem and provided different solutions to past discrimination, resulting in very different configurations between law, time, and historical memory. By adopting the use of teleological intent or purpose, I argue, courts such as *US-Carrillo-Lopez* and *United States v. Fordice* (1992) adopt a "dialectical" temporal relationship that takes into account past discrimination in remedying harm to secure a more just future. Adopting Murray's *institutional realist* approach to discrimination, I argue, provides a remedy to the malevolent legality enacted by the court in *Abbott*. An institutional realist approach to discrimination therefore ensures that the history and memory of discrimination is not severed from the law, as in *Abbott*, but brought into a hermeneutic reading of the present.

## Discriminatory Taint: Cases and Contexts

In this section, I take up the question of "whether a subsequent legislative re-enactment can eliminate the taint from a law that was originally enacted with discriminatory intent."[45] Here, I draw upon Murray's "T1/T2" pattern of analysis.[46] If a statute, law, or policy enacted with discriminatory intent by a legislature at Time One (T1) is reenacted at a later Time Two (T2), can policy T1 be "cured" or "cleansed" of its discriminatory taint? If so, what are the requirements for curing a discriminatory statute, law, or policy? Must the legislature considering enactment at T2 first engage in a deliberative process addressing and removing the discriminatory intent and disparate impact of statute T1? Or does "curing" only require a good faith effort acknowledging and considering the merits of amending the offending provision? Or rather, as argued by the Supreme Court in *Abbott*, should we give new legislatures a "good faith presumption" that the prior discriminatory intent of the legislature that enacted the T1 policy cannot be imputed to the legislature that enacts the policy at T2? These possible answers are not the only solutions to the problem of DT cases, but they are some of the answers that have been given within antidiscrimination jurisprudence, which I will address.

In *Hunter v. Underwood*, the Supreme Court invalidated a criminal provision of the Alabama constitution purging individuals from voting rolls convicted of crimes involving moral turpitude (T2) based upon its finding that its legal predecessor from 1901 defining crimes involving moral turpitude was enacted with discriminatory purpose to disenfranchise black voters (T1).[47] Appellees of the case were purged from voting rolls based on their conviction pursuant to the statute, and they challenged the constitutionality of the provision on equal protection grounds. Since the statute itself was racially neutral, the court utilized the *Arlington Heights* factors to examine whether the statute could be said to have an impermissible racial purpose and discriminatory impact upon African Americans. Since the precedent statute was enacted during the Alabama Constitutional Convention of 1901 with an explicit purpose of disenfranchising African Americans and was shown to have disparate impact on them, and there was not sufficient evidence that the legislature at any time addressed the offending statute, the court found that the "original enactment was motivated by a desire to discriminate against blacks on account of race and the section continues to this day to have that effect. As such, it violates equal protection under *Arlington Heights*."[48]

In *Abbott v. Perez*, The Supreme Court narrowly upheld the constitutionality of Texas's revised 2013 redistricting plans (T2) based upon a set of precedent plans from 2011 (T1) which were found to violate the Equal Protection Clause and the Voting Rights Act by a district court.[49] Ruling on the original plans from 2011, the court found the new plans unlawfully discriminatory because "the Legislature did not engage in a deliberative process to ensure that the 2013 plans cured any taint from the 2011 plans."[50] However, in a 5–4 ruling, the Supreme Court disagreed and allowed Texas "to use maps that the three-judge district court unanimously found were adopted for the purpose of preserving the racial discrimination that tainted its previous maps."[51]

In *Ramos v. Louisiana*, the Supreme Court invalidated a Louisiana statute allowing non-unanimous juries in criminal trials (T2) based on its finding that the statute's predecessor was enacted during the 1898 Constitutional Convention with the effect and explicit purpose "to diminish the influence of black jurors" (T1).[52] In *N.C. State Conference of the NAACP v. Raymond*, a US Court of Appeals upheld North Carolina's 2018 Voter Identification law (T2), whose predecessor law (the 2013 Omnibus Law) was found to have discriminatory intent by a district court (T1). In *Harness v. Hosemann*, a district court upheld provisions of the Mississippi State Constitution disenfranchising voters convicted of felonies (T2) based on its finding that a predecessor from the 1890 constitution was enacted with discriminatory intent and racial impact (T1).[53] The court ruled that, unlike in *Hunter*, the state took at least some affirmative action to address the tainted provision by the legislature considering amendments and reviewing election laws in a formal task force. While the legislature never actually amended the specific offending section (§241) nor enacted reenfranchisement for convicted felons, the court nonetheless considered these legislative actions sufficient to meet the burden that "the state would have passed section 241 as is without racial motivation."[54]

In June 2020, Gustavo Carrillo-Lopez was indicted pursuant to §1326 of the Immigration and Nationality Act. INA §1326 is "a statutory provision enacted in 1929 for the purpose of solving "the Mexican problem" by criminalizing unauthorized reentry after deportation from the United States" (Hernandez et al., 2021: 3). Explicitly motivated by nativist, eugenic concerns about the inferiority of Mexican immigrants, the original language of §1326 within the Undesirable Aliens Act of 1929 was "designed to further the Nativists' racist goal of preventing long-term Mexican immigration to the

United States while also preserving agribusiness access to low-cost workers." As part of the McCarran-Walter Act of 1952, Congress reenacted §1326, followed closely by "Operation Wetback," which together resulted in criminal reentry quickly becoming the most prosecuted federal charge by the US government. Today, approximately half of all federal prosecutions are for illegal entry or reentry, costing the federal government over one billion dollars per year, including costs of incarceration.[55]

In 2021, Carrillo-Lopez sought to dismiss the indictment on the grounds that §1326 violated his constitutional right to equal protection under the Fifth Amendment. In 2021, a US district court ruled in favor of Carrillo-Lopez, finding that,

> at no point has Congress confronted the racist, nativist roots of Section 1326. Instead, the amendments to Section 1326 over the past 90 years have not changed its function but have simply made the provision more punitive and broadened its reach. Accordingly, the Court cannot find that subsequent amendments somehow cleansed the statute of its history while retaining the language and functional operation of the original statute."[56]

In stark contrast to the Supreme Court's ruling in *Abbott,* the district court rejected the argument that the legislature that reenacted the statute enjoys a "good faith presumption." In contrast, the court concluded that Congress never removed the discriminatory taint from the statute, and therefore §1326 is unlawfully discriminatory and violates Carrillo-Lopez's right to equal protection under the Fifth Amendment.

## Institutional Realism

Arguably the most thorough treatment and solution to the problem of discriminatory taint has been given recently by Murray.[57] As a critique of antidiscrimination jurisprudence too narrowly focused on finding intent, Murray develops a theory of DT that accommodates harder cases of discrimination where intent is elusive *or* irrelevant to the discrimination in question. As Murray argues:

> The Supreme Court's antidiscrimination doctrine is widely understood as requiring specific, subjective intent to harm because of a protected trait . . . taint can coexist with genuinely pure-hearted T2 decisionmakers. The same facts that concretize the taint concept, however, also indicate that more matters than pure-heartedness when evaluating a tainted T2. That is, properly understood, taint describes a scenario where a decision rule focused on specific intent is uniquely inapt.[58]

Thus, for Murray, good intentions of policymakers should not be given deference in DT cases, since pure-heartedness or good will is often irrelevant to the inquiry into disparate impact of a specific policy. In debates over what exactly is required to cure a tainted T2, varying levels of deference are given to policymakers. In what follows, I outline four different solutions to the problem of curing DT, beginning with the highest level of deference and ending with the lowest level of deference. These different levels concern the level of deference given to the good faith actions required by policymakers in order for a tainted T2 to be considered cured.

The first solution for addressing DT can be seen in *N.C. State Conference of the NAACP v. Raymond*. In this case, the court dismissed a challenge to its 2018 Voter ID laws (T2) on the basis of its finding that the discriminatory taint of T1 (2013 Omnibus Law) was posited without the good faith presumption required by law.[59] Allowing the highest possible deference to policymakers' good intentions in new legislatures, the court addresses DT by effectively severing the T1/T2 relationship by adhering to the good faith presumption that it traces to *Abbott v. Perez*:

> A legislature's past acts do not condemn the acts of a later legislature, which we must presume acts in good faith. *Id.* So because we find that the district court improperly disregarded this principle by reversing the burden of proof and failing to apply the presumption of legislative good faith, we reverse.[60]

In this strategy, the very notion of DT violates the good faith presumption, which is described as an "unmistakable command" by the Supreme Court's decision in *Abbott v. Perez*. Indeed, here DT does not appear as a debate over the criteria of evaluation or a weighing of the evidence of discrimination at all:

> We do not reverse the district court because it weighed the evidence before it differently than we would. Instead, we reverse because of the fundamental legal errors that permeate the opinion—the flipping of the burden of proof and the failure to provide the presumption of legislative good faith—that irrevocably affected its outcome.[61]

Therefore, strict adherence to the good faith presumption as a "command" of the Supreme Court, as the court did here, militates against a finding of discriminatory intent when evaluating the *Arlington Heights* factors.

The second solution to the problem of DT can be seen in *Harness v. Hosemann*. Here, the court considered a tainted T2 to be cured or cleansed by deliberative *consideration* that fell short of acting on the offending section itself in the form of amending, reenacting, removing, etc. It found that the tainted T2 was cured simply by the fact that the legislature *considered* amending the offending section, and that the legislature reviewed the state's election laws, of which the offending T2 was a part. Thus, while not severing the relationship between the T2/T1 pattern of DT, the second strategy gives a high degree of deference to policymakers in terms of the standard of good faith acts required to cure a tainted T2. I call this solution *deliberative consideration* to indicate the minimal level of legislative scrutiny required to cure a tainted governmental policy, law, or statute.

A third response to DT is found in Murray's *institutional realist* approach. For Murray, the problem of DT is about statutory meaning in light of personal and institutional responsibility for harms created by governmental actors. The problem of discriminatory predecessors, Murray writes, "raise questions about whether and when responsibility for past government acts constrains modern government behavior. We cannot answer those questions with a view from nowhere. But we can answer them against the backdrop of widespread legal recognition that continuity informs meaning and responsibility, and in light of widely accepted antidiscrimination commitments."[62] Arguing against intent-based accounts that give deference to pure-hearted policymakers, Murray writes:

> The problems of evasion and lingering effects of past wrongdoing do not disappear simply because multimember bodies have inconstant personnel. An institutional realist approach suggests that institutional continuity helps explain how identity matters, as well as the nature of the responsibility at T2. Taint recognizes responsibility as connected not just to individual decisionmakers but to the institutions of which they are a part.[63]

Given the realities of institutional continuity and responsibility for state-sponsored action resulting in discriminatory effects and disparate impact claims, Murray's institutional realist approach focuses on addressing disparate impact, directing that "courts first ask whether the state can show that the contemporary policy has eliminated any meaningful disparate impact," and if it cannot, courts must give a legitimate reason why pursuing a nondiscriminatory policy outweighs shielding the disparate impact of a tainted policy.[64] On this point, Murray writes:

> Persistent disparate impact does not necessarily doom the policy. But, to purge the taint, governments must offer (1) a legitimate, nondiscriminatory interest that will be substantially impaired absent this policy, (2) direct engagement with the past problematic history, (3) an explanation of why the disparate impact cannot be eliminated, and (4) an explanation of why the legitimate need for this means of pursuing the legitimate interest outweighs the harm of shielding the disparate impact of a tainted rule.[65]

On Murray's account, deliberative *consideration* falls well short of this fuller direct engagement with the specific elements of disparate impact created or posed by a governmental policy. Instead, Murray's model proposes placing the burden of proof upon the state to first demonstrate lack of disparate impact and a demonstration of departure from the discriminatory intent of the predecessor's history. In this respect, *US v. Carrillo-Lopez* can be seen to utilize this basic procedure of Murray's proposal for adjudication.

The fourth answer to the problem of DT can be found in *United States v. Fordice*, which found that Mississippi's revised educational policies in the wake of *Brown v. Board* (T2) still retained segregative effects connected to the "separate but equal" doctrine ruled unconstitutional.

The Supreme Court burden utilized a "state-burden" standard of evaluating DT that is most starkly contrasted with that used in *N.C. State Conference of the NAACP v. Raymond*. Similar to Murray's proposal, the Supreme Court ruled that the burden lays with the state to *disprove* DT in cases where a T1/T2 pattern of disparate impact exists. The court ruled:

> A challenged policy does not survive under the standard we announce today if it began during the prior *de jure* era, produces adverse impacts, and persists without sound educational justification. When each of these elements has been met, I believe, we are justified in not requiring proof of a present specific intent to discriminate. It is safe to assume that a policy adopted during the *de jure* era, if it produces segregative effects, reflects a discriminatory intent. As long as that intent remains, of course, such a policy cannot continue. And given an initially tainted policy, it is eminently reasonable to make the State bear the risk of nonpersuasion with respect to intent at some future time, both because the State has created the dispute through its own prior unlawful conduct...and because discriminatory intent does tend to persist through time. . . . Although we do not formulate our standard in terms of a burden shift with respect to intent, the factors we do consider—the historical background of the policy, the degree of its adverse impact, and the plausibility of any justification asserted in its defense—are precisely those factors that go into determining intent under *Washington v. Davis*. . . . Thus, if a policy remains in force, without adequate justification and despite tainted roots and segregative effect, it appears clear—clear enough to presume conclusively—that the State has failed to disprove discriminatory intent.[66]

Most notable, the Supreme Court in *United States v. Fordice* (1992) clarified that if discriminatory effects are produced and remain from a governmental policy that was discriminatory, then to that extent we have discriminatory intent *regardless* of the presence or absence or subjective intent. What matters for the *Fordice* court is the lingering *effects* or impact of a discriminatory policy T1 as evidenced in a later policy T2.

Taken together, a robust theory of DT would take cues from both Murray's institutional realist approach and the *Fordice* and *Carrillo-Lopez* courts by directing the burden of proof upon the state to disprove any nexus of connection between the discriminatory effects and policy functions of a governmental policy T2 and a predecessor policy T1. This conception does several things. First, it rightfully places the burden of proof upon the state when confronted with policies that government itself is responsible for but has failed to address. Second, it rightfully places the inquiry on the institutional nexus of the government-sponsored T2/T1 pattern regardless of whether *subjective* intent or motive is present or not. While Murray's institutional realism and the *Fordice* framework emphasize disparate impact and discriminatory effect, *Carrillo-Lopez* emphasizes the institutional analysis of the state's policy and rationale. While both elements—disparate impact and institutional policy— are important for interpreting discrimination, both Murray's institutional realist approach and the institutional policy approach of the *Carrillo-Lopez* court provides the best alternative frameworks to the malevolent legality enacted by *Abbott*. Instead of granting a legislature with a discriminatory history a clean presumption of good faith, these institutional realist approaches to discrimination do not sever discrimination from the memory of law. Instead, institutional realist approaches to discrimination bring the memory of discrimination into a reading of the present, in order to address the state's policy goals of remedying historical injustice for which it is partly responsible,

## Teleological Intent: the "Purpose" of Law

The pragmatic canon of statutory construction known as *in pari materia* is a rule utilized to interpret the intent of a statute by analyzing its institutional relationship to a broader holistic purpose within its subject-matter jurisdiction. More specifically, this rule is useful when there are no explicit linguistic references to the intent of the legislature within a statute or when a statute is passed at different times and different legislative sessions. For these reasons, the pragmatic canon is particularly applicable to DT cases since a) the explicit linguistic use of discriminatory intent has been removed from the T2 statute, and b) the T2 statute is usually enacted within a different legislative session from the T1 statute.

The pragmatic canon of *in pari materia* has been utilized in virtually every field of legal interpretation in cases where legislative intent is either unclear or challenged but where other provisions or laws within the subject-matter jurisdiction shed light upon legislative intent. The definition of this rule as it is utilized in statutory construction was succinctly summarized by a Texas Appellate court in 2018:

The doctrine of *in pari materia* is a settled rule of statutory construction concerning statutes that deal with the same general subject, have the same general purpose, or relate to the same person or thing or class of persons or things, even when such statutes contain no reference to one another and even though they were passed at different times or during different sessions of the legislature.[67]

In 1993, the Wyoming Supreme Court addressed the role of the doctrine, writing, "statutory interpretation is a judicial process that emphasizes the functional relation between the parts and the whole."[68] Interpreting intent through examining the functional relationship of part to whole, the court said, implies that

in ascertaining the legislative intent in enacting a statute the court must look to the mischief the act was intended to cure, the historical setting surrounding its enactment, the public policy of the state, the conditions of the law and all other prior and contemporaneous facts and circumstances that would enable the court intelligently to determine the intention of the lawmaking body.[69]

By examining the policy purpose of a statute in this holistic way, the court said, the intent of a statute can be determined: it "must be read *in pari materia* and harmoniously to form a congruous whole."[70] In attempting to give statutes their proper legislative intent, courts "should look first to the words of the statute but if they do not disclose legislative intent, the court must examine the statute as a whole, giving effect to all of its provisions. *Id.* To determine legislative intent the court may also consider such factors as the context of the statute, the subject matter, historical background, its effects and consequences, and its spirit and purpose."[71]

In 2006, the Supreme Court clarified that the principle of *in pari materia* concerns the interpretation of the function of a statute within subject-matter jurisdiction and not venue jurisdiction.[72] This ruling was deduced in part from a previous Supreme Court decision affirming the basic rule of *in pari materia* that Congress will be aware of previous statutes within the same subject matter when enacting new statutes. The court wrote, "The rule is but a logical extension of the principle that individual sections of a single statute should be construed together, for it necessarily assumes that whenever Congress passes a new statute, it acts aware of all previous statutes on the same subject."[73]

There are two crucial implications for the pragmatic canon in DT cases. The first major issue is whether the discriminatory predecessor statute enacted at T1, of which Congress will be aware, can in fact be considered *in pari materia* with the statute enacted at T2. If the statutes are determined to be *in pari materia*, then the inquiry shifts to whether and to what extent the intent from statute T1 may be imputed to statute T2. Once again, the fact that a law has a discriminatory predecessor does not *in itself* doom the law to being impermissible. Therefore, the determination of whether the statutes are *in pari materia* will turn on whether the statutes, "deal with the same general subject, have the same general purpose, or relate to the same person or thing or class of persons or things, even when such statutes contain no reference to one another and even though they were passed at different times or during different sessions of the legislature."[74] Virtually all cases of DT will satisfy this criteria, since the law or policy being enacted is either identical to or a modified version of a previous law or policy. Because of this, T2 statutes, by definition, will be considered *in pari materia* with their predecessors.

Once statutes are considered *in pari materia*, the inquiry would then shift to whether and to what extent the impermissible purpose of statute T1 can be imputed to statute T2. In the case where the T1 statute is reenacted at T2 *without change*, the logic of the rule dictates that the T2 statute adopts the intent of the T1 statute. According to the logic of *in pari materia*, the Congress that enacts the T2 statute *without change* by extension adopts the same interpretation of the T1 statute as constitutionally impermissible, which is indeed as the Supreme Court interprets the application of the rule:

> Congress is presumed to be aware of an administrative or judicial interpretation of a statute and to adopt that interpretation when it re-enacts a statute without change . . . [when] Congress adopts a new law incorporating sections of a prior law, Congress normally can be presumed to have had knowledge of the interpretation given to the incorporated law, at least insofar as it affects the new statute.[75]

This point is crucial in debates over methods for resolving DT. The doctrine of *in par materia* rules out the good faith presumption. In cases of DT, the entire issue is that Congress enacts a statute T2 with the awareness that there is a discriminatory predecessor T1 enacted by a previous legislature, but the rule of *in pari materia* applies to statutes regardless of temporal distance or whether the statutes were enacted by different legislative sessions. Therefore, the presumption, according to the rule of *in pari materia*, is that a new Congress facing a purportedly tainted statute T2 must either a) address and remove any impermissible discriminatory elements before enactment, or b) fail to remove the impermissible discriminatory elements of which it is already aware.

By the same logic, a Congress that enacts the T2 statute without removing the impermissible discriminatory elements inherited from an *in par materia* statute T1 also adopts that interpretation. The court in *US v. Carrillo-Lopez*, for instance, followed the logic of *in pari materia*, finding that the tainted T2 immigration statute (1326) was unconstitutional because "the Court cannot find that subsequent amendments somehow cleansed the statute of its history while retaining the language and functional operation of the original statute."[76] The court assumed that the T2 legislature was aware of the discriminatory history of the statute, and while the linguistic intent had been removed, the court recognized that the statute nonetheless had to be considered as a part of the whole context and history of the T1 statute, of which the T2 Congress was aware, because the intent of the government's T2 policy was *functionally* connected to the T1 policy. To this point, the court ruled that "at no point has Congress confronted the racist, nativist roots of Section 1326. Instead, the amendments to Section 1326 over the past ninety years have not changed its function but have simply made the provision more punitive and broadened its reach."[77] Thus, because of the institutional connection between the unchanged policy and rationale of the T1 and T2 statutes, and because of a lack of evidence that the reenacting legislature expressly wished to remove and replace the discriminatory intent, the court found that the reenacted statute was unconstitutionally tainted.

This treatment of statutes *in pari materia* is consistent with the way the rule is described in statutory construction. Once statutes are considered *in pair materia*, once again, the inquiry is not complete. Considering the background of the T1 statute, "the court must look to the mischief the act was intended to cure, the historical setting surrounding its enactment, the public policy of the state, the conditions of the law and all other prior and contemporaneous facts and circumstances that would enable the court intelligently to determine the intention of the lawmaking body" regarding T2.[78] In this way, the determination of intent focuses on the comparative history, policy, and rationale of statutes T1 and T2. In cases where the history, policy, and rationale of statutes T1 and T2 are closely linked through a showing of evidence, the burden then shifts to the government, which has to demonstrate that the statute T2 is free of taint and has demonstrated, as the Carrillo-Lopez identified, a "change of Congressional intent, policy, or reasoning."[79] In other words, once a functional relationship has been established between the governmental institutional policy and rationale of statutes T1 and T2 considered *in pari materia*, the government has the burden of removing that institutional relationship before enactment.

The principle of *in pari materia* helps elucidate a central aspect of intent that often goes unexplored. Viewing law as composed of parts functioning within a broader policy context, the principle centers the *policy purpose* of law understood as the policy and rationale of the state in view of some historically embedded social goal, issue, or problem. Understood as an element of intent, the policy purpose of a law can in this way be distinguished from both its literal and semantic meaning as well as its consequences or "implicative" meaning. Since laws and policies often generate unintended consequences, such consequences cannot necessarily be considered part of the intent of legislators at time of enactment if they did not consider those consequences. Therefore, analysis of consequences or effects of a law must be distinct from an analysis of its policy purpose. Similarly, the language used in a statute may be ambiguous, vague, under-inclusive, or over-inclusive as to the more general policy or rationale of the statute. As a result, analysis of a statute's policy purpose can be conducted apart from its literal meaning and its effects or consequences.

In this regard, Solum helps us distinguished between what he refers to as the linguistic, implicative, and teleological elements of intent:

> When we ask the question, "What does this provision mean?" we might refer to the linguistic meaning or semantic content. Call this first sense of meaning the semantic sense. But the term "meaning" can also be used to refer to implications, consequences, or applications. Call this second sense of meaning the implicative sense. We might also use the term meaning to refer to the purpose or function of a given constitutional provision. Call this third sense of meaning the teleological sense.[80]

According to Solum, Dworkin utilizes the notion of the "purpose" of a statute by reference to its *teleological* intent, which according to Solum refers to "the goal, aim, or telos of the object of interpretation. The kind of goal that can be a Dworkinian 'purpose' is a goal that provides a normative justification for the practice being interpreted."[81] In this view, Dworkin's statutory construction would have us consider the textual integrity and legislative history of the T2 statute in light of the "unity" of its *teleological* intent or its "true purpose." In *Law's Empire,* Dworkin suggests that this unity of purpose will be found, among other places, by reference to the "life" of the statute and its context within the background principles of justice and fairness. For Dworkin, "judges should construct a statute so as to make it conform as closely as possible to principles of justice assumed elsewhere in the law."[82] This is so because legislators try to respect traditional principles of justice unless indicating otherwise, and because "a statute forms part of a larger intellectual system, the law as a whole, it should be constructed so as to make that larger system coherent in principle."[83] Here, Dworkin can be seen to advance the canon of *in pari* materia in a very limited sense of reading statutes as part of a holistic system of laws aimed at justice. Dworkin insists that his method of statutory construction respects historical research, textual integrity, and legislative history, while also respecting the aims and ends of law "as a whole." For Dworkin, a law's teleological intent—how it forms a part of a harmonious and coherent whole—is the source of unity in legal interpretation.

The analysis of the pragmatic canon of *in pari materia* gives us a clearer picture of teleological intent from a more technical point of statutory construction. Under this view, the statutory construction of the intent of a purportedly tainted statute asks whether the T2 statute can be considered an institutional part of a holistic view of impermissible conduct in a subject-matter jurisdiction. However, this does not mean that every law or policy that has a discriminatory predecessor is because of that fact alone tainted unconstitutionally. As the *Carrillo-Lopez* court clarifies, this approach does *not* mean that "the fact that a prior iteration of a statute was tainted by racial animus necessarily mean[s] that every subsequent reenactment will be."[84] Rather, imputing discriminatory intent from statute T1 to statute T2 involves, among other factors, the discriminatory *policy purpose* of a statute as part of a more holistic understanding of impermissible conduct by the state within a subject-matter.

To this end, I have proposed that the pragmatic canon of *in pari materia* is a useful rule of statutory construction that helps elucidate a practical way of determining the discriminatory intent of a T2 statute purportedly tainted. When applied to cases involving DT, the pragmatic canon of *in pari materia* provides a fuller account of intent that avoids the problems of voluntarist accounts of attitude-based wrongful discrimination. Most importantly, this canon leads to a statutory construction of discriminatory intent that views statutes in light of their *institutional* connection to the governmental policy and rationale of discriminatory predecessors within their subject-matter jurisdiction. Understanding the institutional responsibility of the state, I argue, is a crucial starting point for understanding discriminatory purpose and places emphasis on whether the policy and rationale of the state is legitimate and permissible in light of its functional comparison to state-sponsored discriminatory policies of the past. This analysis is crucial and distinct from analysis of effects of disparate impact, especially in some cases involving DT where there are no effects on which to judge the policy. Here, the function of the law must be taken into account given its structural and operational connection to the policy and rationale of a discriminatory predecessor.

## CONCLUSION

In *Abbott,* the Supreme Court's solution to the problem of past discrimination by a legislature was to simply sever the "constitutional memory" of discrimination from the law, instituting the rule of the "good faith" presumption. This new rule—that legislatures should be given a good faith presumption regardless of their past discrimination—can be traced back to Justice Scalia's arguments in *Edwards v. Aguillard* (1987), explored in chapter 1. In *Edwards*, Scalia had argued that by scrutinizing the implicit, allegedly unconstitutional motives of the legislature, the judiciary was declaring that the legislature "knowingly violated their oaths and then lied about it."[85] Instead, Scalia argued that the acts of the legislature must be interpreted exclusively on the basis of what the text says "on its face." For Scalia, when looking at the text of a legislative enactment, "the question of its constitutionality cannot rightly be disposed of on the gallop, by impugning the motives of its supporters."[86]

This was precisely the textualist argument of the *Abbott* and *Alexander* courts. Since the legislature takes an oath to carry out their duties in good faith to the constitution, the judiciary should not assume they are acting unconstitutionally. Therefore, so the argument goes, the job of the judiciary is to simply take the word of the text enacted by the legislature at face value. As Scalia famously declared in 1986, "Statutes should be interpreted, it seems to me, not on the basis of the unpromulgated intentions of those who enact them . . . but rather on the basis of what is the most probable meaning of the words of the enactment"[87] Unenacted motives or unstated intentions cannot be used to impugn the good faith of the text, only the enacted text rules. The *Abbott* court was recycling Scalia's textualist attack on discriminatory purpose.

In contrast, the *institutional realist* solutions reviewed in this chapter take seriously the *memory* of governmental discrimination as a source of meaning for interpreting the present. In *Carrillo-Lopez*, the function of the statute took the center of analysis, and the function of the statute was analyzed in terms of its historical context within immigration law and the policy and rationale of the statute in light of that history. Given the clear animus from the history and context of the statute within immigration law and policy, the key element the government had to demonstrate to absolve the statute of taint was a "change of Congressional intent, policy, or reasoning."[88] Finding no substantive change, the court found the T2 statute in violation of the Equal Protection Clause. Since the policy and rationale of the state between statute T1 and T2 had not substantially changed, the T2 statute was tainted. The just adjudication and resolution of DT cases, in this view, hinges upon analysis of the connection between the discriminatory governmental policy and rationale of statutes T1 and T2 considered *in pari materia*. The history and memory of discrimination, in other words, is not severed but brought into a hermeneutic reading of the present.

What truly matters in curing discriminatory laws and policies, as I've argued, is *not* the good faith or pure-heartedness of legislatures but instead whether our constitutional memory and collective history has been severed from the reading of the law. When we turn our attention to the *policy purpose* of the law, we center the *historical and cultural memory of the law* that always stands behind the written text. In this way, the institutional realist approaches to discrimination reviewed in this chapter serve as a remedy of "remembering" in contrast to the "forgetting" and severing of the past that was enacted in the Supreme Court's decision in *Abbott v. Perez*.

The dangerous precedent set by the *Abbott* decision, therefore, lies in the court's exclusion of any evidence of discrimination from the past (including legislative history, historical record) as probative for understanding the *present*. As the court said, citing *Mobile,* "past discrimination cannot, in the manner of original sin, condemn governmental action that is not itself unlawful."[89] This startling sovereign exclusion results in a wholesale erasure of the memory of the law or policy in question. This complete severance of the present with the past exemplifies a temporal regime of "forgetting" or "erasure" whereby a discriminatory law is white-washed and given a "blank slate"—as if the history of the law never existed.

As I have shown, Justice Scalia's attack on the purpose of the VRA and the invalidation of Section 5 provided precedent for the court to conclude in *Abbott v. Perez* that the history of discrimination may be excluded from judicial review of a legislature's voting scheme, which amounts to the proposition that the recent history of a legislature's discriminatory actions *have no logical relation* to the meaning of the same legislature's present enactment in the same subject-matter. By barring the use of the congressional history of discrimination to interpreting legal meaning, the *Abbott* court severs the memory of discrimination from the interpretive framework of the law itself.

Without utilizing the congressional history of discrimination when interpreting the law, the legal system loses its own memory. For Francois Ost, this is precisely one of the functions of *stare decisis* or *precedent*—it is the mechanism by which legal systems maintain the integrity of their own memory. [90] Writing in the shadow of the horrors of World War II, Hannah Arendt in *Origins of Totalitarianism* observes that one of the functions of positive law is to serve as a kind of collective memory that guards against the "totalitarian dream" of "forgetting" the past. Arendt writes,

> the boundaries of positive laws are for the political existence of man what memory is for his historical existence: they guarantee the pre-existence of a common world, the reality of some continuity which transcends the individual life span of each generation, absorbs all new origins and is nourished by them.[91]

For Arendt, the lesson of Nazism and the historical experience of World War II imprinted upon her the terrific danger of severing the past from our collective self-understanding. Warning against both the desire to return to a pure idealized past, and the desire to try to escape the past into a purified image of the future, she writes:

> We can no longer afford to take that which was good in the past and simply call it our heritage, to discard the bad and simply think of it as a dead load which by itself time will bury in oblivion. The subterranean stream of Western history has finally come to the surface and usurped the dignity of our tradition. This is the reality in which we live. And this is why all efforts to escape from the grimness of the present into nostalgia for a still intact past, or into the anticipated oblivion of a better future, are vain.[92]

Just as Arendt observed the danger of burying the past, Aleida Assmann notes that building and preserving cultural memory requires an active, performative role of society. As Assmann has elegantly written,

> in order for anything at all to remain present, a huge degree of attention and great cultural efforts are required. What is not, by means of a collective effort, selected, appraised, distinguished, staged, reclaimed, and repeatedly represented, will always fall back into a latent state of forgetting, or into that cotton batten in which we are all so deeply embedded.[93]

## NOTES

1. *Texas v. United States*, 887 F. Supp. 2d 133, 138 (D.D.C. August 28, 2012).
2. See *Perry v. Perez*, 565 U.S. 388, 391 (2012).
3. See *Bush v. Vera*, 517 U.S. 952 (1996), concurring that the RedAppl software was used to create unconstitutional racially gerrymandered districts: "Because Districts 18 and 29 are formed in utter disregard for traditional redistricting criteria and because their shapes are ultimately unexplainable on grounds other than the racial quotas established for those districts, they are the product of unconstitutional racial gerrymandering." See *Vera v. Richards*, 861 F. Supp. 1304, 1341 (S.D. Tex. 1994).
4. *Bush v. Vera*, 517 U.S. 952, 975 (1996).
5. *Bush v. Vera*, 517 U.S. 952, 976 (1996); Furthermore, the district court issued a foreboding warning that "Just as they micro-manipulated the racial composition of Texas congressional districts in 1991, they may be enabled by a new body of statistical data to select their voters even more precisely in 2001." See *Vera v. Richards*, 861 F. Supp. 1304, 1336 (S.D. Tex. 1994).
6. *Texas v. United States*, 887 F. Supp. 2d 133 (D.D.C. 2012).
7. The Voting Rights Act (VRA) prohibits voting changes that diminish minority citizens' "ability . . . to elect their preferred candidates of choice." U.S.C. § 1973c(d) Section 2 prohibits states from imposing electoral practices "which results in a denial or abridgement of the right of any citizen of the United States to vote on account of

race or color" (42 U.S.C. § 1973(a)). Legal challenges to a legislature's redistricting maps may therefore be brought under these provisions.

8. *Abbott v. Perez*, 138 S. Ct. 2305, 201 L. Ed. 2d 714 (2018).
9. *Perez v. Abbott*, 274 F. Supp. 3d 624, 652 (W.D. Tex. 2017).
10. *Perez v. Abbott*, 274 F. Supp. 3d 624, 652 (W.D. Tex. 2017).
11. *Texas v. United States*, 887 F. Supp. 2d 133, 233 (D.D.C. 2012).
12. *Texas v. United States*, 887 F. Supp. 2d 133, 233-34 (D.D.C. 2012).
13. *Perez v. Abbott*, 274 F. Supp. 3d 624, 652 (W.D. Tex. 2017).
14. *Perez v. Abbott*, 274 F. Supp. 3d 624, 651 (W.D. Tex. 2017).
15. *Shelby County v. Holder*, 570 U.S. 529, 532 (U.S. June 25, 2013).
16. *Shelby County v. Holder*, 570 U.S. 529, 531 (U.S. June 25, 2013).
17. *Abbott v. Perez,* 138 S. Ct. 2305, 2310 (U.S. June 25, 2018).
18. *Abbott v. Perez*, 138 S. Ct. 2305, 201 L. Ed. 2d 714 (2018).
19. *Texas v. United States*, 887 F. Supp. 2d 133, 151 (D.D.C. 2012).
20. *Abbott v. Perez*, 138 S. Ct. 2305, 2311 (U.S. June 25, 2018).
21. *Abbott v. Perez*, No. 17-586, at *7 (June 25, 2018).
22. *Mobile v. Bolden*, 446 U.S. 55, 74 (U.S. April 22, 1980).
23. Steven V. Roberts, "Voting Rights Act Renewed in Senate by Margin of 85–8," *New York Times*, June 19, 1982, https://www.nytimes.com/1982/06/19/us/voting-rights-act-renewed-in-senate-by-margin-of-85-8.html?smid=url-share.
24. *Simmons v. Galvin*, 575 F.3d 24, 52 (1st Cir. Mass. July 31, 2009).
25. Roberts, "Voting Rights Act Renewed in Senate by Margin of 85–8."
26. 52 USCS § 10301.
27. *Mobile v. Bolden*, 446 U.S. 55, 74 (U.S. April 22, 1980).
28. *Perez v. Abbott*, 274 F. Supp. 3d 624, 652 (W.D. Tex. 2017).
29. *Abbott v. Perez*, No. 17-586, at 81-82 (June 25, 2018).
30. *Arlington Heights v. Metropolitan Housing Corp.*, 429 U.S. 252, 268 (1977).
31. *Abbott v. Perez*, No. 17-586, at *3 (June 25, 2018).
32. Judith Butler, *Excitable Speech: A Politics of the Performative* (New York: Routledge, 2021), 15.
33. Butler, *Excitable Speech*, 15.
34. *Abbott v. Perez*, No. 17-586, at *3 (June 25, 2018).
35. Butler, *Excitable Speech*, 15.
36. *S.C. State Conference of the NAACP v. Alexander*, 649 F. Supp. 3d 177, 193 (D.S.C. 2023).
37. *S.C. State Conference of the NAACP v. Alexander*, 649 F. Supp. 3d 177, 193 (D.S.C. 2023).
38. Alexander v. S.C. State Conf. of the NAACP, 2024 U.S. LEXIS 2262, *15-17 (U.S. May 23, 2024).
39. Alexander v. S.C. State Conf. of the NAACP, 2024 U.S. LEXIS 2262, *15-17 (U.S. May 23, 2024).
40. Alexander v. S.C. State Conf. of the NAACP, 2024 U.S. LEXIS 2262, *105 (U.S. May 23, 2024).
41. Alexander v. S.C. State Conf. of the NAACP, 2024 U.S. LEXIS 2262, *142-143 (U.S. May 23, 2024).

42. Alexander v. S.C. State Conf. of the NAACP, 2024 U.S. LEXIS 2262, *107 (U.S. May 23, 2024).
43. Alexander v. S.C. State Conf. of the NAACP, 2024 U.S. LEXIS 2262, *107 (U.S. May 23, 2024).
44. Lawrence B. Solum, "The Unity of Interpretation," *Boston University Law Review* 90 (2016): 561.
45. *Johnson v. Governor of Fla.*, 405 F.3d 1214, 1223 (11th Cir. 2005).
46. See Kerrel Murray, "Discriminatory Taint," *Harvard Law Review* 135 (2022): 1190.
47. *Hunter v. Underwood*, 471 U.S. 222, 105 S. Ct. 1916 (1985).
48. *Hunter v. Underwood*, 471 U.S. 222, 233, 105 S. Ct. 1916, 1922 (1985).
49. *Abbott v. Perez*, 138 S. Ct. 2305 (2018).
50. *Perez v. Abbott*, 274 F. Supp. 3d 624, 649 (W.D. Tex. 2017).
51. *Abbott v. Perez*, 138 S. Ct. 2305, 2335 (2018).
52. *Ramos v. Louisiana*, 140 S. Ct. 1390, 1417 (2020).
53. *Harness v. Hosemann, 988 F.3d 818 (5th Cir. 2021).*
54. *Harness v. Hosemann,* No. 3:17-CV-791-DPJ-FKB, 2019 U.S. Dist. LEXIS 228435, at *27 (S.D. Miss. Aug. 7, 2019).
55. Doug Keller, "Re-thinking Illegal Entry and Re-entry," *Loyola University Chicago Law Journal* 44, no. 1 (2012): 67–68.
56. United States v. Carrillo-Lopez, No. 3:20-cr-00026-MMD-WGC, 2021 U.S. Dist. LEXIS 155741, at *62–63 (D. Nev. 18 Aug. 2021).
57. See Murray, "Discriminatory Taint."
58. See Murray, "Discriminatory Taint."
59. *N.C. State Conference of the NAACP v. Raymond*, 981 F.3d 295 (4th Cir. 2020).
60. *N.C. State Conference of the NAACP v. Raymond*, 981 F.3d 295, 298 (4th Cir. 2020).
61. *N.C. State Conference of the NAACP v. Raymond*, 981 F.3d 295, 310-11 (4th Cir. 2020).
62. Murray, "Discriminatory Taint," 1226.
63. Murray, "Discriminatory Taint," 1221.
64. Murray, "Discriminatory Taint," 1197.
65. Murray, "Discriminatory Taint," 1241.
66. *United States v. Fordice,* 505 U.S. 717, 746-47, 112 S. Ct. 2727, 2745 (1992).
67. *Desir v. State*, 543 S.W.3d 865, 866 (Tex. App. 2018).
68. *Parker Land & Cattle Co. v. Wyo. Game & Fish Comm'n*, 845 P.2d 1040, 1043 (Wyo. 1993).
69. *Parker Land & Cattle Co. v. Wyo. Game & Fish Comm'n*, 845 P.2d 1040, 1044 (Wyo. 1993).
70. *Parker Land & Cattle Co. v. Wyo. Game & Fish Comm'n*, 845 P.2d 1040, 1048 (Wyo. 1993).
71. *Jon Blum v. The State of Ariz.*, 171 Ariz. 201, 205, 829 P.2d 1247, 1251 (Ct. App. 1992).

72. *Wachovia Bank, Nat'l Ass'n v. Schmidt*, 546 U.S. 303, 316, 126 S. Ct. 941, 950 (2006).
73. *Erlenbaugh v. United States*, 409 U.S. 239, 244, 93 S. Ct. 477, 480 (1972).
74. *Desir v. State*, 543 S.W.3d 865, 866 (Tex. App. 2018).
75. *Lorillard, Div. of Loew's Theatres, Inc. v. Pons*, 434 U.S. 575, 580-81, 98 S. Ct. 866, 870 (1978).
76. *United States v. Carrillo-Lopez*, 555 F. Supp. 3d 996, 1027 (D. Nev. 2021).
77. *United States v. Carrillo-Lopez*, 555 F. Supp. 3d 996, 1027 (D. Nev. 2021).
78. *Parker Land & Cattle Co. v. Wyo. Game & Fish Comm'n*, 845 P.2d 1040, 1044 (Wyo. 1993).
79. *United States v. Carrillo-Lopez*, No. 3:20-cr-00026-MMD-WGC, 2021 U.S. Dist. LEXIS 155741, at *62-63 (D. Nev. Aug. 18, 2021).
80. Solum, "The Unity of Interpretation," 561.
81. Solum, "The Unity of Interpretation," 560.
82. Ronald Dworkin, *Law's Empire* (Cambridge, MA: Harvard University Press 1986), 19.
83. Dworkin, *Law's Empire*, 19–20.
84. *United States v. Carrillo-Lopez*, 555 F. Supp. 3d 996, 1027 (D. Nev. 2021).
85. *Edwards v. Aguillard*, 482 U.S. 578, 610-611 (U.S. June 19, 1987).
86. *Edwards v. Aguillard*, 482 U.S. 578, 610-611 (U.S. June 19, 1987).
87. Antonin Scalia, Speech on original intent [submitted as part of nomination questionnaire], Delivered at the Attorney General's Conference on Economic Liberties, June 14, 1986, Antonin Scalia papers, LAW, MMC, 291, Series I, Box: 26, Folder: 11, Harvard Law School Library, Historical & Special Collections, 2.
88. *United States v. Carrillo-Lopez*, No. 3:20-cr-00026-MMD-WGC, 2021 U.S. Dist. LEXIS 155741, at *62-63 (D. Nev. Aug. 18, 2021).
89. *Mobile v. Bolden*, 446 U.S. 55, 74 (U.S. April 22, 1980).
90. Francois Ost, *Le Temps Du Droit* (Paris: Odile Jacob, 1999), 91-93.
91. Hannah Arendt, *The Origins of Totalitarianism* (New York: Meridian Books 1962), 465.
92. Arendt, *The Origins of Totalitarianism*, viii-ix.
93. Aleida Assmann and Sarah Clift, *Is Time Out of Joint? On the Rise and Fall of the Modern Time Regime* (Ithaca, NY: Cornell University Press, 2020), 29.

# 6

## *Students for Fair Admission v. Harvard* (2023)
### Colorblindness by Legal Fiat

In this chapter, I argue that the Supreme Court's "race-neutral" textualist reading of the Equal Protection Clause in *Students for Fair Admission v. Harvard* (2023) should be understood as a form of *sovereign exceptionalism*. First, I examine Justice Scalia's views and opinions on race and the law. Second, I reconstruct the court's colorblind interpretation in *Students v. Harvard* and its articulation by Justices Thomas and Barrett. Third, I argue that the court's judicial colorblindness stems *not* from a judge's lack of ethical sensitivity or epistemic virtue but rather from her self-conferral of a sovereign discretionary power to exclude considerations of justice from her interpretation of the law. As Justices Ketanji Brown Jackson and Sotomayor argued, the court's colorblindness should be understood as a selective, sovereign decision to sever historical memory from the text of the law: that is, "by legal fiat." The textualist judge may exercise colorblindness because she is, as Judith Butler says, a "petty sovereign." This institutional function, in turn, sustains the judge's belief that legal interpretation may be a *neutral* or *apolitical* activity. In this sense, the court's colorblindness is a kind of "meta" *malevolent legality*—a controlling precedent for the sovereign decision to exclude legal meaning from the hermeneutic universe of law under the pretext of neutrality.

### SCALIA ON RACE AND THE LAW

In an interview conducted in 1992, Justice Scalia spoke about his undergraduate experience at Georgetown University, where he received his bachelor's degree in history. In that interview, Scalia revealed that, in fact, his first choice was not Georgetown but Princeton University. To Scalia's great disappointment, he was not accepted into Princeton. In the interview, Scalia reflected on his experience:

I always remembered thinking: that was the only instance where I thought my background, I wouldn't say it was discrimination against Italians in particular. But I remember having the interview with a Princeton alumnus and I sort of had the feeling I was just, or he thought I was just not the Princeton kind of a person.[1]

Speaking about his perceived experience of not being "WASPish" enough (White Anglo-Saxon Protestant), Scalia says he felt that he was

Not from the right school, the right family, good club, not WASPish enough. That may be unfair. It was a long time ago, but I did have that feeling and I must say that's the only time I have ever had the feeling that, you know, that being an Italian-American made any difference to my detriment in my life. Anyway, . . . I didn't get into Princeton and Georgetown offered me a full tuition scholarship.[2]

Scalia's reflections on his denial of admission at Princeton might suggest that Scalia would have at least some moderate understanding in favor of affirmative action policies. If there was even some truth to Scalia's intuition about his denial of admission to Princeton, then it follows Scalia himself was a victim of racial discrimination in admissions. However, this experience did *not* translate to Scalia's views on affirmative action. On the contrary, beginning in 1979, Scalia had launched an aggressive attack on the notion of affirmative action, and one of his main arguments against affirmative action was that such policies benefit blacks at the expense of other minority groups such as Italians, Jews, Irish, and Polish immigrants. Scalia writes:

Some of the most vocal opposition to racial affirmative action comes from minority group members who have seen the value of their accomplishments debased by the suspicion—no, to be frank, the reality—of a lower standard for their group in the universities and the professions. This new racial presumption, imposed upon those who have lifted themselves above the effects of old racial presumptions, is the most evil fruit of a fundamentally bad seed. From racist principles flow racist results.[3]

According to Scalia, affirmative action lowers the standards of admission for black applicants, and thereby debases the accomplishments of other minorities. Scalia then speaks about his own background, writing:

My father came to this country when he was a teenager. Not only had he never profited from the sweat of any black man's brow, I don't think he had ever seen a black man. There are, of course, many white ethnic groups that came to this country in great numbers relatively late in its history—Italians, Jews,

Irish, Poles—who not only took no part in, and derived no profit from, the major historic suppression of the currently acknowledged minority groups, but were, in fact, themselves the object of discrimination by the dominant Anglo-Saxon majority. . . . To be sure, in relatively recent years some or all of these groups have been the beneficiaries of discrimination against blacks, or have themselves practiced discrimination. But to compare their racial debt—I must use that term, since the concept of "restorative justice" implies it; there is no creditor without a debtor—with that of those who plied the slave trade, and who maintained a formal caste system for many years thereafter, is to confuse a mountain with a molehill.[4]

For Scalia, affirmative action establishes a "creditor-debtor" relationship that benefits blacks at the expense of other minorities such as himself. Therefore, he concludes:

I am not willing to prefer the son of a prosperous and well-educated black doctor or lawyer—solely because of his race—to the son of a recent refugee from Eastern Europe who is working as a manual laborer to get his family ahead. The affirmative action system now in place will produce the latter result because it is based upon concepts of racial indebtedness and racial entitlement rather than individual worth and individual need; that is to say, because it is racist.[5]

In the above passages, one cannot help but think of Scalia's remarks on his denial from Princeton based on his perceived experience of racism. From these interview comments, it is plausible Scalia counted himself among the "minority group members who have seen the value of their accomplishments debased" by the lowering of standards that Scalia clearly believed were effectuated by affirmative action. The "cure" to this disease, Scalia argued, was to simply get "beyond" race altogether. Therefore, Scalia advanced the argument that to get beyond racism, the cure was to eliminate any legal remedies based on race, including affirmative action. In short, to get beyond racism, we must cease thinking in terms race at all.

Just one year prior to Scalia's 1992 interview, Scalia had argued in *Chisom v. Roemer* (1991) that the Voting Rights Act (VRA) should be interpreted *not* according to its historically remedial purpose to eliminate the vestiges of slavery but through the text's "ordinary meaning." Scalia argued that the VRA

is not some all-purpose weapon for well-intentioned judges to wield as they please in the battle against discrimination. It is a statute. I thought we had adopted a regular method for interpreting the meaning of language in a statute: first, find the ordinary meaning of the language in its textual context; and second, using established canons of construction, ask whether there is any clear indication that some permissible meaning other than the ordinary one applies. If not—and especially if a good reason for the ordinary meaning appears plain— we apply that ordinary meaning.[6]

For Scalia, the Voting Rights Act was a written text, no more, no less. According to textualism, a text should *not* be interpreted according to the "purposes" allegedly contained in the legislative history that led to its enactment. Indeed, since *Edwards* (1987), which I examined in chapter 1, Scalia had aggressively rejected the use of legislative records such as committee reports as a source of interpretation to illuminate the legislative purpose or intent of a text. In a 1986 speech just prior to his nomination to the court, Scalia writes:

> I think the expressions of the congressional committee are no more useful than an excerpt from, say, *Life Magazine* in showing what society thought about the purpose of the law. I think it is a big mistake to rely on original interest because it freezes the legislative process to use congressional hearings and as such give a perpetual content to the statute. Especially since the whole congressional process is now tricked up. I do not know if those of you should know, in the world of business know, but much "legislative history" is artificial so that it is generally impossible to tell what is real and what is staged. There are floor debates when you have no idea who is even on the floor when the debate's being conducted.[7]

Thus, for Scalia, the written text of the VRA should *not* be read in terms of its historically *remedial* purpose to combat the persistence of discrimination in voting, as Congress had documented. Instead, Scalia adopted a narrow textualist reading of the linguistic meaning of the text itself, declaring, "We are here to apply the statute, not legislative history, and certainly not the absence of legislative history. Statutes are the law though sleeping dogs lie."[8] Therefore, according to Scalia, the congressional purpose and history of the VRA was irrelevant. Judges should pay heed only to the "ordinary meaning" of the written words and exclude the history and purpose of the VRA as sources of legal meaning.

Just two years earlier in *Richmond v. Croson* (1989), Scalia had advanced an argument against affirmative action to remedy past discrimination. Scalia argued, "We have in some contexts approved the use of racial classifications by the Federal Government to remedy the effects of past discrimination. I do not believe that we must or should extend those holdings to the States."[9] For Scalia, *any* use of race by state or local government to remedy past discrimination violated the "race-neutral" text of the Fourteenth Amendment's Equal

Protection Clause. For him, the *only* circumstance that state governments may use race to remedy discrimination was the very specific case identified in *Brown v. Board of Education* (1954), where admissions in education were explicitly segregated based on race. Scalia writes,

> In my view there is only one circumstance in which the States may act *by race* to "undo the effects of past discrimination": where that is necessary to eliminate their own maintenance of a system of unlawful racial classification. . . . This distinction explains our school desegregation cases, in which we have made plain that States and localities sometimes have an obligation to adopt race-conscious remedies.[10]

Outside of that specific context, any use of race by state or local governments violated the "race-neutral" text of the Fourteenth Amendment. Most importantly, even if racial discrimination had been perpetuated precisely *through* race-neutral policies, Scalia still claimed that race could never be used to remedy such discrimination. Commenting on race-neutral policies enacted by states that discriminated against blacks, Scalia writes:

> The same thing has no doubt happened before in other cities (though the racial basis of the preference has rarely been made textually explicit)—and blacks have often been on the receiving end of the injustice. Where injustice is the game, however, turnabout is not fair play.[11]

According to Scalia, blacks have been discriminated against precisely through the use of race-neutral policies in which racial preferences were not made "textually explicit." Despite this, states could *never* use race to remedy this discrimination. As Scalia concluded, the Equal Protection Clause mandates race-neutral policies, full stop. Therefore, according to Scalia, all that is warranted by the Equal Protection Clause is the guarantee of "the government's adoption of "wholly neutral admissions" policies."[12]

Scalia's "colorblind" reading of the Equal Protection Clause was made clear in *Schuette v. Coal. To Defend Affirmative Action* (2014). Defending a Michigan state provision that prohibited any race or sex-based preferences in public education, employment, and contracting, Scalia argued, "I would further hold that a law directing state actors to provide equal protection is (to say the least) facially neutral, and cannot violate the Constitution."[13] Here, Scalia advanced an even stronger argument for "colorblindness" than he had in the past. In *Richmond* and *Chisom*, Scalia had appeared to argue that equal protection required only neutral admissions policies but did not warrant "remedial" policies using race. In *Schuette*, however, Scalia advanced the much more radical view that a facially neutral law *cannot* violate the Constitution, *regardless* of an alleged hidden "discriminatory purpose," writing:

> In my view, any law expressly requiring state actors to afford all persons equal protection of the laws . . . does not— *cannot*—deny 'to any person . . . equal protection of the laws,' U.S. Const., Amdt. 14, §1, regardless of whatever evidence of seemingly foul purposes plaintiffs may cook up in the trial court.[14]

In this startling argument, Scalia advanced the view that allegations of a law's "discriminatory purpose" cannot invalidate a facially "neutral" policy enacted by a state government. For Scalia, a neutral policy enacted by a state government, by definition, cannot be judged discriminatory by nine unelected judges, because the judiciary must always respect, "the near-limitless sovereignty of each State to design its governing structure as it sees fit."[15]

Scalia's radical colorblindness in *Schuette* thus indicated a sharpening of the opposition to not just affirmative action but an upheaval of antidiscrimination doctrine in general. Scalia's argument that neutral laws *cannot* violate the Constitution was remarkable. It contradicted one of the most basic premises of the court's antidiscrimination jurisprudence first established in *Yick Wo* (1892): namely, the idea that a facially neutral policy enacted with discriminatory purpose is unconstitutional. Scalia's rejection of this basic notion explicitly undermined the court's "discriminatory purpose" doctrine developed in *Arlington Heights* (1977), a test that enabled judges to examine the historical record, legislative history of a facially neutral policy to determine if it was motivated by unlawful discrimination. Instead, Scalia's radical colorblindness rejected the very premise of this entire inquiry, going so far as to claim that any "foul purposes" of discrimination that are "cooked up" by plaintiffs cannot invalidate a facially neutral law.

## STUDENTS FOR FAIR ADMISSION V. HARVARD (2023)

The legacy of Scalia's textualist colorblindness and consequent attack on the court's "discriminatory purpose" doctrine was palpable in the Supreme Court's invalidation of affirmative action in June 2023. In this case, Harvard and the University of North Carolina's (UNC) admissions policies were challenged on the basis that their limited use of race violated the equal protection guarantee of the Fourteenth Amendment. Harvard and UNC's admissions had followed the "holistic-review process"[16] established in the court's precedent in *Fisher v. Univ. of Texas* (2016) allowing the consideration of race in the same way as other identified "plus" factors such geography, ethnicity, and socioeconomic status. According to the court's own precedents on affirmative action since *Grutter v. Bollinger* (2003), admissions policies may utilize race among many other "soft variables" in a holistic process of review in pursuit of the educational goals of diversity, without defining diversity solely in terms of race or quotas.[17] In this way, Harvard and UNC's admissions policies simply followed Supreme Court precedent by using race "in a limited way with the goal of recruiting, admitting, and enrolling underrepresented racial minorities to pursue the well-documented benefits of racial integration in education."[18]

However, in a 6–3 majority opinion, the court held that the admissions policies' limited use of race violated the Equal Protection Clause of the Fourteenth Amendment. Writing for the textualist majority, Chief Justice John Roberts argued that the constitutional "time had passed" for making distinctions based on race. Citing the court's *de jure* desegregation of public schools in *Brown v. Board of Education* (1954), Roberts writes, "The time for making distinctions based on race had passed. *Brown*, the Court observed, "declared the fundamental principle that racial discrimination in public education is unconstitutional." [19] In its ruling, the majority laid out its race-neutral reading of the Fourteenth Amendment, citing among other precedents Scalia's opinion in *Richmond v. Croson* that evidence of past discrimination cannot be used to advance legal remedies in the form of preferential government programs or policies. The court cited that opinion as standing for the proposition that any legal remedy "must be meant to further a colorblind government, not perpetuate racial consciousness."[20] The court's colorblind reading thus relied heavily upon Scalia's own race-neutral opposition to the use of historical discrimination as evidence for legal remedies of any kind. Indeed, the court concluded that *any* use of race by government to remedy the effects of discrimination is "contrary to both the letter and spirit of a constitutional provision whose central command is equality."[21]

The court's reliance on Scalia's textualist philosophy did not stop there. In a concurring opinion, Justice Thomas argued *against* using the congressional record of the Fourteenth Amendment's remedial purpose. Instead, he advanced an alternative race-neutral reading of the Fourteenth Amendment, declaring in the spirit of Scalia himself:

> Under our Constitution, judges have never been entitled to disregard the plain terms of a valid congressional enactment based on surmise about unenacted legislative intentions. Instead, it has always been this Court's duty "to give effect, if possible, to every clause and word of a statute."[22]

Here, Thomas offered up a completely race-neutral history of the text of the Thirteenth and Fourteenth Amendments, arguing the text itself ensures racial equality *with no textual reference to race whatsoever*. The history of these measures' enactment renders their motivating principle as clear as their text: All citizens of the United States, regardless of skin color, are equal before the law.[23]

The majority often cites Justice Harlan's famous dissent from *Plessy v. Ferguson* (1896) that "Our Constitution is color-blind, and neither knows nor tolerates classes among citizens."[24] However, since *Plessy* was overturned by *Brown v. Board of Education*, the court's citing of Harlan's 1896 colorblind Constitution argued that the Harvard/UNC admissions policies were no different than *de jure* racial segregation in the nineteenth century. By equating Harvard/UNC's holistic review of "soft variables" and limited use of "plus" factors to *de jure* racial segregation, the court constructed a straw-man, arguing that such policies were no less "segregationist" than the Black Codes or Jim Crow laws. Justice Thomas, once again citing Justice Scalia's opinion in *Croson*, argued that affirmative action policies like Harvard's and UNC's were not just unlawful but "invidious," writing that such "race-based solutions have proved pernicious in segregationist circles."[25]

In a lengthy dissenting opinion, Justice Ketanji Brown Jackson argued that the court's textualist's race-neutral reading of the Fourteenth Amendment had effectively severed the history and purpose of the Fourteenth Amendment from the text of the Constitution. By establishing a kind of legally mandated "ignorance of race" upon our understanding of the Constitution, Jackson argued that the court had completely detached itself from American history. Justice Jackson proceeded to not only review the historical purpose of the Fourteenth Amendment in its "original" historical post–Civil War context but also articulated the current and ongoing need for affirmative action. Citing empirical studies of racial disparities in health, wealth, income, education, housing, and more, Jackson writes,

> our present reality indisputably establishes that such programs are still needed—for the general public good—because after centuries of state-sanctioned (and enacted) race discrimination, the aforementioned intergenerational race-based gaps in health, wealth, and well-being stubbornly persist.[26]

Instead, Jackson writes, the majority ignores the history, purpose, and current reality of race in America, seeking to "turn back time" to a moment that never actually existed in the first place. Jackson concludes of the majority, "With let-them-eat-cake obliviousness, today, the majority pulls the ripcord and announces "colorblindness for all" by legal fiat."[27] In a separate dissent, Justice Sotomayor sharply criticized the "perverse, ahistorical, and counterproductive outcome,"[28] concluding:

Today, this Court stands in the way and rolls back decades of precedent and momentous progress. It holds that race can no longer be used in a limited way in college admissions to achieve such critical benefits. In so holding, the Court cements a superficial rule of colorblindness as a constitutional principle in an endemically segregated society where race has always mattered and continues to matter. The Court subverts the constitutional guarantee of equal protection by further entrenching racial inequality in education, the very foundation of our democratic government and pluralistic society.[29]

In each of the dissents, Sotomayor and Jackson noted the court's temporal desire to prevent progress by "turning back time," with Jackson observing:

Turning back the clock . . . the Court indulges those who either do not know our Nation's history or long to repeat it. Simply put, the race-blind admissions stance the Court mandates from this day forward is unmoored from critical real-life circumstances."[30]

## TEXTUALISM AS PETTY SOVEREIGNTY

The court's opinion in *Students v. Harvard* was in many ways a culmination of the success of Justice Scalia's textualist philosophy on the court. For Scalia, antidiscrimination provisions were simply texts that could be used to enforce the status quo, *not* purposive directives to advance progress or much less racial justice. According to Scalia's textualism, judges cannot utilize the "intent" or "purpose" of the law when interpreting the meaning of the law. As early as 1986, Scalia had argued that the purpose of law for a judge was something that did not exist in the first place; only the enacted text rules. Textualism for Scalia meant that the law should not be interpreted by judges to advance progress or the cause of justice. In this way, Scalia's textualism was a kind of sovereign exceptionalism or "petty sovereignty" that gave judges the discretion to exclude race from the law altogether. This led Scalia to argue explicitly that race should never be used to redress historical injustices, even when those injustices were perpetuated under the cover of "neutral" legal texts and policies. Thus, Scalia had long paved the way for the court's conclusion in *Students v. Harvard*.

Perhaps Scalia's most ardent acolyte or "specter" joining the *Students v. Harvard* opinion was Justice Amy Coney Barrett. In its full report strongly opposing Barrett's nomination to the court, the nonpartisan Lawyers Committee for Civil Rights Under Law focused on Barrett's originalism as the driving force behind her record on constitutional rights.[31] Regarding Barrett's adoption of Scalia's originalism, the report notes:

Because, in the originalists' view, constitutional values are frozen at the time the constitutional text was ratified, the originalist theory often gives no voice or consideration to many of the important constitutional issues facing our country today—such as women's rights, LGBTQ rights, and personal privacy—that were simply not contemplated at the time the Constitution was adopted, when the expectations of equality were far different than in our present day.[32]

Barrett's originalism was evident during her service on the Seventh Circuit prior to her nomination in *EEOC v. Autozone* (2017). In this case, Barrett joined a majority opinion ruling that Autozone's intentional maintenance of racially segregated facilities did not violate the Title VII prohibition against racial discrimination in employment.[33] According to Barrett and the court, Autozone's relocation of an African American worker from a "Hispanic store" to an "African American store" did *not* amount to a Title VII discrimination claim because the action did not adversely affect the plaintiff's wages or employment opportunities, as the text of Title VII explicitly says. As the dissent pointed out, Barrett's majority ruling had the effect of instituting a "separate but equal" policy in employment. In this way, the report states, Barrett's originalism was the justificatory scheme upon which she grounds her decisions turning back the clock to enact a "separate but equal" policy in employment.

The report also reviews a revealing discrimination case in which Barrett penned the majority opinion, *Smith v. Illinois Department of Transportation* (2017).[34] In this case, Barrett found for a majority panel that Smith's supervisor's use of the "n-word" directed toward him at work was *not* sufficient for a successful Title VII racial discrimination claim. In a revealing passage, Barrett writes:

> The n-word is an egregious racial epithet. . . . That said, Smith can't win simply by proving that the word was uttered. He must also demonstrate that Colbert's use of this word altered the conditions of his employment and created a hostile or abusive working environment. . . . To be sure, Smith testified that his time at the Department caused him psychological distress. But that was for reasons that predated his run-in with Colbert and had nothing to do with his race. His tenure at the Department was rocky from the outset because of his poor track record. He clashed with his supervisors over pay, and they confronted him with foul language. As early as August—the first month of his employment—he sent memoranda to the Department complaining of a "hostile work environment." On Smith's own account, his supervisors made him miserable throughout his employment at the Department. But as we have already discussed, he has no evidence that his supervisors were lashing out at him because he was black.[35]

Scalia would have been proud. Barrett's opinion in *Smith* was almost identical to Scalia's opinion in *Carter v. Duncan-Higgins* (1984), explored in chapter 2. In that case, Scalia had also faced an employment discrimination claim involving a racial slur, also just a few years before his nomination to the Supreme Court. Remarking on the use of the racial slur used against the plaintiff in *Carter* (1984), Scalia had stated:

> Even assuming she had established discrimination . . . the plaintiff had further to establish that the reason for that discrimination was her race. She offered nothing to support that point—neither direct evidence, nor circumstantial evidence, statistical or otherwise—except the single racial slur.[36]

The similarities are striking. Scalia and Barrett were relying on an interpretation of Title VII that places the burden of proof on the plaintiff for proving *intentional* discrimination *because* of race. However, as Judge Richard Posner had observed, requiring plaintiffs in employment discrimination cases to meet such a high burden of proof was asking the impossible. Posner had observed:

> Defendants of even minimal sophistication will neither admit discriminatory animus nor leave a paper trail demonstrating it . . . alternative hypotheses (including that of simple mistake) will always be possible and often plausible. . . . The law tries to protect average and even below-average workers . . . but . . . it is so easy to concoct a plausible reason for not hiring, or firing, or failing to promote, or denying a pay raise to, a worker who is not superlative. A plaintiff's ability to prove discrimination indirectly, circumstantially, must not be crippled by evidentiary rulings that keep out probative evidence because of crabbed notions of relevance or excessive mistrust of juries.[37]

In this way, Scalia's textualist influence animated Barrett's majority opinion in the *Smith* (2019) case, once again limiting antidiscrimination provisions designed to protect African Americans and other racial and ethnic minorities. Textualist-originalism, it seemed, animated Scalia's and Barrett's opinions on race. For this reason, the Lawyers Committee for Civil Rights Under Law concludes with this following assessment of the temporal significance of Barrett's originalist connection to Scalia:

> Judge Barrett is a strict textualist and originalist, an approach that can limit the Court's willingness to uphold and enforce measures designed to protect people of color, women and other marginalized groups. This has serious implications for issues of concern to the civil rights community. Originalists look to the world as it existed in 1787. But we live in the 21st century. An originalist will read the Equal Protection Clause, the Due Process Clause, and the

Bill of Rights generally based on the views, to the extent they can be ascertained, of the society at the time these clauses were adopted. There is no doubt that in many areas fundamental to our current understanding of liberty and equality the views of these earlier societies were much narrower than our own. Without a more expansive reading of the Constitution, *Brown v. Board of Education*, *Griswold v. Connecticut*, *Roe v. Wade*, *Obergefell v. Hodges*, and many other landmark rulings, would have reached a different result.[38]

In this way, the court's turning back the clock on matters of race, as Justice Jackson observes, should be understood in light of the specific temporal regime enforced by textualist-originalism. In *Students v. Harvard*, the majority's ruling that the Equal Protection Clause as "a wholly race-neutral text" should be understood in terms of textualism's sovereign exceptionalism that facilitates the *exclusion* of the historical meanings of the Fourteenth Amendment. The Supreme Court's colorblindness should therefore be understood as an intentional and deliberate sovereign exclusion of the race-conscious legal history of the meaning of the law. The court's colorblindness is best described as a "petty sovereignty" granting judges the discretion to sever or exclude race from the meaning of law.

Indeed, just as the court in Dino's case had selectively excluded the definition of "male" that would have given Dino legal standing, and just as the court in *Yates* (2015) excluded other competing definitions of "fish" that did not comport with its textualist reading, the court in *Students v. Harvard* exercises a sovereign exceptionalism by excluding and severing precisely those rich social and historical meanings and memories of the Fourteenth Amendment that explain its origin, purpose, and current relevance to race in America. It is only through this sovereign exclusion of the social meanings of race from the universe of legal meaning that the court can comfortably conclude that the Equal Protection Clause is a "wholly race-neutral text". In this regard, the court's colorblindness can be seen as an extension of the "sovereign power" in the institutional system of liberal government. As Butler writes:

> Petty sovereigns abound, reigning in the midst of bureaucratic army institutions mobilized by aims and tactics of power they do not inaugurate or fully control. And yet such figures are delegated with the power to render unilateral decision, accountable to no law and without any legitimate authority. The resurrected sovereignty is thus not the sovereignty of unified power under the conditions of legitimacy, the form of power that guarantees the representative status of political institutions. It is, rather, a lawless and prerogatory power, a "rogue" power *par excellence*.[39]

According to Butler, sovereign power is exercised in the modern state through delegating sovereign authority to make unilateral decisions to a network of "petty sovereigns." In turn, the function of these petty sovereigns is the self-allocation and justification of the legitimacy and authority of the state. As I noted in the introduction, Justice Scalia himself acknowledged the arbitrary "sovereign" power of federal judges, remarking in his 2012 treatise *Reading Law* that, "Only in the theater of the absurd does an aristocratic, life-tenured, unelected council of elders set aside laws enacted by the people's chosen representatives on the ground that the people do not want those laws."[40] While Scalia was criticizing "purposivist" theories of interpretation (which he rejected), he failed to acknowledge that his *own* theory of interpretation was especially vulnerable to the same criticism: namely, that textualism allows the judge an extremely wide hermeneutic universe of meaning in which he may exercise the arbitrary, unilateral decision of sovereign power over legal meaning for *all* individuals.

In this way, the court's decision in *Students v. Harvard* utilizes Scalia's own brand of textualist-originalism in exercising a sovereign exceptionalism that *requires* the court to exclude those social meanings of law from the universe of legal meaning "by legal fiat." The result was therefore a "race-neutral" text, severed from the historical purpose and memory of the law.

## COLORBLINDNESS AND EPISTEMIC INJUSTICE

The account just discussed is that the Supreme Court's colorblindness should be understood as an intentional sovereign exclusion of race-conscious justice considerations from the meaning of law. That is, my account holds that judicial colorblindness is fundamentally a political-institutional problem of a sovereign decision whereby the judge self-confers the power to arbitrarily exclude the history and memory of discrimination from the interpretation of the law. Therefore, the problem for a textualist judge is *not* her lack of ethical sensitivity or epistemic virtue but rather her self-conferral of sovereign discretionary power to exclude considerations of the very memory and history of discrimination itself. The textualist judge may exercise colorblindness because she is, as Judith Butler says, a "petty sovereign."

However, it is important to note that this account of legal colorblindness should be distinguished from the "interpersonal" account of colorblindness provided by Jose Medina, Josue Pineiro, and others within the "epistemic injustice" framework. Writing within this framework, Medina takes care to distinguish legal-institutional theories of colorblindness from the "interpersonal dimension of the phenomenon of color blindness, that is, on how this alleged blindness figures in face-to-face interactions and on its cognitive and affective aspects."[41] Medina is concerned not with legal theories of interpretation or judicial ideology but rather interpersonal claims such as "*I do not see color.*" For Medina, these kinds of interpersonal (nonlegal) colorblindness result in part from colorblind subjects being epistemically ignorant of their own *social positionality*. According to the lens of epistemic injustice, social positionality refers to one's *situatedness* or location in a particular social position, which in turn produces "habits of expectation, attention, and concern" that structure the limited way one views reality.[42] As a result, one's situatedness gives rise to a partial and limited *ignorance* of the way the world is experienced by others who do not inhabit one's one social position. For Medina, then,

> Color blindness requires being actively ignorant of social positionality, which involves a double epistemic failure with respect to race: a failure in racial self-knowledge and a failure in the racial knowledge of others with whom one interacts. These two failures go together because the lack of familiarity and critical awareness of one's social positionality involves not knowing oneself in relation to one's relevant others, that is, not knowing how one's racialized perspective in the world positions itself vis-à-vis differently situated others and their racialized perspectives.[43]

Thus, for Medina, colorblind subjects in the interpersonal context are guilty not of exercising their institutional power to exclude justice considerations in interpreting law but simply of a failure of "self-knowledge" or awareness of one's own limited knowledge of the world.

For Medina, this epistemic ignorance of one's own positionality results in a lack of awareness of the justice implications of one's actions. He writes:

> Given that the ideology of color-blind is chosen and explicitly proclaimed, it may seem paradoxical to call the subjects who profess it meta-ignorant or meta-blind. Are they not fully aware of their blindness? They are indeed aware of the cognitive stance they are choosing to adopt in their social agency, but they are not at all aware of the presuppositions and consequences of such cognitive posture. . . . The meta-ignorance that color blindness breeds has immediate consequences for responsible agency: it undermines the subject's capacity to be sensitive and responsive to racial harms and disadvantages. . . . In color blindness, the evasion of responsibility goes very deep: the recalcitrant form of ignorance that operates at the meta level renders the color-blind subject unable to take responsibility for racial injustices, which are not even registered and felt (at least not qua injustices); it results in a numbness or insensitivity to racial matters that limits the agent's capacity to respond to wrongs and to improve ethically or politically, since the subject is unable to recognize such limitation.[44]

For Medina and Pineiro, interpersonal colorblindness is therefore described as a kind of "meta-ignorance."[45] Under normal epistemic conditions, when subjects are presented with race-based claims of harm, "good faith" subjects recognize the uptake of the particularity of race-related harms. However, with colorblindness, the "normal" epistemic conditions are disrupted such that subjects fail to recognize the justice implications of race-related harms. This is an injustice that is "hermeneutic," that is, injustice derived from *distortion of meaning*.

In her book *Epistemic Injustice*, Miranda Fricker defined *hermeneutical injustice* as "the injustice of having some significant area of one's social experience obscured from collective understanding owing to persistent and wide-ranging hermeneutical marginalization."[46] According to Fricker, hermeneutical marginalization refers to cases where "there is unequal hermeneutical participation with respect to some significant area(s) of social experience."[47] Applied to cases of interpersonal colorblindness, Josué Piñeiro argues that in cases of colorblindness,

> meta-ignorance gets in the way. Any race-based information that they proffer as evidence is denied on the basis that it is race-based. The hermeneutical filter produced by the meta-level colorblindness prevents whites from understanding the demand as a race-based demand. This causes them to either ignore the racial injustice as a racial injustice and therefore as an injustice, or to misunderstand the demand as one that exists but must not be about race. That is, the numbness or insensitivities towards racial difference and racial matters that Medina points out prevents them from reciprocating the attempted act of communication by taking up the grievance or concern seriously and are thus prevented from understanding the content of the n this strategy when a colorblind subject is presented with information that when analyzed from a race-based perspective will likely undermine the colorblind perspective, the subject would preemptively refuse to carry out the analysis on this basis, circumventing arriving at the conclusion that the colorblind perspective is mistaken.[48]

This epistemic lens therefore views interpersonal colorblindness as primarily a problem of epistemic agents failing to have the right epistemic *virtues* that facilitate normal epistemic conditions. When epistemic agents fail to have the right epistemic virtues, distortions of meaning are produced that lead to epistemic injustices. Thus, according to Medina and Pineiro, interpersonal (nonlegal) colorblind subjects lack sensitivity to and awareness of justice considerations, preventing them from even registering their actions as an "injustice" in the first place. This lack of ethical sensitivity to the consequences and justice implications of their actions and views produces a "meta" form of ignorance: the inability to be aware of the real world consequences of one's own ignorance.[49] Therefore, because colorblind subjects are unaware of the justice implications of their actions, interpersonal colorblindness is primarily an *ethical* and *epistemic* problem.

Medina and Pineiro's analysis of interpersonal colorblindness provides a good contrast with *legal* or judicial colorblindness on the Supreme Court. Whereas interpersonal colorblindness results from subjects failing to *register* their actions as unjust, judicial colorblindness often openly acknowledges the injustice that results from their own interpretations. As I showed in the preceding chapters, Justice Scalia himself acknowledged that "neutral" laws can be used to harm blacks and openly described this as "injustice." The problem, however, is that Justice Scalia did *not* think that the role of the judge was to pursue justice. Therefore, Justice Scalia's colorblindness rejects the application of the fundamental premise of the *epistemic justice* literature and framework—namely, the idea that the interpretation of the law should conform to the requirements of justice. For him, the interpretation of the law is *not* a collective epistemic and ethical project in which the epistemic resources of the community should be distributed equally. Rather, a good judge specifically *excludes* considerations of justice in his interpretation of the law.

Here, we return to the case of Dino, where the liberal textualist Judge Alvarez said that, despite the "sad" and "unfair" outcome, she was simply applying the "ordinary meaning" of the text. Justice had nothing to do with her interpretation of the law. Judge Alvarez wrote:

> Although I agree that the Texas Family Code's definition of man results in an incredibly unfair situation for Villarreal, this court is bound by the language of the statute and not by what we think is fair. . . . Although Villarreal's inability to legally establish standing to assert his parental rights over these children is heart-wrenching and sad, an appellate court is bound by the law and not emotions."[50]

Indeed, the same is true of Scalia. These cases demonstrate that textualist judges often openly recognize the injustice of their own hermeneutic practices but deny that justice is an applicable consideration of legal interpretation. Consequently, it is inaccurate to describe such cases as instances of ignorance or "meta-ignorance" as defined by Medina. In these cases, judges are acutely aware of the injustice that results from their own interpretive theory of the law, but they claim *they* are not responsible for this injustice, since their judicial and institutional role precludes them from making legal decisions on the basis of moral notions like justice, compassion, sympathy, "and the like." Therefore, as Medina rightly points out, legal-institutional forms of colorblindness should be distinguished from interpersonal colorblindness.

For the same reasons, neither can legal colorblindness be properly described as "willful hermeneutical ignorance." As Pohlhaus has argued, "ignorance is not something to which one is doomed because of social position, but rather something one chooses to maintain."[51] When agents *choose* to maintain this ignorance, Pohlhaus argues, the result is willful hermeneutic ignorance. He writes:

> When epistemic agents refuse to allow the development of or refuse to acknowledge already developed epistemic resources for knowing the world from situations other than their own, they contribute to epistemic injustice and maintain their own ignorance about whole parts of the world.[52]

Therefore, applied to the phenomena of colorblindness, one might argue that colorblind judges are engaging in willful hermeneutical ignorance by choosing to maintain their own ignorance about or refusing to acknowledge the race-conscious history of laws such as the Fourteenth Amendment. By stripping the historical meaning of discrimination from the text of the law, the argument might go, the court is committing a *hermeneutical injustice*. In this way, the literature on epistemic injustice suggests that "colorblindness" could be described as a kind of hermeneutic injustice.

However, this would be a misleading characterization. For Pohlhaus, even so-called "willful" hermeneutic ignorance refers to cases of "self-imposed" distorted meaning due to one's particular situatedness or lack of experience. As Pohlhaus argues, "when judging situations in areas where one has little experience, one would do well to suspect that one's perception may be distorted."[53] However, even his conception of willful hermeneutic ignorance still focuses on cases of injustice that are due to cognitive dysfunction resulting in lack of full knowledge. For this reason, the term *willful* hermeneutic ignorance is somewhat misleading. Neglecting to take into account the race-conscious history of law is *not* the same thing as explicitly choosing to exclude race-consciousness as a way of interpreting the law altogether. The Supreme Court's colorblindness is *not* the result of the failure or neglect of judges to acquire the necessary epistemic tools for knowing parts of the world experienced by marginalized knowers. On the contrary, the court's colorblindness is the result of a calculated, decades-long sustained rejection of race-conscious legal history from the perspective of marginalized knowers. The Supreme Court is not refusing to acknowledge race-conscious legal history. On the contrary, it acknowledges race-conscious legal history only to roundly reject that history as a legitimate source of interpretive legal meaning. Indeed, the court's colorblindness stems from the rejection of the very idea that the meaning of law can or should be influenced by marginalized knowers at all. According to the court's colorblind jurisprudence, the meaning of the law is determined by the race-neutral text and not by the racial congressional purposes that one might find "lurking" in the Congressional Record. Legal colorblindness, therefore, results from the sovereign discretionary power to exclude the history of discrimination from the meaning of the law. It is wrong to say that the court is refusing to acknowledge the history of racial discrimination. The court is *not* ignorant. On the contrary, it intentionally selects the history of racial discrimination *as the exception* to exclude from the meaning of the law.

While illuminating important epistemic kinds of injustice that may result from the court's colorblindness, the lens of epistemic or hermeneutical injustice fails to capture and diagnose the intentional and deliberate decisionism of the court's race-neutral colorblind reading of the Fourteenth Amendment. For Fricker, varieties of epistemic injustice are viewed within the framework of virtue epistemology. As a result, Fricker's analysis focuses on forms of injustice that are due to an *epistemic* or *cognitive* failure instead of an *intentional* sovereign performance of legal speech and tactics. The lens of epistemic injustice has been criticized on this point, since for Fricker, epistemic agents *themselves* are not perpetrators of injustices such as hermeneutical injustice. As he states, "No agent perpetrates hermeneutical injustice—it is a purely structural notion."[54] Whereas the malevolent legalities examined in this book, such as the court's colorblind race-neutral textualism, are intentional, sovereign performances of legal speech and tactics, the cases of epistemic injustice Fricker examines are often described in terms of a *negligence* of an epistemic duty. Fricker describes the testimonial injustice of knowers, for example, as a "failure in their duty to make the proper testimonial judgment."[55] Elsewhere, epistemic injustice is described again as "a gross epistemic failure."[56] Indeed, the lack of healthy epistemic functioning that leads to epistemic injustice is described as "an ongoing failure to gain knowledge . . . by preventing [one] from developing certain intellectual virtues."[57] That is, within the framework of epistemic injustice, injustices will be approached primarily as an *epistemological failure* or *negligence*. This epistemological approach to injustice is strikingly similar to the approach taken by Sophia Moreau, for whom "direct" discrimination refers to the subjective intention to discriminate, known as "disparate treatment," whereas "indirect discrimination" is defined as a negligence to take into account the discriminatory outcomes of one's action.[58] Within discrimination law, if there is not sufficient evidence of "direct" discrimination (which there rarely is), then discrimination may be understood in terms of a *negligence* to take into account to "indirect" effects of one's actions. Moreau writes:

> I think it is helpful for us to think about discrimination as a form of negligence, not because this one idea can specify the full extent of an agent's obligations, but rather because it draws us away from an exclusive and narrow focus on the agent's intentions and aims, and instead broadens our gaze, out towards the many things that the agent has failed to notice and failed to do, and out towards the many effects of his policy on the victims of discrimination, which make the policy into something that the agent ought to have scrutinised further and altered.[59]

However, as mentioned in the introduction, the forms of malevolent legality examined in this book are *not* performed simply through *negligence*. On the contrary, forms of discrimination examined in the book are *not* due to epistemological failure or cognitive negligence, but—as Justice Sotomayor suggested in *Abbott v. Perez*—through the selective, sovereign, and intentional exclusion/inclusion of certain social meanings of the law. The problem posed by malevolent legalities (i.e., *performative discrimination*) is precisely that "bad faith" legal actors strategically mask evidence of direct discrimination (disparate treatment) while insulating themselves from claims of indirect discrimination (disparate impact). Because of this, the kinds of performative discrimination examined in this book are performed by actors directly responsible for the injustice produced by their "bad faith" intentional manipulation of the law and legal speech. In contrast, as Jose Medina confirms, Fricker maintains that individuals may be blamed for failing to be virtuous listeners but *not* for the broader injustice of the epistemic system itself.[60] At most, epistemic injustices are due to knowers not being virtuous enough in their ways of knowing, but they are not, under Fricker's analysis, responsible for the broader institutional norms that govern the epistemic system of knowing within which hermeneutical injustice occurs. This is true even for Polhaus in cases of willful hermeneutic ignorance. While such ignorance may said to be self-imposed, there is clearly a substantive difference between "choosing" through negligence to maintain one's ignorance about the race-conscious history of the law and explicitly barring all race-conscious interpretation from being utilized in understanding constitutional law. The Supreme Court's colorblind jurisprudence has adopted the latter, a much more "activist" institutional agenda barring race-conscious remedies and interpretations. This institutional power granted to federal judges enables the sovereign decisions that control the current meaning of the Constitution for all US citizens. Therefore, the court's colorblind jurisprudence is not simply a case of neglecting to adopt the epistemic tools of marginalized knowers but rather a sovereign decision made within the enabling context of the institutional and political framework of the state. It is therefore a kind of "meta" *malevolent legality*: a controlling precedent for the intentional sovereign decision to exclude certain social meanings of the law in performing the "neutrality" of legal texts.

## CONCLUSION

The Supreme Court's colorblindness in *Students v. Harvard* was the culmination of a broader, calculated, decades-long assault on and sovereign exclusion of the historical purpose and policy of the Voting Rights Act, the Equal Protection Clause, Civil Rights Act, and other antidiscrimination provisions. Furthermore, the sovereign exclusion of the history of discrimination from the meaning of law can be traced to the performative tactics of Scalia's judicial philosophy. In this sense, the court's race-neutral reading of antidiscrimination texts is grounded in the sovereign exclusion of the very social meanings and memories that ground the purpose of antidiscrimination law. Here, the injustice that results from this sovereign exclusion is *not* due to epistemic failure or negligence to consider the outcomes of the court's race-neutral colorblindness. On the contrary, Scalia's textualism is a theory of legal interpretation operating within the institutional-political framework of the state that confers upon judges the discretionary power to decide on which legal meanings to "exclude" from legal interpretation. As Jeffery Rosen has observed, in 1995, Scalia had joined three other justices on the court in using their race-neutral reading to launch an assault on affirmative action and the Voting Rights Act. As Rosen noted:

> Clarence Thomas, Antonin Scalia, William Rehnquist, and Anthony Kennedy committed themselves to the principle that government can almost never classify citizens on the basis of race. They paved the way for the judicial invalidation of most forms of affirmative action by insisting that all racial preferences are presumptively unconstitutional unless narrowly designed as a remedy for past discrimination. They signaled their readiness to declare the Voting Rights Act unconstitutional by declaring that the Fourteenth Amendment forbids states from using race as the "predominant purpose" in drawing electoral districts.[61]

In this way, Scalia's textualism deliberatively rejected the very social meanings of the law that generate race-neutral interpretations. These injustices are therefore *not* the result of an epistemological or cognitive failure to listen or hear the experiences or knowledge of other interlocuters or marginalized groups but rather the product of the sovereign decision of exclusion/inclusion of particular social meanings of law. The injustice at issue in the Supreme Court's colorblindness, therefore, is the product not of *negligence* to consider the outcomes of one's interpretation: it is *built into* the sovereign exceptionalism of textualist judicial philosophy itself. The best tools for understanding the Supreme Court's colorblindness, therefore, are not virtue epistemology or epistemic injustice but jurisprudence, constitutional law, and political theory.

One way constitutional legal scholars have described the temporal effects of textualist-originalist interpretation is by examining legal interpretation as an *erasure* of "constitutional memory."[62] Reva Siegel writes that constitutional memory is forged when interpreters "tell stories about the nation's past experience to clarify the meaning of the nation's commitments, to guide practical reason, and to help express the nation's identity and values."[63] Thus, for Siegel, *any* theory of constitutional interpretation is by definition a cultural and political act whereby collective memory is inscribed in law. Because of this, the stakes of constitutional interpretation are doubly political, both serving a legitimizing function for law and a function of political representation. As Siegel writes, "Constitutional interpreters produce constitutional memory as they make claims on the past that can guide decisions about the future. It is the role of constitutional memory to legitimate the exercise of authority."[64] However, this means that constitutional memory is a fundamentally *contested* activity. As Siegel observes, "Constitutional memory is entrenched, yet open and contestable—it is a field of meaning in which we continuously negotiate who we are and what we are to do together."[65] For Siegel, American constitutional interpretation has for most its history excluded and erased the voices, perspectives, and power of women, even in its decision upholding the rights of women:

> The Supreme Court scarcely mentions the Nineteenth Amendment when interpreting the Constitution. Nor do Supreme Court opinions mention those who led women's quest for political voice or the constitutional arguments they made in support of women voting, even though these arguments spanned two centuries. There is no method of interpretation that the Justices employ with sufficient consistency to account for this silence in our law.[66]

For Siegel, the erasure of women's voices from American constitutional law demonstrates the difference between constitutional rights and constitutional memory. Constitutional rights, such as equal protection on the basis of sex, may nonetheless be established by erasing constitutional memory of the history of women's struggles for equality. In more egregious cases of erasure, such as the Court's *Dobbs* (2022) decision overturning *Roe v. Wade*, Siegel notes that the court simply excluded both the history *and* legal precedent of women's rights based on a Scalia-inspired originalism that is backwards-looking. Indeed, just as Scalia had argued that at the time of the adoption of the Constitution abortion was criminal and thus unconstitutional,[67] the *Dobbs* court relied on originalism to argue that abortion was criminalized in 1868 and therefore was not protected by the Fourteenth Amendment. Tracing Scalia's influence on the court's originalism on the issue of abortion, Siegel writes of the *Dobbs* decision:

> Counting states that banned abortion in 1868 was not a neutral or disinterested measure of the Constitution's meaning; the method expressed the interpreters' values as it perpetuated political inequalities of the past into the future.[68]

For Siegel, the court's originalist arguments were selected strategically as a vehicle to secure the values sought by the majority—precisely the same way that Scalia had selectively used originalist methods. Siegel writes that in advancing these claims on constitutional memory, Scalia was choosing how to be bound, singling out and characterizing historical facts that, he asserted, decided the case before him—even as he creatively depicted himself as constrained.[69]

The *Dobbs* court advanced Scalia's originalist erasure of women's struggles for equality and overturned half a century of legal precedent upon which women relied. In contrast, Siegel writes, judges should instead draw upon the *constitutional memory* of women's struggles as a form of constitutional argument itself, adding[70] that Justice Ginsburg's opinion in *United States v. Virginia* (1996) exemplified this approach in drawing upon the struggles for women's suffrage to argue for heightened scrutiny in equal protection claims based on sex.[71] In this way, Siegel argues that constitutional interpretation must reorient its thinking by acknowledging that women are constitutional meaning-makers themselves and a fundamental part of the interpretive process.

Jack Balkin, in his analysis of conservative brands of originalism, argues that originalism is itself its own regime of "constitutional memory." He writes:

> At stake in constitutional memory is which historical figures and movements will count as makers of constitutional meaning for the present. If the memory of the adoption of the Constitution and its amendments features only a small group of white men as the central actors, the American constitutional tradition belongs to them and it is their views that matter. Women and racial minorities have constitutional rights only because these white men allowed them to have them.[72]

For Balkin, Scalia's brand of originalism is a regime of constitutional memory that functions through what he refers to as "selective remembering" or "forgetting," adding that according to Scalia's brand of originalism,

> those persons who did not participate in the framing and adoption of the Constitution, including those who could not have participated, like women and enslaved people, are not constitutional meaning makers. To interpret the Constitution correctly it is not especially important to remember their views or their experiences, except, of course, to the extent that these contributed to the understandings of the Framers and adopters. Thus, originalist argument creates authority through a selective remembering—foregrounding some people, positions, and events and not others. Conservative originalism is a practice of erasure, because it finds large portions of the American experience (and the American population) irrelevant to the Constitution's original public meaning.[73]

Therefore, Balkin argues we must reject the forgetting of originalist regimes of law and adopt instead a "dialectic" view of constitutional memory that reflects the plurality and multiplicity of views, perspectives, and experiences that constitute the diverse fabric of the nation.[74] As an example of a dialectic constitutional memory, Balkin suggests that statutes involving citizenship be interpreted according to the constitutional memory gained from testimony of those individuals who were *denied* citizenship:

> To understand what citizenship is, one might want to listen to the views of those denied it. The testimony of slaves and the conventions of free Blacks petitioning for redress of grievances might inform the construction of all three Reconstruction Amendments. The experience of Black citizens whose rights to vote were slowly strangled and snuffed out by decades of Jim Crow politics might be useful testimony for the construction of the Fifteenth Amendment.[75]

In this way, Balkin argues that we can expand our constitutional memory of the law by admitting into meaning of law the testimony of those the law excluded or harmed in the past. This procedure of "expanding" constitutional memory is in this way much more of a dialectic or conversation about the historical meaning of law rather than a unilateral, sovereign decision about the "correct" interpretation of a provision.

Thus, to the extent we exclude these kinds of testimonial evidence and legal struggles for justice from the meaning of law, we are severing historical memory from the text of the law. For Balkin, the unilateral, exclusionary approach to interpretation adopted by originalism is thus a kind of forgetting that "erases" our constitutional memory. Aleida Assmann and Sarah Clift concur: "What is not, by means of a collective effort, selected, appraised, distinguished, staged, reclaimed, and repeatedly represented, will always fall back into a latent state of forgetting."[76]

In this way, Balkin's and Siegel's assessments of Scalia's originalism as a kind of erasure of constitutional memory provides strong support for the thesis of the book, namely that textualist-originalism requires the interpreter to include/exclude legal meanings through a sovereign exceptionalism. As Justices Jackson and Sotomayor appeared to argue in *Students v. Harvard*, the majority's race-neutral, textualist reading of the Fourteenth Amendment performed an erasure of constitutional memory by legal fiat. The backwards-looking, originalist method thus performs a sovereign exclusion of constitutional memory in order to manipulate reality into an image of an "original" founding and fixed point in an imaginary past. This demonstrates, as I've argued, that Scalia's textualism is grounded in a kind of sovereign exceptionalism or "petty sovereignty" that reserves for itself the discretionary power to unilaterally exclude the history and memory of discrimination by legal fiat.

## NOTES

1. Antonin Scalia, interview conducted by Judith R. Hope, *Esquire*, December 5, 1992, Oral History Project, The Historical Society of the District of Columbia Circuit (2019), 8, https://dcchs.org/wp-content/uploads/2019/03/Scalia-Interview.pdf.
2. Scalia, interview conducted by Judith R. Hope.
3. Antonin Scalia, "The Disease as Cure: In Order to Get Beyond Racism, We Must First Take Account of Race," 1979 *Washington University Law Quarterly* 147 (1979): 156, https://openscholarship.wustl.edu/law_lawreview/vol1979/iss1/17.
4. Scalia, "The Disease as Cure," 152.
5. Scalia, "The Disease as Cure," 153–54.
6. *Chisom v. Roemer*, 501 U.S. 380, 404 (1991).
7. Antonin Scalia, John M. Olin Lecture Series on Political Economy, Wharton School, University of Pennsylvania, April 25, 1986, Antonin Scalia papers, LAW, MMC, 291, Series III, Box: 76, Folder: 28, Harvard Law School Library, Historical & Special Collections, 18.
8. *Chisom v. Roemer*, 501 U.S. 380, 406 (1991).
9. *Richmond v. J. A. Croson Co.*, 488 U.S. 469, 521, (1989).
10. *Richmond v. J. A. Croson Co.*, 488 U.S. 469, 524 (1989).
11. *Richmond v. J. A. Croson Co.*, 488 U.S. 469, 523-24 (1989).
12. *Richmond v. J. A. Croson Co.*, 488 U.S. 469, 525 (1989).
13. *Schuette v. Coal. to Defend Affirmative Action*, 572 U.S. 291, 318 (2014).
14. *Schuette v. Coal. to Defend Affirmative Action*, 572 U.S. 291, 331-32 (2014).
15. *Schuette v. Coal. to Defend Affirmative Action*, 572 U.S. 291, 327 (2014).
16. *Fisher v. Univ. of Tex.*, 136 S. Ct. 2198, 2203 (2016).
17. *Grutter v. Bollinger*, 539 U.S. 306, 311 (2003).
18. *Students for Fair Admissions, Inc. v. President & Fellows of Harv. Coll.*, 143 S. Ct. 2141, 2239 (2023).
19. *Students for Fair Admissions, Inc. v. President & Fellows of Harv. Coll.*, 143 S. Ct. 2141, 2160 (2023).
20. *Students for Fair Admissions, Inc. v. President & Fellows of Harv. Coll.*, 143 S. Ct. 2141, 2186 (2023).
21. *Students for Fair Admissions, Inc. v. President & Fellows of Harv. Coll.*, 143 S. Ct. 2141, 2174 (2023).
22. *Students for Fair Admissions, Inc. v. President & Fellows of Harv. Coll.*, 143 S. Ct. 2141, 2220 (2023).
23. *Students for Fair Admissions, Inc. v. President & Fellows of Harv. Coll.*, 143 S. Ct. 2141, 2177 (2023).
24. *Plessy v. Ferguson*, 16 S. Ct. 1138, 1146 (1896).
25. *Students for Fair Admissions, Inc. v. President & Fellows of Harv. Coll.*, 143 S. Ct. 2141, 2196 (2023).
26. *Students for Fair Admissions, Inc. v. President & Fellows of Harv. Coll.*, 143 S. Ct. 2141, 2278 (2023).
27. *Students for Fair Admissions, Inc. v. President & Fellows of Harv. Coll.*, 143 S. Ct. 2141, 2277 (2023).

28. *Students for Fair Admissions, Inc. v. President & Fellows of Harv. Coll.*, 143 S. Ct. 2141, 2279 (2023).
29. *Students for Fair Admissions, Inc. v. President & Fellows of Harv. Coll.*, 143 S. Ct. 2141, 2225-26 (2023).
30. *Students for Fair Admissions, Inc. v. President & Fellows of Harv. Coll.*, 143 S. Ct. 2141, 2225-26 (2023).
31. Lawyers Committee for Civil Rights Under Law, "Report on the Nomination of Judge Amy Coney Barrett as an Associate Justice of the United States Supreme Court," Washington, D.C., 2005.
32. Lawyers Committee for Civil Rights Under Law, "Report on the Nomination of Judge Amy Coney Barrett as an Associate Justice of the United States Supreme Court," 2.
33. *EEOC v. AutoZone*, 875 F.3d 860 (7th Cir. 2017).
34. *Smith v. Illinois Department of Transportation*, 936 F.3d 534 (7th Cir. 2019).
35. *Smith v. Ill. DOT*, 936 F.3d 554, 561 (7th Cir. Ill. August 21, 2019).
36. *Carter v. Duncan-Huggins, Ltd.*, 234 U.S. App. D.C. 126, 727 F.2d 1225, 1247 (1984).
37. *Riordan v. Kempiners*, 831 F.2d 690, 697-98 (7th Cir. 1987).
38. Lawyers Committee for Civil Rights Under Law, "Report on the Nomination of Judge Amy Coney Barrett as an Associate Justice of the United States Supreme Court," 10.
39. Butler, "Indefinite Detention," 56.
40. Scalia and Garner, *Reading Law,* 408.
41. José Medina, "Color Blindness, Meta-Ignorance, and the Racial Imagination," *Critical Philosophy of Race* 1, no. 1 (2013): 40.
42. Gaile Pohlhaus, "Relational Knowing and Epistemic Injustice: Toward a Theory of Willful Hermeneutical Ignorance," *Hypatia* 27, no 4 (2012): 717.
43. Medina, "Color Blindness, Meta-Ignorance, and the Racial Imagination." 43.
44. Medina, "Color Blindness, Meta-Ignorance, and the Racial Imagination," 47.
45. Josué Piñeiro, "Colorblindness, Hermeneutical Marginalization and Hermeneutical Injustice," *Southwest Philosophy Review* 38, no. 1 (2002): 115–22.
46. Miranda Fricker, *Epistemic Injustice: Power and the Ethics of Knowing* (Oxford: Oxford University Press, 2007), 154.
47. Fricker, *Epistemic Injustice*, 153.
48. Piñeiro, "Colorblindness, Hermeneutical Marginalization and Hermeneutical Injustice," 115–22.
49. Medina, "Color Blindness, Meta-Ignorance, and the Racial Imagination," 38–67; Pohlhaus, "Relational Knowing and Epistemic Injustice," 715–35.
50. In re Sandoval, No. 04-15-00244-CV, 2016 Tex. App. LEXIS 754, at *14 (Tex. App. Jan. 27, 2016).
51. Pohlhaus, "Relational Knowing and Epistemic Injustice," 731.
52. Pohlhaus, "Relational Knowing and Epistemic Injustice," 733.
53. Pohlhaus, "Relational Knowing and Epistemic Injustice," 731.
54. Fricker, *Epistemic Injustice*, 7, 159.
55. Fricker, *Epistemic Injustice*, 29.

56. Fricker, *Epistemic Injustice*, 26.
57. Fricker, *Epistemic Injustice*, 49.
58. Sophia Moreau, "The Moral Seriousness of Indirect Discrimination" in *Foundations of Indirect Discrimination Law*, ed. Tarun Khaitan and Hugh Collins (Oxford: Hart Publishing, 2018), 123–48.
59. Moreau, "The Moral Seriousness of Indirect Discrimination," 144.
60. Jose Medina, "Varieties of hermeneutical injustice," in *The Routledge Handbook of Epistemic Injustice* (New York: Routledge, 2017), 41–52.
61. Jeffrey Rosen, "The Color-Blind Court." *American University Law Review* 45, no.3 (February 1996): 791.
62. See Reva B. Siegel, "The Politics of Constitutional Memory," *Georgetown Journal of Law & Public Policy* 20, no. 1 (2022): 19–58; Jack M. Balkin, "Constitutional Memories," *William & Mary Bill of Rights Journal* 31, no. 2 (2022): 307.
63. Siegel, "The Politics of Constitutional Memory," 21.
64. Siegel, "The Politics of Constitutional Memory," 22.
65. Siegel, "The Politics of Constitutional Memory," 22.
66. Siegel, "The Politics of Constitutional Memory," 23.
67. Antonin Scalia, "Judges as Propounders of Transcendent Moral Law," 2005, Antonin Scalia papers, LAW, MMC, 291, Series III, Box: 73, Folder: 3, Harvard Law School Library, Historical & Special Collections, 10.
68. Reva Siegel, "The History of History and Tradition: The Roots of *Dobbs*'s Method (and Originalism) in the Defense of Segregation," *Yale Law Journal* 133 (2024): 147.
69. Reva Siegel, "The History of History and Tradition," 141.
70. Siegel, "The Politics of Constitutional Memory," 54.
71. *United States v. Virginia*, 518 U.S. 515 (1996).
72. Balkin, "Constitutional Memories," 308.
73. Balkin, "Constitutional Memories," 330.
74. Balkin, "Constitutional Memories," 331.
75. Balkin, "Constitutional Memories," 351.
76. Aleida Assmann and Sarah Clift, *Is Time out of Joint? On the Rise and Fall of the Modern Time Regime* (Ithaca, NY: Cornell University Press, 2020), 29.

# Conclusion
## 303 Creative LLC v. Elenis (2023): The Specters of Scalia

During the 2022–2023 term, Justice Sotomayor penned three back-to-back dissenting opinions in which she noticed a disturbing aspect of the current majority's judicial philosophy. In *Students v. Harvard* (2023), the court had struck down affirmative action policies based on an "ahistorical," "race-neutral" reading of the Fourteenth Amendment. For Sotomayor, the court's "colorblind" reading of the Equal Protection Clause indicated an opposition to racial progress by "turning back time." Sotomayor wrote:

> Superficial colorblindness in a society that systematically segregates opportunity will cause a sharp decline in the rates at which underrepresented minority students enroll in our Nation's colleges and universities, turning the clock back and undoing the slow yet significant progress already achieved.[1]

In *Dobbs v. Jackson Women's Health* (2022), the court overturned the constitutional right to abortion under *Roe v. Wade* by giving an originalist argument that abortion was not a right according to the "consensus of state laws in effect in 1868."[2] Justice Sotomayor noted again the court's "originalist" temporal posture:

> The majority's core legal postulate, then, is that we in the 21st century must read the Fourteenth Amendment just as its ratifiers did. . . . If the ratifiers did not understand something as central to freedom, then neither can we. Or said more particularly: If those people did not understand reproductive rights as part of the guarantee of liberty conferred in the Fourteenth Amendment, then those rights do not exist.[3]

Here, Sotomayor had identified the originalism of the court that Scalia had famously championed. The results of applying Scalia's originalist arguments to constitutional rights, however, were devastating for historically marginalized populations. As Sotomayor noted:

Those responsible for the original Constitution, including the Fourteenth Amendment, did not perceive women as equals, and did not recognize women's rights. When the majority says that we must read our foundational charter as viewed at the time of ratification (except that we may also check it against the Dark Ages), it consigns women to second-class citizenship.[4]

For Sotomayor, there was a clear, disturbing pattern that had emerged in the court's majority view of constitutional rights. If constitutional rights must be interpreted according to Scalia's brand of originalism, then it followed that *all* populations historically excluded from full and equal participation in political life would necessarily be excluded *now*, in the present.

For Sotomayor, the court's willingness to go down the dark path of redefining constitutional rights according to an "original" point in the distant past was illustrated in *303 Creative LLC v. Elenis* (2023). In this case, a graphic design business in the State of Colorado refused to provide business services to a same-sex couple. According to the Colorado Antidiscrimination Act (CADA), any business providing services to the public is prohibited from refusing service to individuals or groups "because of disability, race, creed, color, sex, sexual orientation, gender identity, gender expression, marital status, national origin, or ancestry."[5] However, the owner of the graphic design business claimed that she "will not produce content that 'contradicts biblical truth' regardless of who orders it . . . [and] that marriage is a union between one man and one woman is a sincerely held conviction."[6] Therefore, the owner of the business claimed that her refusal of service to the couple was "free speech" protected by the First Amendment. In remarkable 6–3 majority opinion written by Justice Gorsuch, the court ruled in favor of the business, concluding:

> The First Amendment's protections belong to all, not just to speakers whose motives the government finds worthy. In this case, Colorado seeks to force an individual to speak in ways that align with its views but defy her conscience about a matter of major significance. . . . But abiding the Constitution's commitment to the freedom of speech means all will encounter ideas that are "misguided, or even hurtful."[7]

Since the business owner claimed her actions were "religious speech," the court provided cover for the otherwise discriminatory conduct under the protection of the First Amendment. In the eyes of the Supreme Court, a public-facing business may lawfully deny service to same-sex couples simply by claiming that their actions are "religious speech."

For Gorsuch, this was a perplexing conclusion to be writing for the majority opinion. For just two years earlier, Gorsuch had penned the majority opinion in *Bostock v. Clayton County* (2020). In that case, the court held that an employer who discriminates against homosexual or transgender employees violates the Title VII prohibition against discrimination on the basis of sex.[8] Therefore, Gorsuch had written majority opinions (a) protecting the rights of homosexual and transgender individuals against discrimination in the workplace, and (b) protecting a business's right to discriminate against homosexual individuals in the marketplace. Thus, according to the Supreme Court, homosexual individuals were equals in the workplace but not necessarily in the marketplace.

Justice Sotomayor penned a lengthy dissent in *303 Creative,* echoing her common refrain during the 2022 term that the court was "turning back time" to a dark era of our nation's history, writing:

> Today is a sad day in American constitutional law and in the lives of LGBT people. The Supreme Court of the United States declares that a particular kind of business, though open to the public, has a constitutional right to refuse to serve members of a protected class. The Court does so for the first time in its history. By issuing this new license to discriminate in a case brought by a company that seeks to deny same-sex couples the full and equal enjoyment of its services, the immediate, symbolic effect of the decision is to mark gays and lesbians for second-class status. In this way, the decision itself inflicts a kind of stigmatic harm, on top of any harm caused by denials of service. The opinion of the Court is, quite literally, a notice that reads: "Some services may be denied to same-sex couples."[9]

Citing Justice Scalia's dissent from *Romer v. Evans* (1996), examined in chapter 3, Sotomayor identified once again the originalism at work in the court's reasoning. Instead of following decades of the court's historical progress made on issues of discrimination, Sotomayor wrote, "Today, however, we are taking steps backward. A slew of anti-LGBT laws have been passed in some parts of the country, raising the specter of a 'bare . . . desire to harm a politically unpopular group.'"[10] In a stark warning note, Sotomayor concluded her dissent by writing, "I fear that the symbolic damage of the Court's opinion is done. . . . Every business owner in America has a choice whether to live out the values in the Constitution. Make no mistake: Invidious discrimination is not one of them."[11]

Rather than accepting the long-standing principle of antidiscrimination jurisprudence that "there can be no social castes,"[12] Sotomayor argued that the court enacted a "new license to discriminate" by replicating what they had also done by invalidating affirmative action: "turning the clock back and undoing the slow yet significant progress already achieved."[13]

Justice Sotomayor recognized the temporal relation between the majority's view on constitutional rights and constitutional time. For Sotomayor, by "turning back the clock" to a fixed point in time when such discrimination was lawful, the majority was enacting a regime of "static law" in which "novel" constitutional additions such as antidiscrimination laws were seen as "sweeping," "coercive," and overbroad. As Scalia had argued in his originalist opinion of *Romer v. Evans*, the founding generation did *not* consider hostility or animus toward homosexuals as "discrimination," so therefore "tradition" dictates that what the court calls discrimination is not *really* discrimination. Similarly, in *Windsor* (2013), Scalia had argued in dissent that the Defense of Marriage Act's exclusion of same-sex couples from federal marriage benefits was not technically "discrimination" at all since American "traditions" had upheld this exclusion. As Scalia wrote, "That is not animus—just stabilizing prudence."[14]

Ten years after Scalia's dissenting opinion in *Windsor*, however, his dissent had been forcefully resurrected by the court in *303 Creative*. Despite the court's decision in *Obergefell v. Hodges* (2015) requiring states to recognize same-sex marriages,[15] *303 Creative* now carved out a special "license to discriminate," in the words of Justice Sotomayor. As a result of that decision, a Texas judge refused to officiate same-sex weddings based on her religious beliefs,[16] and in 2023, the Texas Supreme Court heard arguments on whether that judge has a constitutional right to do so.[17] In this way, Scalia's resurrected reasoning in *303 Creative* has made discrimination itself almost a badge of freedom, since exercising one's "religious speech" is seen as a particularly "American" mode of individual freedom. Discriminatory conduct, therefore, is itself not seen as an act of discrimination but rather a unique expression of American religious expression.

## SPECTERS OF CONSTITUTIONAL EVIL

As Justices Jackson and Sotomayor have warned, these "specters" of Scalia's backward-looking originalism give individuals *today* a new license to discriminate *as if historical progress did not exist*. By turning back the clock to a fixed point in time, the court's "regime of static law" therefore provides a cover and justification for new and renewed forms of invidious discrimination by persuading the populace that invidious discrimination is not *really* discrimination. If the United States returns to a time in history in which businesses, judges, and private individuals enjoy a constitutional right to exercise their individual, religious, or personal conscience in discriminating against a protected class of individuals, then discrimination ceases to be discrimination. "Animus" does not equal "animus." Malevolent legality is not "malevolent," just a kind of "stabilizing prudence."

Justices Sotomayor's and Jackson's keen observations on the dramatic transformation of the Supreme Court's temporal relationship to constitutional rights should awaken not simply Americans but world citizens from their slumber. In the wake of the January 6 insurrection at the US Capitol and the resurgence of white nationalism across the globe, slogans such as Donald Trump's "Make America Great Again" have been adopted and further radicalized by figures such as Argentinian president Javier Milei, who has promised to "Make Argentina Great Again" through imposing a radical libertarian economic shock to the country.[18] The common theme of such movements is the desire to "return" the nation to a "former glory"—a static point in time that is at once completely fictional and constructed on the "stabilizing" image of homogeneity, purity, and borders that separate "us" from "them." The banning of "diversity" programs, the war on Critical Race Theory, and the banning of books—all modes of "stabilizing prudence" seeking to return to a fixed, static point in time that provides a safe harbor from the interconnected world of diversity and plurality that characterizes reality.

In this way, the "specters" of Scalia's textualist-originalism continue to haunt our present reality, perhaps more today than ever. The textualist-originalist desire to read the text as if we can turn back the clock is simultaneously a desire to erase the constitutional memory of law and sanction a legion of renewed malevolence and discrimination from the darker pages of history. In the words of Hannah Arendt, it is a desire to destroy the plurality of the world in which we live—the very fact of reality itself. Speaking about the lessons of World War II, Arendt writes in *The Origins of Totalitarianism*:

> We can no longer afford to take that which was good in the past and simply call it our heritage, to discard the bad and simply think of it as a dead load which by itself time will bury in oblivion. The subterranean stream of Western history has finally come to the surface and usurped the dignity of our tradition. This is the reality in which we live. And this is why all efforts to escape from the grimness of the present into nostalgia for a still intact past, or into the anticipated oblivion of a better future, are vain."[19]

As Peg Birmingham notes, for Arendt, the necessary condition for the evils of totalitarianism to flourish is the transformation of historical interpretation (hermeneutics) into the *poesis* of *manipulation*: "a ποίησις that handles the factual matter in a manner that produces a new, albeit deceptive, reality."[20] For Arendt, Birmingham reminds us, "the fundamental condition of totalitarianism [is] . . . the institution of a 'lying world order' whereby reality is replaced with a lie."[21]

Justice Sotomayor's warning regarding the court's turning back the clock, therefore, can also be read as a warning about the evils of historical erasure and deception that for Arendt always prefigure totalitarian forms of political and social control. However, if the Supreme Court's dominant interpretive theory is at least partly responsible for enacting a "deceptive" narrative of historical erasure, then it follows that constitutional law *itself* is at least partly responsible for certain kinds of evil. In *Constitutional Redemption*, constitutional legal scholar Jack Balkin addresses this concern by articulating the problem of "constitutional evil." According the Balkin, "The problem of constitutional evil is the possibility that the Constitution, as it operates in practice, permits or even requires great injustices."[22] For Balkin, the American faith and quasi-religious awe for the Constitution is haunted or threatened by the reality that the Constitution interpreted *correctly* results in injustice. This is the problem of constitutional evil.

As part 1 of the book demonstrated, Justice Scalia himself acknowledged the problem of evil flourishing in and through the law. As he said in a speech in 1986:

> We have seen the careless, the avaricious, the criminal, the profligate, the foolhardy, parade across the pages of the case reports. We have seen evil punished and virtue rewarded. But we have also seen prudent evil flourish and foolish virtue fall. We have seen partners become antagonists, brothers and sisters become contesting claimants, lovers become enemies.[23]

For Scalia, however, the task of lawyers and judges consisted of using the instruments of law to enforce the *process* of law, and to use "discipline and self-abnegation" to *refrain* from engaging the substance or justice of the law.[24] The remedying of substantive issues of injustice or "evil" were questions for the legislature, not an unelected judiciary. As Scalia would write in his treatise *Reading Law*, the mature and responsible judge must reject "the false notion that the quest in statutory interpretation is to do justice."[25] However, Scalia's position implied that textualist judges are prohibited from using principles of justice to remedy injustice in the law. Such a position suggested that a textualist judge who recognizes "prudent evil" flourishing in the law is required to exercise "discipline" in applying the legal process but restraining oneself from applying principles of justice or remedying the substantive issues of evil in the law. In part 1 of the book, I referred to this position as "Scalia's Argument for Textualist Injustice."

In *Constitutional Redemption,* Balkin makes sense of Scalia's position in terms of the "hidden" narratives of constitutional interpretation. As he notes, constitutional law is an activity that is always infused with narratives of progress or stasis, justice or injustice, memory and forgetting, restoration and redemption.[26] For Balkin, one of the sources of *constitutional evil* are the "hidden" narratives that also lie behind the constitutional interpretations of judges themselves. In addition to the constitutional "stories," Balkin writes,

> there are also stories behind individual decision and practices of constitutional interpretation. It may well be that there lies a narrative, sometimes hidden and sometimes overt, a story about how things came to be, injustices fought or still to be rectified, things "we" (the People) did before, things we still have to do, things that we learned from past experience, thing that we will never let happen again.[27]

Because theories of constitutional interpretation themselves often contain behind them "hidden" narratives, Balkin suggests that "Judges may be the most obvious vehicles of constitutional evil, but they are not the heroes of the story."[28] The distinct danger of the quasi-religious American "fidelity" to the Constitution, Balkin argues, is therefore that of "constitutional idolatry"—treating an imperfect human construction as "superhuman or divine."[29] In this way, constitutional idolatry is "the confusion of a morally compromised Constitution with justice and good government."[30] Commenting on Sanford Levinson's 1988 work on *Constitutional Faith*, Balkin observes how Levinson "gave up his constitutional faith" and now argues that the fixed features of the Constitution "make the Constitution a modern-day agreement with hell."[31] As Balkin explains, for Levinson, the institution of the Senate, the presidential veto, Electoral College, and other fixed features make the Constitution "incorrigibly undemocratic and block necessary reforms."[32] However, the real value of Levinson's book on constitutional faith, Balkin suggests, is the exploration of the *dangers* of constitutional faith in the form of what Balkin calls a form of theodicy or *apology*. For him, the danger of American constitutional faith or fidelity is that any form of injustice or evil that results from the law will be justified in a kind of *apology* that functions as a *legitimation* role for the sacredness or goodness of the Constitution. If one truly has faith in the Constitution, Balkin writes, "One apologizes for evil and injustice to make it appear acceptable and justified."[33] According to him, this is precisely the connection between faith and legitimacy, since "it is reflected in the fact that the verb *legitimate* has a dual meaning: it means to make something legitimate and to apologize for or mystify its injustices and its illegitimacy."[34] From this, Balkin concludes:

> From the standpoint of law, the question if whether the belief in the Constitution or in the rule of law is a worthy thing or whether such faith might ultimately be a form of apology for the kinds of oppression and injustice that are wrought through the forms and practices, the technical arguments, and the devices of law and lawyering.[35]

This skepticism should lead us, he says, to a "hermeneutics of suspicion in law," given that the legal form of technical arguments, procedures, and methods have historically been wielded for manifestly unjust and evil ends. As he reminds us:

> Here again slavery is an apt example. The institution of slavery was supported and defended by the ablest legal minds of their time, who justified it as a sovereign right of states and as a sacred form of private property, and who drew upon their considerable talents to protect it, maintain it, and even expand it. If well-trained lawyers could have done this on behalf of so great an evil as slavery, what does this say about what equally well-trained lawyers might be doing today?[36]

In this way, Balkin writes, law is implicated in legal forms of injustice: "Lawyers are rhetors who manipulate and wield rhetoric in order to persuade others and promote the interests of their clients."[37]

Balkin's characterization of lawyers as *manipulators* of legal instruments and speech touches on a central theme in the work of Hannah Arendt. The crucial difference between "manipulation" and "interpretation" for Arendt, as Peg Birmingham reminds us, is that while interpretation refers to the hermeneutic *praxis* of establishing the meaning of the *facts* of the past in light of the present, manipulation is a *poesis* that seeks to *remake* or *erase* the past in forging a new, deceptive reality. Birmingham writes that for Arendt,

> it is important to distinguish between "interpretation" and "manipulation." As the above passage indicates, for Arendt each generation has the right to its interpretation of the facts; each generation must engage in the hermeneutical task of establishing the meaning of the facts, and in this way factual truth will, for each generation, take on new hues and tones. "Manipulation," on the other hand, is literally a "handling" of the matter itself. In other words, manipulation is not concerned with the meaning of factual truth (hermeneutics) but actively transforms the matter into something else entirely. Manipulation is a ποίησις that handles the factual matter in a manner that produces a new, albeit deceptive, reality. Arendt's distinction between ποίησις and πρᾶξις is helpful in grasping the difference between "manipulation" and "action." While manipulation appears to be an action insofar as it introduces something new, it more closely resembles ποίησις insofar as its real intent is to produce a new (although deceptive) reality, using as its means ideology and image-making.[38]

Applying Arendt's distinction between interpretation and manipulation to the arguments advanced in the book, the following conclusion is unavoidable: Scalia's textualist-originalist method of interpretation is *not* a praxis of interpretation at all but rather a *poesis* of manipulation. Such a conclusion is not reached lightly, but the argument I advance in this book is that textualism entails a *sovereign exceptionalism* that requires the interpreter to include/exclude social meanings of law by unilateral, arbitrary decisions. Consequently, the best description of a sovereign textualist judge is *not* one who engages in a hermeneutic *praxis* of interpreting the past in light of present conditions (a "living constitutionalist" approach that Scalia rejected) but rather one who selectively includes/excludes or erases the past to *remake* the present in the manufactured image of some "original," founding moment from 1787 or 1886 or 1953. In terms of Francois Ost's typology of temporal regimes, originalism is therefore a kind of "founding time" that does not interpret but *remakes* the present through a *manipulation* of the past. Scalia's originalism thus seeks to "prevent progress" by manufacturing what he had called a "regime of static law." Part 2 of the book referred to this position as "Scalia's Argument to Prevent Progress."

There is little doubt that Scalia's brand of textualist-originalism is now, at least for the 6–3 majority, "the Court's dominant interpretive theory."[39] As long as this is the case, the "specters" of Scalia will continue to haunt the method and substance of the court's proceedings. If the arguments of this book are persuasive, however, then the court's decisions cannot be understood by simply reading the text of the court's opinions themselves. Rather, as I have argued, the court's textualist judicial philosophy must be understood as a kind of *pretext*—a hidden temporal narrative of "founding time" disguised by the apparent neutrality of the text itself. In other words, the explicit *logos* published by the court must be understood first by paying attention to its *preludes*.

In this way, the book concludes by returning to the beginnings or "origins" of the path where we first began: the Athenian stranger in Plato's *The Laws*, who noted, "All speeches, and whatever things involve the voice, are preceded by preludes."[40] If the argument I advance in this book is successful, I hope that one would agree with the Athenian that laws cannot be fully understand without hearing their preludes:

> the laws that we say are political, no one has either given voice to a prelude, or composed one and published it, as if it were natural for there not to be one. It seems to me, though . . . that it is natural; and the laws stated in double fashion seemed to me just now not to be double in a somehow simple way, but rather to be two things: a law and a prelude to the law.[41]

## NOTES

1. *Students for Fair Admissions, Inc. v. President & Fellows of Harv. Coll.*, 143 S. Ct. 2141, 2260 (U.S. June 29, 2023).

2. *Dobbs v. Jackson Women's Health Org.*, 597 U.S. 215, 223 (U.S. June 24, 2022).
3. *Dobbs v. Jackson Women's Health Org.*, 597 U.S. 215, 372 (U.S. June 24, 2022).
4. *Dobbs v. Jackson Women's Health Org.*, 597 U.S. 215, 373 (U.S. June 24, 2022).
5. C.R.S. 24-34-601.
6. *303 Creative LLC v. Elenis*, 143 S. Ct. 2298, 2307 (U.S. June 30, 2023).
7. *303 Creative LLC v. Elenis*, 143 S. Ct. 2298, 2307 (U.S. June 30, 2023).
8. *Bostock v. Clayton Cty.*, 140 S. Ct. 1731 (U.S. June 15, 2020).
9. *303 Creative LLC v. Elenis*, 143 S. Ct. 2298, 2341 (U.S. June 30, 2023).
10. *303 Creative LLC v. Elenis*, 143 S. Ct. 2298, 2341-2342 (U.S. June 30, 2023).
11. *303 Creative LLC v. Elenis*, 143 S. Ct. 2298, 2342 (U.S. June 30, 2023).
12. *303 Creative LLC v. Elenis*, 143 S. Ct. 2298, 2343 (U.S. June 30, 2023).
13. *Students for Fair Admissions, Inc. v. President & Fellows of Harv. Coll.*, 143 S. Ct. 2141, 2260 (U.S. June 29, 2023).
14. *United States v. Windsor*, 570 U.S. 744, 797 (U.S. June 26, 2013).
15. *Obergefell v. Hodges*, 576 U.S. 644, 644 (U.S. June 26, 2015).
16. *Dianne Hensley v. State Commission on Judicial Conduct*, Supreme Court of Texas, No. 22-1145.
17. Mike Scarcella, "Texas justices weigh lawsuit by judge censured over same-sex marriage stance," *Reuters*, October 25, 2023, https://www.reuters.com/legal/government/texas-justices-weigh-lawsuit-by-judge-censured-over-same-sex-marriage-stance-2023-10-25/.
18. David Biller and Daniel Politi, "The lion, the wig, and the warrior. Who is Javier Milei, Argentina's president-elect?" *Associated Press*, November 20, 2023, https://apnews.com/article/javier-milei-profile-argentina-election-82488d49cca5aee10d4b911bde530922?utm_source=copy&utm_medium=share.
19. Hannah Arendt, *The Origins of Totalitarianism* (New York: Meridian Books 1962), viii–ix.
20. Birmingham, "Elated Citizenry: Deception and the Democratic Task of Bearing Witness," 206.
21. Birmingham, "Elated Citizenry: Deception and the Democratic Task of Bearing Witness," 199.
22. Jack Balkin, *Constitutional Redemption: Political Faith in an Unjust World* (Cambridge: Harvard University Press, 2007), 7.
23. Antonin Scalia, speech on nature of being a lawyer [submitted as part of nomination questionnaire], 1984, Antonin Scalia papers, LAW, MMC, 291, Series I, Box: 26, Folder: 7, Harvard Law School Library, Historical & Special Collections, 5.
24. Antonin Scalia and Bryan A. Garner, *Reading Law: The Interpretation of Legal Texts* (St. Paul: Thomson/West, 2012), 348.
25. Scalia and Garner, *Reading Law*, 347.
26. Balkin, *Constitutional Redemption*, 2.
27. Balkin, *Constitutional Redemption*, 3.
28. Balkin, *Constitutional Redemption*, 80.

29. Balkin, *Constitutional Redemption*, 11.
30. Balkin, *Constitutional Redemption*, 11.
31. Balkin, *Constitutional Redemption*, 75-76.
32. Balkin, *Constitutional Redemption*, 76.
33. Balkin, *Constitutional Redemption*, 77.
34. Balkin, *Constitutional Redemption*, 77.
35. Balkin, *Constitutional Redemption*, 77–78.
36. Balkin, *Constitutional Redemption*, 85.
37. Balkin, *Constitutional Redemption*, 86.
38. Birmingham, "Elated Citizenry: Deception and the Democratic Task of Bearing Witness," 206.
39. William Nichol Eskridge, Brian G. Slocum, and Kevin Tobia, "Textualism's Defining Moment," *Columbia Law Review* 123, no. 6 (2023): 1611.
40. Plato, *The Laws*, trans. C. D. C. Reeve (Indianapolis, IN: Cambridge, 2022), 722d2, 131.
41. Plato, *The Laws*, 722d5.

# Bibliography

Agamben, Giorgio. *State of Exception*. Chicago: University of Chicago Press, 2005.
Alexander, Larry. "Hellman, Deborah, and Moreau, Sophia, eds. Philosophical Foundations of Discrimination Law." *Ethics* 125, no. 3 (2015): 872–79.
Alexander, Larry, and Emily Sherwin. "Deception in Morality and Law." *Law and Philosophy* 22 (2003): 393–450.
Araiza, William D. *Animus*. New York: NYU Press, 2017.
Arendt, Hannah. *The Promise of Politics*. New York: Schocken Books, 2005.
———. *The Origins of Totalitarianism*. New York: World Publishing Company, 1962.
Aristotle. *Art of Rhetoric*. Translated by J. H. Freese. Loeb Classical Library 193. Cambridge, MA: Harvard University Press, 1926.
Assmann, Aleida. *Is Time out of Joint? On the Rise and Fall of the Modern Time Regime*. Translated by Sarah Clifton. Ithaca, NY: Cornell University Press, 2020.
Austin, J. L. *How to Do Things with Words*. Oxford: Clarendon Press, 1962.
Barron, A., Yueguo Gu, and Gerard Steen. *The Routledge Handbook of Pragmatics*. New York: Routledge, 2017.
Balkin, Jack. *Constitutional Redemption: Political Faith in an Unjust World*. Cambridge, MA: Harvard University Press, 2007.
———. "Constitutional Memories, *William & Mary Bill of Rights Journal* (2022): 307–60.
Baude, William. "The 2023 Scalia Lecture: Beyond Textualism?" *Harvard Journal of Law and Public Policy* 46 (2023): 1331–51.
Beiser, Frederick C. *The German Historicist Tradition*. Oxford: Oxford University Press, 2011.
Bernasconi, Robert. "The Fate of the Distinction between Praxis and Poiesis." *Heidegger Studies* 2 (1986): 111–39. https://doi.org/10.5840/heideggerstud198629.
Biller, David, and Daniel Politi, "The lion, the wig, and the warrior. Who is Javier Milei, Argentina's president-elect?" Associated Press, November 20, 2023. https://apnews.com/article/javier-milei-profile-argentina-election-82488d49cca5aee10d4b911bde530922?utm_source=copy&utm_medium=share.
Birmingham, Peg. "On Violence, Politics, and the Law." *The Journal of Speculative Philosophy* 24, no. 1 (2010): 1–20. https://doi.org/10.5325/jspecphil.24.1.0001.
———. "On Deception: Radical Evil and the Destruction of the Archive." In *Difficulties of Ethical Life*, edited by Shannon Sullivan and Dennis J. Schmidt, 195–212. New York: Fordham University Press, 2008.

———. "A Lying World Order: Deception and the Rhetoric of Terror." *The Good Society* 16, no. 2 (2008): 32–37. https://doi.org/10.1353/gso.0.0016.

———. "Elated Citizenry: Deception and the Democratic Task of Bearing Witness." *Research in Phenomenology* 38, no. 2 (2008): 198–215. https://doi.org/10.1163/156916408x286969.

Bjork, Collin, and Frida Buhre. "Resisting Temporal Regimes, Imagining Just Temporalities." *Rhetoric Society Quarterly* 51, no. 3 (2021): 177–81.

Black, Henry Campbell, Joseph R Nolan, and Michael J Connolly. *Black's Law Dictionary: Definitions of the Terms and Phrases of American and English Jurisprudence, Ancient and Modern*. St. Paul: West Pub. Co, 1990.

Buell, Samuel W. "Good Faith and Law Evasion." *UCLA Law Review* 58 (2011): 611–66.

Butler, Judith. *Excitable Speech: A Politics of the Performative*. New York: Routledge, 1997.

———. *Precarious Life: The Powers of Mourning and Violence*. New York: Verso, 2004.

———. "Categories by which we try to live." *European Journal of Philosophy* 31, no. 1 (2023): 283–88.

Chung, Andrew, and John Kruzel. "Supreme Court to Hear Trump Appeal on Colorado Ballot." Reuters, January 6, 2024. Accessed January 6, 2024. https://www.reuters.com/legal/us-supreme-court-hear-trump-appeal-colorado-ballot-disqualification-2024-01-05/.

Colonna Dahlman, Roberta. "Conveying Meaning in Legal Language – Why the Language of Legislation Needs to Be More Explicit than Ordinary Language." *Journal of Pragmatics* 198, no. 198 (September 2022): 43–53. https://doi.org/10.1016/j.pragma.2022.05.009.

Constable, Marianne. "Law as Claim to Justice: Legal History and Legal Speech Acts." 1 *University of California Irvine Law Review* 631 (2011).

Cornell, Drucilla, Michel Rosenfeld, and David G. Carlson. *Deconstruction and the Possibility of Justice*. London: Routledge, 1993.

Davis, Deborah, and Richard A. Leo. "Interrogation Through Pragmatic Implication: Sticking to the Letter of the Law While Violating its Intent." In *The Oxford Handbook of Language and Law*, 354–68. Oxford: Oxford University Press, 2012.

Denning, Brannon P., and Michael B. Kent. "Anti-Anti-Evasion in Constitutional Law." 41 *Florida State University Law Review* 397 (2014).

Derrida, Jacques. *Limited Inc*. Evanston: Northwestern University Press, 2008.

———. "Force of Law: The 'Mystical Foundation of Authority.'" In *Deconstruction and the Possibility of Justice*, edited by Drucilla Cornell, Michael Rosenfield, and David G. Carlson, 3–67. New York: Routledge, 1992.

Domaneschi, Filippo, Francesca Poggi, and Eleonora Marocchini. "Why Lawyers are More Logical Than Ordinary Speakers and When They are Not." *International Journal of Language & Law* 11 (2022): 121–41.

Dorsen, David M. *The Unexpected Scalia: A Conservative Justice's Liberal Opinions*. Cambridge: Cambridge University Press, 2017.

Dotson, Kristie. "Conceptualizing Epistemic Oppression." *Social Epistemology* 28, no. 2 (2014): 115–38.
Durant, Alan, and Janny H. C. Leung. "Pragmatics in Legal Interpretation." In *The Routledge Handbook of Pragmatics*, edited by Anne Barron, Peter Grundy, and Yueguo Gu, 535–49. New York: Routledge, 2017.
Elmers, Glenn. "'Conservatism' Is No Longer Enough." *The American Mind*, September 24, 2021. https://americanmind.org/salvo/why-the-claremont-institute-is-not-conservative-and-you-shouldnt-be-either/.
Eskridge, William, Brian Slocum, and Kevin Tobia. "Textualism's Defining Moment." *Columbia Law Review* 123, no. 6 (2023): 1611–98.
Foucault, Michel. *Security, Territory, and Population. Lectures at the Collège de France, 1977–1978*. New York: Palgrave Macmillan, 2007.
———. *The History of Sexuality*. Vol. 1, *An Introduction*. New York: Random House, 1991.
Fricker, Miranda. *Epistemic Injustice Power and the Ethics of Knowing*. Oxford: Oxford University Press, 2007.
Geraldo, Magela Cáffaro. "The Preface as Stage: The Theatrical Trope and the Performance of Authorial Identities in the Nineteenth Century." *Ilha Do Desterro: A Journal of English Language, Literatures in English and Cultural Studies* 70, no. 1 (January 27, 2017): 265–74. https://doi.org/10.5007/2175-8026.2017v70n1p265.
Grice, Paul. *Studies in the Way of Words*. Cambridge, MA: Harvard University Press, 1989.
Hart, Jr., Henry M., and Albert M. Sacks. *The Legal Process: Basic Problems in the Making and Application of Law*. Westbury, NY: Foundation Press, 1994.
Harvard Law School. "The 2015 Scalia Lecture | a Dialogue with Justice Elena Kagan on the Reading of Statutes." *YouTube*, November 25, 2015. https://www.youtube.com/watch?v=dpEtszFT0Tg.
Hasen, Richard L. *The Justice of Contradictions: Antonin Scalia and the Politics of Disruption*. New Haven, CT: Yale University Press, 2018.
Hellman, Deborah. *When Is Discrimination Wrong?* Cambridge, MA: Harvard University Press, 2011.
Hellman, Deborah, and Sophia Moreau. *Philosophical Foundations of Discrimination Law*. Oxford: Oxford University Press, 2013.
Holmes, Oliver Wendell. "The Path of Law." *Harvard Law Review* 10 (1897): 457–78.
Husserl, Gerhart. *Recht und Zeit: fünf rechtsphilosophische Essays*. Frankfurt am Main: Vittorio Klostermann, 1955.
———. "Justice." *International Journal of Ethics* 47, no. 3 (1937): 271–307.
———. *Der Rechtsgegenstand: Rechtslogische Studien zu einer Thoerie des Eigentums*. Heidelberg: Springer Berlin, 1933.
———. *Recht und Welt*. Halle a. d. S.: M. Niemeyer, 1929.
Hunt, L. W. "Legal Speech and Implicit Content in the Law." *Ratio Juris* 29 (2016): 3–22.
Jolowicz, H. F. *Roman Foundations of Modern Law*. Oxford: Oxford University Press, 1957.

Kamp, Allen. "The Counter-Revolutionary Nature of Justice Scalia's 'Traditionalism.'" 27 *Pacific Law Journal* 99 (1995).
Karnowski, Steve. "Justice Barrett Expresses Support for a Formal US Supreme Court Ethics Code in Minnesota Speech." Associated Press, October 17, 2023. https://apnews.com/article/supreme-court-justice-amy-coney-barrett-ethics-908 8cbf33256ff6995b740087f78c698.
Keller, Doug. "Re-Thinking Illegal Entry and Re-Entry." *Loyola University Chicago Law Journal* 44, no. 1 (2012): 65–140.
Kennedy, Duncan. *A Critique of Adjudication (Fin de siècle)*. Cambridge, MA: Harvard University Press, 1997.
Kent Jr., Michael B., and Brannon P. Denning. "Anti-Evasion Doctrines in Constitutional Law." *Utah Law Review* 1773 (2012).
Langford, Catherine L. *Scalia v. Scalia: Opportunistic Textualism in Constitutional Interpretation*. Tuscaloosa: University of Alabama Press, 2017.
Lanctot, Catherine J. "The Defendant Lies and the Plaintiff Loses: The Fallacy of the Pretext-Plus Rule in Employment Discrimination Cases." 43 *Hastings Law Journal* 57 (1991).
Langton, Rae. "Subordination, Silence, and Pornography's Authority." In *Censorship and Silencing: Practices of Cultural Regulation*, edited by Robert Post, 261–83. Los Angeles: Getty Research Institute for the History of Art and the Humanities, 2008.
Lawyers Committee for Civil Rights Under Law. "Report on the Nomination of Judge Amy Coney Barrett as an Associate Justice of the United States Supreme Court." Washington, D.C.: Lawyers Committee for Civil Rights Under Law, 2005.
Litman, Harry. "Originalism Divided." *The Atlantic*, May 25, 2021. https://www.theatlantic.com/ideas/archive/2021/05/originalism-meaning/618953/?utm_source=copy-link&utm_medium=social&utm_campaign=share.
Lloyd, Harold Anthony. "Law's 'Way of Words': Pragmatics and Textualist Error." *Creighton Law Review* 49, no. 2 (2016): 223.
Markovitz, Daniel. "Good Faith as Contract's Core Value." *Michigan State Law Review* 1 (2021).
Marmor, Andrei. *The Language of Law*. Oxford: Oxford University Press, 2014.
———. "Can the Law Imply More than It Says? On Some Pragmatic Aspects of Strategic Speech." In *Philosophical Foundations of Language in the Law*, edited by Andrei Marmor and Scott Soames, 83–104. Oxford: Oxford University Press, 2011.
———. *Social Conventions: From Language to Law*. Princeton, NJ: Princeton University Press, 2009.
———. "The Pragmatics of Legal Language." *Ratio Juris* 21, no. 4 (December 2008): 423–52. https://doi.org/10.1111/j.1467-9337.2008.00400.x.
McAuley, Alex. "Officials and Office-Holding." In *A Companion to Ancient Greek Government*, edited by Hans Beck, 176–90. Oxford: Wiley-Blackwell, 2013.
Medina, José. "Varieties of hermeneutical injustice." In *The Routledge Handbook of Epistemic Injustice*, 41–52. New York: Routledge, 2017.
———. "Color Blindness, Meta-Ignorance, and the Racial Imagination." *Critical Philosophy of Race* 1, no. 1 (2013): 38–67.

Melissaris, Emmanuel. "The Chronology of the Legal." 50 *McGill Law Journal* 839 (2006): 839–61.
Moreau, Sophia. *Faces of Inequality: A Theory of Wrongful Discrimination*. Oxford: Oxford University Press, 2020.
———. "The Moral Seriousness of Indirect Discrimination." In *Foundations of Indirect Discrimination Law*, edited by Tarun Khaitan and Hugh Collins, 123–48. Oxford: Hart Publishing, 2018.
Maslov, Boris. "The Real Life of the Genre of *Prooimion*." *Classical Philology* 107, no. 3 (2012): 191–205. https://doi.org/10.1086/665621.
Murphy, Bruce Allen. *Scalia: A Court of One*. New York: Simon & Schuster, 2015.
Murray, Kerrel. "Discriminatory Taint." *Harvard Law Review* 135 (2022): 1190–270.
Niou, E. M. S., and P. C. Ordeshook. *Strategy and Politics: An Introduction to Game Theory*. New York: Routledge, 2015.
Nourse, Victoria. "Power." In *Justice Scalia: Rhetoric and the Rule of Law*, edited by Brian G. Slocum and Franics J. Mootz, 35–48. Chicago: University of Chicago Press, 2019.
Ost, François. *Le Temps Du Droit*. Paris: Odile Jacob, 1999.
———. *L'instantané ou l'institué? L'institué ou l'instituant? Le droit a-t-il pour vocation de durer?* In *Temps et droit. Le droit a-t-il pour vocation de durer?* Sous la direction de François Ost et Mark Van Hoecke, 7–14. Bruxelles: Bruylant, 1998.
Ost, François, and Michel van de Kerchove. "Pluralisme temporel et changement. Les jeux du droit." In *Nouveaux itinéraires en droit. Hommage à François Rigaux*, 387–411. Bruxelles: Bruylant, 1993.
Piñeiro, Josué. "Colorblindness, Hermeneutical Marginalization and Hermeneutical Injustice." *Southwest Philosophy Review* 38, no. 1 (2022): 115–22.
Plato. *Laws*. Edited by C. D. C. Reeve. Indianapolis, IN: Hackett Publishing, 2022.
Poggi, Francesca. "Against the Conversational Model of Legal Interpretation." *Revus* 40, no. 40 (August 14, 2020): 9–26. https://doi.org/10.4000/revus.5694.
Pohlhaus, Gaile. "Relational Knowing and Epistemic Injustice: Toward a Theory of Willful Hermeneutical Ignorance." *Hypatia* 27, no. 4 (2012): 715–35.
Post, Robert, and Art And. *Censorship and Silencing: Practices of Cultural Regulation*. Los Angeles: Getty Research Institute for the History of Art and the Humanities, 1998.
Pozen, David E. "Constitutional Bad Faith." *Harvard Law Review* 129, no. 4 (2016): 885–955.
Preus, Anthony. *Historical Dictionary of Ancient Greek Philosophy*. New York: Rowman & Littlefield, 2015.
Ramsey, Michael D. "Beyond the Text: Justice Scalia's Originalism in Practice." 92 *Notre Dame Law Review* 1945 (2017): 1945–76.
Reinsmith, Laina R. "Proving an Employer's Intent: Disparate Treatment Discrimination and the Stray Remarks Doctrine After Reeves v. Sanderson Plumbing Products." 55 *Vanderbilt Law Review* 219 (2002).
Roberts, Steven V. "Voting Rights Act Renewed in Senate by Margin of 85–8." *New York Times*, June 19, 1982. Available at https://www.nytimes.com/1982/06/19/us/voting-rights-act-renewed-in-senate-by-margin-of-85-8.html?smid=url-share.

Rose, Henry. "Arlington Heights Won in the Supreme Court but the Fair Housing Act's Goal of Promoting Racial Integration Saved the Low-Income Housing." 35 *Touro Law Review* 791 (2019).

Rosen, Jeffrey. "The Color-Blind Court." *American University Law Review* 45, no. 3 (1996): 791–801.

Sabo, Mike. "Christian Nationalism Isn't Going Away." *The American Mind*, February 27, 2024. https://americanmind.org/salvo/christian-nationalism-isnt-going-away/.

Scalia, Antonin, and Bryan A Garner. *Reading Law: The Interpretation of Legal Texts*. St. Paul: Thomson/West, 2012.

Scalia, The Honorable Antonin, and John F. Manning. "A Dialogue on Constitutional and Statutory Interpretation." 80 *George Washington Law Review* (2012): 1610–19.

Scalia, Antonin. "Common-Law Courts in a Civil-Law System: The Role of the United States Federal Courts in Interpreting the Constitution and Laws." In *A Matter of Interpretation: Federal Courts and the Law: An Essay by Antonin Scalia*, edited by Amy Gutmann, 3–48. Princeton, NJ: Princeton University Press, 1997.

———. "Response," in *A Matter of Interpretation: Federal Courts and the Law,* ed. Amy Gutman (Princeton, NJ: Princeton University Press, 1997), 129–50.

———. "The Disease as Cure: In Order to Get Beyond Racism, We Must First Take Account of Race." *Washington University Law Quarterly* 147 (1979): 147–57.

———. Speech on "Realism and the Religion Clauses." 1982. Antonin Scalia papers. LAW, MMC, 291, Series III, Box: 73, Folder: 2. Harvard Law School Library, Historical & Special Collections, 1.

———. John M. Olin Lecture Series on Political Economy, Wharton School, University of Pennsylvania. John M. Olin series, April 25, 1986. Antonin Scalia papers. LAW, MMC, 291, Series III, Box: 76, Folder: 28. Harvard Law School Library, Historical & Special Collections.

———. "U.V.A. Federalist Society Introduction." Federalist Society Symposium, Charlottesville, March 4, 1988. Antonin Scalia papers. LAW, MMC, 291, Series III, Box: 79, Folder: 1. Harvard Law School Library, Historical & Special Collections.

———. Speech on "The Rule of Law." 1970–1982. Antonin Scalia papers. LAW, MMC, 291, Series I, Sub-Series I, Box: 8, Folder: 7. Harvard Law School Library, Historical & Special Collections, 12.

———. Speech to the Federalist Society, January 30, 1987. Antonin Scalia papers. LAW, MMC, 291, Series III, Box: 77, Folder: 14. Harvard Law School Library, Historical & Special Collections.

———. "Use of Legislative History: Judicial Abdication to Fictitious Legislative Intent." Miscellaneous 4-2, Legislative history, circa 1987–1993. Antonin Scalia papers. LAW, MMC, 291, Series VIII, Box: MISC-4, Folder: 2. Harvard Law School Library, Historical & Special Collections.

———. Speech on original intent [submitted as part of nomination questionnaire]. Delivered at the Attorney General's Conference on Economic Liberties, June 14, 1986. Antonin Scalia papers. LAW, MMC, 291, Series I, Box: 26, Folder: 11. Harvard Law School Library, Historical & Special Collections.

———. Speech on nature of being a lawyer [submitted as part of nomination questionnaire]. 1984. Antonin Scalia papers. LAW, MMC, 291, Series I, Box: 26, Folder: 7. Harvard Law School Library, Historical & Special Collections.

———. "Federal Constitution Guarantees of Individual Rights in the United States of America." July 28, 1993. Antonin Scalia papers. LAW, MMC, 291, Series III, Box: 73, Folder: 9. Harvard Law School Library, Historical & Special Collections.

———. "The Two Faces of Federalism." April student seminar, New Haven Federalist Society. 1982. Antonin Scalia papers. LAW, MMC, 291, Series I, Sub-Series I, Box: 18, Folder: 19. Harvard Law School Library, Historical & Special Collections, 3–4.

———. "Reflections on the Constitution." University of Kentucky Law lecture, September 14, 1988. Antonin Scalia papers. LAW, MMC, 291, Series III, Box: 79, Folder: 22. Harvard Law School Library, Historical & Special Collections, 1.

———. "Judges as Propounders of Transcendent Moral Law." 2005. Antonin Scalia papers. LAW, MMC, 291, Series III, Box: 73, Folder: 3. Harvard Law School Library, Historical & Special Collections, 9–10.

Scarcella, Mike. "Texas justices weigh lawsuit by judge censured over same-sex marriage stance." Reuters, October 25, 2023. https://www.reuters.com/legal/government/texas-justices-weigh-lawsuit-by-judge-censured-over-same-sex-marriage-stance-2023-10-25/.

Schmitt, Carl. *Political Theology: Four Chapters on the Concept of Sovereignty*. Translated by George Schwab. Chicago: University of Chicago Press, 2005.

Schroeder Jr., Oliver, and David T Smith. *De Facto Segregation and Civil Rights: Struggle for Legal and Social Equality*. Buffalo: W. S. Hein, 1965.

SCOTUSblog. "Justice Kennedy: The Linchpin of the Transformation of Civil Rights for the LGBTQ Community," by Paul Smith, June 28, 2018. https://www.scotusblog.com/2018/06/justice-kennedy-the-linchpin-of-the-.

Shardimgaliev, Marat. "Implicatures in Judicial Opinions." *International Journal for the Semiotics of Law - Revue Internationale de Sémiotique Juridique* 32, no. 2 (2019): 391–415. https://doi.org/10.1007/s11196-018-09601-4.

Siegel, Reva. "The Politics of Constitutional Memory." *The Georgetown Journal of Public Policy* 20, no. 1 (2022): 19–58.

———. "The History of History and Tradition: The Roots of *Dobbs*'s Method (and Originalism) in the Defense of Segregation." 133 *Yale Law Journal Forum* (2024): 99–160.

Silverstein, Shel. "Fish?" In *So Many Heads, So Many Wits: An Anthology of English Proverb Poetry*, edited by Janet Sobieski. Burlington: University of Vermont Press, 2005.

Slocum, Brian G, and Francis J Mootz. *Justice Scalia: Rhetoric and the Rule of Law*. Chicago: University of Chicago Press, 2019.

Slodysko, Brian, and Eric Tucker. "Supreme Court Justices and Donors Mingle at Campus Visits. These Documents Show the Ethical Dilemmas." Associated Press, July 11, 2023. https://apnews.com/article/supreme-court-ethics-donors-politics-4b6dc4ae23aac75d4fccb1bcff0b7e0b.

Solum, Lawrence B. "The Unity of Interpretation." *Boston University Law Review* 90, no. 2 (2010): 551–78.
Sullivan, Shannon, and Dennis J Schmidt. *Difficulties of Ethical Life*. New York: Fordham University Press, 2008.
Sunstein, Cass R. "Originalism for Liberals." *The New Republic*, September 28, 1998. https://newrepublic.com/article/64084/originalism-liberals.
———. "Constitutional Myth-Making: Lessons from the Dred Scott Case." University of Chicago Law Occasional Paper, No. 37 (1996).
Taylor, Diana. *Performance*. Chapel Hill, NC: Duke University Press, 2016.
*New York Times*. "Full Transcript: Read Judge Amy Coney Barrett's Remarks." September 26, 2020. https://www.nytimes.com/2020/09/26/us/politics/full-transcript-amy-coney-barrett.html?smid=url-share.
Tiersma, Peter Meijes, and Lawrence Solan. *The Oxford Handbook of Language and Law*. Oxford: Oxford University Press, 2012.
Torres, Felipe. *Temporal Regimes: Materiality, Politics, Technology*. New York: Routledge, 2022.
Tsiaperas, Tasha. "Constitution a 'Dead, Dead, Dead' Document, Scalia Tells SMU Audience." *Dallas Morning News*, January 28. 2013.
van de Kerchove, Michel, and François Ost. *Le système juridique entre ordre et désordre*. Presses Universitaires de France, Paris, 1988.
van Hoecke, Mark. "Time & Law - Is It the Nature of Law to Last? A Conclusion." In *Time and Law (Le Temps et Le Droit)*, edited by F. Ost, 451–69. Brussels: Bruylant, 1998.
von Savigny, Friedrick Charles. *Of the Vocation of Our Age for Legislation and Jurisprudence*. Translated by Abraham Hayward. London: Littlewood & Co. Old Bailey, 1831.
Walton, Douglas, Fabrizio Macagno, and Giovanni Sartor. *Statutory Interpretation: Pragmatics and Argumentation*. Cambridge: Cambridge University Press, 2022.
———. "Pragmatic Maxims and Presumptions in Legal Interpretation." *Law and Philos* 37 (2018): 69–115.
Watson, Alan. *Legal Origins and Legal Change*. London: Hambledon Press, 1991.
Wood, Gordon S. "Comment" in *A Matter of Interpretation: Federal Courts and the Law*, edited by Amy Gutman, 49–64. Princeton, NJ: Princeton University Press, 1997.
Zartaloudis, Thanos. *Birth of Nomos*. Edinburgh: Edinburgh University Press, 2018.

# Index

Abortion, 5, 147, 154, 170–71;
the *Dobbs* decision as originalist argument against the right to, 5, 227–28, 233
Affirmative action, 171, 207–29
Agamben, Giorgio, 15–16, 51, 141
Alito, Justice Samuel, 5, 30, 181–82
Animus, 27, 31–32, 35, 59, 61, 68n110, 69n112, 83, 117;
racial, 200–201, 217, 236;
Scalia on, 110, 135, 142–50
Anti-Evasion Doctrines (AEDs), 33, 114, 128
Anti-Progressivism, Originalism as, 169–74
Arendt, Hannah, xi, 34, 50–53, 202–3, 237–40
Aristotle, xi, 136
*Arlington Heights* factors, the, 28–30, 87–88, 90, 99–100, 183–85
Austin, J. L., 45–48

Birmingham, Peg, 49–53, 237, 240
Bad Faith, 2, 4, 61, 63;
in employment law, 108–31;
legal Doctrines of, 24–26, 31–34, 38;
in Legal Pragmatics, 53, 57–59;
in Speech-Act theory, 45–46
Balkin, Jack, 228–29, 238–40
Bork, Robert, 7, 146
Butler, Judith:
on Sovereign Power, 15–16;
on Performativity, 46–52, 116–19, 185

Christianity, 1, 88
Civil Rights Act of 1964, the, 7, 60, 85–86, 109–10, 113, 116, 125, 225
Claremont Institute, The, 1
Colorblindness, xii, xiii, 1, 3, 6, 33, 36–37, 49, 62–63;
and affirmative action, 207–29
Coney Barret, Justice Amy, 4–6, 215–17
Constitution, unwritten, 10, 19, 23, 43–44, 77, 135–50
Constitutional:
evil, 236–41;
faith, 239;
interpretation, xi, 5–11, 21–23, 83, 135–50, 153–56, 226–28, 238–39;
memory, 2, 34, 53, 63, 155, 200–201, 226–29, 237
Conservativism, 1, 3, 6–8, 13, 21–23, 34, 41–42, 140
Critical Legal Studies, 3

Defense of Marriage Act, the, 144, 236
Derrida, Jacques, 47–52
Deconstruction, and Textualism, 45
Discrimination:
and colorblindness, 212–25;
and historical memory, 177–203;
legal history and doctrines of, 24–35;
theories of, 35–38
Discriminatology, the method of, 35–60
Discriminatory taint, 61–63, 177–230
Dworkin, Ronald, 199
Diversity, 1, 213, 237

Equal Protection Clause, the, 26–27, 87, 98–99;
  "colorblind" reading of, 32, 49, 169, 207–29;
  Scalia's reading of, 75, 91–98, 139–42, 147, 168
Epistemic Injustice, 62, 219–26

Federalist Society, the, 79–81, 138, 140
Foucault, Michel, on Sovereign Power, 14–16
Fourteenth Amendment, the, 87, 91–92, 142, 158, 178;
  "race-Neutral" reading of, 207–29
Fricker, Miranda, 221, 224–25
Fuller, Lon, 75–76, 139, 141

Gerrymandering, 30, 126, 178–83, 186–88, 203n3
Ginsburg, Justice Ruth Bader, 1, 4, 18, 31–32, 63, 158, 161, 228;
  and the Voting Rights Act, 164–67
Gorsuch, Justice Neil, 5, 7–8, 234–35
Grice, Paul, 54–57, 122–28

Hart, Jr., Henry M. and Albert M. Sacks, 82–84, 157
Husserl, Gerhart, 35, 39–40, 61, 150, 154, 157, 171
Hydra, The Lernaean, 1–2, 32, 63

Indeterminacy, of legal rules, 4, 33, 53, 56–57
Interpretation, Legal, 33, 66–67, 79–100;
  versus Manipulation, 50–53, 237, 240

Jackson, Justice Ketanji Brown, 6, 62, 207, 214
Judicial activism, 2–3, 7, 17, 40, 61, 63, 140–41, 153–56, 158–59, 169, 171

Kagan, Justice Elena, 8, 18–19, 23, 187

Kennedy, Justice Anthony, 8, 142–44, 226
Kennedy, Duncan, 3

Law:
  and game theory, 120;
  and language, 54–60, 94–98;
  and lying, 105–19, 119–31;
  and music, ix–xi;
  and performativity, 44–53, 119–21;
  and temporality, 39–44;
  as war, 120
LGBTQ Rights, 7–8, 37, 216
Legal Pragmatics, 36, 53–60, 63–64;
  and Manipulative Speech, 121–31;
  and Textualism, 95–98.
  *See also* Pragmatics
Liberal Jurisprudence, 3, 6–8, 12, 18, 21, 23

Malice, Expressed versus Implied, 24–26
*Mala fide*, acts performed, 24–35;
  colorblindness as, 207–29;
  lying as, 119–31;
  pretext as, 108–19
Malevolent legality, as domain of study, 24–35
Manipulative speech, 53, 56–58, 105, 121–31
Marmor, Andrei, 53–59, 61, 105, 120, 122, 126–29;
  on the critique of textualism, 126
Medina, José, 219–25
Meaning, Legal:
  explicit, x, 2, 9, 10, 28, 32–34, 55–59, 76–83, 90–100, 195, 211;
  implicit, ix, x, 53–60, 91–93, 127
Moreau, Sophia, 35, 37, 224–25

O'Connor, Justice Sandra Day, 7–8, 99
Originalism:
  as Antiprogressivism, 169–74;
  as Discriminatory Justification, 145–50, 215–19;

Justice Amy Coney Barrett's, 215–18;
Justice Scalia's. *See* Textualist-
originalism;
as Original Intent, xi, 47–48, 146,
148, 163–64, 171;
as Original Meaning, xi, xii, 7, 10,
21, 42–44, 94, 145, 148, 153–55,
168;
as temporal regime, 145–48, 153–56,
227–29, 233–41
Ost, François, 42, 52, 137, 146, 149,
188, 202, 241

Pretext, ix–xiii, 13–14, 21–25, 58–60;
in textualist-originalism, 11–14,
168–69;
in Employment Law, 116–31
Pretext Plus Doctrine, The, 105–34
Performance, ix–xi, 34, 50–52,
59–62;
juridical, 35–38, 41–42, 45–46;
versus performativity, ix–x
Performativity:
Derrida on, 47–52;
J. L. Austin on, 45–47;
Judith Butler on, 15–17, 46–52,
116–19, 185, 207, 218–19;
versus performance, ix–x
Performative Discrimination, x, 1, 45,
61–62, 118, 225
Petty sovereignty, 16–17, 52, 207;
textualism as, 215–19, 229
Plato, ix–xii, 5, 95, 241
Pragmatics, Legal, x, 3, 35–36, 53–60,
94–98, 195–203
Public Meaning, 4, 19, 44, 141, 155
Purposivism, in legal interpretation, xii,
3, 17–18, 79–88, 157–58

Race:
and affirmative action, 207–25;
in Employment Law, 105–31, 155;
and Gerrymandering, 177–88;
remedial use of, 91, 209–15;
neutrality. *See* Race Neutrality;

Scalia's view of, 91–92, 110–16,
207–12;
and the Voting Rights Act, 157–74
Race Neutrality, xiii, 3, 5–6, 26, 33,
62–63, 91–93, 98–100, 207–25
Reagan, Ronald, xii, 6–7, 79, 143
Roberts, Justice John, 5, 30, 68n110,
166, 186, 213

Same-Sex marriage, 7, 142–44, 234–36
Scalia, Justice Antonin:
and the attack on purposivism,
79–94;
on the Civil Rights Act, 159, 169,
109–16;
critiques of, 21–24, 95–98, 169–70;
on discrimination, 90–94, 207–12;
influence on current US Supreme
Court, 153–56, 177–41;
legal ontology of, xii, 2, 60, 88–94;
on originalism, 10–11, 145–48,
153–56;
on pretext in Employment Law,
105–34;
on Race. *See* Race;
on Rule of Law, 75–78, 141;
on textualism, 10–11, 75–82, 88–94;
on the Voting Rights Act. See *The
Voting Rights Act*
Schmitt, Carl, 15–16, 20, 50–52, 141
Seigal, Reva, 53
Solum, Lawrence, 85, 94–95
Sotomayor, Justice Sonia, 183–86, 188,
207, 214–15, 225, 229, 233–37
Speech, Legal:
Manipulative. *See* Manipulative
Speech;
strategic, 30, 33, 53, 56–58, 62–63,
105, 122, 126, 129–30
Sovereign Power:
Carl Schmitt on, 15–16, 20, 50–52;
Judith Butler's critique of, 15–17;
Michel Foucault on, 14–15;
as sovereign textualism, 20, 142, 241
Sovereign exceptionalism, 8, 14–24

Strategic speech. *See* Speech
Substantive Due Process, 154
Sunstein, Cass, 145–46, 171

Taylor, Diana, 36
Temporality, 3, 35–36, 39–44, 171–74
Temporal Regimes:
   customary, 43–44, 76, 137–39, 149, 155;
   dialectic, 43;
   founding, 42–44, 146–48, 154–55, 241;
   promethean, 43
Textualism, 2, 4–5, 8–11;
   and injustice, 76–77, 105–34;
   and legal pragmatics, 94–98;
   as performativity, 44–48;
   as Scalia's theory of interpretation, 74–104;
   as sovereign exceptionalism, 14–24;
   and the unwritten constitution, 135–54;
   versus purposivism, 79–91
Textual skepticism, xii, 24, 27, 34, 59, 64, 83, 90, 129
Thomas, Justice Clarence, 5, 18, 23, 171, 226
Trump, Donald, 4, 5, 7–10, 237

*Volkgeist*, 2, 10, 23, 43, 61, 77, 135–38
*Volksrecht*, 139, 140
von Savigny, Frederick Charles, 10, 23, 43, 61, 77, 135–42
Voting Rights Act, the, 1–3, 61, 63, 90, 93–94;
   Scalia's attack on, 157–74;
   Scalia's influence on, 177–83, 190, 209–10, 225–26

# About the Author

**Kevin S. Jobe** is an assistant professor of philosophy at the University of Texas-Rio Grande Valley in Edinburg, Texas. Prof. Jobe holds a PhD in philosophy from Stony Brook University and a masters of jurisprudence (MJur) from the School of Law at St. Mary's University.